I0793483

MECHADEMIA 9

Origins

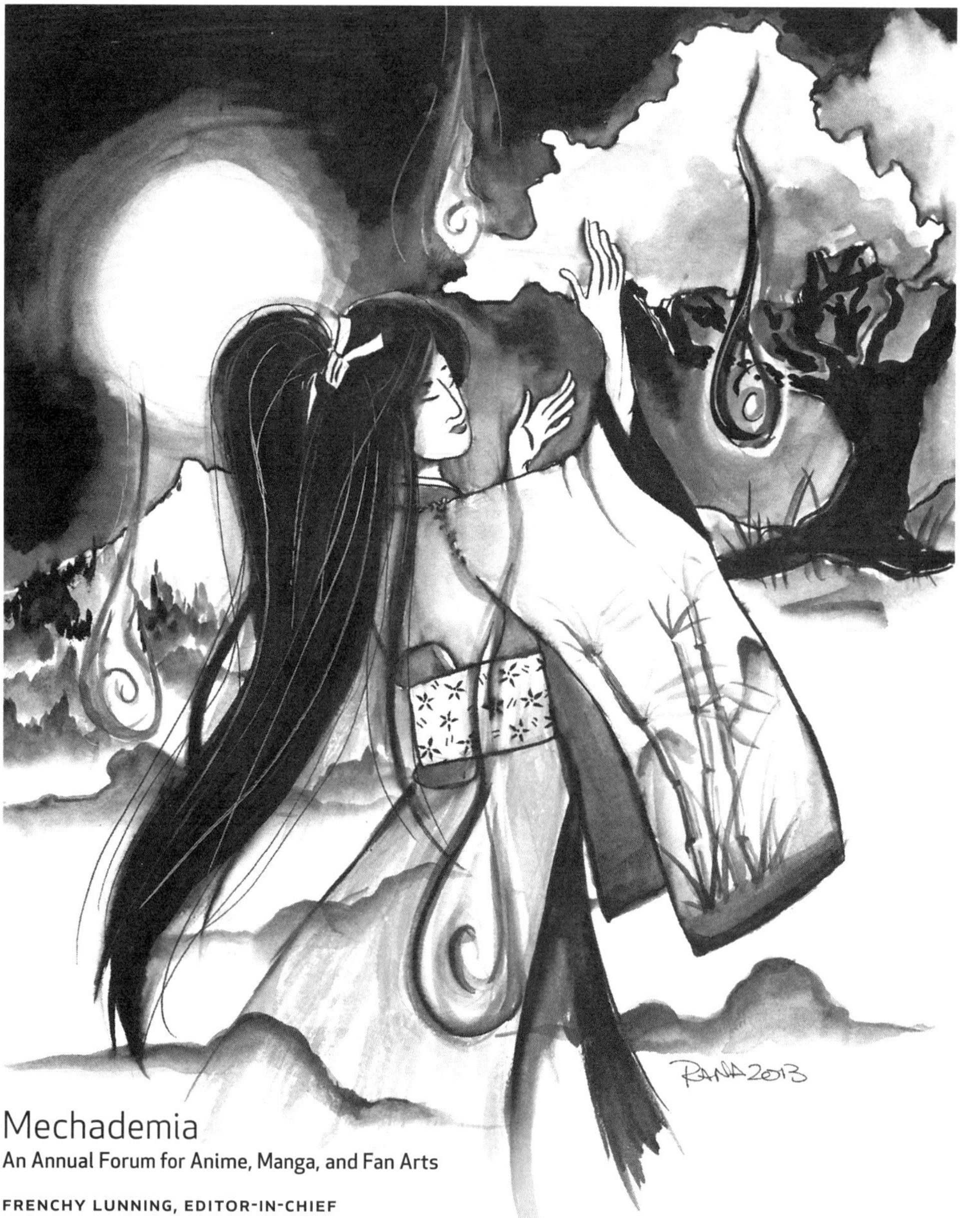

Mechademia

An Annual Forum for Anime, Manga, and Fan Arts

FRENCHY LUNNING, EDITOR-IN-CHIEF

Mechademia is a series of books published by the University of Minnesota Press devoted to creative and critical work on anime, manga, and the fan arts. Linked through their specific but complex aesthetic, anime, manga, and the fan arts have influenced a wide array of contemporary and historical culture through design, art, film, and gaming. This series seeks to examine, discuss, theorize, and reveal this unique style through its historic Japanese origins and its ubiquitous global presence manifested in popular and gallery culture. Each book is organized around a particular narrative aspect of anime and manga; these themes are sufficiently provocative and broad in interpretation to allow for creative and insightful investigations of this global artistic phenomenon.

Mechademia 1: *Emerging Worlds of Anime and Manga*
Mechademia 2: *Networks of Desire*
Mechademia 3: *Limits of the Human*
Mechademia 4: *War/Time*
Mechademia 5: *Fanthropologies*
Mechademia 6: *User Enhanced*
Mechademia 7: *Lines of Sight*
Mechademia 8: *Tezuka's Manga Life*
Mechademia 9: *Origins*

MECHADEMIA 9

Origins

Frenchy Lunning, Editor

UNIVERSITY OF MINNESOTA PRESS MINNEAPOLIS • LONDON

http://www.mechademia.org

Spot illustrations by Rana Raeuchle

"From Street Corner to Living Room: Domestication of TV Culture and National Time/Narrative" is an abridged translation of "Terebi ga ie ni yatte kita: Terebi no kûkan, terebi no jikan," originally published "Terebijon saikô (TV Reconsidered)," *Shisō* 956 (2003).

Published by the University of Minnesota Press
111 Third Avenue South, Suite 290
Minneapolis, MN 55401-2520
http://www.upress.umn.edu

Printed in the United States of America on acid-free paper

20 19 18 17 16 15 14 10 9 8 7 6 5 4 3 2 1

Mechademia Editorial Staff

Contents

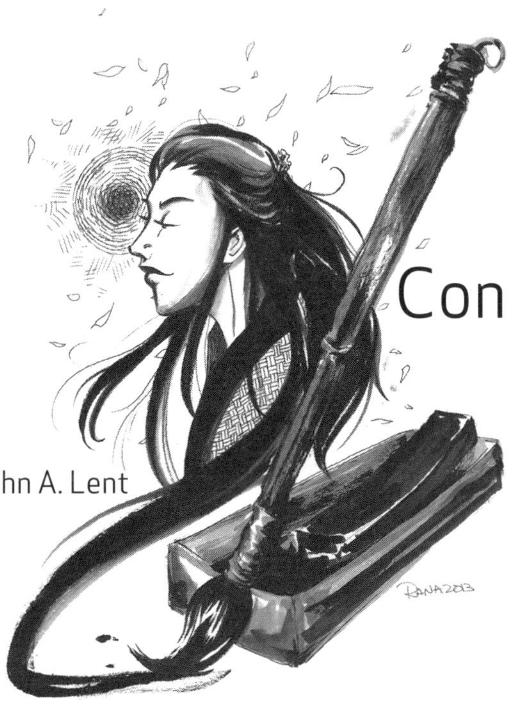

Repetition, Remediation, Adaptation

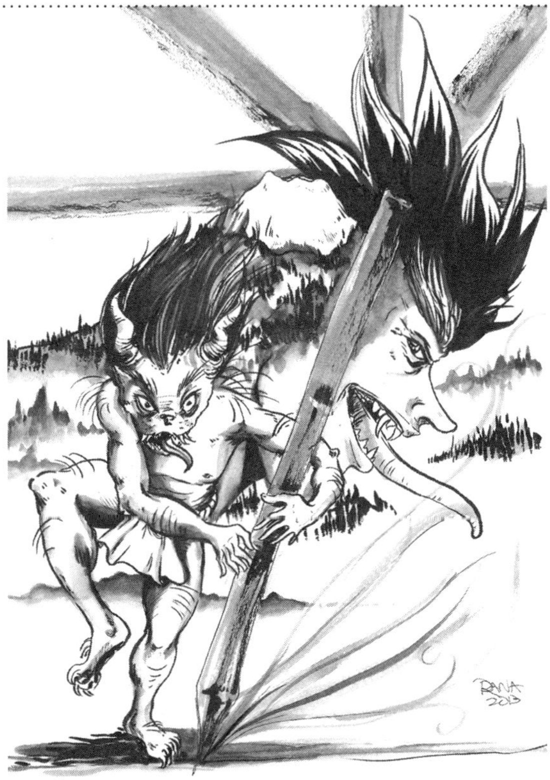

Dedication to Dr. John A. Lent

Dr. John A. Lent represents one of the early origins in the research of Asian comic and animation history and practice. Much like the early images of lone traveling scholars in the early Chinese scrolls, John Lent has journeyed extensively across Asia, interviewing and researching the artists of comics and animation long hidden from global view, tucked away in obscure locations, frequently in danger and/or under censure, and woefully underrepresented in scholarly and popular media. Lent has been a stalwart editor, colleague, and friend of *Mechademia*, and always a strong supporter of young and emerging scholars. The list of his accomplishments is astounding, and we thought it appropriate that we celebrate this wandering scholar and his work in this volume dedicated to the origins of manga and anime.

Lent has been teaching mass communications at the university and college level since 1960. He received a PhD in mass communication from the University of Iowa in 1972 and has held the title of professor since 1976. In 2000, he was the Rogers Distinguished Professor of Media Studies at the University of Western Ontario, Canada. From January 2002 to January 2005, he was guest professor at Shanghai University, and is now professor in charge of PhD dissertations at the Animation School of the Communication University of China. He has been a consultant to different educational and governmental groups, has served on international cartoon and animation competition juries, and has given hundreds of speeches, academic papers, and lectures to all types of groups all over the world.

His publications include the astounding sixty-five books and monographs he has authored or edited, three of which have won the Pat and Ray Browne Popular Culture Book Award and the Broadcast Industry Conference Award. Among his latest books are *Cartooning in Latin America*, *Cartooning in Africa*, *Animation in Asia and the Pacific*, *Illustrating Asia*, and a ten-volume bibliography on comic art worldwide. Most of his books were the first to explore Asian mass communications such as broadcasting, newspapers, film, popular culture, cartooning, animation, and media bibliography. Other areas covered by his books include media and the international division of labor, transnational communications, new world communication and information order, cartoons and comics, animation, women and mass communications, videocassettes worldwide, and so on. He also has written more than eight hundred articles and critical reviews for a variety of journals and periodicals on every continent.

Additionally, Dr. Lent has actively engaged in either starting or fostering professional activities in various areas. He founded and edits the *International Journal of Comic Art*; for twenty-six years, he edited *Berita*, a periodical on Malaysia/Singapore/Brunei studies. From 1987 to 2001, he was founding managing editor of *Witty World International Cartoon Magazine*, and since 1994, editor of *Asian Cinema*. He chairs the Asian Cinema Studies Society, the Asian Popular Culture Group of the Popular Culture Association, and the Comic Art Working Group of International Association for Media and Communication Research. He founded the latter two groups and had a hand in the launching of the Asian Cinema Studies Society. He also is coorganizer of the Silver Fly Animation Workshop in Florence, Italy.

Dr. Lent serves or has served on many association and editorial boards, including the Popular Culture Association, *Comics Journal, Journal of Asian Pacific Communication, Crossroads, Human Rights Quarterly, Jurnal Komunikasi, Asian Thought and Society* (where he was also associate editor), *ImageText: Interdisciplinary Comics Studies,* Seoul International Cartoon and Animation Festival, *Mechademia,* and many others.

Dr. Lent has done so much for both the international artists whose work he preserves and for the scholars whose work he supports that the editors at *Mechademia* wish to honor this stellar leader in our field by dedicating this volume to him.

Wendy Goldberg
Frenchy Lunning

Introduction

CHRISTOPHER BOLTON

For a volume on origins, a volume that simultaneously enacts and questions the search for fixed starting points, perhaps it is appropriate to start with the beginnings of *Mechademia* itself. The annual process of building each of these volumes sometimes feels like a construction montage from a mecha anime: from the blueprint of the call for papers the framework rises, then the body slowly takes form as individual essays are machined, polished, and bolted on. Finally we throw the power, the various moving parts mesh with one another, and the machine stirs to life.

After nine iterations, this annual process has become familiar. But in fall 2003, when Frenchy Lunning pitched her idea for an academic journal about manga and anime to me and some other attendees at the third Schoolgirls and Mobile Suits conference, the idea seemed as improbable as it was exciting—the academic equivalent of a giant walking robot. At that time there were a number of good books on anime and manga for general audiences, but the first academic volumes on these topics were just beginning to appear.[1] So I was both delighted and surprised when plans for the series went forward and *Mechademia* 1 appeared just three years later, an invitational volume that included articles by members of the editorial board and other critics who were writing about anime and manga at the time. Subtitled *Emerging Worlds of Anime and Manga,* it was a snapshot of an academic field that was just then getting off the ground.

Since then *Mechademia* has published something in the neighborhood of a million words, and comparing that first volume with this one, it is striking how much the field has expanded. *Mechademia* 9 contains contributions by senior and junior scholars not only from North America and Japan but also from Korea, Spain, and the United Kingdom, and the variety of fields and methodologies represented extends from literary and media studies to art history, anthropology, folklore, and musicology. Target texts and media include not only mainstream Japanese manga and anime but alternative Japanese animation, video games, nineteenth-century novels and newspapers, television programming, devotional art, Buddhist sculpture, tourism, and Hollywood film, while several metacritical articles analyze popular culture criticism itself.

But while the range and variety of approaches and perspectives are continually expanding, one could say that the question critics have asked about popular media like anime and manga has largely remained constant and in some sense conservative: "where does it come from?" If the first, incomplete answer is Japan, then the question inevitably becomes "where in the Japanese historical or cultural context (or the global one) do we find the origin of anime or manga's particular qualities?" It is easy to respond to this question with reductive generalizations about Japanese culture—to explain these media with various essentialized theories of Japaneseness. But the more interesting answers let these media challenge our present understanding of what Japan is, or lead us to understand the extent to which "Japan" is in fact an idea produced by anime, manga, and other texts, rather than the reverse.

Another version of this query about the origins of anime or manga asks the question from the perspective of media: what other media is anime related to (and is it a medium at all, or a genre of animation, or something in between)? This provokes us to ask in turn what tools we can use to read these texts. Can we analyze manga with the methods of film criticism? Can the plot of an anime be interpreted in the same way as the plot of a novel? Again, the most interesting answers point to the complexity of these media origins, leading us to think about the effects and meanings anime and manga can produce that no other medium can precisely duplicate, and the ways we must adapt existing critical modes in order to read these new kinds of texts.

All the essays in this volume start from these kinds of intuitive questions about the origins of Japanese popular culture and media, but none arrive at simple answers. They invoke a wide range of theoretical work to think through the notion of the origin: media theory, feminist criticism, Japanese fanthropology, poststructuralist textual criticism, postcolonialism, art history, film theory, phenomenology, and more. But in one way or another they all productively question the notion of origin itself. They are arranged in five sections, each corresponding to a different kind of origin: epistemological, biological, national, historical, or textual.

In the first essay of the volume, Margherita Long describes the focus on epistemological uncertainty that has dominated academic literary criticism in recent decades, and the resulting skepticism of original or decisive meanings. Long asks what lies behind and beyond this skepticism, which she examines through prevailing models of desire and their idea that, in her words, "it is only after some original, physical object goes missing that we can begin to desire its substitute," an uncertain, constructed, or textual artifact cut off from the original. Reading Hagio Moto's manga against Japan's ongoing nuclear disaster at Fukushima, Long asks if we could not recover a meaningful notion of desire's object, and with it the promise of meaningful intervention in the world, by a sophisticated reformulation of desire that focuses on ontological presence rather than absence. The other pieces in this section, "Subjects of Desire," likewise ask if desire is to be located in the desiring subject or a desired object or somewhere in between. Fujimoto Yukari analyzes the subjects and objects of lesbian desire in early shōjo manga to reveal the limits and possibilities for female agency depicted in these texts. Seth Jacobowitz looks at the nineteenth-century beginnings of Japanese discourses on the mechanical body that run through contemporary popular culture; he traces the anxieties and desires focused on male, female, and mechanical bodies, and also the substitutions whereby woman and machines act as mediators for a homosocial desire that is originally between men.

The next section, "Bodies in Motion," picks up from Jacobowitz by considering anime's connection to the body. Steven R. Anderson and Paul Roquet both investigate the relationship between the notion of a stable body as origin, and anime's power to transform that body. Anderson examines the anime *Mushishi* through the lens of disability studies and argues that it inverts the notions of "able" and "disabled," while Roquet looks at Tsuji Naoyuki's charcoal-drawn animation and the interplay between the malleability of Tsuji's animated figures and the concrete physicality of the medium: the texture of the charcoal line, the trace of Tsuji's own hand. Finally, Joon Yang Kim probes the discourse surrounding Korean animation and subcontracting work on Japanese anime, in particular the hierarchical division between the conceptualization performed by the designer or artist's brain and the drawing or execution performed by the hand of the artist or subcontractor. Kim provocatively overturns that hierarchy, suggesting that the brain follows the body as much as the body follows the brain, and in the process he complicates our understanding of the origin and direction of the global cultural flows that create these works.

Kim's essay also introduces the question of whether anime, even explicitly "Japanese" anime, really originates within Japan's borders or any border. That question occupies the writers in the third section, "Boundaries." Writing in 1938, Imamura Taihei discusses the portrayal of the moving body in animated cartoons and looks to Japanese art traditions going back to the twelfth century to suggest ways that Japanese animators can compete with American cartoons like Disney's. Shun'ya Yoshimi takes this idea of media competition with countries outside Japan and effectively turns it inside out, asking to what extent mid-twentieth-century Japan formed and defined its borders through media, in particular how early television subdivided time, urban space, and ethnicity. Kukhee Choo examines the relationship between Japanese anime produced by Korean subcontractors and animation for the Korean market produced at the same time. Choo questions the stereotype that Korean animators simply plagiarized Japanese stories and styles, arguing instead that their adaptations were a pointed and ironic comment on the Japanese originals. Finally, Brian Ruh seeks to move beyond national geography with a delocalized definition of anime as a "fantasy datascape," a distributed database of media and elements that are assembled creatively and locally by each user wherever she or he happens to be.

The fourth section, "Rescripting History," shifts the coordinates from space to time, with three essays that all ask how historical origins are depicted by popular media or, more radically, how those historical scripts can be rewritten. Laura Miller looks at popular culture incarnations of the third-century female ruler Himiko and the systematic differences between the historical anthropological record and the contemporary media one. Matsumoto Nobuyuki describes an exhibition he curated at the Tokyo National Museum that displayed premodern Buddhist statuary alongside pages from Tezuka Osamu's manga account of the Buddha's life, and the surprising conclusions that resulted from that juxtaposition. And Dale K. Andrews describes fans' attempts to rewrite the history of the Hachiman Shrine in Shirakawagō to remake it as the fictional Furude Shrine from the anime *Higurashi no naku kokoro ni*. The rewriting that Andrews examines takes place on devotional plaques that are purchased by temple visitors, who draw on them and leave them for display at the temple; Andrews argues that the nature of fans' rewriting and entering into the anime world can be understood only by a careful reading of this novel medium.

Andrews's examination of media translation forms a transition to the volume's final section, "Repetition, Remediation, Adaptation." The essays in this section look at the way texts (particularly canonical ones) have made the transition to different markets or media. Rayna Denison takes up the 2008 Hollywood film adaptation of *Speed Racer*, including the contested ways that the idea of "adaptation" was interpreted and how this influenced the film's reception. Alexandra Roedder discusses the first U.S. localization of *Kiki's Delivery Service* and the ways Hisaishi Joe's soundtrack was rescored by Paul Chihara, concluding that the two versions of the film speak very different musical languages. Forrest Greenwood looks at dating simulations, a video game genre that seems to represent a decisive replacement of reality by representation, and argues that something can be recovered or regained by reinterpreting the dating simulation in the medium of animated film. And my own essay examines the ways the *Akira* anime and manga tell similar stories but seem to inhabit two very different visual and political worlds. Finally, *Evangelion* is well known for repeatedly reinventing itself with new film releases that cover the same story, but Andreu Ballús and Alba Torrents show how this quality of repetition exists in a nested, fractal way even at the level of the original series.

In the process of creating *Mechademia*, the introduction is written last, a kind of retroactive beginning. To the extent that it describes a call (for papers) and a response, it has a constructed quality: in the end, the essays often define the topic as much as the planned topic determines the content. Perhaps the introduction itself should acknowledge this circularity. So to conclude my summary of the volume, I will point out that the last two essays (by Ballús and Torrents and myself) relate anime of the 1990s with a contemporary textual turn in literary criticism that sees the world as an unstable text in which putatively "original" meanings are continually rewritten—the very position that Margherita Long introduces and challenges at the outset. *Mechademia* 9 thus ends where it began, which only seems fitting for a volume that simultaneously enacts and questions the search for fixed starting points.

Note

1. Susan Napier's breakthrough book, *Anime: From "Akira" to "Princess Mononoke"* appeared in 2001 (New York: Palgrave). In 2002, Thomas Lamarre edited a special issue of *Japan Forum*, "Between Cinema and Anime" (vol. 14, no. 2), and later that year Istvan Csicsery-Ronay Jr., Tatsumi Takayuki, and I coedited a special issue of the journal *Science Fiction Studies* (no. 88) on Japanese science fiction, with several articles on anime. At the time, anime was popular with students, and anime criticism was definitely topical, but even as I was editing our volume, I was not certain what the long-term prospects for this kind of criticism might be.

Subjects of Desire

起源

MARGHERITA LONG

Hagio Moto's Nuclear Manga and the Promise of Eco-Feminist Desire

In April 2012 the leading shōjo manga artist Hagio Moto published a collection of five new works in response to the Fukushima nuclear disaster. Titled *Nanohana* (Rape blossoms), the volume was hailed by a review in the *Mainichi* newspaper as proof that manga subculture responds to societal problems "more quickly and more incisively than any other medium" (Figure 1).[1] But the *Mainichi* review, like those in the *Yomiuri* and *Asahi Weekly*, stopped short of spelling out the exact nature of Hagio's insight.[2] And there were also disgruntled otaku bloggers who complained that *Nanohana* merely repeats the same antinuclear slogans ("It's not safe!") we have already been hearing for decades.[3]

In this essay I propose that what is interesting about Hagio's contribution to Japan's denuclearization debates is the way she connects the problem of the nuclear with the problem of desire. In "Purūto fujin" (Madam Pluto) and "Ame no yoru: Uranosu hakushaku" (A rainy night: Count Uranus), radioactive elements take human form and become irresistible to everyone but a tiny minority who refuse to forget their chemical properties. With wry precision, Hagio equates the ability to be humanly wanted with the inability to be materially questioned or acknowledged. The target of her critique is our dominant

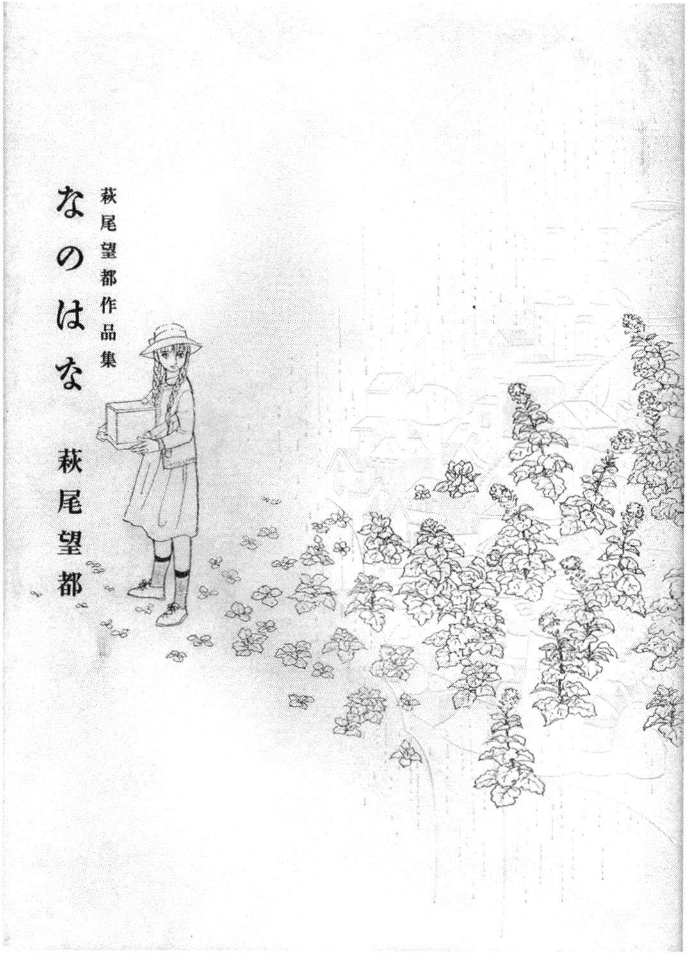

FIGURE 1. Cover image from the first edition of *Nanohana* (Rape blossoms) (Shōgakukan, 2012).

model of desire, in which it is only after some original, physical object goes missing that we can begin to desire its substitute, which is de facto entirely cultural.

This essay expands my reading of *Nanohana* by drawing out its affinity with an earlier and much longer work by Hagio, *Sutaa Reddo* (1980, Star Red). Here Hagio not only sharpens her critique of desire-as-usual but offers a brilliant alternative. The heroine Sei is a galaxy-traveling shōjo who refuses to accept "love" as compensation for the destruction of her beloved planet, Mars. In the process, she teaches her lover Erg how to go back to his own culture's dead planet. There, at her insistence, he relearns human love by reawakening his capacity for human/nonhuman interaction. The result is joyously eco-positive—the rebirth of a planet! And yet, in the rich body of

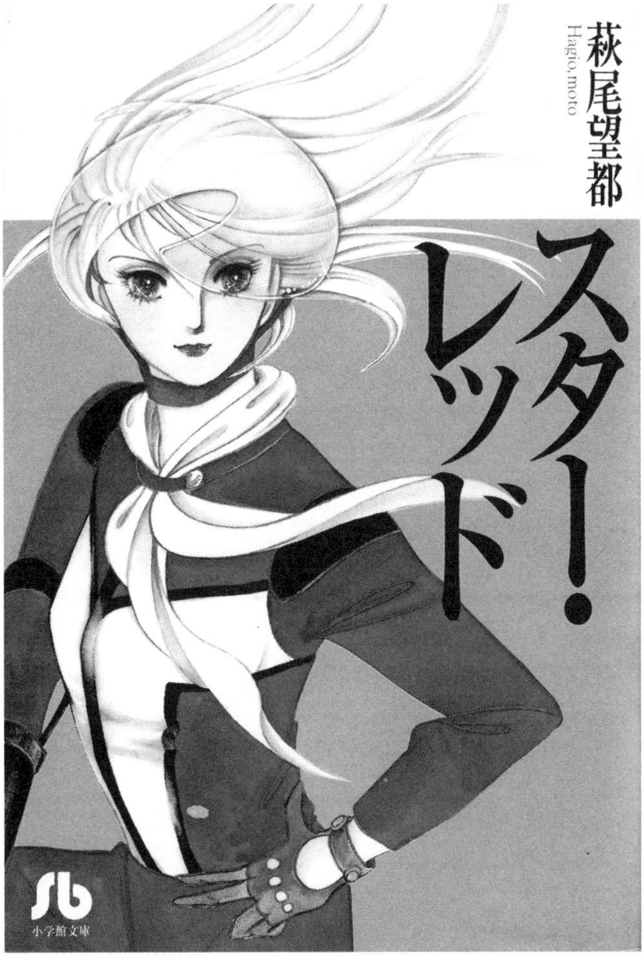

FIGURE 2. Cover image from a later edition of *Sutaa Reddo* (1980, Star Red) (Shōgakukan Bunko, 1995).

Japanese feminist writing on Hagio, this eco-critical element has gone mostly unremarked (Figure 2).

At stake, I think, is how we conceive our relation to material origins. What does it mean to love a planet the way Sei loves Mars? Do we really need to sever our relation with the physical object before we can begin to make sense of it? Desire it? Desire each other? Indeed, what would it mean for intra-human relations if they were not founded in a prior sacrifice of the material world? These are questions that a group of North American feminists has recently begun to ask under the rubric of "new materialism."[4] What I propose in this essay is that a similar set of questions is key to a rich but tantalizingly incomplete debate that has been swirling around Hagio's work since the 1980s: the debate about the hyper-girl.

"Hyper-girl" (*chōshōjo*) is a term coined in 1984 by critic Miyasako Chizuru in her study of Hagio's early manga, *Chōshōjo e* (1984, Toward the hyper-girl). Miyasako argues that we can situate Hagio's heroines along a continuum of feminist progress from the shōjo demanded by patriarchy, to the *hishōjo* (anti-girl) of works like *Heart of Thomas* (1974, *Tōma no shinzō*) and *Pō no ichizoku* (1972, The Poe clan), who seizes agency as a "boy with no genitals."[5] Then, even more positively, we have the *chōshōjo* of *Star Red,* who takes the stage emphatically as a girl. The *chōshōjo* draws her identity from a set of hyper-powers (*chōnōryoku*) that, according to Miyasako, honor a "feminine principle" (*josei genri*) of receptivity to alterity. In her 1995 afterward to Shōgakukan's bunko edition of *Star Red,* Kotani Mari credits Miyasako's "hyper-girl" concept with capturing "the power of the heroine's vital force, something we might even call the assertiveness of her female corporeality (*josei shintai no sekkyokusei*)."[6] In 2001, in a major public forum on Japanese popular culture, Kotani posited the hyper-girl as an important feminist alternative to Saitō Tamaki's "beautiful fighting girl" (*sentō bishōjo*), with whom she is often confused.[7] However, on the pages of *Mechademia* in 2006, Kotani lamented that the hyper-girl had failed to attain critical visibility:

> Oddly, after the publication of *Star Red* in 1980, Hagio Moto never again worked with the figure of the hyper-girl. Moreover, despite its genuine interest, Miyasako's conception of the hyper-girl never came to be widely accepted.[8]

Where did the hyper-girl go? It is not hard to guess that her disappearance had something to do with the vexed terms ("feminine principle," "female corporeality") that critics have used to describe her. Associated with "biological essentialism," such terms fell out of favor in both Japan and North America with the shift to the cultural constructivist paradigm in feminist theory. Reading Hagio after Fukushima, is it time to reinterpret them? That is, can we redefine "biologism" as the opposite of determinism? As a kind of receptivity to biologies, climates, and, indeed, entire galaxies, that are never directly knowable in their materiality, but that nevertheless exert tremendous pressure for cultural change? Both *Nanohana* and *Star Red* make it obvious why this pressure would be felt most urgently by girls. But Hagio never stipulates that only girls can feel it. She entices all her readers to embrace the *chōshōjo* state of mind that, at the time of this writing, may finally be opening Japan to a nonnuclear future.[9]

NANOHANA: THE PROBLEM OF THE NUCLEAR IS THE PROBLEM OF DESIRE

The opening and closing stories of *Nanohana* feature a shōjo struggling with loss after being evacuated from her Fukushima home. In contrast, the middle three stories parody the far more powerful national and international characters who find ways to justify nuclear power despite the reality of accidents. Let me focus on the first two of these three, which Hagio calls her "personification of radiation" trilogy.[10]

In both "Madam Pluto" and "A Rainy Night: Count Uranus," a radioactive element takes glamorous human form. Using the Greek names of the associated planets, Uranus and Pluto, uranium and plutonium appear before a body of judges. In the first story this body is a cross-section of affluent Japanese society assembled in a stately mansion on a rainy night. In the second, it is a group of Western gentlemen assembled in what looks like a nineteenth-century British court of law. As the would-be judges begin to speak, we realize they are so smitten with their respective defendants that they can utter nothing but starry-eyed admiration ("He's beautiful!" [72]; "She's heaven!" [36]). Only a tiny minority uses the element's chemical name and reminds the group that they are dealing with a radioactive substance harmful to humans.

What Hagio satirizes is how masterfully Count Uranus and Madam Pluto deflect these criticisms with an over-the-top discourse of love. "But I love you all!" says Count Uranus, "I received my power from you." "I want to repay your kindness by putting it all at your disposal!" (72, 77). To her own "dear humans" (56) Madam Pluto purrs, "Take it! Take all my love!" (42). Readers sense how ridiculous it is for radioactive elements to make proclamations of love to humans, and the most trite sorts of heterosexual love at that. But they also sense how familiar it is for humans to consider the "thing itself" obsolete and to proceed on the assumption that culture, discourse, and desire are all that matter when it comes to how the world makes sense. In the humanities, we tend to associate this mode of thinking with what Jacques Derrida called the absence of an "outside the text." Here, Hagio points to the limits of such thinking for pondering the nuclear. In both "Count Uranus" and "Madam Pluto," it is impossible to put the elements on trial because what was required for them to be humanly wanted in the first place—to be "discovered" and sold to the public—was their complete transformation from the "nature" of plutonium and uranium to the "culture" of Madam Pluto and Count Uranus.

Consider the story "Rainy Night: Count Uranus." Here the culture that replaces the "thing itself" has a strong Japanese inflection. Count Uranus offers his interlocutors "anything and everything, just as they wish" (73), and there ensues an orgy of consumer indulgence reminiscent of the bubble economy of the 1980s. Up pop not only factories, airports, hospitals, and roads but also Ferraris, Parisian Opera Houses, and diamond earrings. The only person who resists is a young woman named Ann, who asks for "clean water, food, and soil, free from nuclear contamination" (77). This is of course the one wish the Count cannot grant. What is interesting is that Hagio has his admirers defend him with lines that could easily have been borrowed from one of Japan's best-known nuclear advocates, Nakasone Yasuhiro. In April 2011, Nakasone told the *Asahi* newspaper that, although the Fukushima accident was regrettable, the economy remained just as dependent on nuclear energy as in the immediate postwar period, when it allowed Japan to avoid the fate of a "fourth-rate agricultural nation." He emphasized that most of the world was not against nuclear power, that "solar and wind are not capable of meeting even one tenth of Japan's energy needs," and that today's Japanese have a responsibility to history to recover from the disaster in the same way as "Japanese of the past" (*kako no Nihonjin*).[11] Using similar language, a nationalist grandmother in "Count Uranus" rejects green energy with "Don't be daft!" "Wind and solar can't make Japan a first-rate nation!" She continues, "If we don't get rich from Count Uranus's gifts like other nations, we'll be letting Japan alone fall behind! It would be an affront to our ancestors!" (79).

Next, Ann cites the problem of nuclear waste and its potential rogue use in nuclear weapons. This time the Count's devotees counter with the discourse of "completely peaceful nuclear applications" (*akumademo kaku no heiwa riyō,* 80) that played a key role in Japan's acquiescence to nuclear power in the 1950s.[12] But perhaps the most "Japanese" of all the Count's lovers is a boy named Tarō, who illustrates Murakami Takashi's point about otaku being one of the few postwar contingents to own up (albeit too enthusiastically) to the magnitude of Japan's World War II nuclear trauma.[13] For Tarō, the term "peaceful applications" immediately conjures the inverse it is meant to disavow. Playacting a giant detonation, he shouts gleefully, "mushroom cloud!" This prompts the oldest member of the gathering, a sickly grandfather, to wake from a nap and shout angrily "Hi-ro-shi-ma!" "Na-ga-sa-ki!" (80). No one pays attention; it is as if the only person old enough to have had a corporeal encounter with Japan's nuclear past is too close to death to make his opinion matter.

Still, what about Japan's nuclear present, at Fukushima? Ann points out that the cesium contamination there is one hundred times worse than at

Hiroshima. But Count Uranus upstages her, in a virtuoso performance of how easily Fukushima's lessons can remain unlearned. In a speech as eloquent as it is preposterous, the Count propounds the necessity of sacrifice for a world of peace and wealth. He concedes that, globally, nuclear accidents may well take place every twenty-five years. But, he says, this is a small price to pay for the absence of war. "Tens of millions died in World Wars I and II" (82), he intones, "but the world is now rich thanks to the massive heat I generate" (78), and we know that "people only fight when we have poverty and disparities in wealth" (81). "Quite right!" affirms one of his lovers, a company president. "You've completely eradicated hunger, even war!" (82). With bitter irony, Hagio indicts the way our first-world love affair with nuclear rhetoric simultaneously justifies and erases the material realities of places like Iraq, Afghanistan, and East Africa. And she goes further. She also indicts the way we cover over this structure of sacrifice by calling the result "love." Comforting a woman who is frightened about Fukushima, Count Uranus pulls her teary face toward his in a classic pre-kiss close-up. Looking up into his eyes, she is weak and confused. Looking down into hers, he is reassuring:

> **WOMAN**: It's scary! I don't like worrying. I want to live a beautiful life!
> **URANUS**: You can! Go ahead and forget it, this "accident."
> **WOMAN**: Forget?
> **URANUS**: Yes! Focus on everyday life! . . . If you are injured I can satisfy you with my wealth.
> **WOMAN**: Oh Count Uranus, how thoughtful of you to take care of us!
> **URANUS**: It's because I love you all so much! (87–88)

With this scene, Hagio draws a connection between the most clichéd formulations of heterosexual "love" and a philosophy of desire that comes dangerously close to predicating the meaningfulness of everyday life on an extreme prior injury that must be disavowed.

One of the things I love most about *Nanohana* is how Hagio exposes the starkly different positions that men and women are required to assume in these cliché formations. In "Count Uranus," the personified nuclear substance appears as a fully clothed figure of rhetorical authority and active desire. In "Madam Pluto" she is a send-up of what we might call the pornification of women. Scantily clad in a dominatrix outfit, she trades the Count's honorifics for the debased vernacular of a sex worker. "You want me, don't you?" she beckons. "Isn't it me you crave?" (41). On hands and knees, with her mouth open and her ass in the air, she belies her dominant persona with a series of submissive poses, and her appeal to those who would judge her follows suit. She praises man for his transcendence over animals, by means of fire, weapons, language, writing, and mathematics. And she says she is indispensable to him, because his history of increasingly powerful technologies—soon to culminate in stem-cell science that will master death—can only be powered by an equally eternal energy source: herself. Hagio's joke is that one does not have to change much about men's fantasies of either the ideal woman or the ideal energy source to make the analogy work. Both are endlessly available, endlessly compliant, and endlessly "hot." What is more, they are endlessly specular, rewarding every glance with the reflection of man's god-like omnipotence.

The biggest difference between the "Pluto" and "Uranus" stories is that, whereas Count Uranus seduces everyone with his discourse of love, Madam Pluto stumbles. Is it because she is never fully a subject of that love? Only its object? The assembled gentlemen charge her with the scission of human DNA and announce that she will have to be buried underground. At this she becomes enraged and, in a bizarrely wonderful basketball interlude, scores four goals of 24,000 points to teach them about her half-life. It will take 96,000 years for her poison to begin to dissipate! As many of us realized keenly after Fukushima, this is a unit of time that tends to exceed human understanding.[14] By attempting to score what are essentially extradiscursive points against her interlocutors, Madam Pluto emphasizes that she has never fully completed the journey from nature to culture. And so it turns out that she cannot be fully wanted by humans, because she cannot speak a language of desire that fully divorces itself from its material outside.

In this way, *Nanohana* makes a very specific point about desire and about nuclear energy. Hagio is saying that desire-as-usual seals itself off from the contingencies of nature, and at great human peril. But she is not saying that by simply embracing the alternative, and maintaining our relation with materiality, we will necessarily keep ourselves or our planet safe. Hers is a much more nuanced eco-politics, a politics she develops with astonishing scope over the 526 pages of *Star Red*.

PLANET LOVE AND THE ECO-POLITICS OF THE HYPER-GIRL

Serialized in 1978–79, *Star Red* is set three centuries in the future, in the year 2276. Writing at the peak of the U.S.–Soviet arms race, Hagio imagines a future in which nuclear humans have remained in charge. They have not yet

> HAGIO'S JOKE IS THAT ONE DOES NOT HAVE TO CHANGE MUCH ABOUT MEN'S FANTASIES OF EITHER THE IDEAL WOMAN OR THE IDEAL ENERGY SOURCE TO MAKE THE ANALOGY WORK. BOTH ARE ENDLESSLY AVAILABLE, ENDLESSLY COMPLIANT, AND ENDLESSLY "HOT."

destroyed the Earth with radiation, but a war to control satellite defense missiles (anticipating Ronald Reagan's "Star Wars" by four years) has come close, so that each and every city is protectively domed, and all suburbs are abandoned. Even before the doming of the cities, overpopulation has prompted an increasingly ambitious set of colonizations, first of planets in Earth's own solar system, and then in the stellar systems of Proxima, Alpha Centauri, Barnard's Star, and Sirius. To convey the brutality of this "glorious age of galactic development," Hagio offers the sad example of Mars.[15]

Poor Mars! Originally settled by Earth in 2050, it is converted to a penal colony in 2070, when high fetal mortality makes it hard to sustain the colonial population. Focusing on more exploitable planets, the people of Earth begin to ignore the Martian prisoners, and by 2150 they have been left to die. But they do not die. In symbiosis with Mars's atmosphere, their women start giving birth to babies who deal with the lack of water and oxygen by means of *chōnōryoku* or hyper-powers, the scope of which increases exponentially with each generation. When Earth becomes interested in recolonizing Mars in 2264, scientists are shocked to find a thriving population of fourth- and fifth-generation Martians whose DNA differs significantly from humans'. In this new species, we have Hagio's answer to the question, "What would happen if we did not sever our relation to material reality?" Rather than engineer, pollute, and abandon an ever-expanding set of environments, the Martians have stayed put, used less, and adapted. And the result is not that they are nontoxic or eco-balanced but simply that they are different, even while they themselves cannot control this difference or predict its implications. The protagonist, Reddo Sei (Red Star), or Sei for short, is one of the few fifth-generation Martians to have survived Earth's recolonization of her planet. Accordingly, her *chōnōryoku* abilities are the most powerful in the text, and overtly feminized. That is, *chōnōryoku* evokes *chōshōjo* and vice-versa, with both "hyper-powers" and "hyper-girl" serving as metaphors for the ability to sustain a human–nonhuman interaction.

The people of Earth, in their ignorance, imagine that this interaction is simple. Hagio gives us two different versions of their mistake. The first comes from Anju, a woman who works for a government agency that wants to appropriate Martian powers "for the betterment of society" (270). Anju and her colleagues take Sei into custody, examine her, and remark with envy on her three main powers: telepathy (*kannōryoku*), teleportation (*seishindō*), and telekinesis (*nendōryoku*). As Kotani Mari explains, American science fiction had been depicting all three since at least the 1950s.[16] In Japan as in the United States, readers had come to equate them with domination—with the certainty that one can read someone else's mind in terms legible to oneself (telepathy), that one can fit naturally wherever one projects oneself (teleportation), and that one can use the power of the mind to remake the material world according to one's own will (telekinesis). None of the three abilities admits of any uncertainty, any acknowledgment that the object acted upon might exert its own force in return. Anju holds fast to these definitions, certain that telepathy especially can attain a high "safety index" and be used for things like solving crimes and preventing accidents (269). But Anju is bitterly disappointed. Feeling trapped and misunderstood, Sei inadvertently explodes Anju's government agency with the power of her unconscious. When she telekinetically transports everyone in the unit back to the "soil that birthed them" (*shusshōchi*), her hyper-powers seem to assert that their true usefulness is for communing not with one's government but with one's environment (318).

Yet if hyper-powers do not ensure mastery over the material world, neither do they ensure subordination. Hagio critiques this idea by means of a second Earth character named Paveman. As head of an agency called the "Bureau of Information, Department of Martian Research," Paveman must make sure Earth's resettlement of Mars remains safe from the renegade fourth- and fifth-generation populations who have been driven from their sacred capital and into the hinterlands. He carries out his duties sadistically, using biological experiments on live Martians in an attempt to neutralize their hyper-powers. Unlike Anju, he knows these powers are incompatible with the status quo—that they represent a divergent human future. But he is unable to conceive of that future as anything but "regression." He rants:

> Their power of vision is zero! They apprehend things with extrasensory perception! Their eyes are completely unnecessary. And isn't it true that people who have the power to move objects by telepathy can go perfectly well without fingers or hands? They can teleport, so what do they need with legs? They have telepathy, so why would they need vocal cords? Right? What do they need with words? Before long they will stop needing noses, mouths, ears . . . And how will that be? When people just rattle around the face of the earth like mineral deposits? Even thinking will become obsolete. And living! If this is not regression, what is it? (306–8)

Paveman's speech is remarkable for the forced logic of his conviction that their hyper-powers will turn Martians into rock formations. It seems ludicrous given the vitality of *Star Red*'s Martians. But he is constrained by what Miyasako Chizuru calls "limitless allegiance to the linearity of his own temporal thinking."[17] Paveman locates humans at the end of an evolutionary timeline beginning billions of years ago with tiny sea organisms, and shouts, "It is completely unacceptable for anyone but humans to rule the universe!" (309). It is a highly un-Darwininian understanding of evolution, an understanding in which all nature's adaptations can be charted teleologically along a single temporal axis with "Man" at its frozen endpoint. Although Paveman knows hyper-powers seek different destinations, in his schema there is nowhere to go but backward, to an original, mineralized "nature" that is inert and unchanging.

NATURE/CULTURE AND THE "DEAD" PLANETS OF ZESNUSERU

This view of nature is amplified by the villains in the second half of *Star Red*, where Sei learns that the Earth–Mars conflict is but the most recent chapter in a much older conflict between a group of victorious "Zesnuseru" and the red planets (*sekishoku keisei*) they have been persecuting for thirty thousand years (Figure 3).[18] According to the Zesnuserians, the only way to keep the universe safe for humanity—for "wisdom, virtue, and reason" (394)—is to seal away the demons (*mamono*) that lodge in the hearts of all who dwell on red planets (398). They accomplish this by blowing up the offending planets, relocating the inhabitants, and "regulating" them with locks or "seals" (*fūin*) on their hyper-powers. Like the people of Earth, the Zesnuserians believe there are "any number of livable planets" (396) in the universe, and that what defines humanity as such is its consciousness—indeed, a consciousness that becomes human in direct proportion to its freedom from planetary input. In a brilliant third gesture of historical framing, Hagio has the Zesnuserians trace their fear of red planets to an even more ancient civilization reported to have been destroyed by *chōnōryoku* (Figure 3). The ruins of this civilization occupy some two hundred planets that the Zesnuserians have designated "Zero Ward," placed off limits, and declared officially dead.

How are we to understand this death? One thing that makes *Star Red* a compelling contribution to Japan's denuclearization debates is the parallel between one of the pro-nuclear faction's main arguments and this Zesnuserian ideal of humanity divorced from planetary input. We often hear that the

	Time Period Relative to the Year 2276	Dominant Ability (*Nōryoku*) Race	Persecuted Hyper-ability (*Chōnōryoku*) Race
First Frame (First Half of *Star Red*)	The last 226 years	People of Earth Representative: Paveman	People of Mars Representative: Sei
Second Frame (Last Half of *Star Red*)	The last 30,000 years	People of Zesnuseru	People of "Red Planets" Representative: Erg
Third Frame (Prehistory)	Between 900,000 and one million years ago	An "ancient civilization" that tried to master chōnōryoku but failed	

FIGURE 3. The narrative frames of *Star Red.*

Fukushima disaster cannot be allowed to dictate nuclear policy because of the *sōteigai* or "unforeseeable" status of the earthquake and tsunami that caused it. According to Tokyo Electric Power Corporation and its government sponsors, since tectonic plates and the Pacific Ocean are unlikely to deliver such a devastating combination again, the disaster is statistically irrelevant. With arguments like this, are they not telling us, like the Zesnuserians tell their victims, to put a lock on our receptivity to the inexplicability of the material outside? Are they not saying that, when it comes to planning for humanity's future, any force of nature that exceeds our imagination is prohibited from exerting pressure on our decisions? It is the sort of resolute anthropocentrism we have heard steadily since Fukushima, as when economics minister Yosano Kaoru remarked in August 2011, "We thought that human beings—the Japanese—can control nuclear by our intelligence, by our reason. With this one accident, will that philosophy be discarded? I don't think so."[19]

In *Star Red,* Sei's definitive gesture as hyper-girl is to insist on traveling to the most ancient of the Zesnuserian's off-limits planets and seeing for herself whether it is really dead. Hagio stages this journey as Sei's reaction to learning that the Zesnuserians plan to blow up Mars. Rather than save her home planet, which may be impossible, Sei wants to challenge the premise that mandates the destruction of all "red" planets. She wants to challenge the premise that nature's force must be foreclosed, declared inert, for human culture to evolve and flourish.

As part of the new materialism debates in North American feminism,

IT IS NOT A MATTER OF KNOWING DIRECTLY WHAT THE FORECLOSED ORIGIN HAS TO SAY. RATHER, FOR THE HYPER-GIRL, IT IS A MATTER OF FINDING OUT WHAT WE OURSELVES CAN SAY DIFFERENTLY AS A RESULT OF ORIENTING OURSELVES TO IT, AND RESPONDING TO ITS PROVOCATION.

Elizabeth Grosz has argued that feminists themselves come close to adopting such a premise when we rely exclusively on theories of cultural constructivism to understand how gender and culture evolve over time. In an essay called "The Nature of Culture," Grosz offers a sympathetic account of cultural constructivism's post-1968 resistance to prevailing naturalisms that justified divisions of labor, sex, and race by attributing them to the laws of nature. But Grosz points out that we lose important political and conceptual resources if we recognize only culture as productive and generative, and accept the conservative view of nature as invariable, universal, or predictive. If feminists want to understand all the ways culture can change, and if we want better to effect that change, Grosz says we need to understand nature as something that "bequeaths . . . a series of problems or provocations which each cultural form must address, in its own way, even if it cannot solve them."[20] She writes:

> the natural is *not* the inert, passive, unchanging element against which culture elaborates itself but the matter of the cultural, that which enables and actively facilitates cultural variation and change, indeed that which ensures that the cultural, including its subject-agents, are never self-identical, that they differ from themselves and necessarily change over time.[21]

In *Star Red*, what is depressing about the Zesnuserians is that they have remained self-identical (for thirty thousand years!) precisely by sealing themselves off from the dynamism of their environment. Worse, they have projected their denial of nature's generativity backward in time, to the million-year-old civilization that Sei visits. It comes as no surprise that when she arrives there she feels the planet "resonate" and declares, "nothingness and death each have their own kinds of meanings" (436).

What kind of meanings? As *Star Red* soon shows, it is not a matter of knowing directly what the foreclosed origin has to say. Rather, for the hyper-girl, it is a matter of finding out what we ourselves can say differently as a result of orienting ourselves to it, and responding to its provocation. Grosz calls it "the force of an outside that induces thinking," "that incites culture."[22] In *Star Red*, the result is nothing short of a new set of definitions for desire and sexual difference.

REENGAGING THE ZERO-POINT OF THE UNIVERSE: A NEW MODE OF DESIRE

At the same time that Sei learns the Zesnuserians plan to destroy Mars, she also receives a confession of love from a shōnen named Erg. Because Erg has been Sei's loyal fellow-traveler since the start of the adventure, readers are well disposed toward him. The problem is that Erg has been brainwashed by the Zesnuserians. Although he too has hyper-powers, having grown up on a red planet, he willingly gave them up when his planet was destroyed six thousand years earlier, installing the required lock and declaring himself safe from "nothingness, darkness, and madness" (520). Visually and conceptually, Erg's salient feature is the form this lock takes: a short, sturdy horn on the top of his head, like a unicorn's. The horn is distinctly phallic, and as Erg spells out the terms of his love for Sei, we realize that *Star Red* is setting them up as the foils for a vastly superior alternative.

Faced with the loss of Mars, Sei declares her intention to die there with it. But Erg cites the Zesnuserian Law (*okite*) that one can never go home again, and says she should find a new planet, like he did (400).[23] Surprised, Sei presses him on the location of this new planet:

> **SEI**: You . . . where were you able to find your new home (*furusato*)?
> **ERG**: In you. I've been looking for you all this time.
> Without a doubt.
> Will you be my Mars? (403–4)

Sei's second quintessentially *chōshōjo* gesture in the text is to reject Erg's proposal out of hand. For what would it mean to "be Erg's Mars"? Like Erg's horn, which represents the loss of his hyper-powers, Erg's "Mars" would also represent a lack, the exploded planet. It is this strange status as the symbolization-of-lack that makes both the horn and Erg's would-be lover phallic. Because they point simultaneously to the existence of some prior state of wholeness and to its eternal prohibition, they function as classic examples of the master signifier of desire in Lacanian psychoanalysis.

In an essay called "Refiguring Lesbian Desire," Elizabeth Grosz points out that lack-based desire is not unique to Lacan. Tracing it as far back as Plato, for whom desire "is a lack in man's being, an imperfection or flaw in human culture," Grosz reminds us that Hegel is also an important antecedent:

> Hegel conceives of desire as a lack, a unique one that, unlike other lacks, can only function if it remains unfilled, a lack, therefore, with a peculiar object

> all of its own . . . The only object desire can desire is one that will not fill the lack or provide complete satisfaction.[24]

Grosz posits two main consequences of the dominance of this model of desire, with its impossible object. In *Star Red,* Hagio can be seen to skewer both of them by means of Erg's proposal. The first consequence Grosz notes is the model's usefulness to capitalist and other modes of perpetual acquisition. Consider the Earth's acquisition of Mars, which was merely the first in a series that included Jupiter, Neptune, and Pluto, as well as planets in the systems of Proxima, Alpha Centauri, Barnard's Star, and Sirius.[25] Given that the text defines planetary "desire" as a galactically scaled, imperial capitalism constantly cycling through the consumption, manipulation, dissatisfaction, and (in the Zesnuserian case) destruction of successive planets, Erg's request that Sei "be his Mars" could hardly be more terrifying. Even assuming she avoids the worst, if desire is inherently unfillable, then Erg's taking her as his replacement home planet is destined to be just the first in a long chain of decidedly unloving substitutions.

A second consequence of lack-based desire is sexual difference, or, more accurately, the fake difference we get when a dominant group covers over humanity's origin and defines what remains exclusively in terms of the impossible master signifier that takes its place. Erg's horn is a perfect example. When Sei asks him if what the Zesnuserians say could really be true—that the existence of beings with hyper-powers is meaningless, superfluous—Erg hedges. "I don't know" (read: yes). "No one knows. But doesn't it mean something that you and I are here like this in conversation?" (400). Erg tries to redirect Sei to a conversation he calls "love," but he is only willing to have it if he can count on his horn to keep him sealed away from her defining difference. Like the discourse of "love" in *Nanohana,* it is premised on the exclusion of what matters most about the other.

We see Hagio's alternate model of love when Sei asks Erg to remove his horn, and he agrees. Readers can't help regretting that Hagio waits until the final fifty pages of *Star Red* to make this happen. We want more time in this new world of phallus-free desire! We want more time not least to appreciate the two powerful events of rebirth that it enables.

The first is the regeneration of the ancient dead planet the Zesnuserians call "Zero Ward." Erg has traveled there with Sei and has fearfully witnessed her receptivity to its resonance. Ultimately, that resonance absorbs her, body and mind, and she is teleported from Zero Ward to a limbo-space far from Erg. Left alone on his planet, he begins to reconsider his definition of love, and it is in his desperate solitude and yearning that he decides to remove his horn. As soon as he does, we see the Zesnuserians panic at the geophysical data emerging from Zero Ward. The amount of carbon is exploding. The surface temperature is rising. Within three thousand revolutions, the planet will regenerate its swamps, and organic life will flourish. If we read the scene literally, it is a miracle that human receptivity can beget such spectacular rebirth. But if we read it metaphorically, it is a vibrant symbol of the dynamism that nature has possessed all along, independent of human willingness to acknowledge it.

The second rebirth is Sei's. Stuck in limbo after being absorbed by the resonance of the dead planet, she reconnects with an old Martian ally, the third-generation shōnen Yodaka. From the start Yodaka has been helping her in her struggles against Paveman and the Zesnuserians. But his own hyper-receptivity to the spirit of death has landed him, too, in this limbo, which Hagio depicts as a black, galaxy-dappled backdrop to their floating bodies. From here they continue to exercise telepathy, channeling the grief of a group of Martians gathered around Yodaka's comatose body. It is at this point that the two decide to use hyper-powers to inhabit this body together, with Yodaka growing a uterus and Sei becoming a fetus. In some of the text's most quoted lines, Yodaka intones, "Sei! Just make yourself tiny! Be small and tuck yourself in here. I'll help you . . ." (501). In this way Yodaka becomes "Yodaka Mama," and *Star Red* ends with a sixth-generation "Junior Sei" still gestating inside him but already blessed with a remarkably queer set of committed parents. As Miyasako Chizuru points out, these parents include the newly transgendered Yodaka, an anticapitalist Egyptian man Labaaba who takes Yodaka as his wife, and even the watchful spirit of a cross-dressing fourth-generation Martian named Kuroba, who has given her life for Sei.

Miyasako calls these parents "sexual outlaws" in a Zesnuserian world, people whose "extraterritorial sexuality" remains impossible so long as society assigns the work of deciding what is dead and not dead exclusively to shōnen like Erg.[26] She writes:

> At the zero-point, the modern shōnen stands rigid, as if frozen, but the *chōshōjo* does not falter. Having arrived at this point . . . Hagio Moto represents a "feminine principle" that discerns a source of rebirth in the zero-point deemed "nothingness" by linear temporal thinking.[27]

Miyasako derives her term "zero-point" both from "Zero Ward" and from her argument that linear temporal thinking charts a static course for men's lives toward what Erg refers to memorably as "the conclusion called death" (408). Although many have interpreted Miyasako's as a biologically essentialist point—namely, that the "feminine principle" avoids this conclusion because women are the "sex that gives birth"—I take her to be making a much more nuanced argument about the relation between material origins and the conditions of possibility for sexual difference. We know that, for Erg-as-modern-shōnen, the horn (the dead-lock!) both determines what is desired (woman-as-lack) and regulates what is sexually legible (the other as substitute origin). Therefore, to break this deadlock and make "outlaw" sexualities possible, it is not enough simply to struggle against the terms mandated by the horn, from within its cultural sphere. The answer lies instead with renegotiating the relation to origin—with discovering what Miyasako calls "a source of rebirth at the zero-point"—in order to break the cycle of prohibition and substitution, and replace lack-based desire with something much more productive. In *Star Red,* that something goes by the name *chōnōryoku.*

Let me clarify this point by means of two critics who would seem to disagree with Miyasako. In his 1989 essay, "'Umu sei' to shite no shōnen—'Seisa no shōjo mangashi' no tame ni" (Shōnen as the "sex that gives birth": Toward a shōjo manga history of sexual difference), preeminent popular culture critic Ōtsuka Eiji emphasizes that there are two crucial rebirths in *Star Red*: of Erg's planet, first, and of Sei as Junior Sei, second. For Ōtsuka, it is essential that *both* are carried out by young men.[28] Affirming Ōtsuka's point, feminist Fujimoto Yukari writes, "it is emphatically not Sei who gives birth to a child and in this way regenerates life. *Star Red*'s plot does not depend on facile maternal myths but rather on straightforward miracles." We should note that Japanese feminism has waged a long and important battle against the modern state's abuses of the "maternal myth" (*bosei shinwa*) of mothers as naturally selfless caregivers.[29] But we should also consider whether we do mothers a disservice when we reassign their reproductive capacities to men and call it a feminist victory. This runs the risk of becoming a reappropriation of origin, rather than a renegotiation with it.

It also runs the risk of misreading *Star Red,* since the rebirths accomplished by Erg and Yodaka are not miracles but culminating instances of the *chōnōryoku* for which Sei has been fighting from the start. What is more, they are both the direct results of Sei's having said no to becoming Erg's Mars and perpetuating lack-based desire. It is true that Erg is responsible for the regeneration of his planet. But it is also true that he would never have gone there had it not been for Sei, and would never have chosen to open his hyper-powers to his planet's resonance if she had not insisted it was the only way he could love her without annihilating her. Similarly, Yodaka is clearly the mother of

Junior Sei. But Hagio explicitly positions his use of hyper-powers as the result of having telepathically witnessed Erg remove his horn and cry, "Sei! I love you!" (498–99). In other words, it is only because Yodaka is so moved by Erg's affirmation of material origins, and the new love it enables, that he is prompted to suggest the pregnancy that will allow Sei, via Junior Sei, to make her way back to Erg.

How, when, and even whether this reunion will happen is left uncertain at the end of Hagio's text. Likewise, we do not know whether our beloved Red Planet characters will continue to evade their persecutors. What we do know is that it is the *chōshōjo*, more than anyone, who offers them all their best and most open-ended chances. This is because *Star Red* looks ultimately to the hyper-girl to accomplish rebirth—of girls, of love, and of planets—by means of an eco-feminist desire as productive as it is unpredictable.

Notes

I would like to thank Kotani Mari for her encouragement and intellectual generosity. Kotani Sensei wrote the *Mechademia* 1 essay that first spurred my interest in the hyper-girl. She also introduced me to Hagio's *Nanohana* in 2012 and served as discussant for an earlier version of my work on *Star Red* at the Association for Asian Studies meeting in Atlanta in 2008. Thanks also to Anne McKnight and Brian Bergstrom for being inspiring panel mates in 2008 and to Christopher Bolton for his expert editing.

1. "Konshū no hondana: Shinkan *Nanohaha—Hagio Moto sakuhinshū*" (This week's bookshelf: New publication *Nanohana—A collection of works by Hagio Moto*), *Mainichi shinbun*, May 6, 2012, http://mainichi.jp/feature/news/20120506ddm015070028000c.html.

2. The *Asahi Weekly* offers an intriguing if ultimately unsatisfying interpretation, likening radioactivity in *Nanohana* to vampirism in Hagio's *The Poe Clan*. See Tomiyama Akiko, "Wadai no shinkan: Hagio Moto sakuhinshū *Nanohana*" (New titles in the news: Hagio Moto's anthology *Nanohana*), *Asahi Weekly,* May 13, 2012, http://book.asahi.com/reviews/column/2012051300003.html. For the *Yomiuri* review, see "Shinkan nabi: Manga to anime" (Navigating new titles: Manga and anime), *Yomiuri shinbun*, April 26, 2012, http://www.yomiuri.co.jp/book/comic/sinnavi/20120426-OYT8T00575.htm.

3. "Sōshoku kata, kagakusei kihaku na wadaisaku *Nanohana*" (Thick on ornament, thin on science: The much discussed title *Nanohana*). Karasumaru no kurukuru kaiten toshokan kōendōri bunkan (The Kōendōri annex of Karasumaru's revolving library), Book and Manga Review Blog, http://karasumaru.txt-nifty.com/kurukuru/2012/04/post-818c.html.

4. Some key titles in the new materialism debates are Stacy Alaimo and Susan Hekman, eds., *Material Feminisms* (Bloomington: University of Indiana Press, 2008); Jane Bennett, *Vibrant Matter: A Political Ecology of Things* (Durham, N.C.: Duke University Press, 2010); and Diana Coole and Samantha Frost, eds., *New Materialisms: Ontology, Agency, and Politics* (Durham, N.C.: Duke University Press, 2010). See also my essay on nuclear politics

and material feminism, "What Kind of Science? Reading Irigaray with Stengers," in *Philosophy after Irigaray,* ed. Mary Rawlinson, Danae Mcleod, and Sara McNamara (Albany: State University of New York Press, forthcoming).

5. Miyasako Chizuru, *Chōshōjo e* (Toward the hypergirl) (Tokyo: Shūeisha Bunko, 1989), 200. Miyasako defines "*hishōjo*" in contradistinction to the way Honda Masuko defines "shōjo" in the "Hira hira" (Fluttering) chapter of her book *Ibunka toshite no kodomo* (The child as another culture) (Tokyo: Chikuma Gakugei Bunko, 1992). For an overview in English of Honda's book, see Aoyama Tomoko, "*Nodame* as 'Another Culture,'" *U.S.–Japan Women's Journal* 38 (2010): 25–42. Honda's "Fluttering" chapter has been translated by Aoyama and Barbara Hartley as "The Genealogy of *Hirahira:* Liminality and the Girl," in *Girl Reading Girl in Japan,* ed. Tomoko Aoyama and Barbara Hartley (New York: Routledge, 2010), 19–37.

6. Kotani Mari, "Sutā Reddo no watashitachi" (We who are Star Red), in *Sutā Reddo, by Hagio Moto* (Tokyo: Shōgakukan Bunko, 1995), 530.

7. Kotani Mari, "Ota kuiin wa, ota kuia no yume o mita wa" (The queer dream of an ota-queen), in *Mōjō genron F-kai* (Net discourse version F), ed. Azuma Hiroki (Tokyo: Seidosha, 2003), 122. Kotani delivered this paper at a symposium on postmodern otaku sexuality organized by Azuma Hiroki and featuring Saitō Tamaki, Nagayama Kaoru, Itō Gō, and Takekuma Kentarō.

8. Kotani Mari, "Metamorphosis of the Japanese Girl: The Girl, the Hyper-Girl, and the Battling Beauty," *Mechademia* 1 (2006): 166.

9. See Hiroko Tabuchi, "Japan Sets Policy to Phase Out Nuclear Power Plants by 2040," *New York Times*, September 14, 2012, http://www.nytimes.com/2012/09/15/world/asia/japan-will-try-to-halt-nuclear-power-by-the-end-of-the-2030s.html. But see also Hiroko Tabuchi, "Japan Backs Off Goal to Replace Nuclear Power by 2040," *New York Times*, September 19, 2012, http://www.nytimes.com/2012/09/20/world/asia/japan-backs-off-of-goal-to-phase-out-nuclear-power-by-2040.html.

10. Hagio Moto, "Nanohana to" (On the title *Nanohana*), afterword to *Hagio Moto sakuhinshū: Nanohana* (Rape blossoms: A collection of works by Hagio Moto) (Tokyo: Shōgakukan, 2012), 157. Hereafter, page numbers will be given parenthetically in the text. I read the third story in the trilogy, "Salome 20xx," as an amplification of themes in the first two. In this story, Hagio casts Plutonium as the perverse female hero of Oscar Wilde's 1891 play *Salome.*

11. Nakasone was prime minister from 1982 to 1987 and, as a Diet member in the 1950s, influential in setting up Japan's nuclear power infrastructure. See Nakasone Yasuhiro, interview with Yoshida Takafumi, "Genshiryoku to Nihonjin" (Nuclear power and the Japanese), *Mainichi shinbun*, April 26, 2011. A partial translation appeared as "INTERVIEW/ Yasuhiro Nakasone: Learn Lessons from Fukushima Crisis and Continue to Promote Nuclear Energy," *Asahi Shimbun Asia and Japan Watch*, May 23, 2011, http://ajw.asahi.com/article/0311disaster/opinion/AJ201105232599.

12. Since March 11, 2011, there have been a number of essays in the online journal *Japan Focus* about the process by which Japan was persuaded to accept nuclear energy in the early and mid-1950s, after having been the target of nuclear attacks in 1945. Peter Kuznick quotes a Defense Department consultant to Eisenhower's 1953 United Nations "Atoms for Peace" speech advising the president, who needed nuclear fuels and technologies for the arms race with the Soviet Union, "the atomic bomb will be accepted far more

readily if at the same time atomic energy is being used for constructive ends." See Yuki Tanaka and Peter Kuznick, "Japan, the Atomic Bomb, and the 'Peaceful Uses of Nuclear Power,'" *The Asia-Pacific Journal: Japan Focus* 9, no. 18 (May 2, 2011), article no. 1, http://www.japanfocus.org/-Yuki-TANAKA/3521. Oguma Eiji notes that the countries that have promoted nuclear energy's "peaceful applications" from the Cold War to the present day are the same ones whose nuclear arsenals play the biggest role in their international diplomatic standing: "International opinion poll surveys in response to Fukushima demonstrate that Japan, Germany, and Italy indicate a preference for breaking away from nuclear power generation, while the United States, France, Russia, China, and others adhere to their standpoint of nuclear power promotion. In other words, the standing members of the UN Security Council, who armed themselves with nuclear weapons after winning World War II, maintain their position of promoting nuclear power." Oguma Eiji, "The Hidden Face of Disaster: 3.11, the Historical Structure and Future of Japan's Northeast," trans. Kyoko Selden, *The Asia-Pacific Journal Japan Focus* 9, no. 31 (August 1, 2011), article no. 6, http://www.japanfocus.org/-Oguma-Eiji/3583.

13. Murakami Takashi, "Earth in My Window" (Mado ni chikyū), trans. Linda Hoaglund, in *Little Boy: The Arts of Japan's Exploding Subculture* (New Haven, Conn.: Yale University Press, 2005), 123.

14. This point is elaborated compellingly in Peter C. van Wyck, *Signs of Danger: Waste, Trauma, and Nuclear Threat* (Minneapolis: University of Minnesota Press, 2005), 33–76.

15. Hagio Moto, *Sutaa Reddo* (Star Red) (Tokyo: Shōgakukan Bunko, 1995), 120. Hereafter, page numbers will be given parenthetically in the text.

16. Kotani, "Sutaa Reddo no watashitachi," 532.

17. Miyasako, *Chōshōjo e*, 264.

18. Translating an essay by Kotani on Japanese women's science fiction, Miri Nakamura uses "Zesnusers" for the plural of "Zesunuseru." Here, I use "Zesnuserians." Kotani Mari, "Space, Body, and Aliens in Japanese Women's Science Fiction," trans. Miri Nakamura, in *Robot Ghosts and Wired Dreams: Japanese Science Fiction from Origins to Anime*, ed. Christopher Bolton, Istvan Csicsery-Ronay Jr., and Takayuki Tatsumi (Minneapolis: University of Minnesota Press, 2007), 58.

19. Quoted in Evan Osnos, "The Fallout—Seven Months Later: Japan's Nuclear Predicament," *The New Yorker* (October 17, 2011): 61.

20. Elizabeth Grosz, "The Nature of Culture," in *Time Travels: Feminism, Nature, Power* (Durham, N.C.: Duke University Press, 2005), 51.

21. Ibid., 47.

22. Ibid., 48.

23. There is a strong affinity between this Zesnuserian law and the Lacanian framework Deborah Shamoon reads in Takemiya Keiko's 1977–1980 science fiction series *To Terra* (*Tera e*). See Deborah Shamoon, "Humanity Grows Up," in *Manga and Philosophy*, ed. Josef Steiff and Adam Barkman, 149–59 (Chicago: Open Court, 2010). For a reading of Hagio and Takemiya's contrasting approaches to the politics of desire, again defined psychoanalytically, see Midori Matsui, "Little Girls Were Little Boys: Displaced Femininity in the Representation of Homosexuality in Japanese Girls' Comics," in *Feminism and the Politics of Difference*, ed. Sneja Gunew and Anna Yeatman, 177–96 (San Francisco: Westview Press, 1993).

24. Elizabeth Grosz, "Refiguring Lesbian Desire" in *Space, Time, and Perversion* (New York: Routledge, 1995), 176.

25. We know that Neptune and Pluto have been colonized because Sei wonders if Erg might be from either of them, before she learns of his true origin in the Zesnuserian Galaxy. And we know that Jupiter has been colonized because Erg carries a fake passport from there, or rather from its moon Ganymede, to fool the Martian immigration authorities.

26. Miyasako, *Chōshōjo e*, 276.

27. Ibid., 277.

28. Ōtsuka Eiji, "'Umu sei' to shite no shōnen—'Seisa no shōjo mangashi' no tame ni" (Shōnen as the "sex that gives birth": Toward a shōjo manga history of sexual difference), in *Kodomo ryūritan: Sayonara "kodomo" tachi* (Tales of the exiled wanderings of a child: Goodbye children) (Tokyo: Shin'yōsha, 1990), 180.

29. Fujimoto's essay on Hagio appears in a volume of Ueno Chizuko's six-volume *New Feminism Review* series. Titled *Bosei fashizumu* (Maternity fascism), this volume is edited by women's historian Kanō Mikiyo and features essays on successful efforts by both the state and nationalist feminists to appropriate maternity for right-wing ends. Fujimoto Yukari, "Seishoku kara no tōsō, aruiwa, sekai no saisei: Hagio Moto o chūshin ni" (Escape from reproduction, or, the world's regeneration: With a focus on Hagio Moto), in *New Feminism Review 6: Bosei fashizumu: Haha naru shizen no yūwaku* (Maternity fascism: The temptation of mother-as-nature), ed. Kanō Mikiyo (Tokyo: Gakuyō Shobō, 1995), 134. Interestingly, the same volume, which came out nine years after Chernobyl, features two pieces actively critical of both German and Japanese antinuclear activism that rallied around "mothers who give birth to life, protecting life" (seimei o umidasu hahaoya wa, seimei o mamoru) (183). This is an important context for Fujimoto's constructivist reading. Kanō Mikiyo, "Hangenpatsu undō no naka no bosei: Kansha Taeko *Mada maniau no nara* o chūshin ni" (Maternity in the anti–nuclear power movement: With a focus on Kansha Taeko's *Is it Too Late?*), in *New Feminism Review 6*, 180–85; Kanō Mikiyo and Claudia Von Werlhof, "Bosei wa sekai o sukuu? Yōroppa hangenpatsu undō no shimesu mono" (Will maternity save the world? What Europe's anti–nuclear power movement shows), in *New Feminism Review* 6: 166–78.

FUJIMOTO YUKARI

Translated by Lucy Fraser

Where Is My Place in the World? Early Shōjo Manga Portrayals of Lesbianism

I have often been asked about the lack of lesbians depicted in shōjo manga, especially compared with the numerous depictions of gay men. At one event I spoke with a lesbian woman for a long time, and the heart of the issue finally became vividly clear to me: "Why is it that there are so few lesbian shōjo manga?"[1]

I attempted to respond with this explanation: "Lesbianism introduces reality into the work." After all, doesn't Hagio Moto say that when she was writing "Jūichigatsu no gimunajiumu" (1971, November gymnasium)—which was the model for her masterpiece *The Heart of Thomas* (1974, *Tōma no shinzō*), that set *shōnen'ai* in motion—doesn't she say that at the draft phase, she tried writing both a female and a male version, and she gave up the female version because it was too raw and fleshy?[2] Girl readers do not want to embrace female bodies; they want to create a distance between themselves and sexual love. If that is indeed the case, then girls have no reason to desire lesbianism.

The lesbian woman I was speaking with responded: "Yet before the war the world of 'S' that Yoshiya Nobuko created was so well supported by girls. I can't believe that there is no demand from readers for that kind of work now."[3]

I could not produce an answer that completely satisfied this particular woman, and I continued to wrangle with the issue: "Why can't love between

> THE HEART OF THE ISSUE FINALLY BECAME VIVIDLY CLEAR TO ME: "WHY IS IT THAT THERE ARE SO FEW LESBIAN SHŌJO MANGA?"

women provide sufficient fantasy for girls today?"

One explanation that I might give is that the closed, girls-only time and space that comprised Yoshiya Nobuko's world does not exist as a communal object any more. Of course there are still girls' schools now, and in those places there are still wavering emotions between girls, and this is reflected in works such as Yoshida Akimi's *Sakura no sono* (1985–86, The cherry orchard).[4] However, these works do not replicate the experiences of the general masses, and although girls' schools may exist, these days they are substantially influenced by the outside world. The schools can no longer exist as maidens' gardens (*otome no sono*).[5]

Most important, in Yoshiya's time, girls' schools provided a temporary respite before marriage. Marriage was usually something parents imposed on girls with or without the girls' agreement. Therefore in the limited time before marriage, girls desired the only love that they could freely choose for themselves: the fantasy of love between girls. And they savored it. However, as the concept of freedom in romantic relationships was popularized, *romantic* relationships with the opposite sex surfaced as a means for girls to choose their own paths *through* marriage. We label this concept "modern romantic love ideology." This powerful fantasy drove out all other fantasies.

Thinking through my explanation, I have come to realize that my first instinct, that "lesbianism introduces reality into the work," conceals an essential issue. I would like to consider that issue here, by examining some of the few shōjo manga that actually portray lesbianism, starting with the origins of this phenomenon in the early 1970s.

DARK ENDINGS IN LESBIAN WORKS

The earliest and most famous shōjo manga work portraying lesbians is Yamagishi Ryōko's "Shiroi heya no futari" (1971, The two of the white room).[6] This is the tragic love story of Simone and Recine, who are assigned a shared room in their school dormitory. When Simone is called on in class, she recites a Rainer Maria Rilke poem that is not in the textbook:

> I must die because I have known her
> Die for the indescribable radiance of her smile
> For her light hands I must die, for her . . .[7]

It is a very affecting poem. Simone then leaves Recine murmuring mysteriously, "I was looking at you as I said it."

Backing up slightly, the story begins with Recine, who has just lost her parents in an accident, coming into the dormitory of the girls' school. Her roommate, Simone, is beautiful and an all-around sports star, but she breaks the rules and constantly goes out at night. She is a "bad girl," which alienates her from her classmates. At first Recine is spun about by Simone and feels at a loss, but then she learns that Simone's rough lifestyle is her way of acting out to her mother, a famous actress who goes from one man to the next and who has dumped her daughter in boarding school. After this revelation, Simone and Recine are rapidly drawn to each other; Recine, although confused, allows Simone to kiss her. However, Recine is then shocked to hear rumors that she and Simone are lesbians and tries to distance herself from Simone, who tells her, "You just don't want to sully your name. You don't want to lift yourself out of the tracks of ordinary society. But I won't run away from the truth. I love you, Recine. I love you!!" Simone tries to follow Recine, but Recine brushes her off and runs into the rain. She arrives at her aunt's house and faints with a fever; when she recovers it is to be notified of Simone's death, from what amounts to a suicide.

"Shiroi heya no futari" set off a fascinating phenomenon: over the next few years in the early 1970s, the writers who were to become the leading figures in shōjo manga published works that followed the same pattern. While not portraying lesbians as their subject, these works clearly deal with lesbian relationships (though, because they were published in shōjo manga magazines, they do not involve any actual sex). The works include Ikeda Riyoko's "Futaribotchi" (1971, Just the two of us) and *Oniisama e . . .* (1974, Dear elder brother . . .), Ichijō Yukari's "Maya no sōretsu" (1972, Maya's funeral procession), and Satonaka Machiko's *Ariesu no otometachi* (1973, Maidens of Aries).[8] In fact they form a set: in all of them, lesbian relationships develop between sisters who have been raised in separate households.

In Ikeda Riyoko's early work "Futaripotchi," two girls are engaged in a bitter feud (Figure 1). (Reiko is a rich girl with long curly hair, Kaoru is poor with short hair; it is very much a product of its strange time.) Then the girls' single parents marry, and the girls become stepsisters. At first the two repel each other at every turn, but Reiko comes to acknowledge that she is drawn to Kaoru; after that the two rapidly become intimate. At that point, it comes to light that their remarried parents, Reiko's father and Kaoru's mother, were once lovers. So, does that mean that while Reiko and Kaoru may have different mothers, they are actually sisters . . . ? No, in a sudden twist, they learn

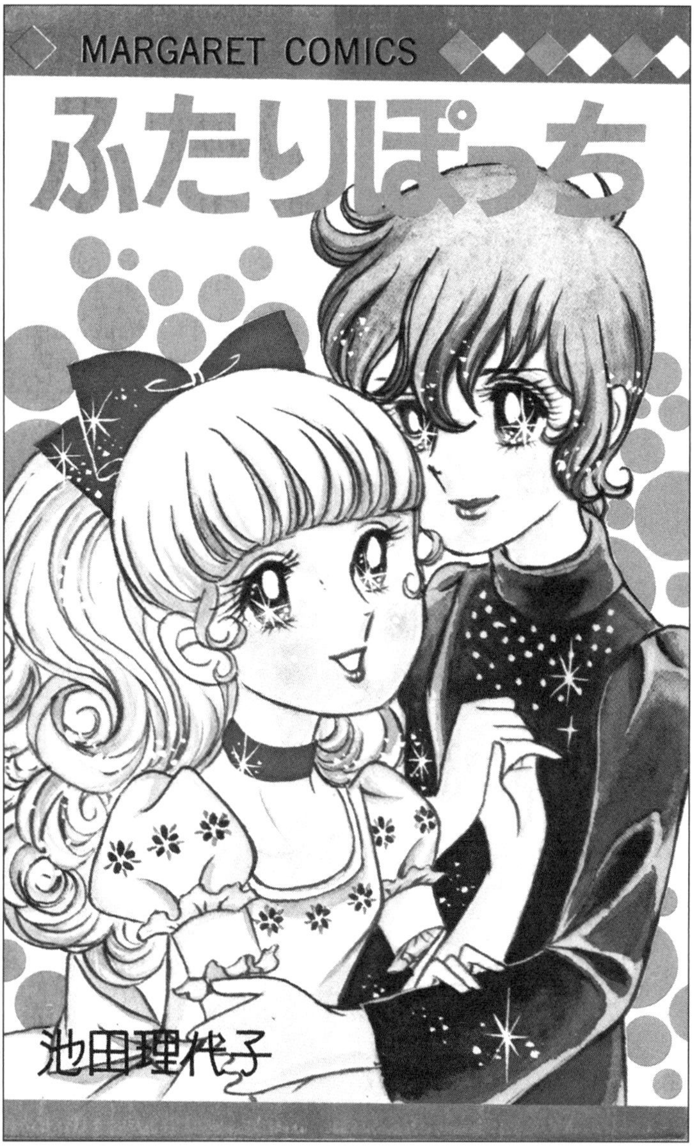

FIGURE 1. Cover image for Ikeda Riyoko's *Futaripotchi* (1971), from the 1971 Margaret Comics paperback edition.

that the revelation that Kaoru's new stepfather was actually her biological father was a lie told by Kaoru's mother to bring stability to her life. The truth is that Kaoru was conceived when her mother was forcefully impregnated by a robber-murderer. When Reiko and Kaoru learn this, they lose all hope for a happy future and commit suicide together.

Oniisama e . . . has a slightly more complicated plot. The heroine Nanako has entered an exclusive private school for young ladies that has a sorority for selected students. Nanako is not a typical invitee, but she becomes a member because the sorority leader, Ichinomiya Fukiko (respectfully nicknamed "Miya-sama") takes a liking to her (Figure 2). However, there is something strange and jarring in the relationship between Fukiko and another student—Asai Rei (nicknamed "San Jusuto no Kimi" or Saint-Just), with whom Nanako has fallen in love at first sight. The story revolves around Fukiko and Rei's relationship, but others become entangled: Rei's good friend Orihara Kaoru (nicknamed "Kaoru no Kimi"), as well as Shinobu Mariko, a proud solitary girl who hates men and is deeply attached to Nanako.[9] Finally, it is revealed that

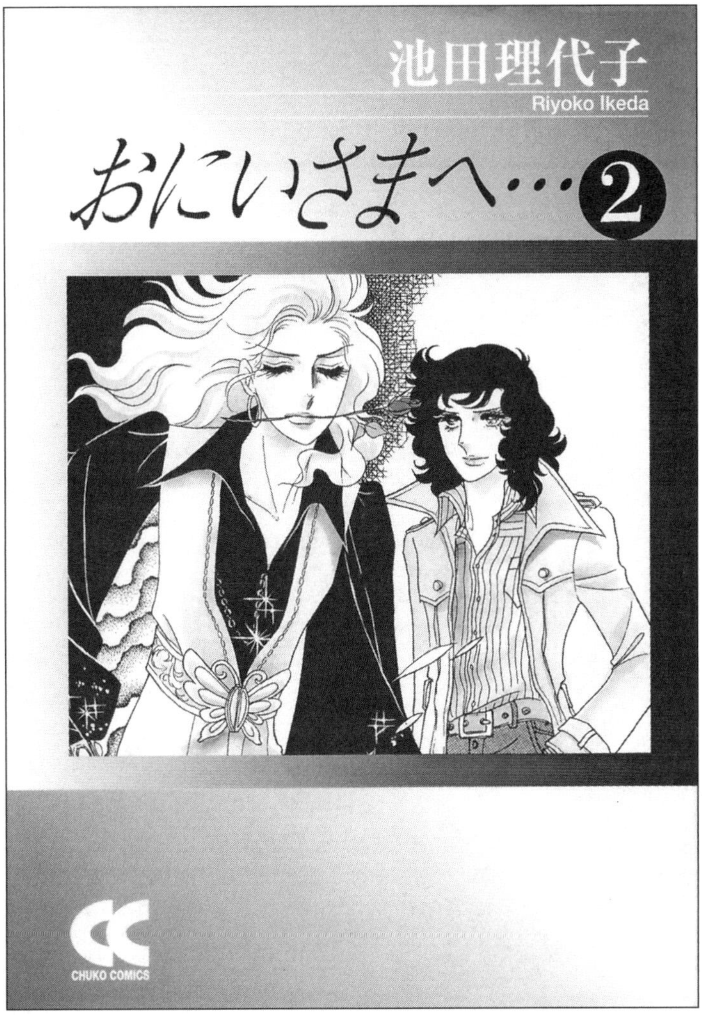

FIGURE 2. Cover image for Ikeda Riyoko's *Oniisama e . . .* (1974, Dear elder brother . . .), from volume 2 of the 2002 Chūkō Bunko paperback edition.

the scar on Saint-Just's right wrist was a cut made by Fukiko, who told her "I will die together for you." Rei and Fukiko are also revealed to be sisters sharing both mother and father. (Fukiko had known that Rei was the illegitimate child of her father's mistress, but then discovers she has the same mother.) Then the enraged Fukiko informs Rei that she does not have a single feeling of love for her, that she was only using Rei to enhance her own sense of superiority. The next day at school they are notified of Rei's suicide.

"Maya no sōretsu" is basically the same in its tragedy involving a (possible) sister/lesbian couple (Figure 3). Reina is the privileged daughter of a family in the jewelry trade. She visits her family's holiday home after a long absence and encounters a beautiful woman, Maya, who has some kind of shadow hanging over her. Maya, too, was once the happy daughter of a jeweler family, but her parents were killed by Reina's parents, who destroyed the business belonging to Maya's family by burning their building; Maya and her elder sister were permanently marked with burns and now seek revenge. Maya moves steadily closer to her revenge, but even so, Reina and Maya are strongly drawn to each other. When the story reaches the crucial closing act of vengeance, Maya learns from Reina's mother that Maya and Reina are sisters by the same father. Reina's mother was abandoned by Reina's father, so out of spite the mother killed him and took the jewelry business. Maya, having achieved her revenge, leaves only Reina behind and disappears into the flames.

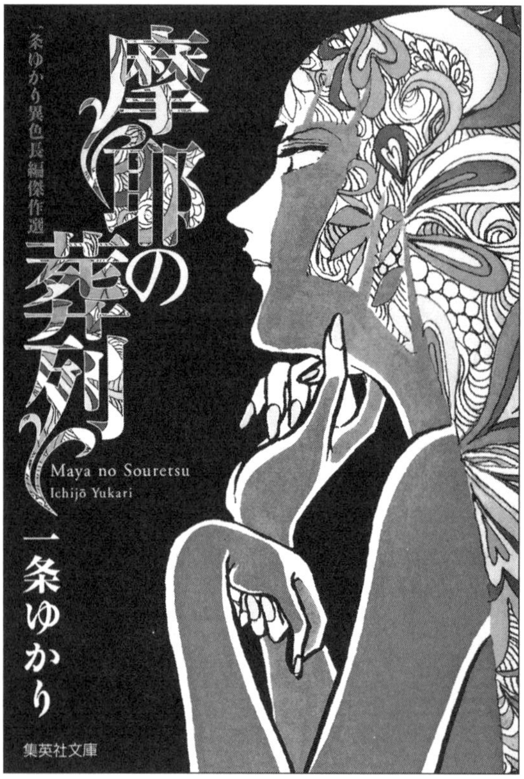

FIGURE 3. "Maya no sōretsu" (1972, Maya's funeral procession) is the title manga for this 2005 Shūeisha Bunko paperback collection of Ichijō Yukari's work.

As you can see, each one of these works reaches a dark conclusion. The one exception is Satonaka Machiko's *Ariesu no otometachi*. In this story, Ekubo does not realize that the dashing, fiery, and outspoken Romi (also a talented horseback rider) is her own sister (Figure 4). The text is the same as the others up to the point where the two main characters experience a powerful mutual love and admiration even though they are of the same

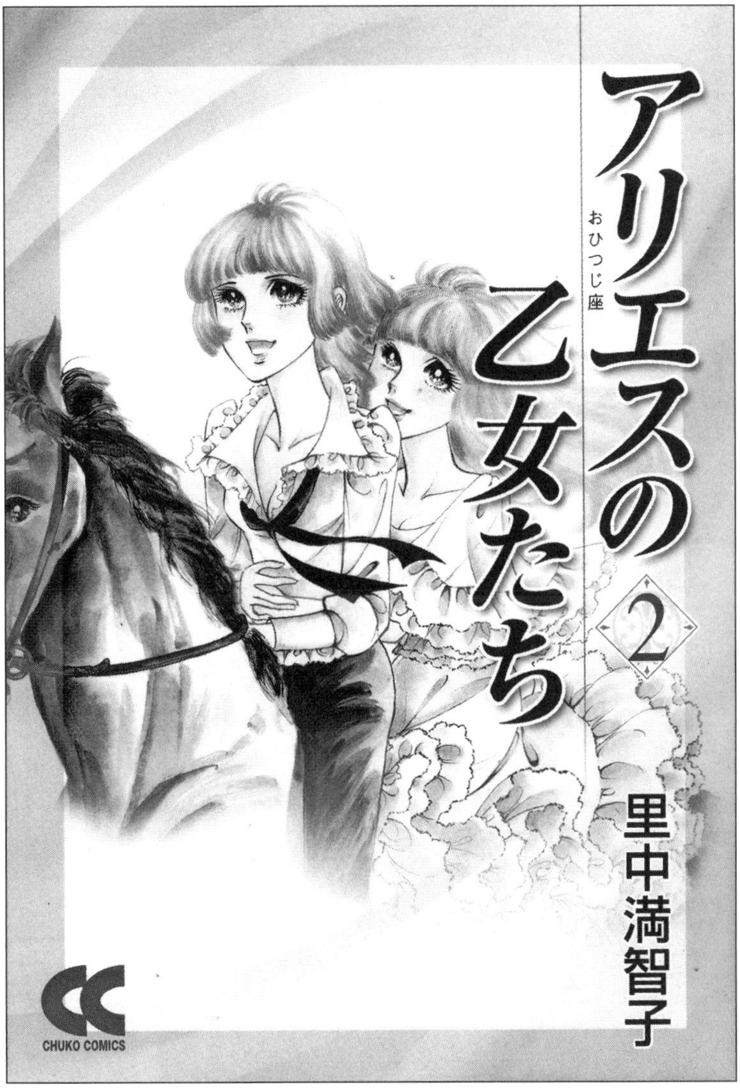

FIGURE 4. Cover image for Satonaka Machiko's *Ariesu no otometachi* (1973–, Maidens of Aries), from volume 2 of the 2005 Chūkō Bunko paperback edition.

gender. However, when they discover that they are sisters, their relationship changes. (In other words, they come to a realization that they were drawn to each other because they share the same blood.) In fact after that point, the narrative shifts to focus on their rivalry over the same boy. As a result, the tragedy worthy of a classical painting that characterizes each of the other texts is absent here.

What I want to establish is that while the subject of *Ariesu no otometachi* is not "lesbians" (as it is, for example, in "Shiroi heya no futari") and while the girls' intense emotions are explained away as "blood ties," it is clear that the girls' relationship was bound to end in tragedy if it had not changed to another form.

THE CRIMSON ROSE AND THE CANDY GIRL

Skipping ahead a few years to the mid- to late 1970s and early 1980s, a number of lesbian works were published in *Sebuntiin* (Seventeen), a magazine aimed at an older bracket of shōjo readers and a forerunner of the ladies' comics genre. Examples include Fukuhara Hiroko's *Kurenai ni moyu* (Blazing crimson) and *Hadashi no Mei* (Barefoot Mei), and Kashi Michiyo's *Kanojotachi* (Those girls). A little more recently, in the mid-1980s, Nagahama Sachiko's *Ibutachi no heya* (Eve and the others' room) was serialized in *Gyaruzu komikku* (Girls comic).[10] In keeping with publications aimed at an older readership, the stories included not only kisses but also actual sexual relations. However, all of these works with lesbians as their subjects (including "Shiroi heya no futari," discussed above) are surprisingly similar on a structural level.

The two main characters in every work are invariably a beautiful, cool superwoman with a bold personality matched with an extremely girly, artless type. I will refer to the former as the "Crimson Rose" and the latter as the "Candy Girl." Both these protagonists—but particularly the Rose—are burdened with unhappy homes. While not every Candy Girl suffers from this particular problem, she is always dosed with some measure of unhappiness, and the unhappier the Candy Girl is at home, the more she is inclined toward the Rose. (One exception to the rule is the Candy Girl in *Kanojotachi*, Misono, who has a supportive family.)

These lesbian relationships are consistently gossiped about and treated as a scandal by the cruel characters surrounding the protagonists. The threat of exposure as lesbians through photographic evidence is a common device. The late 1980s work, *Ibutachi no heya*, is no exception: even though it is set at a girls' high school where students simper over fellow girls about as regularly as they eat meals, when the two main characters are discovered to have serious feelings, they are the sudden victims of slander and backbiting comments such as "Ew, so they're lesbians. That's so disgusting," and "How far do you think they'll take this lesbo thing?" As a result the Rose—trying to protect her Candy Girl even if she cannot protect herself—either kills the blackmailer then herself (in *Kurenai ni moyu*), or loses all hope and undergoes a death that is near suicide (in *Kanojotachi* and "Shiroi heya no futari"). Whatever the events, it seems that the Rose is fated to die in every story.

The circumstances surrounding these dark endings and deaths are the same as in the sister/lesbian stories of the early 1970s texts. The only real difference is that, in the earlier works, lesbianism is not cited as the direct reason for the death. Rather than slander and outside pressure, the death is the result of complicated circumstances arising from the secrets surrounding the character's birth and origins.

Even when the characters do not actually die, the specter of suicide is still present. In *Hadashi no Mei* the two characters do not precisely enter a lesbian relationship, so neither one dies; but the Rose protagonist is the survivor of a previous lesbian double suicide, so that element is still inserted into the story. In *Ibutachi no heya* the Candy Girl loves the Rose, but unable to stand the slander, she betrays her and decides to marry. On the day of the wedding, the Rose sneaks into the bridal dressing room and demands the Candy Girl take poison and commit suicide with her. The Candy Girl takes the poison mouth-to-mouth from the Rose, but the latter reveals that it was a ruse; having confirmed that the Candy Girl still loves her, the Rose departs and leaves her at the ceremony.

Texts that portray male homosexuality—which I believe are the essential opposite of these lesbian texts—do not deal similarly with the censoring gaze of society, rumor and gossip, or taboo. This contrast illustrates the fact that shōjo manga about male–male relationships are not attempting to portray "homosexuality." At heart, these texts attempt to portray not men whose sexual orientation makes them capable of loving only other men but the extreme opposite. These works are an attempt to remove the existing symbolism and imagery that has surrounded heterosexuality, and to portray the shape of a more purified sexual love. Therefore, even if characters face interior conflict because their love is not easily accepted, on the outside they do not work out problems of being different or being judged for being a male attracted to other males.

On the other hand, the fact that lesbian works cannot escape from society's gaze is proof that they are dealing with "reality." This is the reason lesbian texts cannot expand into the territory of fantasy. They exist in opposition to the male homosexual texts, which adopted the figures of boys in order to soar away from reality and acquire the excitement and fascination of human relationships removed from everyday experience.

There are a very small number exceptions to the patterns describe here, and in any case, as I have already pointed out, shōjo manga that treat lesbianism are very few to begin with.[11] Other manga that might touch on the subject all involve beautiful-girl-in-boy's-clothing types. There is Rosalie's admiration and affection for Oscar in *The Rose of Versailles* (1972–73, Berusaiyu no bara); Romantsa's confession of love for her girlhood friend Valentino/a, the female sovereign of Venice disguised as a man, in Morikawa Kumi's "Sukyandaru mūn wa yoru no yume" (The scandal moon is a night dream); and the love between the male-dressing Queen Erminia and the servant Fiona in *Parosu no ken* (1986–87, The sword of Paros).[12] That is about the extent of it, and what's more, all three of these couples are still Crimson Rose–Candy Girl combinations. Comparing these few works with the profusion of talent in male homosexual shōjo manga is like comparing earth with heaven.

THE CAGE OF REALITY

So why on earth is it that reality is bound to intrude upon lesbian works, and why is it that they cannot then break away from stereotypical portrayals? Why is it that the minute the protagonist dresses up as a boy, shōjo are released from reality and a free world full of excitement is created? It can only be that for shōjo, and also for women, *being a woman* is the most insurmountable symbol of reality. And sadly, for shōjo this particular reality is difficult to accept.

First and foremost is the fear of sexuality. The majority of girls cannot feel 100 percent open to the idea of sexual maturity. It is something they want to look forward to as well as something to put off. These works, beginning with the *shōnen'ai* I have discussed and encompassing the great variety of shōjo manga that experiment with transgressing gender boundaries, are in fact flowers that have bloomed from an earth made fertile by girls' inability to experience positive affirmation and acceptance of their own sexuality as women. We see this in the misogynistic remarks dropped by the protagonists of *shōnen'ai* works, but girls' dispositions toward their own sexuality are most clearly represented in the prototypes that gave birth to all these texts that depict gender transgression: that is, the works that explore "the girl in boy's clothing." The figure of the boy is a disguise for the souls of those girls who want to put off being women. In most cases these girls accept their own female sexuality with the appearance of a member of the opposite sex whom they like: they remove their male costume and fall into the arms of the one they love. (Of course I am speaking metaphorically here.) This act echoes a wish to "be a woman only in front of the person I love." There are not many women who do not experience this wish.

Considered from another angle, this means that there is *only one way* a woman can affirm her own sexuality: "being loved by a man (whom I love)." The structure of this belief is also connected to the fantasy that "someday my prince will come." In contrast to their apparent sweetness, these fantasies cannot be neatly dismissed as girls' dreams and yearnings: at their root is a desire that concerns the very foundations of existence.

IT IS NO EXAGGERATION TO SAY THAT THE WORDS "WHERE IS MY PLACE IN THE WORLD?" MAY BE USED TO REPRESENT THE THEME OF NEARLY EVERY SHŌJO MANGA.

For the last thirty years, I have absorbed shōjo manga at about the same rate as I absorb oxygen, and what preoccupies me deeply is the extreme degree to which girls cannot help but want their own identities to be confirmed by another. The girls keep shouting "Somebody love me. Someone tell me that it is alright for me to be alive!" While much of this desire takes the form of a longing for heterosexual love, sometimes it is voiced directly to parents. It is no exaggeration to say that the words "Where is my place in the world?" may be used to represent the theme of nearly every shōjo manga. And the wonder drug that resolves this anxiety about the existence and acceptance of sexuality is a member of the opposite sex, someone you love telling you that he loves you and affirming your own existence. It is at that moment that the negative marker "woman" is changed dramatically into a positive one, and, it seems, the moment the woman begins to shine.

However, the structure of this apparent "wonder drug" conceals the way the fantasy itself actually exacerbates women's anxieties about their own existence. Why does a woman become so desperate to be loved? No other affirmation can rescue her from these anxieties; if she achieves love from a man then she is fine, but if not she will never be able to reconcile herself with the reality of her existence as a woman.

This is the message of the modern romantic love ideology: "Couple. If you do not couple you are nothing."[13] A woman is of no value in and of herself. A woman who is not loved by a man is second-rate—no matter how successful she might be in society. Women are constantly exposed to this threat. They have been impelled to suffer a variety of disadvantages because their sexuality has been judged essentially inferior, and love with a man is the only means of improvement and the only way to finally have their place in society recognized. Women have internalized this process, and it has manifested itself as an evasion of our own inner sexuality. It has become the single-minded belief that a man's sympathy and deep love can rescue a woman from her anxiety.

This process of anxiety and desire, discernible when we consider the gaps in the portrayal of lesbianism in shōjo manga, certainly gives me the shivers. It reveals a dexterous form of control in which male-dominated society has imprinted girls with an anxiety about themselves and then led them to believe that only men can save them from their anxiety. Yet is there anyone who can renounce this belief and escape it?

The question of "Where is my place in the world?" is the powerful theme of shōjo manga; it is the desire for self-affirmation through the other, and it is especially emphasized in lesbian works. Two souls are called together by their mutual loneliness and unhappiness at home. For example, in *Kurenai ni moyu*, Reina (the Candy Girl) says:

> I've finally found a place to belong
> I had been searching for it since I was small
> somewhere that will care for my heart
> a place that will warm my loneliness
> where time is easy on me . . .

If this were a comic about heterosexual love, this would be the ultimate happy ending. Readers would expect Reina and her partner to overcome the obstacles keeping them apart, and the writer would meet those expectations. But in manga about lesbians, this cannot be. For one thing, even if a girl's spiritual hunger for someone to affirm her existence is sated, the second function of affirmation by the opposite sex cannot be fulfilled—that is, the male's function as a passport to becoming a regular member of society.

Furthermore, because the medium is shōjo manga, neither the protagonists nor the readers are yet conditioned as responsible adults who can consciously choose lesbianism. Inevitably, the period where the shōjo can believe that "a man will appear who can save me from everything" is the quintessence of shōjo manga. On the other hand, when she has lost hope and realized that "no man will save me," the reader becomes independent, or assumes a ladies' comic attitude where all she desires from men is the guarantee of social status, sex, and entertainment. If all that is the case, then for girls who cannot discard the hope of "someday, somewhere," lesbianism can only ever be an emergency escape.

Before their suicide pact in *Hadashi no Mei*, the girl protagonists' classmates speculate that their "indecent relationship" is the result of their unhappy upbringings. The words Misaki (the Rose) shouts back at them are characteristic of lesbian shōjo manga:

> We're two children who didn't know our fathers, whose homes are troubled, and well, our hearts didn't fit in with everyone else's. One day we met, and comforted one another, warmed one another, and made a world just for the two of us. Even though we knew that having our own private world created a bigger and bigger distance between us and everyone else, we couldn't let go of the warmth we had finally found. Don't you get it? For a truly lonely person, if you find someone who will fill your loneliness you don't care who they are!

In essence, she describes a closed existence into which the girls retreat to nurse each other's wounds. Of course this is not a realistic portrayal of lesbian relationships. However, because the vehicle is shōjo manga, and because the shōjo's fantasy that "a man will save me" is still being perpetuated, the works cannot move past this image.[14]

The existence of women reminds girls unavoidably of "the cage of reality." Whether it is imagining love with a male, or imagining oneself as a male as in *shōnen'ai,* girls cannot escape from that cage unless the medium is that symbol known as "a man." Unconscious or not, this feeling is at the heart of the issue.

EMOTIONAL EXCHANGE BETWEEN WOMEN

As I have written elsewhere, from the 1990s onward, lesbian works all at once became more bright and cheerful.[15] But in this earlier period of the 1970s and '80s, where does lesbianism exist apart from sexual taboo, a mutual nursing of wounds in a closed space, and pornography? On which horizon does it have new meanings? I will consider the answer to my final question through a discussion of Kimura Minori's *Umibe no Kain* (Cain of the seaside), published in *Mimi* in 1980–81 (Figure 5).[16] (*Mimi* was one of the first magazines of the genre now known as "young ladies"—shōjo manga magazines marketed to the upper age bracket—but unfortunately it ceased publication in 1996.)

The story begins with Mori Nobuko, who works as a waitress or sings and plays guitar in late-night cafés; she is what is now known as a "freeter."[17] Nobuko comes to a seaside town and gets to know Sano-san, a children's clothing designer. The women form a close friendship, and Nobuko confides in Sano-san about the emotional wounds inflicted by her mother. Through Sano-san's advice and support, Nobuko is able to straighten out her feelings and visit her parents for the first time in a long time.

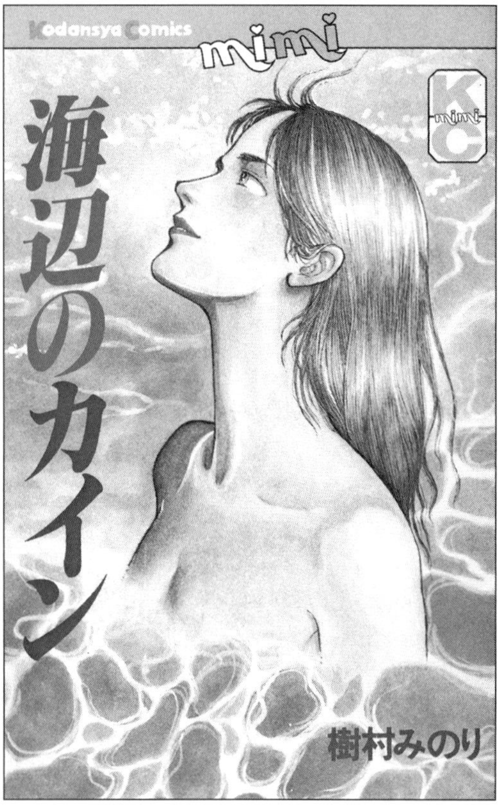

FIGURE 5. Cover image for Kimura Minori's *Umibe no Kain* (1980–81, Cain of the seaside), from the 1981 Kōdansha Comics Mimi paperback edition.

One night, that same Sano-san who understood Nobuko's feelings so well invites Nobuko to bed with her. In reply, Nobuko confesses that: "I have always loved you, I think from the time I first met you, but I was worried that I didn't love you for yourself, that I was loving you in replacement for my mother. But now I have reconciled with my mother, so there is no reason for me to feel guilty about my feelings for you." Sano-san's expression changes slightly, and after that night she rejects Nobuko, saying that Nobuko's "intentions" "disgust" her. "I was acting out of curiosity . . . a woman loving a woman," she says. "You are unnatural. It's abnormal."

In a desperate whirl of emotions, Nobuko realizes that, as with her mother, she is "angry when the other person does not love me." She goes to meet Sano-san again. This time Sano-san invites her inside and presses her with, "It was curiosity for you too, you know." Nobuko wonders, "Does she want me to say yes?" She tries to answer but the tears stream down her face, and she cannot say anything. The final lines conclude with, "I left the town by the seaside, and never returned."

While some might read Sano-san's rejection of Nobuko as showing the taboo against lesbianism, others might feel that nothing really happens in the story. Kimura Minoru later published *Hahaoya no musumetachi* (Mother's daughters), which depicts a situation very similar to the one in *Umibe no Kain*.[18] That is, a woman (who feels that her mother didn't love her) admires an older woman and shares her bed once, at the older woman's invitation, but is then treated coldly. In *Hahaoya no musumetachi* the psychology of the older woman is explicated: another female friend explains to the protagonist, "She just wanted to tease you a little. She was surprised when she found your feelings were serious."

The title *Hahaoya no musumetachi* proves that mother–daughter relationships are among Kimura Minori's personal interests. As I have already shown, in shōjo manga, conflicts with parents, unhappiness at home, and loneliness are the foundations through which people connect. The same elements are also emphasized in the portrayal of male–female relationships. So what exactly is new about Kimura's portrayal of lesbianism? What is the element that is unique to love between women that cannot be narrated through analogies with male–female love? I believe that it is the subtle *exchange* of feelings made possible because what we might call the pressure of their emotions is equalized between both partners. The similarity of their experience as women is what allows their emotions to permeate the barriers between them. That mutual exchange is not possible if one of the partners is male.[19] Regardless of the final break between the two characters, this is what Kimura's work has captured.

Here we are finally emancipated from the Crimson Rose–Candy Girl pairing. A glance at the illustrations shows that the two characters do not have especially alluring figures; they are ordinary women one might find anywhere. For example, Sano-san's distorted feelings about problems in her design career are something that, on the whole, we would rather not see. However, Nobuko views Sano-san as "someone who is honest about her feelings" and says "sometimes Sano-san has an incredibly lonely look on her face." In fact, on the inside, Sano-san shares Nobuko's feeling that her sexuality is not accepted. She says, "I think I'm probably someone other people don't love," and Sano-san's rejection of Nobuko is colored by her experience, long ago, of having sex with a man who then stopped contacting her and dumped her.

This reminds me of Yoshida Akimi's *Sakura no sono.* Yoshida's work also portrays that subtle exchange of feelings enabled because both partners are female. "If we do this it makes our breasts less obtrusive," Shimizu-san explains to Kurata-san as she sews ribbon into her costume; and I cannot think of two stories more heartbreaking than the ones Shimizu-san relates in this scene. She says, "I have large breasts too, and I've worried about them since I was small . . . I thought I had done something wrong," and again, "I still remember clearly the vivid red stain on my underpants, as though someone had swept a crimson crayon across them. I washed my body again and again in the bathroom. And while I washed, I cried."

Here we find that two girls can understand each other because they are both female, because they both share the same realities, and because they share the same level of emotion, their feelings are able to permeate into each other. As a result, through their exchange of sensations and feelings, women are able to accept the existence of their own sexuality in a way that does not use the existence of men as its medium.

> HERE WE FIND THAT TWO GIRLS CAN UNDERSTAND EACH OTHER BECAUSE THEY ARE BOTH FEMALE, BECAUSE THEY BOTH SHARE THE SAME REALITIES, AND BECAUSE THEY SHARE THE SAME LEVEL OF EMOTION, THEIR FEELINGS ARE ABLE TO PERMEATE INTO EACH OTHER.

In times when women enjoyed less freedom, there was a period when their one hope was a "modern love relationship" with a man who understood them. However, today the thought that this relationship is the only path available is trapping women in anxiety. When women can affirm their own sexuality as women, or better, affirm their own existence as women, a completely new horizon will open. That is an image of a new society that no one has yet seen. In the world of manga written for women, there are some texts such as Yoshimura Akemi's *Kirin-kan gurafiti* (Kirin Hall graffiti) that, while they may not be lesbian, feature women who meet one another through men and join together to transcend the existence of men and affirm one another's existence. These provide us with a vivid image of an ideal world created by women.[20]

"Woman-loving" means women affirming their own sexuality from within themselves. The possibilities that accompany love between women exist not within fantasy but within women's shared ownership of the same reality. And this sharing allows women to forge connections that may work toward changing that reality.

Notes

1. [This text is an abridged translation of "Rezubian: Onna de aru koto o aiseru ka" (Lesbianism: Can We Love Our Own Existence as Women?), a later chapter from Fujimoto's book *Watashi no ibasho wa doko ni aru no? Shōjo manga ga utsusu kokoro no katachi* (Where is my place in the world? The shape of the heart reflected in girls' comics) (Tokyo: Gakuyō Shobō, 1998). For a translation of the preceding chapter see: "Transgender: Female Hermaphrodites and Male Androgynes," trans. Linda Flores and Kazumi Nagaike, *U.S.–Japan Women's Journal* 27 (2004): 76–117. For other English translations of Fujimoto's work, see "Takahashi Macoto: The Origin of Shōjo Manga Style," trans. Matt Thorn, *Mechademia* 7 (2012): 24–55; "Historical Shōjo Manga: On Women's Alleged Dislike," trans. Jaqueline Berndt, in *International Journal of Comic Art*, 13, no. 2 (2011): 87–102; "A Life-Size Mirror: Women's Self-Representation in Girls' Comics," trans. Julianne Dvorak, *Review of Japanese Culture and Society* 4 (1991): 53–57. For an English-language outline of shōjo manga scholarship in Japan, see Takeuchi Kayo, "The Genealogy of Japanese Shōjo Manga (Girls' Comics) Studies," *U.S.–Japan Women's Journal* 38 (2010): 81–112.—Trans.]

2. Hagio Moto, "Jūichigatsu no gimunajiumu" (November gymnasium), in *Seera Hiru no seiya* (Sara Hill's holy night), season 1, vol. 4 (Tokyo: Shōgakukan, 1977), first published in *Bessatsu shōjo komikku,* November 1971; Hagio Moto, *Tōma no shinzō*, season 1,

vols. 11–12 (Tokyo: Shōgakukan, 1978); translated as *The Heart of Thomas* by Matt Thorn (Seattle: Fantagraphics, 2013); Yoshimoto Takaaki and Hagio Moto, "Jiko hyōgen to shite no shōjo manga" (Shōjo manga as self-expression), *Yuriika* 13, no. 9 (July 1981): 82–119.

3. ["S" describes romances or intimate friendships between girls; Sarah Frederick notes that the letter "can refer to 'sister,' *shōjo,* or the German *schöne*" (68). For more on Yoshiya Nobuko's girl characters see Frederick's chapter, "Not That Innocent: Yoshiya Nobuko's Good Girls," in *Bad Girls of Japan,* ed. Laura Miller and Jan Bardsley (New York: Palgrave Macmillan, 2005), 65–79.—Trans.].

4. Yoshida Akimi, *Sakura no sono* (The cherry orchard) (Tokyo: Hakusensha, 1986).

5. [Apart from playing on Yoshida's title, the phrase *otome no sono* (maidens' garden) has several connotations in the field of shōjo studies. The word *sono* might remind readers of a private, enclosed garden such as is found in Frances Hodgson Burnett's *The Secret Garden* (1910; rpt., London: M. Joseph, 1986), which, in Japanese translation, became one of the classics of the *shōjo shōsetsu* (girls' novels) genre that gave birth to shōjo manga. Also, Honda Masuko, in her pioneering essay on the shōjo, used garden imagery to describe girls' reading: "When I was a girl, there was nothing more important than the infinitely rich 'world of our own.' So those of us who cherished this world joined together and built a small enclosure to protect our secret garden. What did our enclosure protect? Girls today guard their paradise known as the girls' comic. What flowers bloom therein?" Honda Masuko, "The Genealogy of *Hirahira,*" trans. Tomoko Aoyama and Barbara Hartley, in *Girl Reading Girl in Japan,* ed. Tomoko Aoyama and Barbara Hartley (New York: Routledge, 2010), 36.—Trans.]

6. Yamagishi Ryōko, "Shiroi heya no futari" (The two of the white room), vol. 28 of *Refuto ando raito Yamagishi Ryōko zenshū* (Left and right, complete works of Yamagishi Ryōko) (Tokyo: Kadokawa Shoten, 1986). First published: *Ribon komikku* (Ribbon Comic), February 1971.

7. [Yamagishi's text shifts from the more generalized "we" or "one," and the plural object "them" common in English and Japanese translations to the more personal "I" and "her," which may be a deliberate change by Yamagishi/Simone.—Trans.]

8. Ikeda Riyoko, "Futaribotchi" (Just the two of us), *Maagaretto* (Margaret), no. 23–27, 1971; reprinted in *Aizōhan Ikedo Riyoko chūhenshū II* (Classic Ikeda Riyoko, central volume II) (Tokyo: Chūo Kōronsha, 1989); Ikeda Riyoko, *Oniisama e . . .* (Dear elder brother . . .), *Maagaretto* (Margaret), no. 12–39, 1974; reprinted in *Aizōhan Ikedo Riyoko chūhenshū I* (Classic Ikeda Riyoko, central volume I) (Tokyo: Chūo Kōronsha, 1989); Ichijō Yukari, "Maya no sōretsu" (Maya's funeral procession), *Ribon* (Ribbon), May supplement, 1972; reprinted in *Kurisuchiina no aoi sora • Maya no sōretsu • Kugatsu no popii* (Christina's blue sky; Maya's funeral procession; September poppy) (Tokyo: Shūeisha SG Komikkusu, 1991); Satonaka Machiko, *Ariesu no otometachi* (Maidens of Aries), *Shūkan shōjo furendo* (Girl's friend weekly), nos. 33–, 1973; reprinted in 4 vols. (Tokyo: NTT Shuppan Manga Kessakushu, 1996).

9. [Rei's nickname is taken from the ruthless French revolutionary, Louis Antoine Léon de Saint-Just. Kaoru's nickname is taken from Prince Genji's nephew, an ambiguous character in Murasaki Shikibu's eleventh-century classic, *The Tale of Genji.*—Trans.]

10. Fukuhara Hiroko, *Kurenai ni moyu* (Blazing crimson), 2 vols. (Tokyo: Shōgakukan Manga Bunko, 1982); Fukuhara Hiroko, *Hadashi no Mei* (Barefoot Mei) (Tokyo: Shōgakukan

Manga Bunko, 1977); Kashi Michiyo, *Kanojotachi* (Those girls) (Tokyo: Shōgakukan Manga Bunko, 1982); Nagahama Sachiko, *Ibutachi no heya* (Eve and the others' room) (Tokyo: Shufu no Tomo-sha GL Komikkusu, 1983).

11. For two rare exceptions that portray lesbianism with no hint of taboo, see Naka Tomoko's woman-loving protagonist Duchess Vistaria in *Sharutoru kōshaku no tanoshimi* (The Duchess of Chartres's pleasure), 7 vols. (Tokyo: Shogakukan Bunko, 2004), and fashion model Shijō Maki in Ikesumi Chieko's *Kujaku no bishō* (The peacock's smile), first serialized in *Purinsesu* (Princess), 3 vols. (Tokyo: Akita Shoten Purinsesu Komikkusu, 1976–77).

12. Ikeda Riyoko, *Berusaiyu no bara* (The rose of Versailles), *Maagaretto* (Margaret), nos. 21–52 (1972–73); reprinted in 5 vols. (Tokyo: Shūeisha Bunko, 1994); Morikawa Kumi, "Sukyandaru mūn wa yoru no yume" (The scandal moon is a night dream), in *Barenchiino shiriizu* 1 (Valentino series vol. 1) (Tokyo: Take Shobō, 2001); Kurimoto Kaoru (text) and Igarashi Yumiko (illus.), *Parosu no ken* (The sword of Paros), 3 vols. (Tokyo: Asuka Komikkusu, 1987).

13. Ueno Chizuko, Afterword to *Seiairon* (Theory of sexual love) (Tokyo: Kawade Shobō Shinsha, 1991).

14. [Here I have omitted Fujimoto's discussion of two rare exceptions. The first is Ariyoshi Kyōko's important lesbian work *Apurōzu* (1981–82, Applause), which portrays the strong bond and tension between two aspiring actresses. Second, while depictions of lesbianism in the ladies' comics genre for adult readers tend to be pornographic, Tsukumo Mutsumi's *Mūnraito furawaazu* (1989–90, Moonlight flowers) is seemingly a culmination of the shōjo manga portrayals. One of the characters speaks the following line: "[In this era of women's social advancement] Many men find it difficult to accept lesbianism because it encroaches on their privileges. For men, sex, most of all, is the last bastion. Men always believe that 'women are not allowed to have sex without men' and 'women are always waiting for men who will love and desire them.'" Tsukumo Mutsumi, *Mūnraito furawaazu* (Moonlight flowers) (Tokyo: Shūeisha, 1991).—Trans.]

15. [See the chapter that follows this one in *Watashi no ibasho wa doko ni aru no*, "Jidai wa akarui rezubian" (The bright era of lesbian works).—Trans.]

16. Kimura Minori, *Umibe no Kain* (Kain of the seaside) (Tokyo: Kōdansha Komikkusu, 1981).

17. [*Furiitaa* (freeter) is the name for freelancers or people working in casual, usually low-paid jobs, who often exist on the fringes of society.—Trans.]

18. Kimura Minori, *Hahaoya no musumetachi* (Mother's daughters) (Tokyo: Kawade Shobō Shinsha, 1986).

19. [Fujimoto's original metaphor involves the notion of osmotic pressure and osmotic exchange between two fluid solutions.—Trans.]

20. Yoshimura Akemi, *Kirin-kan gurafiti* (Kirin Hall graffiti), 13 vols. + extra edition (Tokyo: Shōgakukan Furawaa Komikkusu, 1987–92).

SETH JACOBOWITZ

Between Men, Androids, and Robots: Assaying Mechanical Man in Meiji Literature and Visual Culture

Despite the seeming ubiquity of androids, robots, and their biomechanical kin in contemporary Japanese popular culture, we are sorely beset by a lack of understanding of their discursive origins. Conventional narratives on the subject all too often breezily skip from eighteenth-century *karakuri* (handmade automata) to postwar icons such as Tezuka Osamu's *Tetsuwan Atomu* (Astro Boy) and beyond, with scant mention of the major developments that transpired between them.[1] Even pioneering studies such as Inoue Haruki's *Nippon robotto sōseiki, 1920–1938* (1993, The genesis of Japanese robots, 1920–1938), which have done much to refocus attention on the intellectual ferment of the interwar years, essentially bypass the half-century of industrialization and technological innovation in the Meiji period (1868–1912).[2] The frequency with which tropes of "machine-like" (*kikai no yōni*) and "mechanical" (*kikaiteki*) human beings are expressed in modern Japanese literature and visual culture, however, necessitates closer scrutiny of the episteme of "mechanical man" that arose during this time. It further raises the question how these notions of mechanization ought to be reconciled with the Meiji ethos of "civilization and enlightenment" (*bunmei kaika*) that placed strong emphasis on Western humanism and Romanticist philosophy. If Meiji thought culminated in calls for emancipated individualism such as Natsume Sōseki's "My Individualism" (1914, *Watakushi no kojinshugi*), it did not forestall the disquieting apprehension of the individual's limits under the conditions of what can rightly be called Japan's first machine age.[3] To that end, this article seeks to assay—I intentionally use this term from the hard sciences to determine the quantity of metallic or biological substance in a given object—the recurrent trope of mechanization that appears in Meiji literature and visual culture. Even as individuality was being discovered in modern Japan, so too were its technologically and socially defined boundaries.

My critical approach is principally informed by the methodological insights of Friedrich Kittler's *Discourse Networks 1800/1900* and Eve Kosovsky Sedgwick's *Between Men*.[4] Kittler identifies a new class of privileged, male authors, protagonists and readers in German Romanticism for whom Woman (not individual women) is elevated to sacred Muse of Nature and Beauty, who does not speak for herself but instead circulates as a signifier in Romanticism's constellation. While we may already detect in this arrangement the internal workings of what Sedgwick calls "homosociality," I wish to argue that the continuum of male–male relationships in Romanticism and its outgrowths is always already tempered by the simultaneous apprehension of machinery as a metaphor for degraded or servile humanity.[5] Accordingly, Romanticism can be seen as much a reaction against mechanical instrumentality as an endorsement of the supposedly innate ties of blood, soil, and spirit.[6]

In Meiji Japan, Romanticism made substantial inroads from the 1890s, effectively transforming the literary landscape with the modern, realist (*shajitsu shugi*) novel and free verse poetry (*shintaishi*) as its primary conduits. At the same time, Western-style typography, lithography, and visual arts began to articulate the promises and perils of a mechanically organized way of life. In the three sections of this article I seek to fill in some of the blanks in this lacuna of origins for mechanical man. The first section examines the origins of the concepts "android" and "robot" in the West that chronologically bracket developments in Meiji Japan; first, to demonstrate the permeability of these two concepts well into our own time, and second, to argue that the literary texts under consideration here owed more to Romanticism per se than to the incipient genre of science fiction. It is particularly with respect to the homosocial question that these texts can be drawn into productive comparison with Meiji representations of mechanical man.

In the second section I analyze several examples from Meiji visual culture that attest to the crisis of the individual under mechanical civilization, first with the convergent arrangements of human bodies and machines in a page of advertisements from the *Tokyo asahi shinbun* (1889), then in the disturbing representation of a tortured mechanical man in Kobayashi Kiyochika's cartoon "The Eye-Rotating Machine" (1885) from the comic journal *Marumaru chinbun*. They constitute the conditions that made it possible for the mechanical man to emerge with the coherence of a discourse, in this case what I am primarily identifying as Meiji-era Romanticism.

The third and final section turns to three literary texts, Tayama Katai's *The Quilt* (1907, *Futon*), Mori Ōgai's "The Dancing Girl" (1890, *Maihime*), and Natsume Sōseki's novel *And Then* (1909, *Sorekara*), to show how a host of machine-driven topoi offer a striking counterpoint to the unfettered notions of individualism typically attributed to Sōseki and Meiji Romanticism more generally.[7] Of equal importance is that all three represent homosociality as that which mitigates anxieties over technology by providing a sympathetic audience of peers with whom to commiserate.

BRACKETING ANDROIDS AND ROBOTS

The fact that "mechanical man" was primarily articulated in Meiji Japan through Romanticist literature and related visual imagery is not altogether surprising when we consider how science fiction has occluded a larger field of discursive relations. Two of the central concepts for humanlike machinery in the sci-fi lexicon did not emerge from within that genre per se, but from European modernism: the "android" from Villiers d'Isle Adam's symbolist novel *Tomorrow's Eve* (1886, *L'Ève future*) and "robot" from Karel Čapek's Czech avant-garde play *Rossum's Universal Robots* (1921, *R.U.R.*).[8] It is thus necessary to revisit these urtexts, however briefly, to observe how they exceed the narrow confines of science fiction and to insist that even its contemporary concepts and categories are not as definitively settled as we might imagine.

Tomorrow's Eve and *R.U.R.* provide quite a few reversals of expectation about the origins of the android and the robot. In the former, the female android Hadaly is created by the great Creator himself, Thomas Alva Edison, as a gift to his male friend Ewald. Romantic irony predominates where the presumptive copy of nature incarnates the beauty of one Alicia Clary, a flesh-and-cold-blooded woman so lacking in mental or spiritual capacity as to drive Ewald to the point of suicide.[9] Hadaly is as much a product of the Symbolist fascination with the fantastic and supernatural (itself an outgrowth of the Romantic imagination) as she is an uncanny product of Edison's techno-scientific prowess. As it turns out, she is not only a mechanical being but is suffused with the spirit of Edison's mystical assistant Sowana, although her premature drowning in the novel's conclusion curtails any development of this intriguing potentiality.

> TWO OF THE CENTRAL CONCEPTS FOR HUMANLIKE MACHINERY IN THE SCI-FI LEXICON DID NOT EMERGE FROM WITHIN THAT GENRE PER SE, BUT FROM EUROPEAN MODERNISM: THE "ANDROID" FROM VILLIERS D'ISLE ADAM'S SYMBOLIST NOVEL *TOMORROW'S EVE* (1886, *L'ÈVE FUTURE*) AND "ROBOT" FROM KAREL ČAPEK'S CZECH AVANT-GARDE PLAY *ROSSUM'S UNIVERSAL ROBOTS* (1921, *R.U.R.*).

Hadaly's scientific-supernatural hybrid makeup notwithstanding, she is, outwardly speaking, closer in type to our contemporary definition of the robot, while Čapek's robots better approximate the definition of androids. In contrast to the nuts and bolts that gird Hadaly's body, the robots of *R.U.R.* are not mechanical at all, but, in fact, mass-produced from a synthetic material that is mixed and kneaded in vats, then assembled in a factory. Although they are not made from the same organic substances as human beings, in one of the first scenes in the play a female robot is mistaken for a human being. But as we may glean from photographs taken from international performances in London and New York in the 1920s, however, it did not take long for Čapek's artificial human beings to be recast as ironclad automatons (Figure 1).[10]

The basic narrative of *R.U.R.* has become the fodder of endless science fiction remakes ever since its debut: the robots are created to serve as slave-laborers, only to rebel and assert their supremacy over humanity. Initially the robots are manufactured without affect and hence no desire to rebel. It is only at the insistence of Helena Glory, a human-rights crusader who becomes the wife of Domin, the general manager of the factory, that one of the scientists enables the robots to experience pain. This in turn leads them to recognize and resent their bondage. It is imperative to point out, however, the entirely male human team of scientists is absolutely devoted to each other, with Helena as the one woman whose presence prevents their male homosocial desire from crossing over into more dangerous territory. No sooner have the scientists assured her that the robots are not being exploited than Domin, standing in for the group, proposes marriage:

> **DOMIN**: Helena, you wouldn't be so cruel as to refuse us.
>
> **HELENA**: But, but—I can't marry all six.
>
> **DOMIN**: No, but one anyhow. If you don't want me, marry Fabry.[11]

Irony is in no short supply here, too, where their collective desire to act in unison and satisfy Helena's sentimental wishes to humanize the robots (much as she humanizes them, homosexual desire is apparently out of the question) is what precipitates the downfall of man.

It would be a mistake to assume contemporary science fiction has erased the ambiguity between robot and android. The "replicant" androids in Philip K. Dick's *Do Androids Dream of Electric Sheep?* (1968) and Ridley Scott's

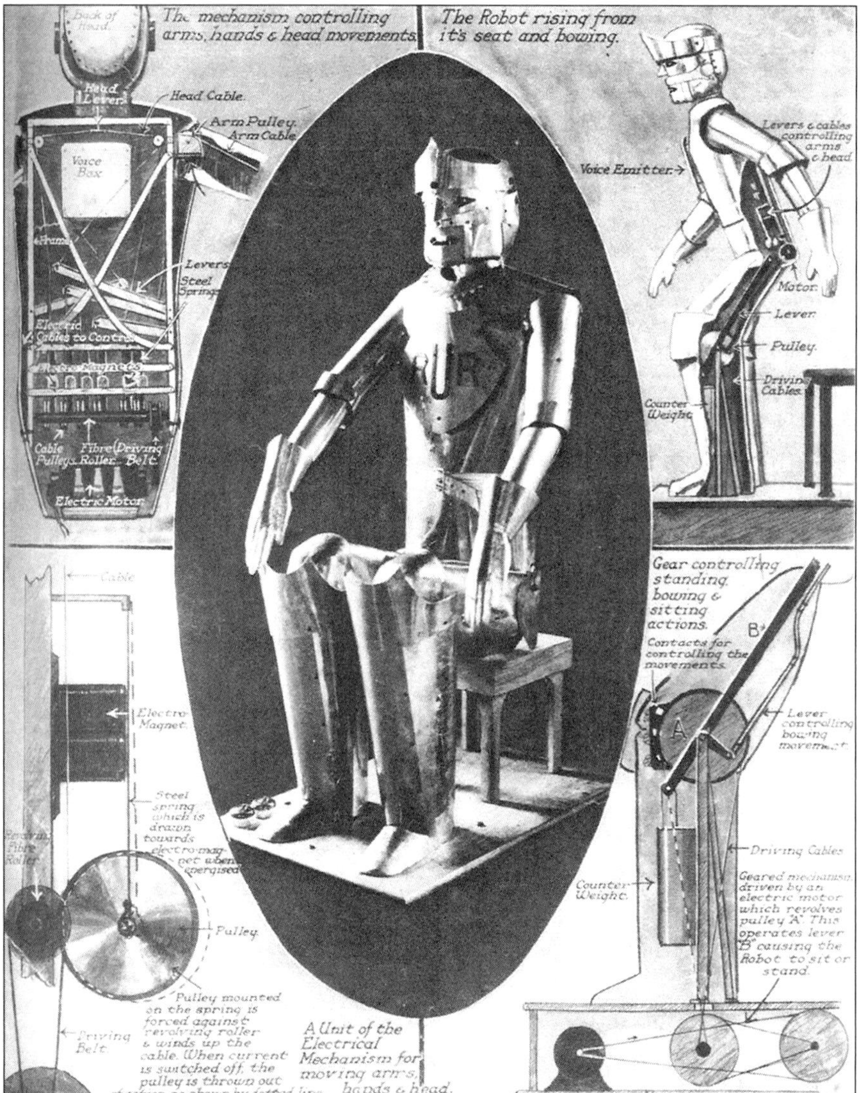

FIGURE 1. *R.U.R.*'s robot as "mechanical man."

film adaptation *Blade Runner* (1982) are physically indistinguishable from ordinary humans, despite possessing superhuman strength and stamina.[12] It is only in the infamous Voight-Kampff test that a physiological response can betray their simulated souls. The androids' lack of innate empathy is offset by implanted false memories that have as their complement the faded evidence of black-and-white photographs (i.e., replicated minds as well as bodies). As if this were not already closer to the spirit of Čapek than Villiers, Dick's novel further alludes to *R.U.R.*-like artificial being by naming the lead android Roy Baty, which all but spells out the connection when the letter "y" (or the "whys") are removed: R-O-B-[O]-T. Although Scott tweaked the lead android's name to Roy Batty as if to indicate his mad desperation to overcome the android's built-in lifespan of four years, *Blade Runner,* too, makes much of the association of androids with lifelike dolls, toys, mannequins, and puppets. Second only to Dr. Tyrell, the master inventor of the androids, is the genetic engineer J. F. Sebastian, who doubles in his spare time as a toymaker. His living/work space—the now-abandoned Bradbury Building in Los Angeles—overflows with Victorian toy soldiers and porcelain-faced dolls, who provide the backdrop for the climactic showdown between the last two androids and the bounty hunter sent to "retire" them.

There is an additional impetus for situating the extensive mechanical tropes of Meiji between the history of androids and robots given that the preferred Japanese translation for robot in the early 1920s was *jinzō ningen*, or "artificial human being." Almost immediately after Čapek's *R.U.R.* made its international debut, scientist-*cum*-science fiction writer Unno Jūza began to employ *jinzō ningen* interchangeably, or rather simultaneously, with the phoneticized *robotto* in order to exploit the full range of ontological ambiguity in the continuum from human to machine.[13] Likewise, as Miri Nakamura has observed of the interwar period:

> Japan saw a "robot boom" during which such popular science magazines as *Kagaku gahō* (Illustrated Magazine of Science) and satirical writers as Mizushima Niou began to feature robots in their texts. . . . The image of *jinzō ningen* (literally, "artificial humans") also became popularized through works such as Mizushima's "Jinzō ningen jidai" (1923, "The Age of Artificial Humans").[14]

Although it is far less common than "robot" in daily usage, *jinzō ningen* nevertheless remains in active circulation today. To cite but one prominent example, in the first episode of the blockbuster television anime series *Neon Genesis*

Evangelion (1997, *Shin seiki Evangerion*), the semi-sentient, humanoid-looking giant robots are repeatedly and matter-of-factly referred to as *jinzō ningen*.[15] My point here is not to project backwards a genealogy from mechanical to artificial human beings, which presupposes a continuous or direct lineage, but rather to underscore the fluidity of the signifiers "robot" and "android" in relation to each other. Moreover, as we shall see in the final section of this essay, what determined "mechanical man" in Meiji was not only a machine anxiety registered in flesh and blood but also a set of shared relations from which women were either exempt or excluded.

EYING MECHANICAL CIVILIZATION

We need look no further than the daily newspaper for evidence of a mechanical civilization of Meiji, replete with juxtapositions of what Mark Seltzer has called the binary "machine process" and "life process" of modern industrial civilization.[16] To borrow a fairly typical advertising page from the August 15, 1889, issue of the *Tokyo asahi* (Figure 2), lithographic illustrations of cog-and-gear-driven mechanisms sit comfortably alongside timetables for the postal service and newspaper delivery, while a smattering of maps, fountain pens, magic lantern shows, and self-instruction manuals in shorthand notation are further reminders of increasingly networked technologies of writing and projection. Pocket watches that reveal the inner workings of cogs and gears appear alongside a medicinal remedy that seeks to prove its efficacy by making visible an anatomical cross-section of the lungs. What transpires in these multiple arrangements is an increased visibility of circulation systems, the shifting of gears and pumping of fluids. Precision machinery and the organic pathways of the human body are thus held up as mutually legible and potentially interchangeable systems. These casual, but increasingly ubiquitous, juxtapositions should not mislead us into thinking the dehumanizing implications of mechanical civilization were easily swallowed even by the most ardent modernizers.

As early as the September 5, 1885, issue of the comic weekly *Marumaru chinbun* new fears of human beings disposed as interchangeable parts in a machine assembly, their humanity reduced to a ghost or tortured body, converge in Kobayashi Kiyochika's cartoon "The Eye-Rotating Machine" (Figure 3). In an abrupt departure from the rosy-hued scenes of daily life in his earlier "light-and-shadow" (*kōsenga*) prints and also at a considerable remove from his later patriotic war prints, Kiyochika's political cartoons of the mid-1880s often

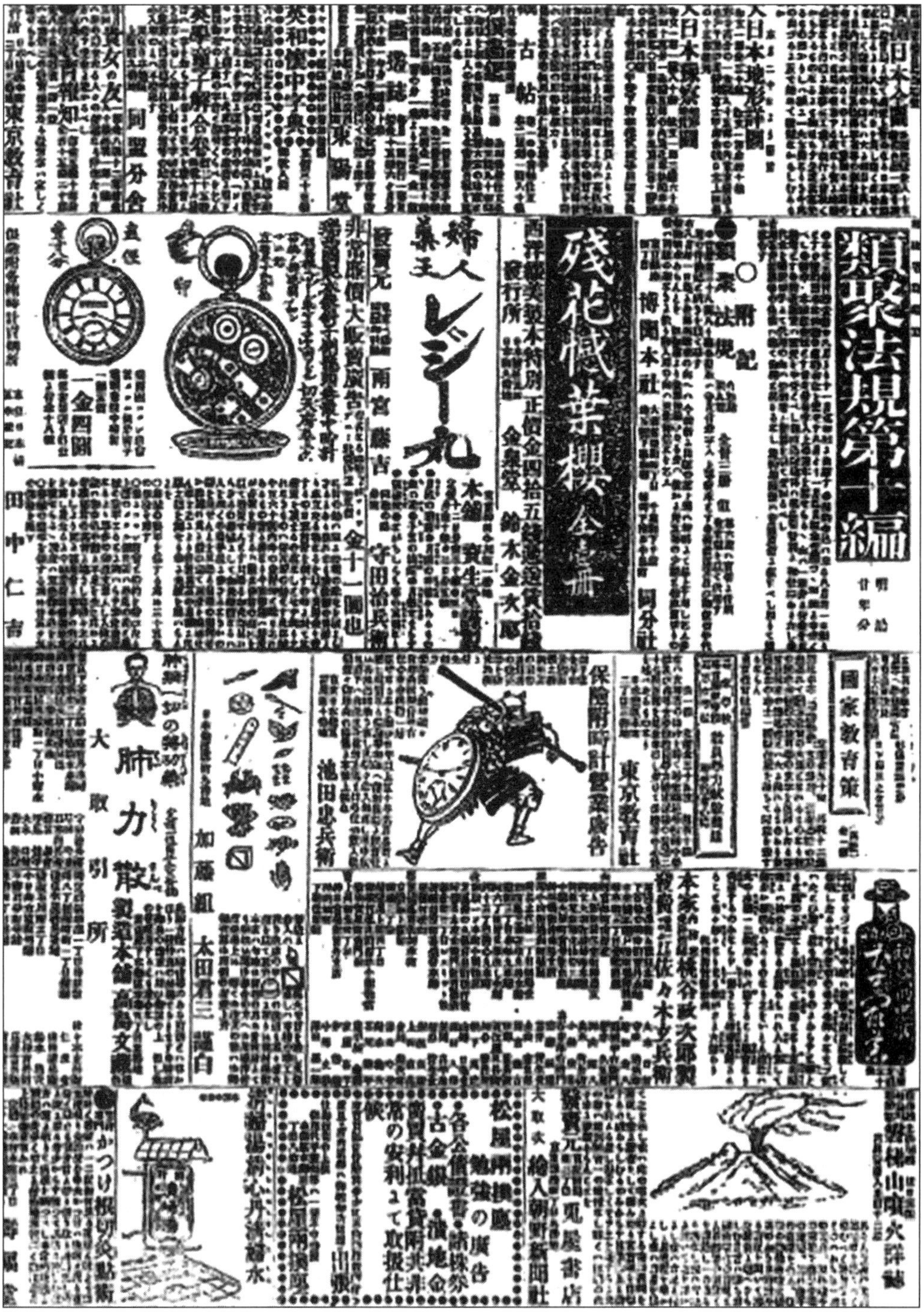

FIGURE 2. The mechanical universe of Meiji visual culture, from the *Tokyo asahi shimbun,* August 15, 1889.

caricatured the excesses of modern bureaucracy and the physical machinery that drove it. “The Eye-Rotating Machine” depicts a civil servant confronted with the ever-growing piles of documents that proliferate with the modern nation-state: taxes, national education, public sanitation, military conscription, and so on. His face contorted with horror, the man throws up his hands as if to fend off the oncoming tide. The caption in English, which corresponds to the Japanese text in the upper-right corner of the picture, further conveys the helplessness of the situation: “‘Mercy!’ Ejaculated the Honorable district magistrate, and kept on his bewilderment by saying, ‘O! busy, busy sir! This [is] too much for us!’”[17] As was standard practice for the political cartoons in the *Marumaru chinbun,* Western and Japanese conventions of word–image relations both apply. In keeping with the former, an English caption is located below the picture frame, while the Japanese text is located within, right alongside the image:

> “Waterwheels on the river Yodo turn and turn. . .” goes the song of the Kakubei dancers. It’s a fine machine, and in this heat there’s plenty of sweat to keep it oiled. So I’ve got to turn, turn. Is something wrong with my eyes?

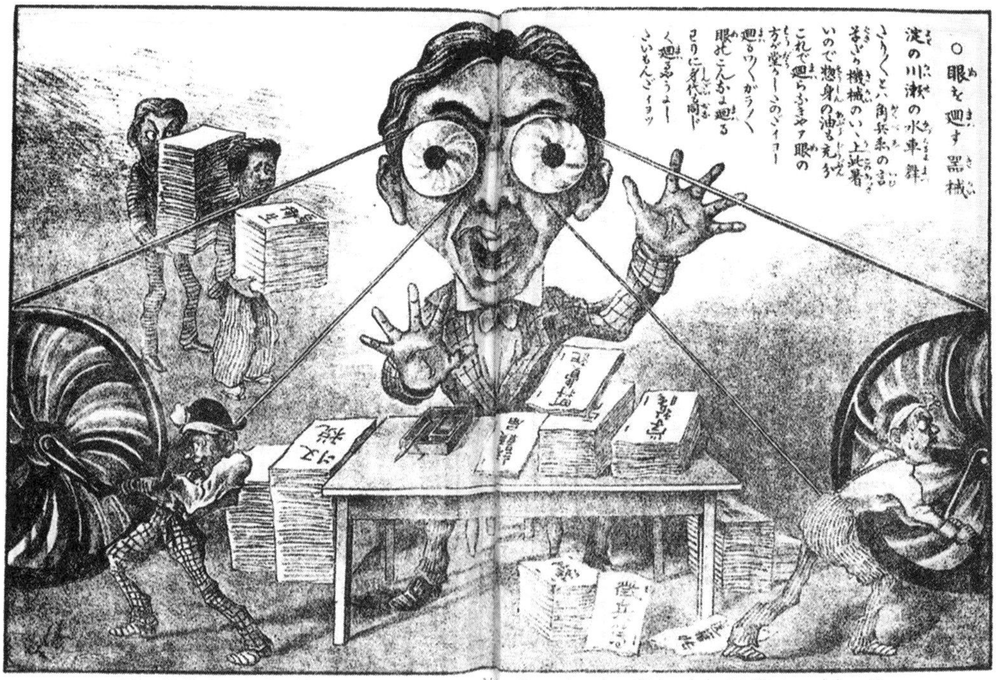

FIGURE 3. Kobayashi Kiyochika’s “Eye-Rotating Machine,” from *Marumaru chinbun,* September 5, 1885.

> Round and round it goes, the wheels turning clatter, clatter. If only my investments would bring in returns as fast as my eyes are turning![18]

Yet it is not the bilingual address that captures the viewer's attention but the hypnotic gaze of the unfortunate bureaucrat's beveled and bedeviled eyes as they are twisted round in his head by two manually operated, wheel-driven pulleys. The machinery of bureaucracy and the printing press are literally hooked up to the sockets of the modern gaze. Kiyochika's grim caricature leaves no question about the impossibility of immersion in machinery without becoming machines ourselves.

THE MACHINERY OF BUREAUCRACY AND THE PRINTING PRESS ARE LITERALLY HOOKED UP TO THE SOCKETS OF THE MODERN GAZE. KIYOCHIKA'S GRIM CARICATURE LEAVES NO QUESTION ABOUT THE IMPOSSIBILITY OF IMMERSION IN MACHINERY WITHOUT BECOMING MACHINES OURSELVES.

SELF-PITYING MACHINES: ROMANTICISM AND MECHANICAL MAN

Concerns about a similar degradation of the human recurs in Meiji Romanticist fiction, where the male protagonists frequently define their mechanization against the love of a woman who is herself outside the alienating forces of modernity. The consistent motif about anxieties over technology is that they are mediated by male homosociality, with male self-pity as the preferred means by which male authors, narrators, protagonists, and readers could readily detect their own conscription into the machinery of the state, industrial, and capitalist apparatuses.

Resonant with Kiyochika's "Eye-Rotating Machine," the spectacle of male self-pity is fed directly into the apparatus of the printing press in the opening scene of Tayama Katai's *The Quilt* (1907, *Futon*). The protagonist, Takenaka Tokio, a small-time romance novelist who dreams of ditching his old-fashioned wife and finding a modern girl to love, earns a living by working in a mapmaking factory. After commuting by suburban trains that expose him on a daily basis to the modern schoolgirls who are both the object of his literary ambitions and his secret desires, he enters the factory, literally passing through the greasy innards of the heavy machinery:

> Every day, then, he would go mechanically along the same route, in through the same big gate, along the same narrow passage with its mixture of

> vibrating noise from the rotary press and smelly sweat from the factory-hands. He would casually greet the employees in the office, climb laboriously up the long and narrow steps, and finally enter that room.[19]

His occupational entrapment within the machine thus established, the narrative of *The Quilt* thereafter traces a meandering path composed of love letters and train lines whose collisions, or at least derailments, determine Tokio and his pupil Yoshiko's fates. This, too, is foreshadowed at the beginning of the novel when Tokio tracks Yoshiko down on a map using the train lines as his guide, gazing at the topography of the map as though it were her own body, and no less amorously studying the contours and style of her writing: "three pages of small characters written laterally in violet ink across blue-ruled Western-style paper."[20] His dominion over her through writing thus established, Tokio is thwarted in achieving a more intimate relation with the girl in the flesh. In the cruelest of reversals, it is Yoshiko who makes good on the carnal possibilities of romantic love without Tokio's knowledge or participation. When her family gets wind of her affair with a young male student, her reputation is ruined and she disappears back to the countryside in disgrace. Yet it is the weeping, pathetic figure of the male protagonist clutching her soiled quilt that concludes the story and seals the novel's identification of the privileged male subject as the truest victim of Meiji enlightenment.

Among the Meiji literati, Mori Ōgai's bona fides regarding science and technology are by far the best established: he studied medicine and hygiene in Germany from 1884 to 1888 and in his career as a military surgeon rose to become surgeon general of the Imperial Japanese Army by 1907. In his early literary career, however, he was no less accomplished as the preeminent Japanese translator and disseminator of German Romanticism. What is apparent, particularly in his literary debut, the novella "The Dancing Girl" (1890, *Maihime*), is how keenly Ōgai grasped the paradoxes of the heroic Romantic individual versus soulless mechanical man. The novella is written from the perspective of an elite Japanese student who is sent to Berlin for legal studies. The protagonist, Toyotarō, who deeply imbibes the atmosphere of German Romanticism immediately upon arrival in Berlin, reflects on his unhappy coming of age in Japan in familiar tropes of mechanization:

> There is always a time when, come what may, one's true nature reveals itself. I had obeyed my father's dying words and had done what my mother had taught me . . . But all that time I had been a mere passive, mechanical being with no real awareness of myself.[21]

Building upon this notion of mechanization-as-enslavement, Toyotarō remarks on the unhappy start of his career in Tokyo: "my department head had obviously tried to turn me into a machine that could be manipulated as he desired."[22] In his studies in Berlin, however, he unexpectedly falls in love with a lower-class German woman—the eponymous dancing girl—and veers from his preordained path. Already engaged in the study of the Romantic canon on the side of his official studies, Toyotarō takes it upon himself to educate the girl, Elis, not only teaching her to read the likes of Schiller but even correcting her faulty (read: lower-class) German pronunciation!

When word of his extracurricular activities reaches his superiors, he is cut off from his scholarship and forced to earn a living as a freelance journalist, writing on issues of culture and politics. For a time this suits him well. While now financially impoverished, his writings on culture, history, and politics provide him a greater sense of satisfaction than he ever felt in his technocratic education. He lives with Elis, who becomes pregnant. Their bohemian idyll is interrupted when Toyotarō's colleague, Aizawa, calls on him to return to his career in the service of the state and patriarchal system. For Ōgai, the tensions between Romantic hero and mechanical man are not only irreconcilable, the decision they force upon Toyotarō can have only one outcome. It reminds us that male–male bonding was not merely a shared idea but a matter of educational formation and compulsory national service.

Toyotarō opts to return to service and leave Berlin for good, a decision that drives Elis insane. Yet consistent with the homosociality of Romanticism, the reader's sympathies are not meant for the abandoned, destitute German woman with an unborn child in her womb but the unhappy Japanese man whose career is once more in ascent. Toyotarō last words are especially telling of the substitution of one set of relations for another, namely the grudging prioritization of the homosocial bond over mere love for a foreign woman: "Friends like Aizawa Kenkichi are rare indeed, and yet to this very day there remains a part of me that curses him."[23]

These crises of the individual as degraded mechanical man come home to roost in Sōseki's *And Then* (1909, *Sorekara*), whose title simultaneously reflects its nature as a serial newspaper novel in the *Asahi* and the ennui-ridden dilemma ("and then?") at the heart of modern existence. The novel revolves around the figure of Daisuke, the dissolute and irresolute second son of a wealthy Meiji industrialist. At age thirty, Daisuke has chosen neither the business path of his father and older brother nor the hardscrabble intellectual life of his former classmates, who scrape by working as editors and translators for newspapers and literary journals like *Teikoku bungaku* (Imperial literature), instead preferring a life of indolence. A bachelor by choice, he fends off the photographs of prospective brides brought by his sister-in-law by complaining about the irregularity of each woman's features. Yet his objections mask a more fundamental problem: he nurtures within him a secret love for Michiyo, the wife of his former classmate Hiraoka.

Although "he loathed the absurdity of shackling himself like a machine" (*kikai no yō ni sokubakusuru no gū o inda*), Daisuke embodies virtually all of the modern anxieties and routines of mechanical man.[24] His existence is made known to him by the morning rituals that start each day, and which set the tone for the beginning of the narrative. Daisuke keeps a watch by his pillow, not to check the time but to measure his pulse upon waking. This is followed by reading the daily newspaper, a trip to the toilet, and grooming—daily acts of composition (*sans* writing) for no greater cause than contemplation of his being. The first waking scene in the novel exposes the automatism of the body that lies outside Daisuke's control and that consequently threatens to erase the dividing lines between the life process and machine process:

> With his hand still on his chest, he tried to imagine the warm, crimson blood flowing leisurely to this beat. This was life, he thought. Now, at this very moment, he held in his grasp the current of life as it flowed by. To his palm it felt like the ticking of a clock. But it was more, it was a kind of alarm that summoned him to death. If it were possible to live without hearing this bell—then how carefree he would be! How he would savor life! But—and here Daisuke shuddered involuntarily. He was a man so attached to life that he could scarcely bear to picture his heart calmly beating to the coursing of his blood . . . Lifting his hand from his heart, he picked up the newspaper beside his pillow. He reached from beneath the covers and with both hands spread out the paper . . . [Later] he carefully brushed his teeth, taking pleasure, as always, in their regularity.[25]

Even as he fantasizes about an embodied possibility beyond the limits of flesh and blood, Daisuke equates these vital "life signs" with a fragile and finite machine: the existential clock ticking from within that cannot be reset or (as yet) replaced. Despite his excellent health and youthful good looks, Daisuke is obsessed with the regularity of these rhythms and fearful of the ease with which they may come undone. Moreover, he is keenly sensitive to the artificiality that represents modern existence and the inner, involuntary rhythms produced by his own body. Of course, as Otto Mayr points out, the equation of the human heart with a clock was nothing new, having served as a basis in seventeenth-century Europe for comparing the human body with that of clockwork automata.[26] What sets this apart from early modern Europe or Japan, however, is not only the existential anxiety that such a comparison elicits but also the host of other mechanical conditions and metaphors to which it is linked.

Further along in the narrative Daisuke suffers a gradual psychological collapse that presents itself to him as confused symbols of writing that undermine the integration of his mind and body. Later he stares at his naked legs in the bath only to find they "no longer seemed to grow from his trunk at all, but rather, completely unconnected, they sprawled rudely before him . . . With hair growing unevenly and blue streaks running rampant, they were terribly strange creatures."[27] The human body (*shintai*) is overlaid with an illegible, even grotesque, written script (*jitai*): the blue veins of his body are a text that no longer makes any sense. This sense of becoming illiterate to the text of one's body is reinforced by Daisuke's estrangement from the printed word. While, in his younger days, foregoing even a single day of serial reading left him with "a vague sense of decay," the pressure to commit to Michiyo builds until he can no longer sustain his powers of readerly concentration. When he sits down to read a book, he finds it incomprehensible: "Daisuke persevered and kept his eyes on the pages for some two hours. Finally, he could stand it no longer. True, as a collection of print (*katsuji no atsumari*) the words projected a certain meaning on his mind. But they showed no sign of circulating to his flesh and blood."[28]

These relations of the human–machine interface also manifest elsewhere in Sōseki's oeuvre. In his later novels *Mon* (The gate, 1910) and *Kokoro* (1914), male protagonists describe a similar state of mental disarray, where their powers of concentration can no longer animate the words on a page or bring the meaning of Chinese characters to mind. In *Kokoro* the metaphor of the clock is also invoked, although this time it is not to affirm the metronome-like qualities of the beating heart but to protest the inherent deceptiveness of human behavior. The misanthropic character known only as Sensei reflexively asks, "Can one expect the complicated mechanism of the human mind to betray its purposes so obviously, as if it were some kind of clock?"[29] Yet even as autonomic nervous system functions are recast in mechanical terms, it is important to recognize that the existential crises read from their signs are always "between men," setting men apart from the women such as Elis, Michiyo, and Sensei's wife.

CONCLUSION

In assaying the origins of mechanical man in Meiji Japan, I have outlined how the dehumanizing effects and anxieties over technology that accompanied Romanticist notions of the modern individual were particularly registered by homosocial appeals to self-pity between men. It is noteworthy that the emergence of the figure of the android in the French symbolist novel and the robot in Czech avant-garde theater, which respectively precede and postdate these developments in Japan, do not derive from the "low" genre of science fiction. These works, too, share in a debt to the homosocial underpinnings that mark male–male, male–female, and man–machine relationships. Accordingly, one need not adopt a defensive posture about the presumed lack of indigenous science (or speculative) fiction in the Meiji era to locate critical insights into the changing human condition vis-à-vis machine technology, to say nothing of the social, capitalist, and industrial relations upon which they are predicated. While the historical avant-garde in Japan developed only in the interwar period alongside a mass culture that no less quickly embraced concepts of robots and the like, the instances provided by Kiyochika, Sōseki, Ōgai, and others underscore the consistency of an episteme already in place by the late nineteenth century in which mechanical man is both a leading indicator of modernity and inevitable consequence wrought by "civilization and enlightenment."

Notes

1. Timon Screech's *The Lens within the Heart: The Western Scientific Gaze and Popular Imagery in Later Edo Japan* (Honolulu: University of Hawai'i Press, 2002) has done much to show the extent to which *karakuri*, clockwork mechanisms, and the precision instruments associated with "Dutch Learning" (*rangaku*) percolated through Tokugawa society in the preceding two-and-half centuries. Nonetheless, there is profound difference between the Edo period's amateur scientists and affluent artisans dabbling with novel technologies and the systematic, and system-wide, national transformations of the late nineteenth and early twentieth centuries.

2. Inoue, Haruki, *Nippon robotto sōseiki, 1920–1938* (The genesis of Japanese robots, 1920–1938), (Tokyo: NTT Publishing, 1993).

3. Sōseki cautions in this famous address against "mechanical knowledge" (*kikaiteki no chishiki*) and uncritical acceptance of received ideas, whether they amount to vulgar nationalism or the supposedly superior opinions of Westerners about poetry and literature. As we will see in this article, what is philosophically expressed to a far greater degree in his fiction is that one's individuality is inescapably constructed from within the confines

of mechanical civilization. See Natsume Sōseki, *"My Individualism" and "The Philosophical Foundations of Literature,"* trans. Sammy I. Tsunematsu (Boston: Tuttle Publishing, 2004).

4. Friedrich Kittler, *Aufschreibesysteme 1800/1900*, trans. Michael Metteer with Chris Cullens as *Discourse Networks 1800/1900* (Stanford, Calif.: Stanford University Press, 1990): 124–73; and Eve Kosovsky Sedgwick, *Between Men: English Literature and Male Homosocial Desire* (New York: Columbia University Press, 1985).

5. As Sedgwick explains in the introduction of *Between Men*, "'Homosocial' is a word occasionally used in history and the social sciences, where it describes social bonds between persons of the same sex; it is a neologism, obviously formed by analogy with 'homosexual,' and just as obviously meant to be distinguished from 'homosexual'" (1).

6. While American scholarship such as Susan Napier's *The Fantastic in Modern Japanese Literature* (London: Routledge, 1995) and Joseph Murphy's *Metaphorical Circuit: Negotiations between Literature and Science in Twentieth Century Japan* (Ithaca, N.Y.: Cornell University Press, 2004) have invoked Sōseki to register generalized anxieties about technology in modern Japan, this article is specifically concerned with the human–machine interface in his work and elsewhere subtended by homosocial bonds.

7. Tayama Katai's *Futon*, trans. Kenneth Henshall as *The Quilt* (Tokyo: University of Tokyo Press, 1981); Mori Ōgai's "Maihime," trans. Richard Bowring as "The Dancing Girl" (*Monumenta Nipponica* 30, no. 2 [Summer 1975]: 151–76); Natsume Sōseki's *Sore kara*, trans. Norma Field as *And Then* (Baton Rouge: Louisiana State University Press, 1978).

8. Karel Čapek, *Rossum's Universal Robots (R.U.R.)*, trans. Claudia Novak-Jones (New York: Penguin Classics, 2004); Villiers de l'Isle Adam, *L'Ève Future*, trans. Robert Martin Adams as *Tomorrow's Eve* (Chicago: University of Illinois Press, 2000).

9. Some significant differences notwithstanding, the desire for an artificial woman can be traced back at least to Mary Shelley's Romantic novel *Frankenstein* (1818). The creature, who relentlessly pursues his maker, demands that he create a female counterpart, an Eve fashioned like him from the animated flesh of corpses, with whom he will flee into the Edenlike jungles of South America—the fulfillment of Enlightenment philosophy's wish to return to the state of nature as noble savages.

10. See also Inoue's *Nippon robotto sōseiki*, chapter 1.

11. Čapek, *R.U.R*, 29.

12. Philip K. Dick, *Do Androids Dream of Electric Sheep?* (1968; rpt: New York: Del Rey, 1987); *Blade Runner*, dir. Ridley Scott (1982), DVD (Warner Bros., 2007).

13. The Chinese characters for "artificial human" (人造人間) are glossed with the katakana syllabary spelling out the reading and simultaneous meaning of "robot."

14. Miri Nakamura, "Horror and Machines in Prewar Japan: The Mechanical Uncanny in Yumeno Kyūsaku's *Dogura magura*," *Science Fiction Studies* no. 88 (2002): http://www.depauw.edu/site/sfs/backissues/88/nakamura.html.

15. Gender and genealogy via Judeo-Christian mysticism play a critical role in the make-up of the artificial humans in *Evangelion* and the human–machine interface required to pilot them. See Mariana Ortega's "My Father, He Killed Me; My Mother, She Ate Me: Self, Desire, Engendering, and the Mother in *Neon Genesis Evangelion*," *Mechademia* 2 (2007): 216–34.

16. Mark Seltzer, *Bodies and Machines* (London: Routledge, 1992): 3–12.

17. Kobayashi Kiyochika, "Me o mawasu kikai," *Marumaru chinbun* 16 (1885): 110–11.

18. Henry D. Smith II, *Kiyochika: Artist of Meiji Japan* (Santa Barbara, Calif.: Santa Barbara Museum of Art, 1988), 76.

19. Tayama, *The Quilt*, 37.

20. Ibid., 40.

21. Mori, "The Dancing Girl," 153.

22. Ibid.

23. Ibid., 166.

24. Natsume, *And Then*, 188.

25. Ibid., 1–2.

26. Otto Mayr, *Authority, Liberty, and Automatic Machinery in Early Modern Europe* (Baltimore: The Johns Hopkins University Press, 1989), 45.

27. Natsume, *And Then*, 78.

28. Ibid., 170–71.

29. Natsume Sōseki, *Kokoro*, trans. Edwin McClellan (New York: Gateway Editions, 1996), 210.

Bodies in Motion

起源

PAUL ROQUET

Carbon as Creation: On Tsuji Naoyuki's Charcoal Anime

Think about where to move the lines to next. Rip off a piece of bread and dab at the paper, pulling the carbon residue off the page. Pick up a stick of charcoal and draw some new lines a little to the side of the ones you just erased. Record this new image onto a few frames of film. Repeat once you decide where to take the lines next.

This is how you create a charcoal anime. This looping method takes anime back to the basics, rooting it to the manual encounter between hand, carbon, and paper. Tsuji Naoyuki (b. 1972) pioneered the style in Japan, at a time when most anime was pushing further into digital technology and increasing layers of electronic mediation. Charcoal anime strips these layers away instead.

After graduating with a degree in sculpture from Tokyo Zōkei University in 1995 and experimenting with stop-motion animation, Tsuji began developing short sequences of monochrome charcoal drawings and recording them on 16mm film. *A Feather Stare at the Dark* (1995–2003, *Yami o mitsumeru hane*) and *Trilogy about Clouds* (2005, *Mittsu no kumo*) both went on to screen at the Directors' Fortnight at the Cannes Film Festival, securing Tsuji's place as a central figure in the burgeoning world of Japanese art animation. Like many working in the field, Tsuji situates his work at a complex remove from

TSUJI'S TURN TO CHARCOAL CAN BE UNDERSTOOD AS A RETURN TO THE HAND, AN ATTEMPT TO INSERT THE PHYSICAL ACT OF DRAWING BACK INTO THE HYPER-MEDIATION AND VISUAL EXCESS OF CONTEMPORARY ANIME PRODUCTION.

the commercial anime industry, presenting it at festivals, screenings, museums, and galleries, but without denying the influence of more mainstream trends in anime style. Inspired as a youth by the manga duo Yudetamago (Shimada Takashi and Nakai Yoshinori), Tsuji initially approached the pair to become their apprentice but, on seeing their original manuscripts in person, found himself overwhelmed by the size and complexity of series like *Ultimate Muscle* (1979–, *Kinnikuman*). Instead, he eventually turned to the more diminutive but carefully crafted world of charcoal anime. Operating at a similar frame rate to limited animation (with several frames of film per still image), Tsuji's work adopts even greater material limitations. Tsuji's turn to charcoal can be understood as a return to the hand, an attempt to insert the physical act of drawing back into the hyper-mediation and visual excess of contemporary anime production.

As W. J. T. Mitchell writes, "drawing remains closest to the center of the vortex of image production [. . .] emanating from and returning to the body."[1] The hand drawn helps to slow down contemporary media's rapid succession of images and renders the initial contact between body and paper perceptible once again. Rosalind Krauss notes "the upsurge of the autographic, the handwrought, in an age of the mechanization and technologizing of the image via either photography or digital imaging."[2] While shared by a number of Japanese art animators, this return to the hand drawn is nowhere more vivid than in Tsuji's charcoal anime, where the residue of each gestural movement of the carbon remains on the page, the bread eraser never completely clearing the trace of what came before (Figure 1).

To make charcoal for drawing, pieces of wood are packed tightly in airtight containers and heated under the subsiding embers of a fire, then cooled slowly. The more prolonged the heating, the softer the charcoal that results. The sticks Tsuji uses are composed of the rough and impure carbon produced by the burnt wood of willow trees, producing particularly dark tones well suited for capture on film. When applied, this charcoal sits rough upon the page, its microscopic flakes splintering and scattering unevenly across the surface of the paper.[3] Charcoal is too coarse a medium for sketching out fine detail or crisp lines, favoring instead broad, vigorous strokes emphasizing mass and movement. Drawing with charcoal often involves articulating not just the hand but elbow and torso as well.

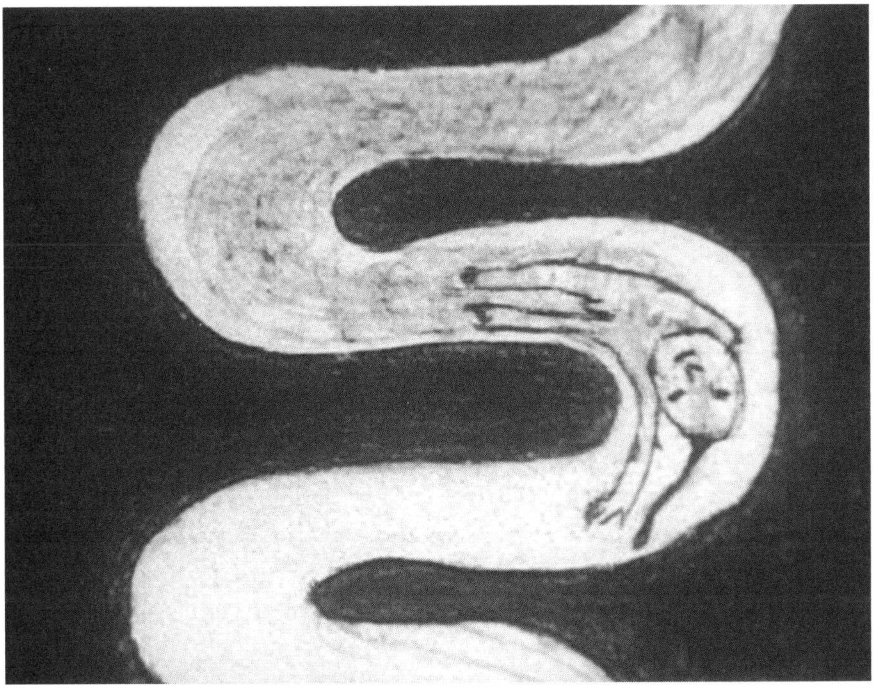

FIGURE 1. The boy in *A Feather Stare at the Dark* moves by being drawn, erased, and drawn again, leaving a trail of charcoal residue in his wake. *Thinking and Drawing: Japanese Art Animation of the New Millennium* (Image Forum Video/Daguerreo Press, 2005).

Charcoal markings do not "dry" in the manner of paint or ink, leaving them continuously malleable on the page. The lines can be erased, smudged, and redrawn, their contour shifted a minute later, a month later, a year later. As a result of this insistent malleability, drawings in charcoal for a long time suffered from a lack of permanence, though they proved quite durable when left alone. Some of the earliest drawings still in existence, at the caves of Altamira and Niaux, are renditions in charcoal. Just barely hanging on to the rock walls, these sketches must now be actively protected as they are just as primed to shift and dissolve now as they were when originally conceived more than ten thousand years ago. The expressive power of charcoal images comes in part from how they preserve the mutability of the initial moment of drawing, resisting the patina of age and decay that sets in with most other materials.

Most charcoal drawings did not have the protection of the caves, of course, and for centuries, charcoal remained but an interstitial medium, a good tool for sketching out a plan but rarely the one used for the final product. Underdrawings and preparatory studies in charcoal were usually tossed aside on the way to more durable media like oil and stone. From the late fifteenth century, however, charcoal drawing achieved greater permanence thanks to the invention of the "fixative," a spray applied to finished works to secure the carbon in place and preserve it from further alteration.

With the emergence of photography, a less invasive approach to fixing charcoal became available. Unlike the fixative spray, the camera's registration of light reflecting off the carbon did not prevent the continued manipulation of the carbon itself. By preserving a space for the hand to come between the drawing paper and the fixative of photographic film, the possibility of both fixing and further moving the charcoal emerged—in other words, the possibility of charcoal animation. With the arrival of the motion picture camera, the movement of charcoal itself could be fixed in a photographic series. As with stop-motion animation, each manipulation of the charcoal image could be recorded on a few frames of film, then shown in sequence to render alterations to the drawing perceptible as continuous movement. By means of film, charcoal could now seemingly move by itself—the hand disappearing into the spaces between the frames even as it leaves its traces everywhere on the canvas.

Oscar Fischinger was the first to develop charcoal animation as a practice, creating his groundbreaking abstract charcoal animation *Studies* (1929–34, *Studie Nr. 2–13*) while working for Fritz Lang in Berlin in the late 1920s. Paired with music, the works screened in theaters in Europe, the United States, and Japan. Canadian animator Ryan Larkin experimented with charcoal animation in the 1960s, and in recent decades William Kentridge brought the medium to wider attention through his widely exhibited *9 Drawings for Projection* (1989–2003), a series of deeply moving ruminations on South African cultural memory.

Part of this diminutive but distinguished lineage of charcoal animators, Tsuji's work is distinctive both for its monochrome austerity and its conscious alignment with anime (as opposed to *animeeshon*) as a form. Tsuji's animations are also unique in their use of close-ups, where the camera cuts in to magnify one portion of the drawing. These shots imitate the grammar of live-action cinema by focusing in on a character's facial expressions. Unlike a live-action close-up, however, the charcoal close-up magnifies not only facial details but also the materiality of the medium itself, revealing in greater detail the grain of the carbon and the paper it rests upon (Figure 2).

Drawing attention to the texture of the paper and the fragility of the medium, Tsuji's work echoes the surface consciousness of the earlier cave charcoals, where the drawn lines often seem to engage directly with the texture of

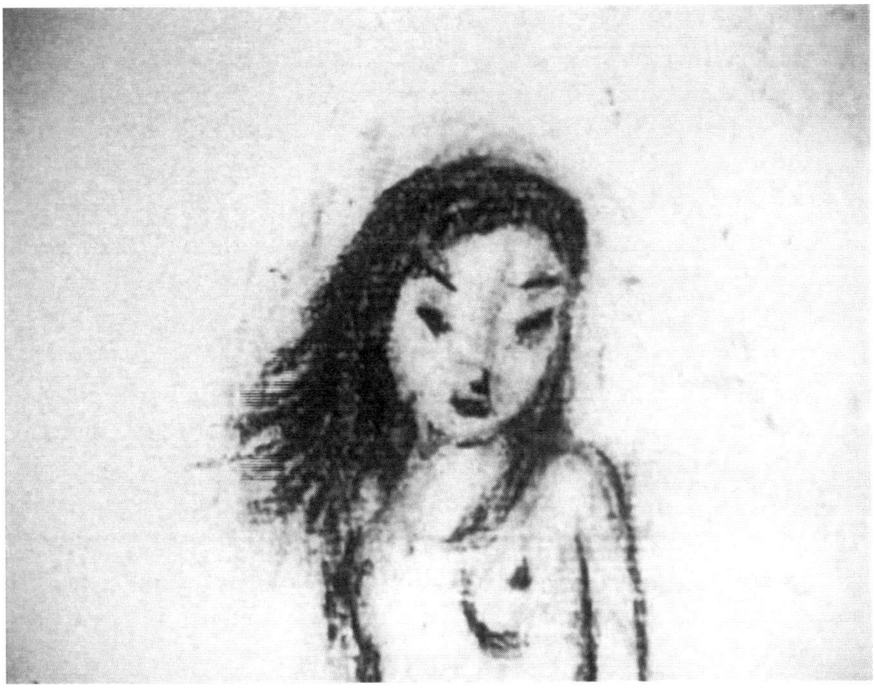

FIGURE 2. The "close-up" from *A Feather Stare at the Dark*, revealing both the woman's body and the texture of the carbon on the page. *Thinking and Drawing: Japanese Art Animation of the New Millennium* (Image Forum Video/Daguerreo Press, 2005).

the walls they sit on. As Maurice Merleau-Ponty wrote of the Lascaux caves, "the animals painted on the walls of Lascaux are not there in the same way as the fissures and limestone formations. But they are not *elsewhere*. Pushed forward here, held back there, held up by the wall's mass they use so adroitly, they spread around the wall without ever breaking from their elusive moorings in it."[4] By drawing the viewer back toward the contours of the paper, Tsuji's work similarly pulls anime back to a focus of the surface of inscription, to the moment of contact between animator and canvas. The charcoal stays close to its origins in burnt wood, and the animated lines stay rooted in the mutual push and pull of paper, hand, and bread.

SLOWING ANIME DOWN

Unlike the cel animator, who assembles a series of drawings to produce the illusion of continuous movement, or the digital animator, who works nonlinearly through a series of software commands, the charcoal animator sticks to a single piece of paper for the entirety of a sequence, manually erasing and redrawing the image over and over to create a film one shot at a time. Cel and digital animation both leave a collection of frames behind, with the potential to use or modify them again later if needed. The draw-shoot-redraw-shoot rhythm of charcoal animation leaves nothing behind but the very last image of each sequence, smudged with the residual traces of lines drawn for earlier shots. As each sequence of a film progresses, the paper is gradually covered over with the shadows of Tsuji's previous lines, so that each new movement arises not from a blank page (or a fresh cel), but out of the foggy carbonate echo of each movement that came before.

The music for Tsuji's charcoal films, improvised on bass guitar by his partner Takanashi Makiko, echoes the slow gestural quality of the medium. In Takanashi's playing, "every stroke of the musician's hand is audible, accentuating the tactile and intimate nature of the drawings."[5] The low rumble of the bass resonates with the dark registers of the charcoal, and the way Takanashi's repeated patterns often slide from the free play of rising and falling melodic lines into a muddle of low tones matches the resistant smudge of the charcoal as it makes its way across the paper.

Like William Kentridge, Tsuji does not use storyboards or other planning tools prior to recording, preferring to allow the state of the drawing at each moment to determine where the film goes next:

> My method is quite simple. I sit in front of the paper and wait for an idea. When I get an idea, I draw it down and click the shutter a few times. Then I erase a bit and redraw and click the shutter a few more times, and so on. So it's random, yet with direction, ordered towards the future. I start with no set idea for the film. Each image I draw and photograph creates suggestions which lead to the next image, and these images build up inside me as the film advances. The reason I take this approach to filmmaking is to pursue the unique possibilities of this particular medium, which doesn't require any special preparation beforehand other than charcoal and paper.[6]

Drawing hints from the flexibility of charcoal itself, Tsuji allows his own embodied intuition to substitute for a more carefully plotted narrative trajectory:

> It might be easier for the audience to understand if I make a precise storyline, but if I do that there isn't much of a point in using charcoal. It feels appropriate to allow more flexibility with the contents of the image, and create together with my own biorhythms.[7]

IN TSUJI'S WORK, CHARCOAL'S MATERIAL RESISTANCE WORKS AS A COUNTER TO ANIME'S USUAL TENDENCY TOWARD METAMORPHIC EXCESS.

In recording the spontaneous modification of a single drawing as he reflects on what came before and how the film might move forward, Tsuji departs radically from the well-plotted temporality of cel animation. His working process renders the time of anime aleatory and imminent, persistently returning to the open-ended encounter between hand and paper. This irreducibly linear style of working gives equal weight to each moment of the film. Whereas cel and digital animators usually focus on "key" frames to articulate the fundamentals of a movement and only later have an assistant or a computer fill in the inbetweens, for charcoal animators every subsequent image presents the opportunity for the film to spin off in a new direction. This causes the flow of the film to stutter at times. A character's movement is momentarily arrested or suddenly switches directions. The carbon's refusal to move smoothly forward repeatedly draws viewer attention back to the labor involved in the act of drawing, redrawing, and photographing by hand.

In her analysis of Kentridge's *9 Drawings for Projection*, Rosalind Krauss notes how "it is this very density and weight of the drawing, this way it has of producing the hiccup of a momentary stillness and thus dragging against the flow of the film, that opens up the gap between [the charcoal] medium and that of film itself."[8] Krauss examines how this weight runs counter to the frequent association (going back to Sergei Eisenstein) of animation and image plasticity. As Eisenstein noted, the near weightless immateriality of the animation cel often tempts animators to indulge in rapid transformations of form, exploring modes of embodiment freed from gravity and the laws of physics. In charcoal animation, however, the linear, labor-intensive process and the insistent materiality of the carbon helps put the brakes on animation's tendency toward swift transformations. Krauss notes Kentridge's "sense that this transformative power needs to have a certain drag placed on it, a certain resistance or pressure exerted against its weightless fluidity."[9] In Tsuji's work, charcoal's material resistance works as a counter to anime's usual tendency toward metamorphic excess. Tsuji's use of 16mm film, with its own manual limitations, lends additional layers of mediated slowness and textural drag.

This insistence on slower forms of materiality works its way into the content of the drawings themselves. Krauss points to Kentridge's repeated focus on the most basic gestural repertoires of the body: small movements of the head and limbs, breathing lungs, and beating hearts. Tsuji's work meanwhile appears obsessed with the effects of gravity, presenting bodies seated, lying down, or walking with slow and deliberate strides. Occasionally, characters overcome the weight of the body through winged flight or by transforming their body into a gaseous state, only to later come crashing, Icarus-style, back down to earth.

Film critic Kitakōji Takashi recalls that when Tsuji was asked why he chose to study sculpture in college, he half-jokingly described wanting to use sculpture to "develop his body." Kitakōji takes him at his word, observing how this early sculptural attention to weight and volume carries over to inform Tsuji's approach to animation.[10] Tsuji's films draw on the materiality of charcoal to depict the tension between anime's promise of physical transcendence, and the weight and drag of the human body in all its stubborn inertia.

STARING AT THE DARK

This tension is particularly evident in Tsuji's first major work of charcoal anime, *A Feather Stare at the Dark*. The character designs in this work echo the late nineteenth-century charcoal "noirs" of Odilon Redon: angels, skeletal demons, and winged orbs with human faces float across symbolist landscapes governed by a pantheon of naked mythic creatures. The film's central focus is on the construction and destruction of worlds. Tsuji provides a partial summary of the first few minutes of the film on his blog:

> Male and female gods with large wings make a baby as they fly through the sky. After a while a boy is born, and the male god creates a world for his son. One time while the son is sleeping his left hand turns into a woman, who goes off somewhere. The boy sets off travelling in search of the woman, wandering through a newly created woods. He looks through a hole in one of the trees and glimpses a different world [*betsusekai*] beyond it. He crawls into the hole to go to the other world, but falls asleep before emerging out the other end. A dead skeleton god pulls the boy fully into this other world . . . [11]

The rest of the seventeen-minute film further extrapolates on this mythic search for the woman, freely mixing different religious and folkloric iconographies. At moments the film appears to reference charcoal's own ability to imagine new universes, as when the boy reaches the other world by passing through a tree.[12]

After waking up in this other world, the boy discovers a volcano that begins to erupt profusely, covering him and the surrounding landscape. The film cuts back to the winged father god, now giant in size. The skeleton returns and transforms into a demon woman, who flies to the god's genitals and quickly brings him to a giant orgasm. The semen begins to spill out continuously in an unstoppable flood, covering the forest and giving instant life to hundreds of small humans (Figure 3) as well as a city for them to live within.

A Feather Stare at the Dark includes persistent nudity and the frank depiction of sexual pleasure, sexual pain, and bodily excretions. The latter include not just semen but the ingestion and defecation of the human characters by the giant gods. As Tsuji hints in an interview, the seeming innocence and imprecision of the charcoal medium allows him to get away with these kinds of images, presenting them not as something vulgar or scatological but as part of what Kitakōji calls the broader "ecological thought" running through his work.[13] The use and reuse of the black carbon particles to depict these physical transformations lend an organic unity to this rapid circulation of energies.

However, the film shows how these unbounded transformations quickly begin to undermine themselves in their very excess. The boy takes revenge

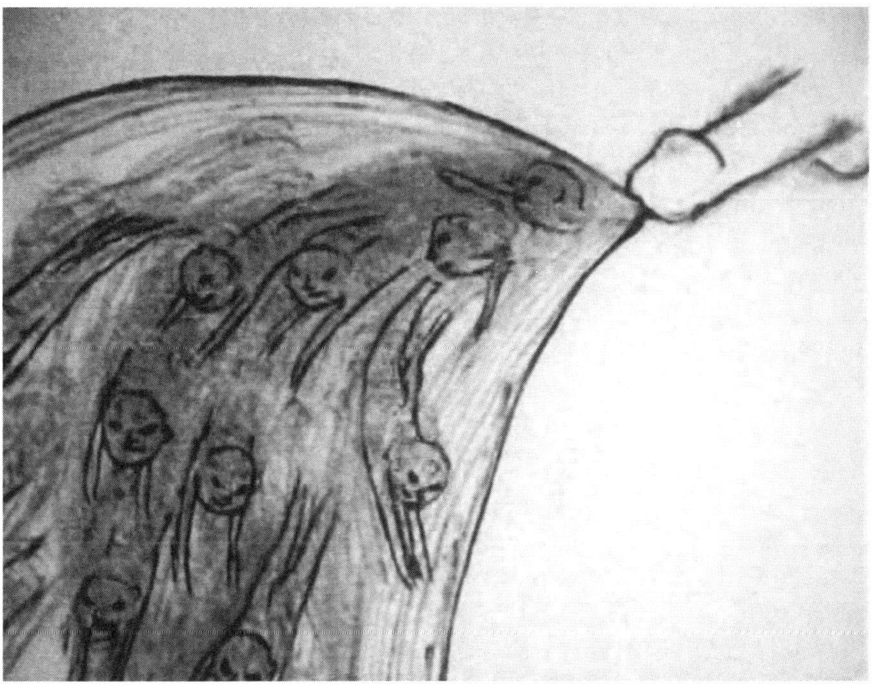

FIGURE 3. The father god's inadvertent but ultra-productive orgasm, miming the unwieldy creative potential of the charcoal stick. *Thinking and Drawing: Japanese Art Animation of the New Millennium* (Image Forum Video/Daguerreo Press, 2005).

on his father, cutting off the giant god's wing in exchange for the earlier loss of his own arm. This act of revenge triggers a spiraling apocalypse where the world gradually begins to crumble, only to give way to new worlds in turn. These transitions feature rapid shifts of scale and swift physical metamorphoses, in familiar anime style. Yet the film also attends closely to the fatigue that follows from these orgasmic bursts of productivity. As noted above, the boy falls asleep on his way to the other world, a scene the film returns to in its ending credits. The god's facial expression shows not pleasure but annoyance at the spilling of his seed. And at the end of the film, after the cosmic upheaval, we witness the various gods assembled in a room inside the sun for a kind of apocalyptic after-party, sitting around a dining table and sharing a bottle of wine. The boy, clearly bored with the gathering, gets up and heads for the door. In moments like these, the film introduces doubts about anime's desire for transformative freedom, presenting tired, heavy bodies as if they were bearing the fatigue of Tsuji's own fecund imagination.

This questioning of anime's omnipotent fantasies of creation and destruction has its roots in the artist's struggle to make sense of the apocalyptic desires driving violent behavior in Japan and overseas during the years Tsuji was working on the film. Enthusiastic about new age forms of spirituality during his college years, Tsuji recalls his shock at the transformation of Aum Shinrikyō from a yoga-practicing new religion into a terrorist doomsday cult. The group launched their sarin gas attack on the Tokyo subway in March 1995, just as Tsuji was about to graduate from art college.[14] This stark reminder of the dark side of the mythic imagination cast a pall over his early work on *A Feather Stare at the Dark*, and for a time he stopped working on the film entirely. After finally moving to continue with the work in the early 2000s, the 9/11 terrorist attacks and the subsequent war in Iraq again forced him to confront the tragic hubris of fantasies of world creation and destruction. Looking back on the film, he describes it as the trace of his own confused "search for the world" amid these unsettling events around the turn of the millennium.[15]

The final scene of the "good" and "evil" gods relaxing together with a bottle of wine radically relativizes the apocalyptic struggle acted out earlier in the film: the little people may have had their whole world destroyed, but the gods in charge appear to have enjoyed putting on the show (Figure 4). The boy, neglecting to touch his wine, unceremoniously leaves the gods at the table and opens the door to look outside. There, floating in a peaceful pastoral landscape, he finds a floating dark mass of charcoal. This soon resolves into the form of the woman born from his arm (Figure 5).

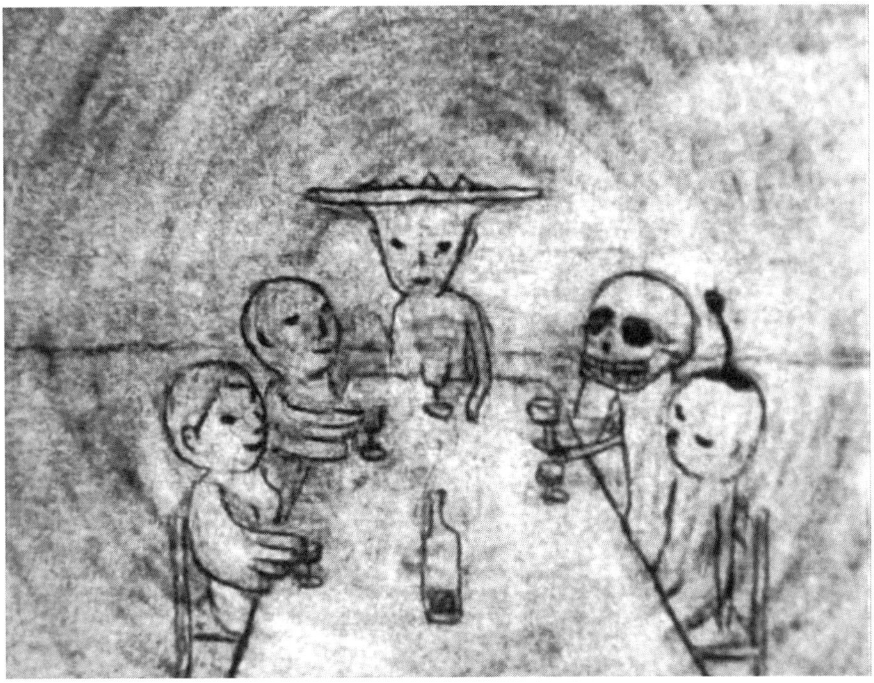

FIGURE 4. The dinner party of the gods, with the bored boy seated at right. *Thinking and Drawing: Japanese Art Animation of the New Millennium* (Image Forum Video/Daguerreo Press, 2005).

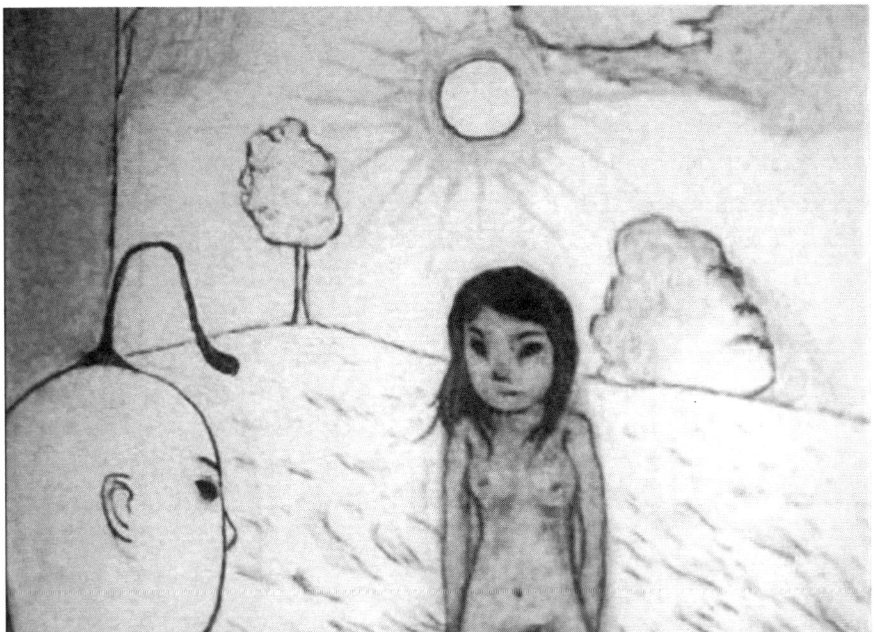

FIGURE 5. As the boy looks on, the dark mass of charcoal resolves itself into the figure of the woman. *Thinking and Drawing: Japanese Art Animation of the New Millennium* (Image Forum Video/Daguerreo Press, 2005).

REJECTING APOCALYPTIC FANTASY, THE FILM HEARKENS BACK TO AN OLDER FANTASY FROM THE AGE OF ROMANTICISM, ROOTED IN THE MORE FAMILIAR PHYSICALITY OF CARBON-BASED LIFE-FORMS.

The boy's turn from the violent play of the gods to the more contained physicality of his naked female companion—born from his own (drawing?) hand—stages Tsuji's rejection of anime's imaginative excesses in both aesthetic and gendered terms. The intemperate male potency portrayed earlier in the film contrasts with the immanent physicality of the pastoral female nude, as the guiding desire shifts from one of mythic world creation and destruction to a search for the restorative embrace of woman-as-charcoal-as-nature. Rejecting apocalyptic fantasy, the film hearkens back to an older fantasy from the age of romanticism, rooted in the more familiar physicality of carbon-based life-forms. Unlike the continuous and often violent movements of the gods, the woman stands still, patiently and smilingly accepting the boy's gaze. The subject of the film's earlier (and only) close-up, she finally pulls the film away from animation and back to the welcoming simplicity of the still image.

While other contemporaneous anime also grappled with questions of physical transcendence and apocalyptic desire, *A Feather Stare at the Dark* is unusual in pursuing these questions so deeply into the materiality of drawing itself.[16] Diminutive and slow in an age of imaginative excess, the film distances itself from anime's tendency toward free-form transformation, seeking instead to reestablish the unadorned and unmediated body as the source of every animated line. Tsuji's charcoals push anime to continually return to its founding gestures of drawing and erasing, while never forgetting the dark afterimage of so much carbon shifted around the page.

Notes

1. W. J. T. Mitchell, "Architecture as Sculpture as Drawing: Antony Gormley's Paragone," in *Antony Gormley: Blind Light,* eds. Anthony Vidler, Susan Stewart, and W. J. T. Mitchell (London: Hayward Publishing, 2007). Quoted in Isobel Harbison and Brian Dillon, *The End of the Line: Attitudes in Drawing* (London: Hayward Publishing, 2009), 6.

2. Rosalind Krauss, "'The Rock': William Kentridge's Drawings for Projection," *October* 92 (Spring 2000): 25.

3. "Kurōzu appu: Mokutanga anime no eizō sakka Tsuji Naoyuki" (Close up: Charcoal anime moving image maker Tsuji Naoyuki), *Yomiuri shinbun,* morning edition, July 4, 2005; Gerald W. R. Ward, ed., *The Grove Encyclopedia of Materials and Techniques in Art* (Oxford: Oxford University Press, 2008), 102.

4. Quoted in Akira Mizuta Lippitt, "*Arche*texts: Lascaux, Eros, and the Anamorphic Subject," *Discourse* 24, no. 2 (Spring 2002): 23; emphasis in original.

5. Harbison and Dillon, *The End of the Line,* 92.

6. Quote from "Naoyuki Tsuji," *Gallery Simon* website, http://www.gallerysimon.net/CV/tsuji_english.html.

7. From a prescreening talk at Image Forum, Tokyo, celebrating the release of Image Forum's *Thinking and Drawing* DVD (an anthology including *A Feather Stare at the Dark*). Quoted in Eichi, "'Kansō' saikin mita eiga, 'Gyakkyō nain' 'Yami o mitsumeru hane' hoka" (Thoughts on recently seen films 'Adversity Nine,' 'Feather Stare at the Dark,' etc.), *Aa, terebi to shinema—zakki* (Ah, Television and Cinema—Scattered Thoughts) blog, http://d.hatena.ne.jp/eichi44/20050813/p2. My translation.

8. Krauss, "'The Rock,'" 10.

9. Ibid., 17.

10. Kitakōji Takashi, "Tsuji Naoyuki 'Mittsu no kumo:' Toraware to kaihō o meguru torirojii" (Tsuji Naoyuki "Trilogy about clouds": Trilogy on captivity and liberation), *Bijutsu techō* 57, no. 868 (August 2005): 123.

11. Tsuji describes it as the boy's left hand but in the film it is clearly his right. Tsuji Naoyuki, "Yami o mitsumeru hane" (Feather Stare at the Dark), *Tsuji Naoyuki* blog, http://cannes.exblog.jp/423227/. My translation.

12. The arboreal basis of charcoal drawing is clearer in Japanese, as the word for charcoal (*mokutan*) begins with the character for tree (*moku*).

13. Tomio Koyama Gallery, "Artist Interview: Tsuji Naoyuki," http://www.tomiokoyamagallery.com/interviews/naoyuki-tsuji-interview-2009/; Kitakōji, "Tsuji Naoyuki 'Mittsu no kumo,'" 123.

14. Numerous commentators have noted the influence of apocalyptic anime and manga narratives on the group's historical imagination. See Miyadai Shinji, *Owarinaki nichijō o ikiro: Ōmu kanzen kokufuku manyuaru* (Living the endless everyday: Complete guide to defeating Aum) (Tokyo: Chikuma Shobō, 1995).

15. Tsuji Naoyuki, Okabe Masao, Miyaoka Hideyuki, and Minamoto Asako, "Tsukuru ~ creation ~ Tsuji Naoyuki o chūshin ni" (Making ~ creation ~ focus on Tsuji Naoyuki), symposium at Doshisha University, Kyoto, November 20, 2008. Transcript at http://1st.geocities.jp/mothermonika/m_works/screening/tsuji_screening.html.

16. While working at radically different scales, *A Feather Stare at the Dark* makes an interesting comparison with the contemporaneous television anime series *Neon Genesis Evangelion* (1995–96, *Shinseiki Evangerion*), which similarly seeks to make sense of the animated apocalypse in post-Aum Japan. *Evangelion* continuously shuttles between the fragile physicality of its young male protagonist and mythical concerns with world creation and destruction. It also presents an infamous sequence in the final episode in which the animation style briefly slips back into rudimentary black ink sketches on white paper, questioning anime's "freedom" to create alternative realities and forcing audiences to confront the hand-drawn origins of the otherwise slickly-produced characters. See Mariana Ortega, "My Father, He Killed Me; My Mother, She Ate Me: Self, Desire, Engendering, and the Mother in *Neon Genesis Evangelion,*" *Mechademia* 2 (2007): 216–32.

起源

STEVEN R. ANDERSON

Powers of (Dis)Ability: Toward a Bodily Origin in *Mushishi*

The anime series *Mushishi* (2005–6),[1] adapted from the manga by Urushibara Yuki, continues anime's tradition of reconfiguring the physical form to expose more than just vital organs. Paul Wells describes metamorphosis as "the constituent core" of animation, and the climactic scene in Ōtomo Katsuhiro's *Akira* (1988), when Tetsuo's psychic abilities finally overwhelm him, stands as one of the most memorable examples.[2] *Akira* proposes a transition from adolescence to adulthood that is directionally inside out, the body its significant origin point. Tetsuo's metamorphosis in the film can be viewed literally, a change of physical form, as well as symbolically, an expression of Japan's own ambivalence toward its economically powerful identity in the late 1980s.[3]

While readings of transformation that link to broader sociocultural themes may appear more promising for analysis, *Mushishi* calls for an analytic gaze that is exceedingly close to the body itself, largely resisting interpretations of Japanese society or identity. The series' quiet tone, minimal aesthetic, historically vague setting, and natural beauty are contrasted with at times shocking depictions of illness, disability, and bodily invasion. Following a type of healer known as a *mushishi* (literally, "insect master") named Ginko, the series depicts consecutive medical mysteries set around the interaction between humans and the creatures known as *mushi*. "Neither beings like us, nor illusions," the *mushi* are described as "a different form of what we consider 'life.'" Pervasive yet visible only to certain individuals, the *mushi* are notable for their uncertain ontological status as well as their role in reconfiguring the boundaries of the human body. One of the central paradoxes of *Mushishi* is that human interaction with the *mushi*—creatures described as deriving from "life itself"—often results in suffering and loss. Characters lose their ability to see, walk, hear, and think because of *mushi*. Yet the suffering and loss of the human characters is often accompanied by curious new powers. In this essay I will argue that for the characters in *Mushishi,* loss and gain, ability and disability, coalesce within the body to form a uniquely *(dis)abled* state.

Inspired by the recent "transdisciplinary" field of body studies, which synthesizes works in psychology, philosophy, disability studies, and medical sociology, I aim to begin from this state of *(dis)ability* and work backward, tracing paths of digression to reconfigure previously held boundaries.[4] Although I hope to challenge the normative body through an inversion of human ability and disability, my larger goal is to utilize theory on the digressive body to situationally locate it in an original space, a "bodily origin" that reveals something about what it even means to *be* a body. Approaching a bodily origin requires us to fearlessly catalog potential states—a broken rib, a dancer's mastery, a cancer that has metastasized to the lungs—to understand both where we came from and where we might be going. Animation has the ability to imagine the human body as a "magical tabula rasa" that can project "both dreams and nightmares of what it is to be human"; through *Mushishi* I will delineate what exactly those dreams and nightmares can be.[5] Then, I will go one step further, approaching the space between the normal and abnormal, the desired and feared, where an ambiguous, (dis)abled other resides—able although disabled, disturbed although magically enhanced. In these interconnected bodily extremes, repulsion and fascination meet in a challenge to human potentiality. There, at what the French psychoanalyst Julia Kristeva describes as the "border" of our existence, lies the bodily origin.[6]

PURE INVADERS: *MUSHI* REPRESENTATIONS

Although described as deriving from life itself, the identity or even symbolic possibilities of the *mushi* remain enigmatic. Insectoid in their ubiquity, diversity, and ephemerality, yet visible only to certain individuals and able to interact with mammals and humans alike, the *mushi* seem to reside in a gray zone that resists most symbolic readings. In the first episode of the series, the *mushishi* Ginko attempts to explain the creatures by presenting his arm as a metaphorical tree of life. Tracing the length of his arm, he ends with his thumb pressed against his heart and says that this is where *mushi* reside, calling it "green matter" (*midori mono*). They exist somewhere "between the living and the dead . . . living, like people, and inanimate, like objects." We later learn that *mushi* are born from a river of light called *kouki* (literally "light wine") that flows beneath the earth. *Kouki* is pure, ancient, and closely connected to life forces, but the exact nature of this "life" is left ambiguous. Are the *mushi* born from the river of light actually living, earthly creatures? Or are they more like ghosts (*yūrei*), gods (*kami*), or monsters (*bakemono*)? In his review of the series, Paul Jackson draws parallels to Japanese mythology to argue that *mushi* may be most closely associated with *kami*,[7] noting in particular the ability of *kami* to enter the human body.[8] Although Jackson notes that the *mushi* are "more elusive" than their direct translation (insect) suggests, examining them as insect-like creatures nonetheless offers us insight into their complex nature, as humans have been assigning characteristics to them for thousands of years.

ALTHOUGH JACKSON NOTES THAT THE *MUSHI* ARE "MORE ELUSIVE" THAN THEIR DIRECT TRANSLATION (INSECT) SUGGESTS, EXAMINING THEM AS INSECT-LIKE CREATURES NONETHELESS OFFERS US INSIGHT INTO THEIR COMPLEX NATURE, AS HUMANS HAVE BEEN ASSIGNING CHARACTERISTICS TO THEM FOR THOUSANDS OF YEARS.

Writing in the second century C.E., the Greek diviner Artemidorus interpreted insects in dreams as symbols of worry and anxiety.[9] Much later, the psychoanalyst Otto Rank, a member of Sigmund Freud's inner circle, theorized that the insect's ability to disappear into small holes in the earth, like the journey by which the spermatozoa and ova unite, may be the origin of all small creature phobias.[10] In contrast, Freud, in *The Interpretation of Dreams* (1900, *Die Traumdeutung*), emphasizes the sexual power of insects, noting that the most important aspect of a patient's dream, which involved various acts of insect mutilation, is the connection between the patient's anxiety about her husband's sexual dysfunction and her act of crushing Spanish flies, a noted aphrodisiac.[11] The biologist and cultural entomologist Barrett Klein, in his 2012 paper on insects and dream mythology, writes further on the power of insects, specifically on their ability to act as "dream vectors" capable of inducing feverish and dream-like states through (often malarial) infection and parasitism.[12]

The simultaneous fear and power associated with insects is depicted in episode 4 of *Mushishi,* in which a man's dreams become infected with a type of *mushi* that, like the pestilent bedbug, gathers in the host's bedding between nightly acts of parasitism. In the beginning, the man's dreams appear to be powerful visions of the future, foretelling the discovery of a well in the village and providing life-saving warning of an impending landslide. In time, however, the man's calamitous dreams become less premonitory and more causal, invading reality until his family and entire village are destroyed by a green mold. Ginko visits the distraught man and explains that although the *mushi* normally reside in the person's dreams at night, they occasionally come out and "become the medium to make the dream the host was having infect reality." The insect-like *mushi* affects both dreams and reality *via* dreams, adding a fantastical element to what Klein has observed as a real-world phenomenon.

Our relationship with insects is characterized by a combination of extremes, with the resulting affinity and repulsion, closeness and distance frequently expressed in works of fiction. Within film and anime, the *mushi* may evoke the jointly adorable and disturbing tree spirits *(kodama)* in Miyazaki Hayao's *Princess Mononoke* (1997, *Mononokehime*).[13] Paul Jackson notes the "enchanting luminescence" that characterizes both *kodama* and *mushi,* although the *mushi* are not nearly as benevolent or even neutral as their *kami* counterparts. Their frequently antagonistic relationship with humans may more closely recall Miyazaki's *Nausicaä of the Valley of the Wind* (1984, *Kaze no tani no Naushika*), yet the pure and natural *mushi* also stand in stark contrast to the segregated and toxic Ohmu that rampage in *Nausicaä.*[14] The difficulty in finding a representational analogue for the *mushi* reveals the divergent symbolic relationships between body and nature, human and creature in *Mushishi.* An example from literature that perhaps better captures this duality is the collector's case filled with butterflies and beetles in Joseph Conrad's *Lord Jim* (1900), which are described as representing the "qualitative extremes of humanity" with their positive (gorgeous, transformative) and negative (ugly, dirty) characteristics, respectively.[15] Teshigahara Hiroshi's *Woman in the Dunes* (1964, *Suna no onna*), in which an entomologist's quest to capture and catalog an elusive sand dune beetle is derailed by his own physical and spiritual entrapment in a sand pit, explores the dehumanizing consequence of our ambivalent associations with insects.[16] In her review of the film, Judith Shatnoff notes that what the entomologist does to insects, "life does to him," a role reversal that resonates primarily through its dissolution of one of the strictest hierarchical boundaries—that between human and diminutive creature.[17]

BODY AS (DIS)ABILITY

Pure and infecting, the *mushi* originate from a stream of light (*kouki*) to impregnate, control, and disable the human body. The paradox of the "pure invader" mirrors the complex associations ascribed to real-world insects. It is therefore not surprising that the result of *mushi*–human interaction is equally complex, neither uniformly positive or negative. In the second episode of the series, "The Light of the Eyelid" ("Mabuta no hikari") a girl named Sui contracts an eye disease that causes a debilitating sensitivity to light. Sui must wear bandages over her eyes and spend most of her time in a windowless shed as a result of her affliction. While talking to Biki, a young boy unaffected by the disease, she tells him that she thinks a *mushi* is the cause of her blindness. She also tells him that the only way for her to experience total darkness is to close her "second eyelid" (*futatsume no mabuta*). In Sui's case, ability has become disability: she is blind not because she can't see but because she sees too well. The power of light is magnified in Sui's eyes, and it is only within utter darkness, from behind a barrier that is unknown to able-bodied individuals (the "second eyelid"), that she gains an ability to see. In one scene, the children play together in the darkness of the shed and Biki complains that he can't close his second eyelid. "Really? You're so uncoordinated (*fukiyou*)," she retorts. Once she closes all four of her eyelids, Sui's surroundings are illuminated by the pure river of light (*kouki*) beneath her, enabling her to see. Although Sui hears the voice of a distant man (Ginko) warning her not to stare at the *kouki* too long, the river of light gifts the otherwise blind girl with an unusually abled body, as well as allows an embodied communication between the two children via the skin, which psychoanalyst Didier Anzieu prioritized as the "intermediary screen" that facilitates interaction between the self and others.[18]

In the episode that follows, "The Tender Horns" ("Yawarakai tsuno"), villagers in a remote snow-covered region become deafened en masse, and Ginko is summoned. After curing the villagers of the afflicting *mushi* residing in the cochlea organs of their inner ears, Ginko meets a boy, Maho, who is not only deafened but has also grown horns. Like Sui in the previous episode, Maho is debilitated and confined to seclusion due to sensory overload, in his case unbearably loud noise that deafens him. Ginko deduces that the rare *mushi* known as *ah* is the cause of Maho's deafness. *Ah* creates horns on the host that detect noises humans can normally never hear. *Ah* hates the sound of the living body, and when using a living body as a host it tries to erase the body's noise, deafening it. This rare creature is ultimately eliminated when one covers the ears with the hands, assaulting it with the sound of one's own body. In these episodes, disability is conceptualized not in terms of a deficit but as a painful acuity: Sui sees light so sensitively that she must not see at all; Maho is assaulted with so much noise that he is immobilized by pain. Heightened ability is perversely transformed into disability in these instances, and it is through this inversion that the ability/disability dichotomy is destabilized.

To question this dichotomy is to question the normative body, which forms the basis of various postmodern, quasi-political academic fields that gained acceptance in universities by the 1990s, such as queer theory, gender and sexuality studies, and whiteness studies. Disability studies, which can be traced to the founding of the Society for Disability Studies in 1986, explicitly rejects the medical model that views disability as inseparable from impairment and interrogates the assumption of normalcy that bifurcates the able from the disabled body. Through the alternatively proposed social model of disability, normativity as it relates to the body becomes the object of study itself.[19] The physicality of the body is erased from the identity of being disabled in this model, broadening the scope of disability from a random group of people who deviate from established norms and into a social category worthy of the same attention as gender, sexuality, or race.[20] Cultural theorists have noted the deeply embedded cultural and social processes of "othering" that separate normal, healthy bodies from those that are deemed abnormal or deficient.[21] These include the ways individuals with disabilities may be physically restricted by the world around them, as well as through less apparent barriers. Sociologist Nikolas Rose identifies Western psychology's "regime of the self" that privileges individualization, autonomy, and inward examination as contributing to a "regulative ideal" that dictates what is normal and abnormal.[22] For Rose, bodily difference can be enacted not only through outright coercion but from the inside out, planted and seeded through a self-centered definition of identity. Disability is threatening precisely because it "exposes the illusion of autonomy, self-government, and self-determination" that is the foundation of the regulative ideal of the healthy, strong, and able-bodied individual.[23] As will be explored, however, the characters of Mushishi do not simply challenge the regulative ideal through the inversion of ability and disability, as illustrated in episodes 2 and 3. Rather, bodily loss and gain are integrated into the subject to create a newly *(dis)abled* state.

CULTURAL THEORISTS HAVE NOTED THE DEEPLY EMBEDDED CULTURAL AND SOCIAL PROCESSES OF "OTHERING" THAT SEPARATE NORMAL, HEALTHY BODIES FROM THOSE THAT ARE DEEMED ABNORMAL OR DEFICIENT.

(DIS)ABILITY AS SUBJECT

The humans in Mushishi are not simply disabled by their interaction with mushi. Characters lose their ability to see in the daytime but gain the ability to see at night. The simultaneous loss and gain that characterizes the (dis)-abled bodies in *Mushishi* is reified through its incorporation into personal identity. In the episodes that follow, I will discuss how (dis)ability is made real in the lives of the characters of *Mushishi,* affecting both their identities and occupations. Through this discussion, I will offer a critique of the traditional social model of disability, which at its most extreme does not acknowledge physical impairment and opposes medical or helping professions that aim to treat disability physically. *Mushishi* provides a critique of this model on two counts: first, in its presentation of disability/ability not as dichotomy but rather as coexistence—what I have termed *(dis)ability*—and second, in the way that nondichotomous ability/disability informs the livelihoods and identities of the affected characters, most notably the series protagonist, Ginko. Prominent scholars within disability studies have noted the constraint that the politically motivated social model of disability places on identity, i.e., that one is either disabled or abled, us or them.[24] Physical impairment, as well as the desire to simply be "normal," apolitical, and not defined by one's disability, is excluded in the social model. Yet *Mushishi,* by presenting identities of (dis)-ability as well as an unremitting acknowledgment of physical impairment, offers a compromise between these two models.

A central example is Ginko's origin story, which is detailed nearly halfway through the anime series in episode 12. Owing to its rarity and importance within the series, Ginko's origin figures prominently in Ōtomo Katsuhiro's 2006 live-action adaptation (*Mushishi*), which weaves together multiple episodes from the series into a feature-length film.[25] Despite being one of the only recurring characters in the series, Ginko's past and internal motivations are rarely explored. The exception occurs in "One-Eyed Fish" ("Sugame no uo"), in which a young Ginko (known as "Yoki" prior to his magical transformation) is shown losing his mother in a landslide and wandering into a forest. There, a stern woman with white hair and only one eye discovers him and becomes his adopted mother figure. The woman, Nui, teaches Ginko her unusual abilities, including the use of a cigarette that can control *mushi* and the ability to see even in complete darkness. Ginko eventually learns why Nui stays close to a pond that emits an eerie glow at night, for as she explains to him, an enormous, fish-shaped *mushi* named *ginko* lives in the pond, feeding on another type of *mushi* known as *tokoyami* (perpetual darkness). The *mushi* cannibalism in the pond results in an "enchanting luminescence" that can permanently disfigure any creature—human or otherwise—exposed to it.[26] Nui lives alone by the pond in search of her husband and children, who she believes were drawn by the enchanting glow. While attempting to prevent Nui from committing suicide at the pond, Ginko comes into contact with the unusual light and loses consciousness. When he awakens, his hair is white, he has only one eye, and he suffers from retrograde amnesia, adopting the name "Ginko" after the *mushi* that transformed him. Ginko's transformation in this episode is an example of ability and disability truly intertwined. His newfound disabilities, which include attracting *mushi* wherever he goes, force him into the peripatetic lifestyle of a *Mushishi.* Yet he has also been magically endowed, able to see otherwise invisible *mushi* and control them with the smoke of his cigarette. The incorporation of identity allows Ginko to live as "a person with disability, rather than being overwhelmed by the disability."[27] This distinction recalls the semantic difference, central to the social model of disability and codified in the American Psychological Association's Style guide, between a "disabled person" and a "person with disability," with the latter preferred for its "person-first" focus.[28]

Episode 20, "A Sea of Writings" ("Fude no umi") describes a woman cursed by a *mushi* that has been sealed into the bodies of her descendants for generations. Ginko meets the woman, Tanyu, who is immobilized by the blackened leg that is the mark of her ancestor's curse. Like many of the characters in *Mushishi,* the woman in this episode is isolated from the outside world, resigned to an existence of specialized work in solitude as a result of her disabled body. The isolating effect of disability can be contrasted with social categories such as ethnicity; yet as Rosemarie-Garland Thomson notes, "like gays and lesbians, disabled people are sometimes fundamentally isolated from each other, existing often as aliens within their social units."[29] Like Tanyu, Ginko is both isolated and alien, wandering from place to place with few discernible friends or family, and marked by both his unusual physical appearance (white hair and only one eye) as well as his modern clothes. Tanyu's leg endows her with the ability to control *mushi* living in strings of Japanese characters. The only way to keep the *mushi* living inside her from killing her is to put it to "sleep" by recording stories of *Mushishi* exterminating *mushi.* However, because she hears only tales of killing, Tanyu is gradually saddened by the visiting *mushishi*'s "arrogance toward tiny, lower life forms" and their "unfounded fears of things different than themselves." The simultaneous loss and gain that Tanyu experiences as a result of her curse is emblematic of the ambiguous state of (dis)ability that affects many of the humans in *Mushishi.*

But there is another layer as well, which is the crystallization of identity that Tanyu's (dis)abled state confers, resulting in an uneasy identification with the very creatures that diminish her life. In short, Ginko and Tanyu's altered bodies inform their altered lives.

BETWEEN SUBJECT AND OBJECT

The (dis)abled body is incorporated into the identity of the subject, creating a feedback loop where selfhood is defined and reinforced by coexisting loss and gain. However, to use a concept developed by the Julia Kristeva in *Powers of Horror* (1980, *Pouvoirs de l'horreur*), the (dis)abled body is also abject. Kristeva writes how the abject is both of the body and not of the body, pushing us to the "border" of our existence through the transgression of previously held boundaries.[30] The human bodies in *Mushishi* are transformed through *mushi* interaction, becoming both abled and disabled. Yet it is precisely because of this coexistence of states—a blurring of boundaries around the regulative ideal—that the (dis)abled body may be viewed as abject. A change of familiarity is key. "Abjection is elaborated through a failure to recognize its kin; nothing is familiar, not even the shadow of a memory," Kristeva writes.[31] Closely related to the body—for what could be more familiar to us?—the abject disrupts our deepest self-familiarity, inspiring revulsion precisely because it lies both within the body and in opposition to it. As Susan Napier notes, when "given access to the secret depths of the body," as in Tetsuo's monstrous transformation at the end of *Akira,* "the viewer cannot quite look away."[32]

THE HUMAN BODIES IN *MUSHISHI* ARE TRANSFORMED THROUGH *MUSHI* INTERACTION, BECOMING BOTH ABLED AND DISABLED.

In episode 21 of *Mushishi,* "Cotton Changeling" ("Watabōshi"), a woman's unborn child is killed in the womb and replaced by a spore-like *mushi.* When the woman, Aki, gives birth a green slime emerges, quickly escaping beneath the floorboards. Mysterious children begin to appear underneath the house, and although Aki raises them as her own, she struggles to reconcile her intense desire to bear children with her knowledge of their inhuman origin. The episode recalls aspects of David Cronenberg's film *The Brood* (1979),[33] in which a woman undergoing "psychoplasmic" therapy gives birth to murderous facsimiles of her daughter Candice. Although even more horrific in tone than episode 21 of *Mushishi,* the two works share a disturbing similarity. Nola, the woman giving birth to the Brood, remains isolated in a cabin throughout the film, seemingly unaware of the presence of her murderous progeny. Her ignorance is questioned by the film's end, however, where she reveals a fetal creature appended to her abdomen, an external womb from which she "births" the Brood in front of her estranged husband. This establishes a familial closeness between Nola and her psychogenic children. As a result of a past miscarriage that led to divorce, Aki shares an immediate affinity with her *mushi* children despite their alien origin. Similarly, in the final scene of Roman Polanski's *Rosemary's Baby* (1968),[34] Mia Farrow's character overcomes repulsion to approach (and presumably comfort) her recently birthed devil child, signaling an acceptance of the inhuman product of her traumatic parturition.[35]

My point in illustrating these examples is that coexistent bodily addition and negation link the (dis)abled body with the abject body. Like the insects described earlier in this paper, the power of abjection lies in its extremities: self and other, repulsion and fascination, "unapproachable and intimate."[36] Insects are symbols of sexual power as well as worry; the birth of a child is an event to celebrate as well as dread. The abject arises from the transgression of boundaries, yet paradoxically, the abject is also what defines us, "what life withstands, hardly and with difficulty, on the part of death."[37]

TOWARD A BODILY ORIGIN

The *mushi* infect, distort, and rob the human characters in *Mushishi,* but they do not merely disable. Ability and disability are inverted and finally consolidated into selfhood to magically *(dis)able* the characters in *Mushishi.* Although the body may now be considered abject due to this boundary transgression, the "plastic corporeality" of these simultaneous bodily states leads me to conclude that the primordial *mushi* function as an origin point from which all possible bodily forms emerge.[38] The development of abject (dis)ability via ostensibly "pure" creatures in *Mushishi* calls into question the purity of origin. At the end of *Powers of Horror,* Kristeva quotes the twentieth-century writer Louis-Ferdinand Céline to argue that the abject ultimately "cancels our existence." My interpretation of this is that the abject, as representing the parts of us we most want to deny, functions as the ultimate revealer of ourselves. In our being, disability is denied and avoided; the abject confluence of ability and disability may be even more threatening. Yet it is there, in that most feared place, that our origin lies.

Notes

1. *Mushishi,* dir. Nagahama Hiroshi, TV series, 26 episodes (2005–6); 4-DVD box set (Funimation Productions, 2011).

2. Paul Wells, *Understanding Animation* (London: Routledge, 1998), 69; *Akira,* dir. Ōtomo Katsuhiro (1988); DVD (Geneon, 2001).

3. Susan J. Napier, *Anime from* Akira *to* Howl's Moving Castle, *Updated Edition: Experiencing Contemporary Japanese Animation* (New York: Palgrave Macmillan, 2005), 40.

4. Lisa Blackman, *The Body: The Key Concepts* (New York: Berg, 2008).

5. Napier, *Anime,* 36.

6. Julia Kristeva, *Pouvoirs de l'horreur*; translated by Leon S. Roudiez as *Powers of Horror: An Essay on Abjection* (New York: Columbia University Press, 1982), 3.

7. Paul Jackson, "The Space between Worlds: *Mushishi* and Japanese Folklore," *Mechademia* 5 (2010): 342.

8. This is also supported in the writings of the early Japanologist Lafcadio Hearn (1850–1904), who details the "madness" that overcomes those affected by fox spirit possession (*kitsunetsuki*), writing how "on some part of the body of the possessed a moving lump appears under the skin, which seems to have a life of its own." Lafcadio Hearn, *Glimpses of Unfamiliar Japan* (1894; rpt., North Clarendon, Vt.: Tuttle Publishing, 2008), 158.

9. Artemidorus Daldianus, *Oneirocritica*; translated by R. J. White as *The Interpretation of Dreams = Oneirocritica* (Park Ridge, N.J.: Noyes Press, 1975).

10. Otto Rank, *Das Trauma der Geburt* (1924); trans. E. James Lieberman as *The Trauma of Birth* (New York: Martino Fine Books, 2010).

11. Sigmund Freud, *Die Traumdeutung* (1900); trans. as *The Interpretation of Dreams,* line 28, http://www.bartleby.com/285/6.html.

12. Barrett A. Klein, "The Curious Connection between Insects and Dreams," *Insects* 3 (2012): 1–17.

13. *Mononokehime,* dir. Miyazaki Hayao, 1997; translated as *Princess Mononoke,* DVD (Walt Disney Home Entertainment, 2000).

14. *Kaze no Tani no Naushika,* dir. Miyazaki Hayao, 1984; translated as *Nausicaä of the Valley of the Wind,* DVD (Walt Disney Home Entertainment, 2005).

15. Joseph Conrad, *Lord Jim* (1900; rpt., New York: Empire Books, 2012); Tony Tanner, "Butterflies and Beetles—Conrad's Two Truths," *Chicago Review* 16, no. 1 (1963): 123–40.

16. *Suna no onna,* dir. Teshigahara Hiroshi, 1964; translated as *The Woman in the Dunes*, DVD (The Criterion Collection, 2007).

17. Judith Shatnoff, "Review: *Woman in the Dunes (Suna no Onna)* by Hiroshi Teshigahara," *Film Quarterly* 18, no. 2 (1964): 43.

18. Didier Anzieu, *The Skin Ego* (New Haven, Conn.: Yale University Press, 1989), 4.

19. *Rethinking Normalcy: A Disability Studies Reader,* ed. Tanya Titchkosky and Rod Michalko (Toronto: Canadian Scholars' Press, 2009), 6.

20. Ibid., 3; Mark Oliver, *Understanding Disability: From Theory to Practice* (New York: Palgrave Macmillan, 1996).

21. Blackman, *The Body,* 60.

22. Nikolas Rose, *Inventing Our Selves: Psychology, Power, and Personhood* (Cambridge: Cambridge University Press, 1998), 3–4.

23. R. G. Thomson, *Extraordinary Bodies: Figuring Physical Disability in American Culture and Literature* (New York: New York University Press, 1997).

24. Tom Shakespeare and Nicholas Watson, "The Social Model of Disability: An Outdated Ideology?" *Research in Social Science and Disability* 2 (2002): 9–28.

25. *Mushishi,* dir. Ōtomo Katsuhiro, 2006; translated as *Mushi-Shi: The Movie,* DVD (Funimation Productions, 2009).

26. Jackson, "The Space between Worlds," 342.

27. Margaret Wangui Murugami, "Disability and Identity," *Disability Studies Quarterly* 29, no. 4 (2002), para. 17.

28. American Psychological Association, *Publication Manual of the American Psychological Association, Sixth Edition* (Washington, D.C.: American Psychological Association, 2010); Ken Davis, "The Social Model of Disability and Its Implications for Language Use" (Glasgow: Glasgow Center for Inclusive Living, 1996).

29. Rosemarie-Garland Thomson, "Disability, Identity, and Representation: An Introduction," in *Rethinking Disability: A Disability Studies Reader,* ed. Tanya Titchkosky and Rod Michalko (Toronto: Canadian Scholars' Press, Inc., 2009), 71.

30. Kristeva, *Powers of Horror,* 3, 5.

31. Ibid., 6.

32. Napier, *Anime,* 46.

33. *The Brood,* dir. David Cronenberg (1979); DVD (MGM, 2003).

34. *Rosemary's Baby,* dir. Roman Polanski (1968); DVD (The Criterion Collection, 2012).

35. Lucy Fischer, "Birth traumas: Parturition and Horror in *Rosemary's Baby,*" *Cinema Journal* 31, no. 3 (1992): 3–18.

36. Ibid., 6.

37. Kristeva, *Powers of Horror,* 3.

38. Blackman, *The Body,* 324.

JOON YANG KIM

South Korea and the Sub-Empire of Anime: Kinesthetics of Subcontracted Animation Production

The relationship in the animation industry between Japan and South Korea has been as close as the geographic distance between the two countries. Since the mid-1960s, South Korean studios and workers have manufactured Japanese animation in a mode of production referred to as *hacheong* in Korean and *shitauke* in Japanese, both of which mean "to subcontract." In the global anime wave that started in the 1990s, this material condition of production has often been neglected or ignored, by academics as well as fans. Meanwhile in South Korea, since the mid-1990s when the government started to promote film and animation as a new national industry, the Korean term *hacheong* has been replaced by the English acronym OEM (original equipment manufacturing), despite no substantional changes in the condition of subcontracted production, as the former term seemed likely to offend many South Koreans' national pride. Indeed, the issue of internationally subcontracted animation production in South Korea has long been viewed and spoken of from a nationalist perspective. While intentionally ignoring the material reality of subcontracted work that has acted on the majority of the country's animation industry, the South Korean mass media has not hesitated to propagate the notion that South Korea is the third-largest producer of animation in the world.

Subcontracted production in the Japanese animation industry, which I will explore in the main part of this essay, was encouraged by politico-economic factors that included location, diplomatic agreements, wage levels, and exchange rates, and then materialized by a Taylorist work organization that went along with technologies of celluloid animation. My focus is, however, not on the perennial issue of developed countries' transnational exploitation of underdeveloped or developing countries' labor. Rather, subcontracted production is widely experienced at a domestic, as well as international, level, and the Japanese animation industry has long used a subcontracted production system within the territory of Japan. What I will bring into focus in this essay is the dominant discourse in this mode of animation production that places manual labor and laborers at a lower rank in the artistic-production hierarchy of brain over hand. Imagined and reproduced internationally through the animation subcontracting between South Korea and Japan (and possibly going further to the United States), this cerebral/manual dichotomy is a discursive construct I wish to call into question, with regard to animation's aesthetics as well as its kinesthetic processes.[1]

ANIME SUBCONTRACTION IN HISTORY

Subcontracted production in South Korea for foreign animation industries traces back to *Ōgon batto* (Golden bat) and *Humanoid Monster Bem* (*Yōkai Ningen Bemu*), first broadcast in Japan in 1967 and 1968, respectively. These were animated TV series produced by the Japanese animation company Daiichi Dōga and subcontracted to a South Korean TV station named TBC (Tongyang Bangsong); this station was part of the South Korean mega-conglomerate Samsung and is currently one of the state-owned TV stations, KBS 2. However, TBC stopped animation production a few years later. As suggested by Jeong Wook in a documentary television program about the South Korean history of cartoon animation, Lee Byung-chul, then chairman of the Samsung Group, did not judge animation to be a promising business because it was contingent on manual labor, noting in particular that Tōei employees in Japan had gone on strike at that time.[2] Today, the Samsung Group is well known for its technology-intensive businesses and for not allowing the activity of labor unions.[3]

Tōei Animation also prevented employees from forming a union. Yamaguchi Katsunori suspects that the Tōei management was concerned about such a movement because it was looking to coproduce animation with the U.S.

FOR ŌKAWA, WHO WAS DREAMING OF TŌEI ANIMATION AS THE "DISNEY OF THE ORIENT," THE UNITED STATES MAY HAVE BEEN A NEW RESOURCE FOR IDEAS TO BE SIMPLY ABSORBED AND THEN MATERIALIZED BY THE ANIMATORS' SKILL.

film company MGM.[4] In 1961, however, Tōei employees succeeded in organizing a union, and management stopped them from coming to work, eventually ordering a lockout. Many employees were forced to leave the studio, and some moved to Mushi Production, established by Tezuka Osamu in 1963.[5] In 1965 Tōei Animation stopped employing regular workers, turning to the policy of hiring temporary workers for discrete projects.[6] Finally, Tōei's ambitions of international coproduction came true in 1966 with *The King Kong Show*, an animated TV series from the U.S. company Videocraft International, which was followed by other coproduced (actually outsourced) projects with Western companies until the 1980s.[7] In his 1960 interview with *Shūkan asahi* (Asahi weekly), Ōkawa Hiroshi, then president of Tōei Animation, referred optimistically to this mode of animation production as a promising business.[8] For Ōkawa, who was dreaming of Tōei Animation as the "Disney of the Orient," the United States may have been a new resource for ideas to be simply absorbed and then materialized by the animators' skill. In contrast with Ōkawa's expectations, however, young animators were not content with merely drawing pictures as ordered, but rather wanted to play a creative role in animation production.[9] One example that makes clear the studio's situation is *The Little Norse Prince* (*Tayō no ōji, Horusu no daibōken*), the 1968 animated feature directed by Takahata Isao. The film was made both creatively and manually by the production crew—all union members—independently of and against the studio's management. This film is well known for the fact that Miyazaki Hayao, who had just started his animation career as an in-between artist, made a much greater contribution than he had in previous roles, providing a lot of creative artistic and technical input.

In 1971, Tōei Animation suffered more substantial changes. Ōkawa passed away, and his once-Disneyesque studio was cut in half in terms of workspace, number of employees, and technical resources.[10] It was in the same year that Takahata left the company with Miyazaki and Kotabe Yōichi, who were to become longtime colleagues. Two years later, the studio's management began outsourcing the manual process of animation production to small overseas studios located in neighboring Asian countries, one of which was South Korea.[11] Along with these changes, the practice of animation was increasingly dealt with as a mechanical skill, not as an artistic activity. A relevant example might be the business run by a Japanese company named Minwasha for a few years until 1974. With the sales pitch of "animation as a second job," Minwasha sold housewives a correspondence course in animating skills and hired some of them, calling them "home staff."[12] The growing fragmentation of animating labor took place in parallel with the growth of subcontracted animation production at home and abroad.

Although continuing to some extent even now, Japanese studios' subcontracted or outsourced animation production for Western companies began to show a sharp decrease in the mid-1980s. Having worked on as many as seventy projects from the United States by 1984, Tōei Animation pulled out of this production business around 1988.[13] This was largely due to the commercial success of *Dragon Ball* and the studio's other animated television series starting in 1986, and at the same time to the waning of the U.S. dollar's strength against the yen during the period of the Japanese bubble economy.[14] On the other hand, the studio paved the way to further outsource its own productions, establishing a studio to handle in-between cels, backgrounds, and finishing in the Philippines in 1986; since the Filipino studio was turned into a subsidiary of Tōei Animation in 1999, it has covered seventy percent of the animation production.[15] In this sense, neighboring Asian animators and animation workers deserve to be recognized as having supported the animation boom in 1980s Japan and the "anime" wave that started in the 1990s.

What is noteworthy is that this new geography of Japanese animation production in Asia was literally effaced in terms of cultural politics. According to Sawada Yukari, the names of Korean animators or in-betweeners were often replaced with fictitious Japanese names in the credits of animated series broadcast on television in the 1980s. It was necessary to disguise overseas subcontracting, given that there were sometimes noticeable visual inconsistencies, supposedly due to overseas animators' not fully controlled labor, in one and the same animated television series.[16] "Made in Japan" did and still does function as a national myth of animation production in Japanese society, and it was not until the mid-1990s that audiences could see many South Korean (and soon Chinese) names in the credits of Japanese animation, while more often the credit titles featured the names of the subcontracting studios (both Japanese and non-Japanese) rather than the names of their workers. The sub-empire called "anime" today is based on these subcontracting structures, set up under specific socioeconomic conditions in Asia.[17] A grotesque vision of those studios and workers is seen in Banksy's controversial 2010 title sequence for the "MoneyBart" episode of *The Simpsons*, in which he imagines a South Korean animation sweatshop, and displays his critical view of the Fox media empire.

I have examined how the manual labor of animating has been marginalized in the anime industry, within and outside of Japan. Now I will proceed to discuss the discourses that pertain to this way of deploying human resources in animation production.

DISCOURSES OF BRAIN AND HAND IN ANIMATION AND ART

In South Korea in the late 1980s there were attempts to change the fact that most of the country's animation production was dependent on foreign industries. Yet, one of the main strategies was centered on the dichotomous hierarchy of brain over hand—in other words, on a strategy for replacing the foreign brain with a national one. The cerebral element of animation production was often described as creativity, ideas, or the ability to write original stories and screenplays. On the other hand, there was no critical discussion of the techniques of animators trained in subcontracted production. First, it was feared that raising these technical issues would hurt animators' professional pride; and second, artistic issues have been regarded as irrelevant to the field of animation because the concept of art in South Korean society has long been one associated with Western "High Art" like classical music or oil painting. In the context of this cerebral/manual split, government institutions and the private sector tried to find a way to combine Korean ideas with the Korean animating skills that could supposedly materialize them. Such a simplistic combination was just an inverted version of what Ōkawa Hiroshi had attempted in dreaming of the internationalization of Tōei Animation in the 1960s.

In South Korea, the quasi-Romantic view placing human mind or spirit over materiality and corporality in artistic production has manifested itself again under the state-led project named BK 21 (BrainKorea21), in which the moving image (along with information technology, life science, design, traditional Korean medicine, and the like) was chosen as an emerging industrial field. The aim of the project is to foster "core experts" in advanced scientific and/or cultural technologies by supporting master's and PhD students in those fields.[18] If not appropriated for three-dimensional computer graphics or mediated by new digital devices, however, the manual labor and skills of animation are unlikely to find their proper place. Higher education tends to be dominated by a traditional Korean value system that has placed manufacturing work below literature for centuries. Much the same view is found among some "brain-oriented" Japanese experts, too. The animation journalist Kakizaki Shundō evaluated South Korean director Lee Sung Gang's 2002 animated feature *My Beautiful Girl, Mari* (*Mari iyagi*) as the result of the simple combination of an outstanding director, with animators trained through subcontracted production. He viewed the animators as having been waiting for just such a talented person.[19] And on a Japanese television talk show which discussed South Korean animation as an emerging competitor, Kubo Masakazu (the Shōgakukan editor and producer who had huge success with *Pokémon*) took a biological-sounding tone: he stated that the "brain," as well as the ability to develop and write scenarios, was not mature in South Korea's animation production.[20]

Such cerebral/manual splits can trace back as far as the Renaissance in Europe, well before the appearance of the modern film industry. E. H. Gombrich suggests that poets who "wrote" with their brains were loved by Renaissance snobs, but the artists who worked with their hands were not.[21] The Renaissance painter Giotto could obtain fame and distinguish himself from shoemakers or other craftspeople only through his scientific pursuit of mathematics and anatomy.[22] Furthermore, Da Vinci argued that the manual labor of a painter working with brushes was not as essential as that of a poet writing with a pen.[23] Gombrich denounces their view as snobbish and points to Aristotle as most responsible for its creation.[24] Likewise, in the field of live-action cinema, Alexandre Astruc proposed the movie camera as a new pen in the first half of the twentieth century.[25] In contrast, at the beginning of the twenty-first century Lev Manovich attempted to introduce the idea of a "kino-brush," in which cinema becomes closer and closer to animation through digital image-processing technology.[26] In his view, animation is located somewhere other than where cinema has been for the last century.

What I am concerned with here is not the distinction or relationship between the two concepts of "cerebral" pen and "manual" brush, which would be too big a project for this essay. Rather, I am interested in how it is possible to get over—in a practical way—the dichotomous hierarchy that seems to remain at work despite Manovich's sophisticated conceptualization of digital filmmaking. The fact is that we can immediately experience something emotional or mental from a series of subtle bodily gestures in an animated character, even if we "know" it to be merely composed of pixel-based, virtually three-dimensional images or flat, discrete, hand-drawn pictures. Such experience tells us that our sensation of animated visuals is not determined simply by cerebral intelligence. Rudolf Arnheim understands the relationship between brain and hand not in a causal way but rather as a structural similarity that allows a resonance between them.[27] He refers to "isomorphism" in discussing

A. Observed Person	
I. State of mind	psychological
II. Neural correlate of I	electrochemical
III. Muscular forces	mechanical
IV. Kinesthetic correlate of III	psychological
V. Shape and movement of body	geometrical
B. Observer	
VI. Retinal projection of V	geometrical
VII. Cortical projection of VI	electromechanical
VIII. Perceptual correlate of VII	psychological

FIGURE 1. Isomorphic Levels from Rudolf Arnheim

perception, stating that there are a series of different levels—psychological, electromechanical, mechanical, and geometrical—each of which is structured to resonate with its neighbors (Figure 1).[28] Significantly, the psychological state of mind does not occupy a privileged, dominating place over the geometrical shape and movement of the body and other physical levels; Level II is not the product but the correlation of Level I.

It should be noted that Level I and V in the observed person are mediated through hypodermic operations that are neural, muscular, and kinesthetic; these are not as visible as bodily shape and movement but not as supposedly mental as mind or perception. In Arnheim's view, dancers or actors are able (and trained) to enact bodily gestures, postures, and facial expressions that adequately correspond to their emotional or mental states through the kinesthetic correlation experienced while they are moving their own bodies.[29] In a phenomenological sense, an observer can experience the kinesthetic and other isomorphic levels of the expressing person's body, through resonance with its geometrical shape and movement. Given that people can become actors of sorts in specific social contexts, Arnheim's two terms, observed and observer, should not be understood as essentially and permanently separated from each other.

It is not strange, then, that animators have often been referred to as actors or choreographers. This type of performing artist expresses her- or himself by animating the extrinsic body-object or body-image of a character, but the central locus of neural, muscular, and kinesthetic operations should be the animator's body in the first place. For example, looking at his own face in a mirror, Peter Lord intentionally moves his lips and facial muscles to the recorded voice of the interviewee Bill Perry, while he is animating the lips of a clay figure that is Perry's representation in his animated documentary *War Story* (1989) (Figures 2, 3, 4, 5, 6, 7).[30] He could have relied on live-action footage of the interviewee telling his own story, but it is obvious that this cannot substitute for the hypodermic levels within the very body of the animator. These levels are required to function as the expressing (not just receiving) intermediary between the photorealistic representation of the interviewee's moving lips, the animator's eyes and hands, and the surface and mass of the clay figure. Another example is Miyazaki Hayao's bodily demonstration seen during the production of his animated feature *Ponyo* (2008, *Gake no ue no Ponyo*).[31] The director moves the entire upper part of his body, including his arms and hands, while talking with an animator about how to show to audiences the movements of a fictitious marine life-form that nobody has ever seen. William Schaffer's investigation of similar practices leads to a post-Cartesian account of the relation between the animating human subject and the animated nonhuman object. He comments:

> The animator finds himself reanimated in turn by the characters he animates and feels himself becoming a cartoon. Resonances of influence are conducted back through the pencil into the vibrating network formed by the strings of the artist's nervous system . . . the multiple strings of the moving puppet are never simply controlled from a single point embodying the "will" of the puppeteer . . . The puppeteer or animator may initiate this dance of strings and displaced bodies; but once in set in motion, it reverberates unpredictably, takes on a life of its own, in which the artist's entire body becomes but one of many dancing limbs.[32]

If more attention is paid to hand-drawn animation that does not deal with characters as physical objects in space, Gilles Deleuze's theory of painting should be taken into account. Deleuze's approach differs from Da Vinci's. In the French philosopher's thought, there is a quality inherent to the painting, something material, physical, and dynamic on the canvas, something that originates from the hands; but we lose the capability of feeling it when the

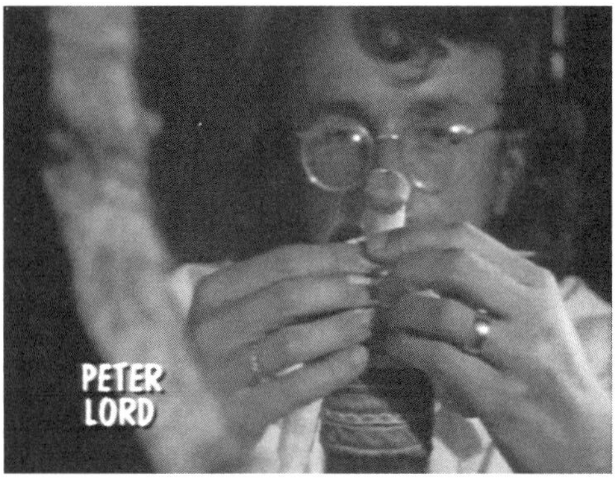

FIGURE 2. Peter Lord with his clay puppet

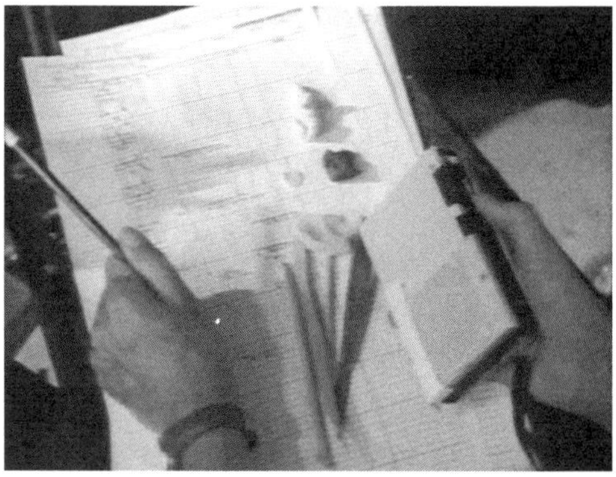

FIGURE 3. A tape cassette player with his right hand

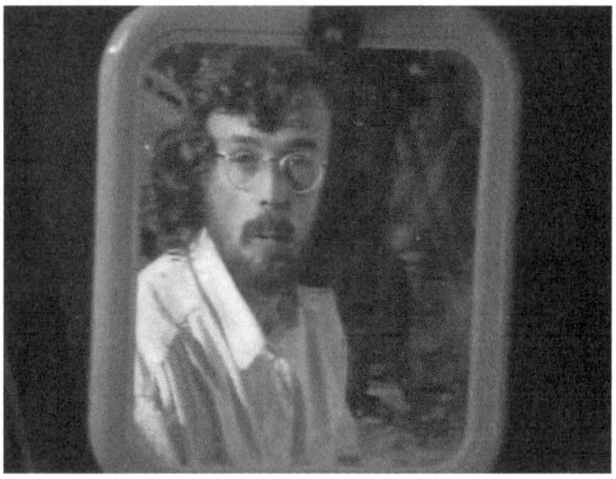

FIGURE 4. His facial movements in front of a mirror

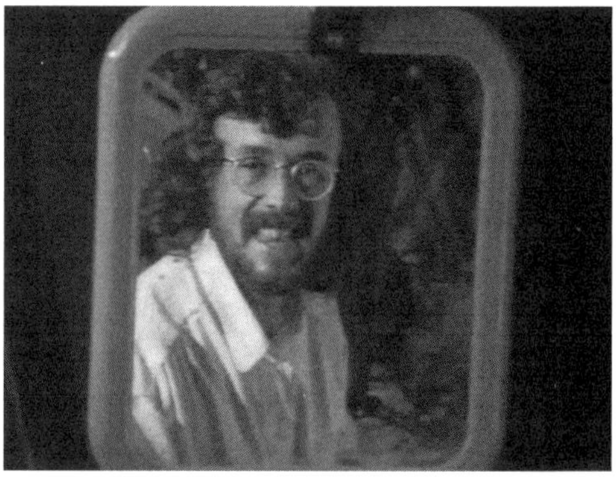

FIGURE 5. His facial movements in front of a mirror

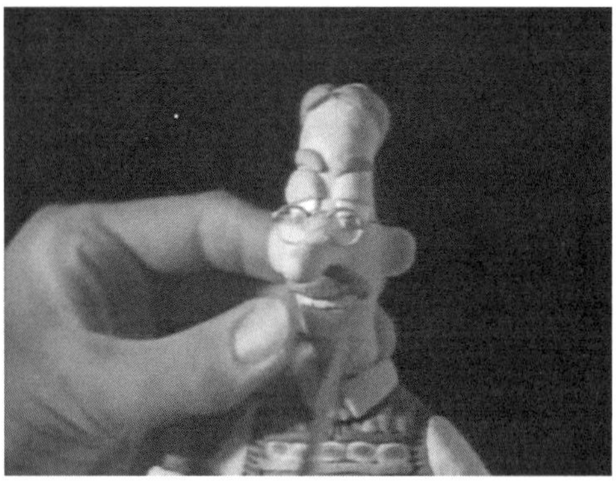

FIGURE 6. Animating the lips of the puppet

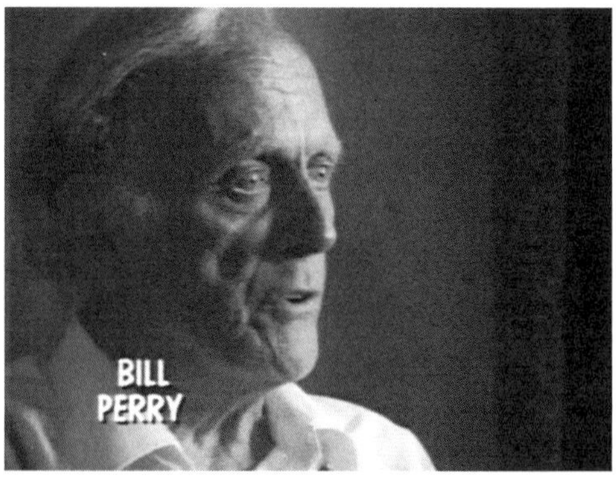

FIGURE 7. Bill Perry, the owner of the voice

manual is neglected by the cerebral.[33] It is impossible to *see* anything on the canvas with the eye, the retina, and the optic nerve, as long as they are dominated by the brain. Remind yourself of the apples of Paul Cézanne or René Magritte, and you are likely to think you *see* apples in their paintings, trained to do that in accordance with your given languages and schemata (apple, *ringo, sagwa, pomme,* and so on), but they are not what you believe you see. Similarly, you might think you *see* Ponyo in Miyazaki's animated feature, but you have never seen *her* before. In drawing the line of flight from such a visual field, you can *see* something tactile, visceral, and motile from the deterritorializing girl-fish and the other protean figures on the screen, then feel it in your retina, neural networks, kinesthesia, and muscles.[34] This mode of sensation is the same for the clay figure of Peter Lord, even when it aims at representing a human interviewee in a documentary film. We can see the mushy clay mass in flux, and the animator's manual marks on/beneath/around its surface, at almost the same time we see a human being smiling or talking. Keeping this in mind, now I will discuss how the global subcontracting structure of animation production can twist and fragment the embodied identity of both the animator and the spectator.

GESTURE AND IDENTITY: HOW TO MOVE AND LOOK LIKE A GENTLEMAN

In 1981, a South Korean national newspaper ran a disturbing story about the economic boom in South Korean animation. With an optimistic tone, an interviewee argued that on-the-job training in overseas productions will help Korean animators learn better techniques and make them more skillful at expressing the emotions of Western people.[35] One of the most important goals required of South Korean animators at that time was not to express their own emotions but the emotions of others—most of whom had never met, nor lived with in the same community. Encouraged by studio owners and the government, and appropriated by subcontracted production, South Korean animators' hands in the 1980s became more and more coded to specific cultural-industrial types of emotional and bodily expression. Their hands were trained to draw lines in the styles demanded by the Japanese and Western animation industries. During this process, the animators' bodies were broken down in time, through the process of breaking down characters' bodily movements, and the former also in-betweened through in-betweening the latter. My suggestion here is that the hand and body of the animator (particularly working in industry) is not entirely autonomous but likely to be controlled by industrial powers. For example, when discussing American animator Chuck Jones's self-referential animated short *Duck Amuck* (1953), William Schaffer points out that animators regularly find themselves to be puppets or cartoon characters manipulated by invisible controlling powers—slaves to the mechanical operation of capital.[36] Working in communist Czechoslovokia, Jiří Trnka also expressed this notion that the animator does not only animate extrinsic objects but is also animated through them, by extrinsic powers. Trnka's last animated film, *The Hand* (1965), portrays a puppet character forced to be a propaganda artist by the hand of a dictator.

The voice heard in the 1981 news story about incorporating animators' or in-betweeners' bodies into the engine of capital was reproduced with a different inflection in a recent interview. The story, which covers a South Korea–based studio owner and his success in working on the U.S. animated television series *The Legend of Korra* (2012), reports:

> His success was backed up by a thorough analysis of the U.S. market. . . . He researched intensively the emotional codes of U.S. audiences. The protagonist of the heroic story . . . was set as a gentleman who covers up for a female partner.[37]

Here, attention is paid not to manual skills but rather to the cerebral ability to analyze a market and research emotional and behavioral codes. The brain-centric logic delivered and reinforced here by the South Korean press looks only at how U.S. audiences prefer a person to act in terms of social norms: a gentleman should cover up for a female partner. It does not seem to have any interest in the way the gentleman will move in terms of gesture. Arnheim suggests that gentleness as a gesture should be embodied in the velocity and acceleration or deceleration of moving limbs, the shape of their curves, and other elements,[38] but these will vary with the identity of each finite and socially situated human being. Heather Crow suggests that the corporeal articulation of gestures is subordinated to the systems of representation (film, stage, social milieu), which make them perceptible and thereby manage their circulation and repetition.[39] She cites film scholar Leslie Stern's notion that gestures are performed but not owned by an individual: directly related to identity, gestures are foreign but familiar, public but private, wandering homeless ghosts that are ready to haunt human bodies.[40]

According to Yoo Sun Young, many Korean audiences in the early twentieth century seem to have been possessed by gestural ghosts invoked in the new medium of film. In her view, their bodies were imbued and animated with the gestures of Hollywood actresses or actors, as they imitated ways of walking and laughing, and came to feel that eating a piece of cake with a fork was more cultured than eating kimchi with chopsticks.[41] Yoo conceptualizes this trend as a process of early Korean modernization under colonization, where people were forced to be "naked" individuals who lost traditional communities.[42] My suggestion is that animation is an optimal medium for examining such wandering and haunting ghosts, because it enables us to deal with bodies not as given from a "real" world but as artificially constructed from discrete elements, in an infinitesimal, differential, and fluxional manner—frame by frame, or even pixel by pixel. At the heart of this discursive practice is the animator as a neurally, muscularly, and kinesthetically processing/processed entity.

This raises two questions regarding the news story about the U.S. code of gentlemanly behavior. The first asks what gestures will be imparted to the heroic gentleman character for U.S. audiences who embrace many different and diverse communities. The second question asks about the attribution of gentlemanly behavior to U.S. society, although the animated story enacts supposedly Asian (male) protagonists against Asian-looking scenery. With this, it seems to follow that such behavior should not be South Korean or Chinese. How many Asian children audiences will agree on such an idea? Certainly, the word, "gentleman" (*shinsa* in Korean) is likely to be associated with the "English gentleman" (*youngguk shinsa*), something foreign in South Korea; but nonetheless the word does not discourage one from imagining such a character as proper to another society. In relation to embodied identities and morals, these issues will be important for many young audiences who are situated in given social contexts (or situate themselves in different, chosen ones). Any of them could be animators in the future.

Notes

1. When the cerebral is spoken of here and other places in this essay, it does not only imply the intellectual but also refers to the brain itself. Indeed, many discourses in artistic production have attributed intelligence to the human brain, as will be shown later in this essay. In them, the brain has been understood as a superior locus, not just as a lump of meat, distinguished from the other biological organs of the human being by virtue of the metaphysical, often transcendental, notion of intelligence. The diametric view has been applied to limbs and their physical operation. But there are theories opposing this deep-rooted, brain-centric view of intelligence. For broader conceptions of intelligence, refer to Howard Gardner, *Frames of Mind: The Theory of Multiple Intelligences,* 3rd ed. (Philadelphia: Basic Books, 2011).

2. Jeong Wook, "Part Two: Bit gwa gurimja" (Light and Shadow), *Hanguk manhwa yeonghwa saship nyeonsa* (Forty years of Korean cartoon animation), TV (Tooniverse, December 19, 1998).

3. Choi Ji Yong, "Interview with the Samsung Union President Park Won Wu," *Oh My News,* July 17, 2012, http://www.ohmynews.com/NWS_Web/View/at_pg.aspx?CNTN_CD=A0001758164.

4. Yamaguchi Katsunori and Watanabe Yasushi, *Nihon animeishon eigashi* (The history of Japanese animation) (Osaka: Yūbunsha, 1977), 68.

5. Ibid., 106–7.

6. Ibid., 132.

7. Ibid., 116; Kusanagi Satoshi, *Amerika de nihon no animeishon wa dō mirarete kitanoka?* (The way in which the USA has seen Japanese animation) (Tokyo: Tokuma Shoten, 2003), 93, 183.

8. Ibid., 35–36.

9. Kimura Tomoya, "Shoki Tōei Dōga ni okeru eizō hyōgen to seisaku taisei no henkaku" (Changes in the production system and the visual expression of early Tōei Animation), *Dōjidaishi kenkyū* 3 (2010): 19–34.

10. Yamaguchi and Watanabe, *Nihon animeishon eigashi,* 132–33.

11. Tōei Animation website, http://corp.toei-anim.co.jp/company/history.php.

12. Yamaguchi and Watanabe, *Nihon animeishon eigashi,* 178–79.

13. Kusanagi, *Amerika de nihon no animeishon wa dō mirarete kitanoka?* 157–83.

14. Ibid., 183.

15. Tōei Animation website, http://corp.toei-anim.co.jp/company/companies.php.

16. Sawada Yukari, "Higashi Asia no manga bunka: grōbaraizeishon no genjō" (Culture of cartoon in East Asia: The current situation of globalization), Tokyo University of Foreign Studies website, July 18, 2003, http://www.tufs.ac.jp/21coe/area/hyoushou/vmg_seminar_030718.pdf.

17. The term "Sub-Empire" is cited from Ueno Toshiya. See Ueno Toshiya, "Japanimation and Techno-Orientalism: Japan as the Sub-Empire of Signs," *Documentary Box* 9 (1996), http://www.yidff.jp/docbox/9/box9-1-e.html.

18. Brain Korea 21 website, http://bnc.krf.or.kr/home/kor/index.do?method=getList.

19. Kakizaki Shundō, "Kankoku anime jijō" (Situation of Korean animation), Argo Pictures website, http://www.argopictures.jp/mari-summer/anime.html.

20. Kubo Masakazu, "*Grōbaru ueibu 2003: Anime ga sekai o kakemeguru*" (Global wave 2003: Anime in focus around the world), TV (NHK BS-1, October 26, 2003).

21. E. H. Gombrich, *The Story of Art* (London: Phaidon Press, 2006), 216.

22. Ibid..

23. Ibid., 223.

24. Ibid.

25. Alexandre Astruc, "The Birth of a New Avant-Garde: La Caméra-Stylo," in *The New Wave,* ed. Peter Graham, (Garden City, N.Y.: Doubleday, 1968), 17–22; first published as "Naissance d'une nouvelle avant-garde: La Caméra-Stylo," *L'Ecran français* 144 (March 20, 1948).

26. Lev Manovich, *The Language of New Media* (Cambridge, Mass.: MIT Press, 2001).

27. Rudolf Arnheim, *Toward a Psychology of Art: Collected Essays* (Berkeley: University of California Press, 1966), 57–63.

28. Perception can be dealt with as distinct from sensation, especially in terms of theorist Gilles Deleuze, whom I will refer to later in this essay.

29. Ibid., 67–70.

30. "War Story" and "State of the Art," in *Aardman Animations*, Laserdisc (Lumivision, 1992).

31. See the documentary television program *Purofesshonaru shigoto no ryūgi supesharu Miyazaki Hayao no subete: Ponyo mitchaku 300 nichi* (Professional, the way of work: All about Miyazaki Hayao with 300-day close coverage of *Ponyo*), TV (NHK, 2008).

32. William Schaffer, "Animation 1: The Control-image," in *The Illusion of Life II: More Essays on Animation,* ed. Alan Cholodenko (Sydney: Power Publications, 2006), 462.

33. Gilles Deleuze, *Francis Bacon: The Logic of Sensation,* trans. Daniel W. Smith (Minneapolis: University of Minnesota Press, 2004), 129.

34. For more on deterritorialization, see Gilles Delueze and Félix Guattari, *Anti-Oedipus: Capitalization and Schizophrenia* (New York: Penguin Classics, 2009), 206.

35. Lee Seong Ju, "Boolhwang sog ui hohwang: manhwa yeonghwa soochul" (A boom in the middle of recession: Export of cartoon animation), *Dong-a ilbo*, January 13, 1981, http://newslibrary.naver.com/viewer/index.nhn?articleId=1981011300209212001.

36. Schaffer, "Animation 1: The Control-image," 474.

37. Min Byeong Sun, "'Pororo' do gongryak mot han nangongbulak mi eni shijang, hanguk gojol gamdog i jeomryeong" (A South Korean director with a high-school diploma overpowers U.S. market where Pororo failed to do that), *Dong-a ilbo*, July 1, 2012, http://news.donga.com/3/all/20120630/47413110/1.

38. Arnheim, *Toward a Psychology of Art,* 59–60.

39. Heather Crow, "Gesturing toward Olympia," in *Animated 'Worlds,'* ed. Suzanne Buchan (Eastleigh, UK: John Libbey Publishing, 2006), 49.

40. Ibid., 49–50.

41. Yoo Sun Young, "Yookche ui gundaehwa: Hollywood modernity ui gagin" (Modernization of the body: The imprint of Hollywood modernity), *Moonhwa gwahak* 24 (2000): 233–50.

42. Ibid.

Boundaries

起源

IMAMURA TAIHEI
Translated by Thomas Lamarre

Japanese Cartoon Films

TRANSLATOR'S INTRODUCTION

Renowned as the author of the world's first book of animation theory, *Manga eigaron* (A theory of cartoon films), first published in 1941, revised and published again in 1948 and 1965, and recently republished in 2005, Imamura Taihei merits special attention for his combination of practical analysis, philosophical inquiry, and Marxist paradigms, which enabled him to develop highly influential theories both of animation and of documentary film.[1]

When Imamura embarked into film theory in earnest in 1934, contributing to the reader's column of *Kinema junpō* and founding and contributing to a film magazine *Eiga shūdan,* a series of mass arrests of communists and others deemed politically suspect (including Marxists) was leading to the collapse of the Japanese Communist Party and to "conversions" (*tenkō*) of intellectuals and artists from Marxism to nationalism, among them Imamura. It is thus difficult to gauge the impact of Marxism on Imamura. Irie Yoshirō calls attention to the Marxist currents of Imamura's film theory, "Imamura's investigations into the essence of cinema began alongside his emerging consciousness of Marxism."[2] In volume 8 of *Mechademia,* Ōtsuka Eiji stresses Imamura's renunciation of Marxism. It is clear, however, that Marxist dialectic analyses of film, especially that of Sergei Eisenstein, appealed to Imamura, evident in his use of concepts such as contradiction, mediation, and synthesis, and in his emphasis on realism.

At the same time, another aim of Imamura's cartoon theory was to reform cartoon and film production in Japan. Imamura's theory thus shows continuity with concerns of prior film criticism for reforming national production, particularly as articulated in the Pure Film Movement that gathered steam from late 1910s through the 1920s in Japan. Yet Imamura's interest in reforming Japanese cartoons took a turn that seems, at least at first, to be at odds with his interest in Marxist social realism. His reflections turned toward how cinema might enable a practical repurposing of traditional Japanese art forms, and he draws inspiration from the aesthetic philosophy associated with the Kyoto School, especially that of Watsuji Tetsurō. The result is a provocative combination of modernism and realism, traditionalism and Marxism, and cultural nationalism and socialism.

Originally published in 1938, the essay translated here, "Nihon manga eiga no tame ni," not only anticipates the arguments of his famous 1941 book but also presents them in a condensed form, making clear the connections between arguments that are sometimes held apart in the book.[3] This essay also addresses a specific moment in the history of animation: the introduction of new techniques for producing a sense of depth in animation, that is, the multiplanar camera system, which received a great deal of popular and critical attention in the context of Disney's *The Old Mill* (1937) and the Fleischers' *Popeye the Sailor and the Forty Thieves* (1937). Imamura would continue to evoke recent American cartoons throughout his career, but there is a sense of historical urgency vis-à-vis questions of the materiality and realism of cartoons at this early stage of his thinking.

Such historical circumstances and social concerns allowed Imamura to build a theory of animation that is highly unusual in two respects: it does not construct a divide between animation and documentary, and consequently, it succeeds in offering a theory of animation as a form of realism, a real experience of life. And this is what makes his account of cartoon films so timely and thought provoking today.

I recently went into a theater for short films, and there was but one cartoon. To my surprise, it was a Japanese cartoon, *Kaeru no kenpō* (1933, Frog sword art).[4] Accustomed to seeing cartoons like Mickey Mouse and Popeye the Sailor, I found Japanese cartoons quite wanting.

HOW IS IT THAT A CRUDE DRAWING DONE WITH HEAVY LINES WITHOUT ANY PARTICULAR CHARM, WHEN SET IN MOTION, APPEARS FULL OF LIFE AND INNER PURPOSE AND, SIMPLY PUT, IS NO LONGER A DRAWING?

Walt Disney's works invariably feel like they're pulsing with life. The little animals on the screen seem to be more than just a drawing, and the most familiar objects around us appear utterly transformed.[5] Even if the background art often looks mediocre, the joy of life overflowing in the moving animals makes for marvels. Whether they are leaping about or lying down, the life force bubbling up on the screen courses through us like wine. Clearly, this is what gives us such a delightful feeling of intoxication. There is nothing like viewing a Disney cartoon for making we moderns understand the festive spirit of ancient Dionysian rites.

These animals truly are modern-day satyrs. Taken one by one, the still images have no particular charm.[6] The still image of a figure like Mickey Mouse tends rather to be unsightly. How is it that a crude drawing done with heavy lines without any particular charm, when set in motion, appears full of life and inner purpose and, simply put, is no longer a drawing?[7] The secret must lie in movement itself, that which moves the drawings. What makes Japanese cartoons so boring lies in this secret of movement. Movement of Disney cartoons is endowed with a dimension of inner purpose, like human psychology. Japanese cartoons lack this dimension. It is painful to watch movement that is not endowed with inner purpose. This is because inner purpose is precisely what we feel to be most vital. Put another way, any movement that has inner purpose will feel full of life. It is delightful when forms that we expect to be animate start to move. Yet it is quite unpleasant if things without animate form start moving or stopping. A body not endowed with the power of movement cannot be considered alive.

Watching cartoons like *Kaeru no kenpō,* one never gets any feeling of the inevitability of movement, that any of these drawn forms have to move. It makes no difference whether these forms move or not. Consequently, they don't really have to have a particular form. Compare the frog in Disney's *The Old Mill* with the one appearing in *Kaeru no kenpō*: Disney's frog has been simplified in a realistic manner, while the latter has no grounding in realism, which makes a transformation from frog into human meaningless because it feels so easy.[8]

Now then, the realism of Disney's cartoons—this wellspring of life force—where does it come from? It comes from that fact that their drawings are not just drawings; they are *drawings combined with photography.*[9] In fact, in cartoons, *photographic techniques prevail over the arts of drawing and painting.*[10]

> THE CARTOON IS SOMETHING FUNDAMENTALLY DIFFERENT FROM PRIOR ARTS OF DRAWING AND PAINTING.

The actions of the drunken mouse in *The Country Cousin* are a good example (Figure 1).[11] It is nothing less than photographic footage of a person in an inebriated state.[12] Each frame of the film has been copied in drawings. Another good example is the depiction of the long takeoff when the Roc takes flight at the beginning of the Fleischers' *Sinbad the Sailor,* which closely resembles the takeoff of a Douglas passenger plane (Figure 2).[13] The realistic movement of the Roc's wings is clearly a pictorial depiction based on parsing the movement of a bird in flight with film photography.[14]

What I wish to make clear here is that, conceptually, the cartoon is something fundamentally different from prior arts of drawing and painting.[15] Of course, each image entails drawing and painting. Yet, taken one by one, the drawings in cartoons do not have any particular artistic significance. Drawing is essentially a spatial art. While the drawings in the cartoon film might be considered spatial, they only become art under conditions that enable them

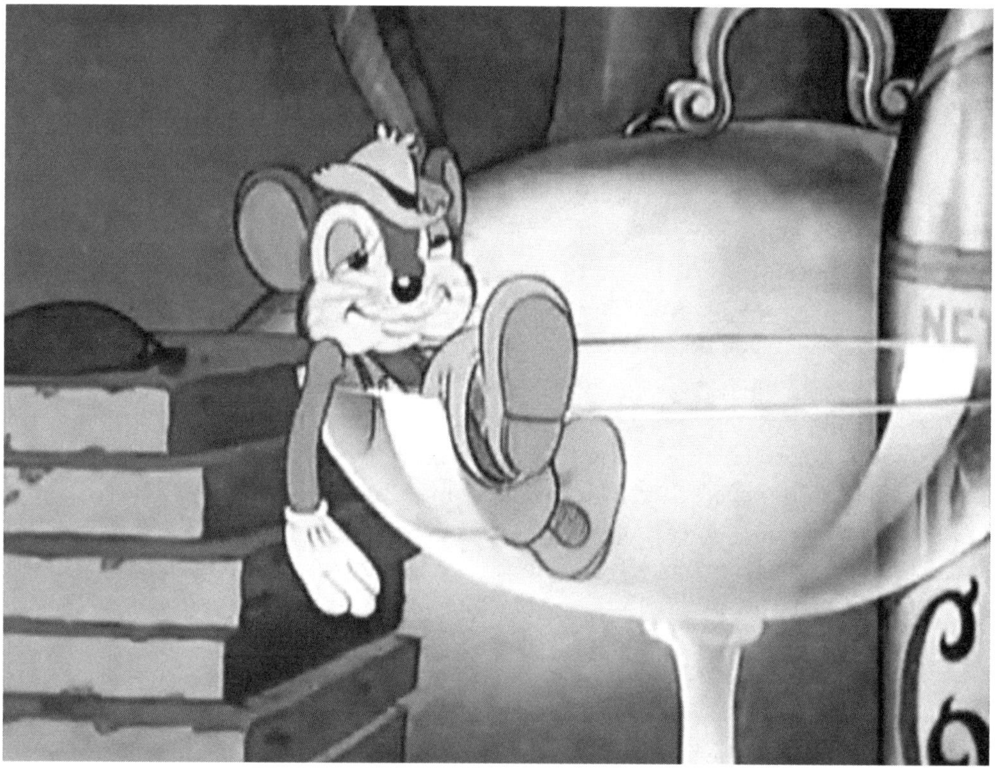

FIGURE 1. An image from *The Country Cousin* (1936), directed by Wilfred Jackson

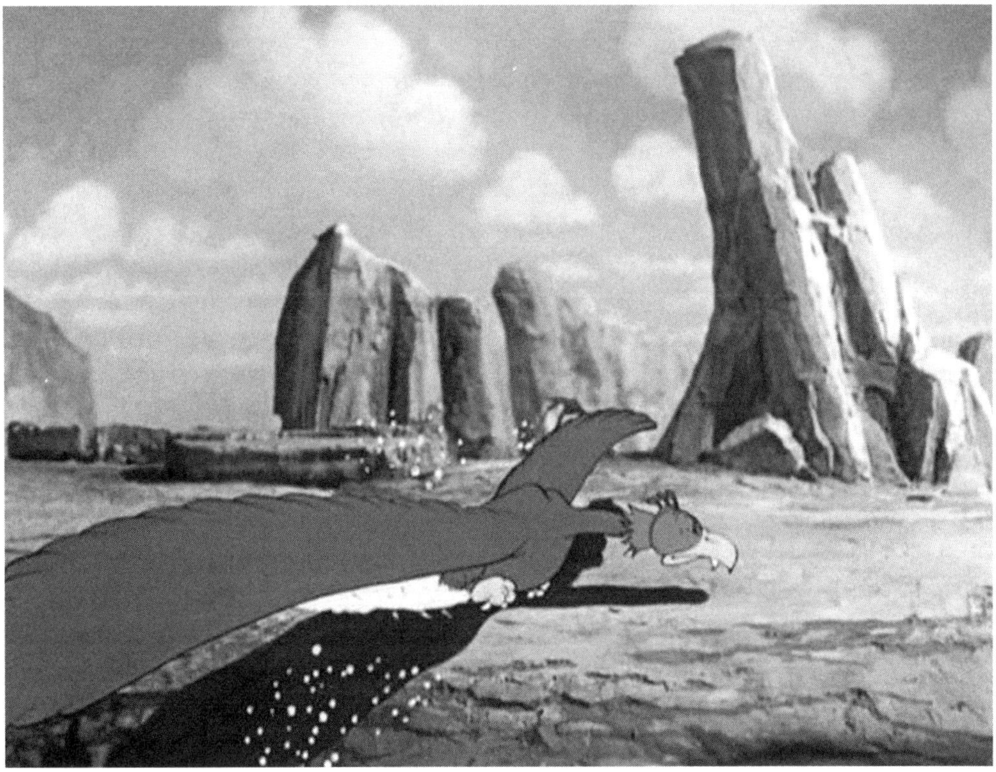

FIGURE 2. An image from *Popeye the Sailor Meets Sinbad the Sailor* (1936), directed by Dave Fleischer

to become *temporal art*. As such, insofar as the arts of drawing and painting in cartoons are grounded in photographic techniques and combined with photography, cartoons come into being as a temporal art, wherein lies their specificity.

Without the use of photography to parse actions instant by instant, it would be impossible to express the liveliness of the mouse, duck, and dog. The use of film photography to parse the entire chain of a living movement brought movement-time to images for the first time.[16] While the realism of Disney's cartoons lies in their reliance on parsing movement with photography, Japanese cartoons today are almost always based on print cartoons in newspapers and magazines. People on the whole seem oblivious of the fact that the reality of movement in Disney cartoons is based on techniques of photographic parsing. This is why Japanese cartoonists are not able to create realistic movement: because they are not combining images with techniques of photographic parsing.

Like images on one of those revolving magic lanterns, movement in Japanese cartoons do not impart any sense of inner motivation because the pictures have been drawn in accordance with techniques of still images.[17] The Japanese cartoon I saw recently was *cartoon as drawing* without any parsing by photography, in contrast to the Disney cartoon, which is *cartoon as photography*. This fundamental difference makes clear why Mickey Mouse and Donald appear so full of life and inner purpose.

The question of why cartoon films have undergone great advances only in America must be considered carefully. We have yet to see anything that rivals Disney. Similarly, confronted with Chaplin, all kinds of American slapstick comedies fell out of favor. Faced with American cartoons, both Reininger's silhouette animations and Starevitch's puppet films fell out of the limelight.[18] Why did this happen? It cannot be explained solely in terms of capital investment. Clearly, the key to such success was their use of techniques that were more cinematic. Capital merely brought them to light. Prior to capital there were more cinematic techniques that beautifully tied into a poetic sentiment. Film criticism then must always address the question of these very cinematic techniques. Disney was a poor artist living in an attic when he first took an interest in cartoons and made his first works. Well before the bank put up the necessary funds, he had already grasped an important principle.

The principle was that of drawing images strictly in accordance with movement as parsed with film photography.[19] This is what "animating" is all about. If I may speculate a bit, it seems likely that he parsed movement through close observation of the dynamics of the actions of various animals and humans. And film photography is the only way to show all the stages of such actions in still images. Thus, he would have carefully observed the continuity of various actions as given on film and copied it into drawings.

In the work *Clock Cleaners*, a dog whose head is gonged [inside the clock tower bell] weaves about unsteadily, vibrating (Figure 3).[20] Surprisingly enough, it is a waltz that accompanies his movements. It is surprising because it is already difficult enough to depict the movement of walking unsteadily as if in a daze. For an actual person, walking in a stupor to the pace of a waltz would be quite a marvelous feat. Such a sequence is not one that could be drawn without an object of reference. In other words, we can well imagine that film photography provided a model for parsing movement, which was drawn in keeping with the tempo of a waltz. The dog's manner of walking especially shows the influence of high-speed filming.[21] It wouldn't have been possible to create the impression of the dog stumbling about while vibrating without recourse to techniques of parsing movement with high-speed filming.

The success of American cartoons is rooted above all in the characteristics of this country, where there are no long established traditions of art,

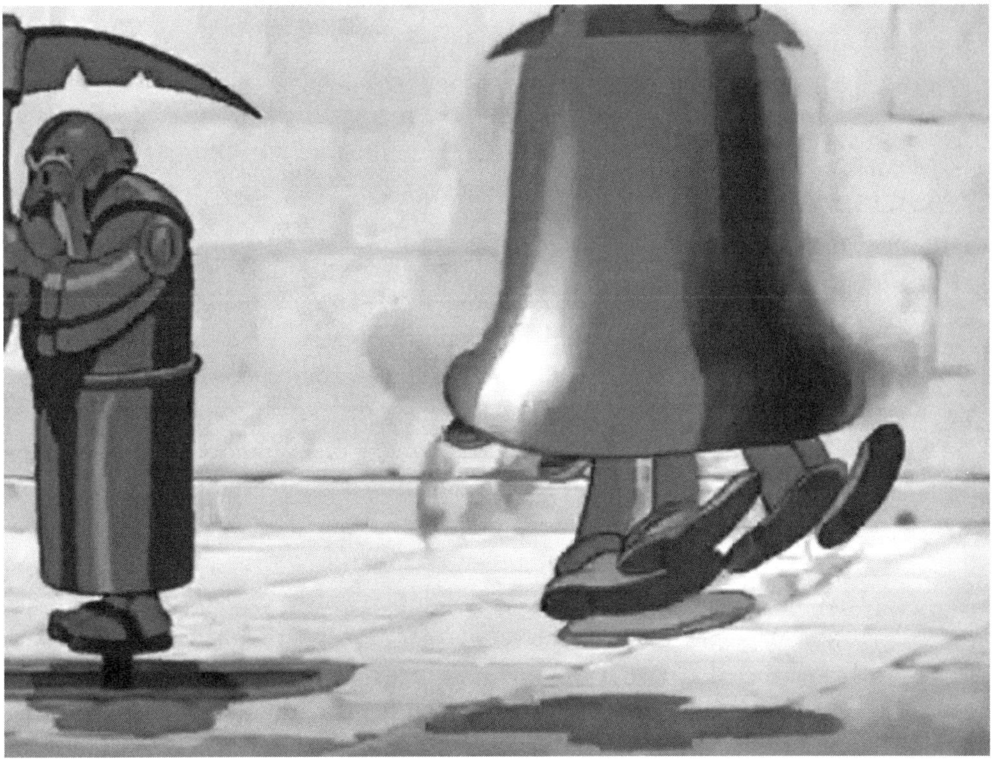

FIGURE 3. An image from *Clock Cleaners* (1937), directed by Ben Sharpsteen

and mechanical techniques are the most highly advanced. Due to the lack of constraining traditions, drawings are most confidently combined with photography. In other words, their art is based on use of the camera for a temporal partitioning of the movement of objects. It was surely Impressionism that first attempted a serious treatment of time within art. We may think of the Impressionist artist who tried to capture the essence of a haystack as it ceaselessly transformed with the changing light as one who investigated time with images.[22] An artist like Degas, who tried to grasp the ballerina's pose in the instant, was another investigator of movement-time within art. Nevertheless, in the fact that not a single creator of cartoon films has appeared in France, we must see the considerable and heavy constraints of that artistic tradition.

Such concerns become especially salient in the case of Japan, insofar as the tradition of Oriental arts is very long. In its deep resistance to photography, Japanese art is quite unlike French art. Such resistance may well be explained in terms of the difference between ink painting and oil painting. The historical development of oil painting techniques has been realistic and materialistic to the point where it shows a tendency toward embossing or relief carving, especially when it comes to modern art.[23] As such, oil painting is

> EVERYONE IS LEARNING HOW TO LOOK AT THINGS WITH PHOTOGRAPHY.

the formative matrix of photography. Rubens and Rembrandt come to mind in such a context. Oil painting itself has moved steadily toward a sort of photography of things.

In contrast, Japanese art—or Oriental art—stands diametrically opposed to photographic realism. Instead of placing great emphasis on the external reality of things, this is of secondary importance. In Japanese art, the tendency is far removed from photography; it is to draw materials from the imagination, materials that could not become objects of the camera. This tradition has been sundered due to the introduction of oil painting techniques, which has made matters excessively complicated. We may have a better understanding of and appreciation for the traditions of Japanese art, and yet, mechanical techniques, not at all different from those in America, are developing all around us; photography is flourishing, and everyone is learning how to look at things with photography. Of course, traditions of Japanese art will necessarily have a perceptible impact on Japanese oil painting and photography, insofar as those who adopt them are Japanese. Such impact can be said to be inevitable, without need for any further deliberation.

Our feeling of being caught between the tradition of Japanese painting and the countertradition of oil painting is identical to the circumstances of contemporary Japanese culture in general. Around the world today, the contradiction between cinema and art has become greater and greater. Judging from trends in modern culture, I think that the received modes of still pictures will continue to undergo transformation into moving pictures. The solitary artist who, like the solitary novelist, retreats into his studio to create still images aloof from the world—has he not lost all significance? Would the most social art not be based in the industrial system, entailing the cooperative work of hundreds of artists, like the production facilities for Disney cartoons?

Is it not the case that a single moving artwork, such as Disney's *Silly Symphonies,* can be enjoyed on screens across the world, in contrast to the individualized appreciation of art exhibitions?[24] It is obvious that, due to the emergence of cinematic techniques, art is moving from the stage of artisanal production into that of mechanical production. A new generation of musicians has become aware of cinematic techniques, and likewise, new artists are becoming aware of cinema. Salvador Dalí, Fernand Léger, and Maurice de Vlaminck are prime examples. In this era in which the contradiction between the spatiality of art and the temporality of cinema is gradually being exposed around the world, the contradiction between Oriental art and Western art will become ever more acute, whence the emerging historical significance of Japanese cartoon films.

The development of Japanese cartoon films necessitates finding a resolution to the contradiction between Japanese art and Western art. All in all, the lack of creativity in Japanese cartoons is a befuddled reflection of the contradiction of contemporary Japanese art. It would be a mistake to set aside an examination of this aesthetic problem and to think that, if we invested as much capital as the Americans, we could make Japanese cartoon films. Such an approach would only make for duplications of Mickey Mouse and Popeye.

Like it or not, to conjoin drawing with photographic techniques, the tradition of Japanese art must assimilate the material pictorial techniques of Western art. In the recent cartoons of Disney and Fleischer, shading has been enhanced, imparting greater dimensionality, and color has become more nuanced, aiming for realistic photography. Take, for instance, the ocean in the background of the opening sequence for *Sinbad the Sailor,* or the desert in the first scene of *Forty Thieves* (Figure 4).[25] The latter picture in particular might well be mistaken for photography. The silhouettes of the forty thieves appear

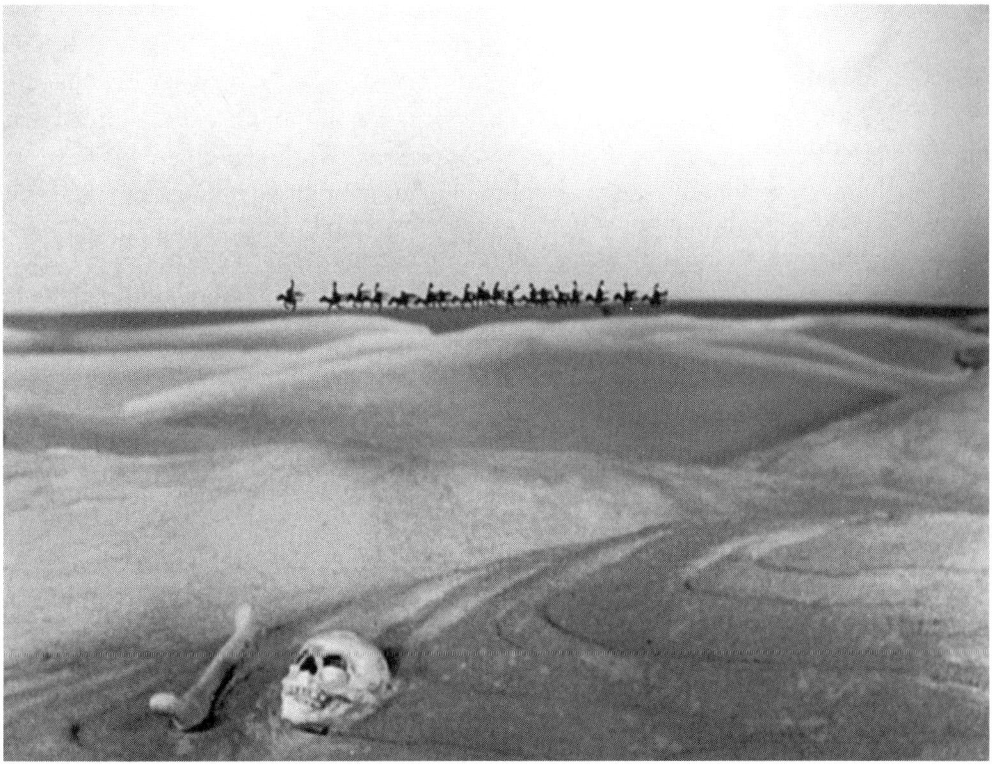

FIGURE 4. An image from *Popeye the Sailor Meets Ali Baba's Forty Thieves* (1937), directed by Dave Fleischer

running across the distant horizon. The subtle shading and perspective used to depict the undulating dunes of the desert and the remains of a skeleton in the foreground are very close to color cinema. Such techniques are on par with *The Old Mill*. As the summer rainstorm tears open the roof of the small windmill amid flashes of lightning, the rain shines brilliantly white. The streams of pouring rain, glowing whitely, do not feel at all like a drawing. With the portrayal of moonlight shining through an old roof in *Lonesome Ghosts* (1937), or the dazzling flood of sunlight in the southern lands of *Hawaiian Holiday*, the images before our eyes are closer to color cinema photography than to conventional oil painting.[26] It is only normal that, as cinema comes as close as possible to actual reality, images in cartoons turn toward *drawings aiming for real photography*.

If Japanese cartoons rest content with simple line drawings or ink painting, they cannot possibly compete with Western cartoons. Perfecting Japanese cartoons will be a matter of conquering Western techniques of material realism from the standpoint of Japanese painting, as well as innovating in various ways with traditions of Japanese painting that agree with the photographic factual way of seeing things. Traditions that are truly carried on as traditions are blessed with renewal through incessant innovation. Traditions not allowing for innovation become formalist, rigid, and decrepit, and perish. Although the tradition of Japanese art is nonphotographic and spiritual in tendency, it will become increasingly permeated with the materialist way of looking at things, as with the camera. Photographic equipment can be found in every household today, along with radio and records. Photographs are indispensible features of newspapers and magazines, for covers and as illustrations. The advance of photography is such that, even in Japan, it is inevitably bringing about new techniques of drawing that parse the movement of things through the mediation of photography.

I have particularly high hopes that the received styles of Japanese art will be artistically combined with photographic techniques within cartoon films. This is because, within the long history of Japanese arts, many splendid techniques suited to today's cartoon films have appeared.

I have said that cartoons are temporal art. Japanese picture scrolls, which rank among the finest of arts, may also be one of the oldest forms of art striving to be temporal. Much like contemporary cartoons, they develop a story with pictures. It is surprising how close they come in that respect to the temporal techniques of cinema. Seen from the standpoint of Western painting, the bulk of such pictures appear utterly chaotic in terms of perspective. One scroll of a warship loaded with warriors, for instance, shows not just the side facing us but the side facing away as well. As a result, the ship looks oddly twisted. To borrow from Hinago Motoo's discussion, it is exactly as if the artist had done a pan with a camera to show us both sides simultaneously.[27] Establishing continuity between two pictorial planes upon a single pictorial plane, then, is just like a type of motion cinematography.[28]

> PERFECTING JAPANESE CARTOONS WILL BE A MATTER OF CONQUERING WESTERN TECHNIQUES OF MATERIAL REALISM FROM THE STANDPOINT OF JAPANESE PAINTING.

The image does not render all parts equally, as in Western painting. For instance, the significant parts of a building are depicted, while the rest of it remains hidden in the clouds. This technique of ellipsis using clouds is very common. It recalls temporal techniques of cinema such as fade-in, fade-out, and overlap. Displays of different space-times within a single picture happen constantly in picture scrolls.

This does not occur only in picture scrolls. Illustrated maps of Kyoto, for instance, which were painted in the Edo period on large folding screens, show a reversal of techniques of perspective. Such a tendency also appears in smaller works of art, and so it is difficult to determine where to look for its conceptual basis. Yet, if you will permit me to speculate, I tend to think that these techniques indifferent to proportion appearing in large-scale works like the illustrated maps of Kyoto are related to the temporal forms found in picture scrolls. For, instead of overall spatial balance and proportion, the artists' goals are *to present distant sites in the same manner as nearby ones.* A small theater in Sanjō Kawara, for instance, had to be drawn as large as the Shimizudera temple complex. What was distant and what was close had to be shown in the same way. As a result, techniques of perspective run haywire. A path may become wider and wider as it goes from foreground into the distance. The image is clearly not drawn from the standpoint of equalizing spatial proportions; rather such techniques are designed to allow for temporal progress related to narrating—and explaining—things here and there in Kyoto. The picture scroll form seems to be one that rejects pictorial space in favor of narrative time. It is much the same with the warped perspective of the actors' faces in Sharaku's woodblock prints.[29]

Such examples lead us to believe that the influence of picture scrolls extends to other kinds of pictures as well, confirming the important role played by picture scrolls in Japanese art. These picture scrolls usually strived to recount unusual events such as battles, or improbable tales of changing fortunes stemming from the religious imaginary. As an art of the fantastic, picture scrolls provide clear historical precedents for the fantastic tendencies of contemporary cartoon films. Japanese cartoon films cannot develop if they do not revive such traditions and call upon the splendid fantastical art in the Tobae lineage.[30]

The ghost appearing in Disney's *Lonesome Ghosts* has a transparent body, not visible to Mickey or Donald. Incredibly gruesome fantasies are also depicted in the *Gaki zōshi* (Scroll of the hungry ghosts) of the Kamakura period.[31] People are polishing grains of rice in the vicinity of a well. Ghouls have come forth, voraciously gobbling up scattered grains of rice and discarded husks in the water. They are ghastly in appearance. The people, however, are not aware of the ghouls alongside them. In *La mort de Tintagiles* and *L'Intruse,* Maeterlinck described that terror of something next to you that you cannot see, but Disney puts it into images in *Lonesome Ghosts*.[32] In Japanese religious art, what captures our attention is the way that illusion and reality are depicted side by side. Were Disney to see these fantastical scrolls in which hungry ghosts, with their swollen bellies and arms and legs skinny as twigs, bend to scoop water from the river to drink, only to have the water burst into flames at their touch, Disney would be as full of admiration for Japanese picture scrolls as Eisenstein was full of wonder over Sharaku.[33]

Nothing quite compares with Tobae for its depiction of animals with simple lines, such as its rabbits and monkeys capering about mounted on deer, yet such beautiful fine lines have appeared in Japanese painting for longer than one can say. There's no reason to doubt that the simple ink strokes of Japanese painting would have a special impact when shown upon the screen. Yet not one of these exquisite treasures of traditional art has been taken up in cinema. Similarly, although nearly half of Japanese films to date are period pieces, it seems fair to say that the artistic traditions of kabuki and noh have hardly ever been consciously taken up in cinema.

Among the techniques of noh drama and puppet theater that had a profound impact on kabuki performance, there are also a couple of significant principles that Japanese cartoons films must adopt. As Watsuji Tetsurō has pointed out, in puppet theater, substantial reality lies in the material body of the puppet.[34] Because the puppeteer manipulates the puppet only with his fingers, the performance is exceedingly limited, largely transmitted into movements of the head and shoulders. The principle of the cartoon film is precisely the principle of puppet theater. Like the puppet, the image that is drawn sheet by sheet is but the material body. If manipulation of this material body is to impart the feeling that it is alive, one must select only the most distinctive actions. As in photography, in cartoons it is not possible to capture all movements equally, so it is necessary to draw the viewers' eyes only to the most significant movements of the actor. Close observation of Disney's animals confirms that the repetition of simple operations similarly has complicated effects on us. If you look at that Donald's action, for instance, the operation consists almost entirely of him wagging his rump back and forth.

In noh drama as well, one finds a mechanical parsing of human actions similar to puppet theater. Noh makes no pretense about being abstract, reducing backdrops and props to the bare minimum. Noh is clearly an imitative art. It should be noted that the renowned artist and theorist of noh, Zeami Motokiyo (ca. 1363–1433), begins his treatise *Sarugaku dangi* (ca. 1430, Talks on *sarugaku*) by writing, "The way of theater is all about the imitation of things."[35] Similarly, in *Kadensho* (1400, Book of transmission of the flower), he opens the second section with a statement that makes evident how much noh aimed for realistic depiction: "It is difficult to set forth the various facets of imitating things. Nonetheless, because they are fundamental to the way, you must try to attain them above all else. *All in all, the aim is to imitate without omitting anything.*"[36] It would seem that stripping away backdrops and props was, in fact, a way to impart absolute power to the performance. It would be no easy matter for the personage standing on the planks, without any of the relevant attire whatsoever, to recreate in all their detail the manners of "wood choppers, grass cutters, charcoal burners, salt scoopers."[37]

There is no way to disagree with Iwasaki Masumi placing noh among Wundt's genre of imitative arts. Noh is an art that is born above all of "imitating things," placing the imitation of things at its very heart, such that "not a single aspect would slip by."[38] Such highly detailed imitation gradually became abstract and practiced consciously, providing a mechanism for the parsing of action.

Watsuji Tetsurō writes, "The noh actor moves into a position to step forward, putting one foot forward and holding it level to the ground, and then suddenly, stomps loudly with the sole of his foot. Such an action parses our natural way of walking into two movements. *It has thus made for a transmutation of an organic way of moving into a mechanical way of moving.*"[39]

It is the same principle that is discovered in the movement of cartoons. Actions in cartoons are also a revival of new life through "negation of natural life."[40] Their actions entail a thorough simplification and mechanization of actual actions, which constitutes a truly striking deformation of reality.

Japanese artistic traditions, in so many respects, have an amazing power of dynamic evocation geared toward imbuing images with movement greater than that of cartoon films.

The extreme combination of image and sound of the kind occurring in

Disney cartoons has striking implications for Japanese dramatic arts.[41] Despite Wagner's efforts, foreign opera has unwittingly exacerbated the split between theatricality and musicality. This is probably due to the remarkable development of autonomous instrumental music. In contrast, Oriental drama generally has developed with close relations between performance and music, and Japanese dramatic arts are one example.

In the case of Japanese music, due to the absence of autonomous instrumental music like that of the orchestra, musical instruments such as the *shamisen* developed as musical accompaniment for performance. As a consequence, in kabuki and puppet theater, it is common for the performance to be enacted with the *accompaniment* of songs performed by musicians and chanters called *degatari* who narrate on stage. A row of *nagauta* vocal performers is on stage in the background, a chorus that provides an ongoing explanation of events, whose appearance recalls the nonindividualized chorus of ancient Greek drama. Cinema has indeed resurrected such dramaturgy. Cine-operetta and musical films are obvious examples, but even in such films as *La Kermesse hérioque* (1935), for instance, the crowd takes on a role like that of the chorus vis-à-vis the film's protagonists.[42]

The problems confronting Japanese cartoon films lie not only in the visual arts. They face similar problems with music. In sum, it is a question of how to create music that will link with the images on screen. *Shamisen* accompaniment like that in *Kaeru no kenpō* is pointless. For marching triumphantly along, Disney cartoons can promptly take up the overture to *Light Cavalry* as accompaniment, but what sort of music is there for Japanese cartoons?[43] Instruments such as the *shamisen, koto,* and *shakuhachi* cannot stand alone as accompaniment. The problem lies in the contradiction between the discordant tones of Japanese music and harmonious Western melodies. The problems entailed in such a contradiction are the same as those entailed in the contradiction between ink painting and oil painting.

The observations presented above make evident that the development of Japanese cartoon films is linked to a number of serious problems. The deficiencies of cartoons imported from abroad offer a fine opportunity for the takeoff of Japanese cartoons. We must review which principles discovered by our ancestors are truly significant from the point of view of cinema.

Notes

1. The most recent collection of Imamura's writings reprints the original 1941 text of *Manga eigaron*: Imamura Taihei, *Imamura Taihei eizō hyōron 5: Manga eigaron* (Tokyo:

Yumani Shobō, 1991). Ghibli Studios recently promoted the republication of the revised 1965 edition: Imamura Taihei, *Manga eigaron*, Ghibli Library (Tokyo: Tokuma Shoten, 2005). Despite his importance, Imamura has hardly been translated. A partial translation of one of the chapters from the revised 1965 edition has appeared: Imamura Taihei, "Japanese Art and the Animated Cartoon," *The Quarterly of Film Radio and Television* 7, no. 3 (Spring 1953): 217–22. Michael Basket recently translated two essays, "A Theory of the Animated Sound Film" and "A Theory of Documentary Film," in *Decentering Theory: Reconsidering the History of Japanese Film Theory,* special issue of *Jōsai University Review of Japanese Culture and Society* 22 (December 2010): 44–51, 52–59.

2. Irie Yoshirō, "Approaching Imamura Taihei," in *Decentering Theory,* 60–61.

3. This essay, originally published in *Eigakai* in 1938, was reprinted in the 1991 collection of Imamura's film criticism. Imamura Taihei, "Nihon manga eiga no tame ni," in *Imamura Taihei eizō hyōron 2: Eiga geijutsu no seikaku* (Tokyo: Yumani Shobō, 1991), 137–59.

4. Presumably the cartoon in question is actually *Kaeru kenpō* (dir. Iwao Ashida, 1933). See, too, the listing on the Toy Film Project website, http://toyfilm.jp/2010/06/post-142.html. Imamura provides only two references within his text, to Iwaskai Masumi (note 36 below) and Watsuji Tetsurō (note 37 below). All other notes are the translator's.

5. The meaning of the Japanese term *e* can be rendered as "drawing," "image," or "picture," and depending on the context, I use all three translations in this essay. But I distinguish *e* from *kaiga,* consistently translating this latter term, which means something like painting and drawing, simply as "art" (and on one occasion as "visual art" when the contrast is necessary), to avoid confusing it with the former term *e.* In sum, the reader can be sure that, when the terms "drawing," "image," or "picture" are used, the Japanese term is *e.* Also, I translate *bijutsu* as "arts" to differentiate it from *kaiga.* Finally, near the end of the essay, Imamura uses the term *eizō* in reference to cinematic or photographic images.

6. Imamura uses the term *seishi-e* for still images or drawings that do not move.

7. In the context of discussing the secret of movement, Imamura uses a series of interrelated terms—*seishin, shinri,* and *kokoro.* Because Imamura is making a fairly familiar argument about how animated figures seem to be self-causing, I have generally translated these terms as "inner purpose" (or in one instance as "motivation"), because it seems to me that although there are implications of a soul, psyche, or even psychology, Imamura is interested in how the appearance of having an inner cause, purpose, or motivation makes animated images appear to be alive, and shows little interest in psychology in the usual sense. Nonetheless I gloss the use of *ningen shinri* later in this paragraph as "human psychology" to offer some indication of the potential nuance of his approach.

8. Walt Disney produced and Wilfred Jackson directed *The Old Mill* (1937) as part of the *Silly Symphonies* series. This animated film is credited as the first to use Disney's multiplane camera system.

9. Imamura uses the phrase *shashin to ketsugōshita e.* There are two or three senses of *ketsugō* implicit in Imamura's usage. The term calls attention to combining the arts of drawing and photography within the image (in the sense of producing a more photographic style of drawing in terms of composition and dimensionality, for instance). It may also imply a combining of images in a cinematic fashion, that is, a series of images or film footage. Finally, Imamura also seems to use *ketsugō* in the stronger conceptual sense of

"synthesis," claiming cartoon films enable a synthesis of drawing and photography that overcomes the contradiction between them.

10. Although the term *hōhō* is more commonly translated as "method(s)," I translate it here consistently as "techniques," for that seems better to convey Imamura's argument, which focuses on the contradictions that arise between different technical determinations, thus flirting with but ultimately avoiding a technological determinism (an "essence" of film photography grounding a teleological progress).

11. I consistently translate *dōsa* as "actions," in contrast to *undō* and *ugoki,* which are rendered as "movement" or "movements." Another entry in the *Silly Symphonies* series, *The Country Cousin,* was produced by Walt Disney and directed by Wilfred Jackson in 1936.

12. The term *shashin* or "photography" is the most difficult in this essay to translate, for photography implies two things for Imamura. On the one hand, he calls attention to the realism of the photographic image, and on the other hand, he uses photography to refer to film photography, that is, shooting a series of images. While I translate the term consistently as "photography," I occasionally add the gloss "photographic footage" when the context seems to demand it. I render *shashin satsuei* as "film photography."

13. *Popeye the Sailor Meets Sinbad the Sailor,* released in 1936, was produced by Max Fleischer and directed by David Fleischer. The plane in question was probably the Douglas DC-2, introduced in 1934, or the DC-3, introduced 1936.

14. I consistently use the verb "parse" for Imamura's *bunkaisuru,* which refers to the process of breaking down or decomposing a movement into a series of instants when filming. I use "parse" to emphasize the analytic and conceptual bent of Imamura's argument.

15. Here I translate *kaiga* fully as "arts of drawing and painting," but subsequently it will simply be "art," for it usually appears modified, for instance as *Nihon kaiga* or Japanese arts of drawing and painting, which I render as "Japanese art."

16. Imamura introduces a hyphenated term *undō-jikan* or "movement-time." In this instance, "film photography" is *katsudō shashin.*

17. "Inner motivation" is *ishi*, that is, motivation or will.

18. Charlotte "Lotte" Reininger is famous for her pioneering work in animation, especially silhouette animations such as *The Adventures of Prince Achmed* (1926), which was a critical and popular success. Ladislaw Starevitch, Russian and French animator, is credited with making the first stop-motion puppet animation, *The Beautiful Lukanida* (1912). Like many subsequent films, it used dead animals (here insects) as "puppets."

19. "Film photography" here is, in fact, *katsudō shashin,* but the translation "moving pictures" would make the phrase unwieldy in English.

20. Directed by Ben Sharpsteen and produced by Walt Disney Productions, *Clock Cleaners* (1937) features Mickey, Donald, and Goofy. This short animation, a critical and popular success, clearly had an impact on Imamura at the time of this essay, for he makes reference continually to Disney's mouse, duck, and dog.

21. "Filming" here is *satsuei.*

22. The reference is to Monet's *Haystacks* (1890–91).

23. Imamura uses the term *ukibori,* relief or embossing, to describe the quality of oil painting. Presumably he wishes to call attention to the thickness of paints and their application in brushstrokes.

24. Imamura here uses the term *ugoku kaiga* (moving art) to refer to cartoons, thus stressing their status as art.

25. *Popeye the Sailor Meets Ali Baba's Forty Thieves,* released in 1937, was produced by Max Fleischer and directed by David Fleischer.

26. Directed by Burt Gillett and produced by Walt Disney Productions, *Lonesome Ghosts* opened in 1937. *Hawaiian Holiday* was directed by Ben Sharpsteen and produced by Walt Disney Productions in 1937.

27. Hinago Motoo, a historian of art and architecture, is especially known for his postwar work on Japanese castles.

28. Imamura uses the term *undō satsuei* or "motion cinematography." When he later revised this argument in his book *Manga eigaron,* he refers to this technique as a form of double exposure, mentioning Cubism and Futurism.

29. Little is known about Tōshūsai Sharaku except that he was actively producing ukiyoe in the years 1794–95. Sharaku is noted for his portraits of kabuki actors and sumo wrestlers.

30. "Tobae" is a lineage of Japanese painting prevalent in eighteenth-century Japan, based on the styles of Toba Sōjō, or more precisely, the twelfth-century frolicking animal picture scrolls attributed to him, *Chōjū jinbutsu giga.*

31. *Gaki zōshi* or "Scroll of Hungry Ghosts" is also a twelfth-century picture scroll, depicting the realm of hungry ghosts, one of the six paths of transmigration within certain strands of Buddhist thought.

32. Belgian playwright Maurice Maeterlinck is renowned for his symbolist plays, many of which were adapted to music in the form of operas, cine-poems, and symphonic poems.

33. Imamura is referring to Sergei Eisenstein's 1929 essay "A Dialectic Approach to Film Form." Eisenstein's comments on Sharaku's late eighteenth-century woodblock prints are worth repeating here, for they suggest a strong relationship between Imamura's dialectic and Eisenstein's in their quest for new forms of temporality: "The secret of his extremely perfected strength of expression lies in the anatomical and *spatial disproportion* of the parts—in comparison with which, our I [roman numeral one] might be termed *temporal disproportion.*" Sergei Eisenstein, *Film Form: Essays in Film Theory,* translated by Jay Leyda (San Diego, Calif.: Harcourt, 1977), 51.

34. Imamura appears to be drawing on Watsuji Tetsurō's essay, "Bunrakuza no ningyō shibai," *Shisō* (August 1935), which is reprinted in *Watsuji Tetsurō zenshū,* vol. 17 (Tokyo: Iwanami Shoten, 1963), 309–15. The term *keigai* is used to stress the materiality of the doll or puppet body, and *jittai* to indicate its substance or reality.

35. I have translated this phrase from the opening sentence of Zeami's *Sarugaku dangi* in such a manner as to convey Imamura's take on it, but basic terms such as *sarugaku* (literally "monkey play"), which Zeami uses to indicate noh (hence "theater" in this translation), and *monomane* ("imitating things") are subject to very different interpretations. For instance, J. Thomas Rimer and Yamazaki Masakazu translate the same phrase as "the way of *sarugaku* is chiefly concerned with Role Playing." Zeami Motokiyo, *On the Art of the Noh Drama: The Major Treatises or Zeami* (Princeton, N.J.: Princeton University Press, 1984), 172.

36. Rimer and Yamazaki offer this translation: "It would be impossible to describe in writing all the various aspects of Role Playing. Yet as this skill forms the fundamental basis of our art, various roles must be studied with the greatest care. In general Role Playing involves an imitation, in every particular, with nothing left out." Zeami, *On the Art of the Noh Drama,* 10.

37. This quote is from the same section of *Kadensho,* at the end of the first paragraph of the second chapter or section.

38. Iwasaki Masumi, "Nōgaku ni okeru kamen shiyō no igi," *Shisō* (February 1933). German psychologist Wilhelm Wundt describes imitative gestures as those that replicate the form of an object—for instance, drawing an object in the air, in a chapter of his multivolume work later published as a book under the title *The Language of Gestures* (1921).

39. Watsuji Tetsurō, "Nōmen no yōshiki," *Shisō* (July 1936), reprinted in *Watsuji Tetsurō zenshū,* vol. 17 (Tokyo: Iwanami Shoten, 1963), 297.

40. Imamura here uses *sei* to refer to life, in contrast to his prior use of *seimei.*

41. "Image" here is *eizō.*

42. *La Kermesse héroique* was released simultaneously in German and English as *Die klugen frauen* and *Carnival in Flanders,* in 1935. It was directed by Jacques Feyder.

43. Franz von Suppé's overture to *Light Cavalry* was used in the 1942 Mickey Mouse cartoon *Symphony Hour,* directed by Riley Thompson and produced by Walt Disney Productions.

SHUN'YA YOSHIMI

Translated by Jodie Beck

From Street Corner to Living Room: Domestication of TV Culture and National Time/Narrative

For postwar Japanese, television was a form of media that had overwhelming influence and special symbolic significance. With rapid growth, our lives came to be surrounded with various types of new media; however, television held a particularly privileged position among them. Even now, Japanese people watch an average of more than three hours of television per day; the most time spent at home next to sleeping is spent watching television. According to a 2002 comparative international survey conducted by the Nippon Hōsō Kyōkai [NHK] Broadcasting Culture Research Institute, about 23 percent of people in Japan watch more than five hours of television a day, a rate significantly higher than in the United States and France at 14 percent. Furthermore, the rate of people who believe that the most important type of communications activity is "watching" stands at 7 or 8 percent in the United States and France, yet in Japan the rate is 28 percent. On the other hand, those who believe that "reading" is the most important type comprise more than a third of respondents in the United States and France, but only 17 percent in Japan. Compared to other countries, then, it seems that Japanese people really love television.

This pattern is more similar to results seen in Thailand than in the West, but Japanese people still love TV more than Thais. In response to the question, "which would you choose if for the next several months you could have only one of the following six items: newspapers, television, cell phone, personal computer, car, or refrigerator?" most Japanese people answered "television" at 23 percent. Most Americans, however, answered "car" at 42 percent, with only 5 percent of respondents answering "television." Among the French, "car" was also the most popular response at 31 percent; only 10 percent chose television, which rated even lower than newspapers at 14 percent. In Thailand, too, compared to the 40 percent for cars and the 23 percent for computers, television only reached 13 percent.[1] This heavy slant toward television in Japan has remained constant since the 1960s, and as I will discuss shortly, a study conducted in the early 1970s showed very similar trends. We can probably say, then, that the privileged value accorded to television has been a consistent feature of postwar Japanese society.

Moreover, the time that Japanese spend watching television has consistently increased since the end of the 1980s; the daily average at present [2003] has surpassed three and a half hours and is approaching four.[2] With all we hear about the end of the era of television, and as new media cultures swirl across borders, as seen with the spread of the Internet in Korea, Japanese society still seems to be attached to the same primary postwar medium of television. Any time a critical event occurs, from the Great Hanshin earthquake and the Aum Shinrikyō incident, to the Gulf War, to the 9/11 attacks in the United States, to the Iraq War, the first thing people do is virtually "become glued to the TV," thus continuing to reimagine the nation through their relationship with this medium. In order for this reimagining to be carried out effectively, television today is developing advanced grammatical, visual, and technical systems that mediate the public and the private in multilayered ways. Individual viewings of information and variety shows, news, and dramas combine in complex ways with our conversations with others, sustaining this simultaneously public and private system of relating known as television.

Once, Shimizu Ikutarō predicted that the appearance of images directly before people's eyes on TV would make it difficult for them to peel themselves away from the reality presented there. Furthermore, as the medium develops technically, the "mechanism gets stronger, so it is easy for its contents to become conservative or reactionary." If that kind of TV-like reality is still deeply conditioning everyday consciousness in Japanese society today, it is worthwhile to go back half a century to the time when this connection began to form and retrace the history of the relationship between television and its audience.

RIKIDŌZAN AND THE STREET AUDIENCE

The streets were the stage on which television made its postwar Japanese debut. Before TV appeared in the living rooms (*chanoma*) of people's homes, it emerged in outdoor spaces such as in front of stations, in busy areas of town, within the grounds of temples and shrines, and in front of department stores and electrical goods shops. This outdoor TV culture began with the televisions installed in various locations on the streets by NTV, the first private television station. At the time, TVs for home use cost about 200,000 yen, while the starting salary of a university graduate was about 8000 yen per month. TVs were luxury items that "middle class" people could not hope to have. Before opening its station in 1953, NTV installed 220 large-size TVs in 55 locations in front of stations and in busy areas around the capital, aiming to give the experience of television to the public, who were likely to be fervently interested in TV broadcasts. This would then generate revenue from program advertisements. By 1957, NTV had installed street TVs in 278 locations.

The importance of street TVs is owed not only to the fact that they triggered the spread of TVs overall but also that they demonstrate the inherent connection between television and the mass imagination in the early postwar period. The strength of street TV was never in its dramas or documentaries but rather its sports broadcasting, and the biggest draw was professional wrestling with Rikidōzan; crowds of several thousand people would cram together around one TV, making the place look like the site of some kind of open-air assembly. With the film technology available at the time, it was not possible in a baseball broadcast to cover the entire area of the field at once. However, professional wrestling was characterized by speedy moves within a small ring, making it the perfect genre to fit the TV screen. The wrestler Rikidōzan, well aware of the camera, made full use of this characteristic. As Inose Naoki has noted, "TV became known through pro wrestling, and pro wrestling became known through TV. Rikidōzan became a hero because of TV, and TV gained viewers because it produced a hero."[3]

Furthermore, in addition to the camera-conscious showmanship he acquired in the United States, Rikidōzan consciously presented himself as a brave, small-built Japanese going against giant American wrestlers who were constantly committing fouls. Regarding the overwhelming popularity of professional wrestling on TV, several years later a commentator in the *Asahi shinbun* newspaper suggested that for people at that time, the idea "that there was a world in which rules could be broken" was incredibly attractive.[4] However, the unprecedented boom in professional wrestling in the 1950s was likely linked to a consciousness of the times that cannot be reduced to an argument about the urge for *communitas* or a general desire for lawlessness. That is, the postwar boom in professional wrestling in Japan was more than anything else a Rikidōzan boom. A determined Kim Shin-rak (Rikidōzan's real name) had crossed the Genkai Sea from the Korean peninsula to Japan and skillfully gave shape to Japanese people's complicated feelings toward America, an enemy country that had become both Japan's occupier and protector. While other postwar pro wrestlers based in Osaka and Kyushu did not see professional wrestling as anything other than a martial art, Rikidōzan understood that it was not simply a sport or a spectacle but rather a national symbolic drama. It is said that in his first tag-team match with the Sharpe brothers in February 1954, massive crowds formed around street televisions, and the scenes in which Rikidōzan sprang into the ring and knocked down these American giants with karate chops raised cheers that resounded like great rumbles in the earth.

Of course, there was more to the overwhelming popularity of Rikidōzan than the idea that he embodied the "anti-American nationalism" deeply felt by postwar Japanese. Superimposing the fictionality of Rikidōzan, who played the part of "a Japanese," and the fictionality of the "sport" of professional wrestling, Kawamura Takashi argues that "watching professional wrestling could be a truer experience of space and time not because it was built on truth but, on the contrary, precisely because it was built on a sensational fiction." From Kawamura's perspective, then, in the fictional space of professional wrestling, the fact that Rikidōzan was not "a Japanese" bestowed even more reality on his performance of the role of the heroic "Japanese." Rikidōzan's background became known publicly after the late 1970s, when Ushijima Hidehiko's detailed reportage was published and *Weekly Playboy* (*Shūkan pureibōi*) publicized the "Rikidōzan boom" occurring in his home country, North Korea; but it seems that in the 1950s his background was generally known by the public from rumors, and certainly by his *zainichi* Korean compatriots. Within this ambivalent mass consciousness of "knowing, but behaving as though not knowing," Rikidōzan's professional wrestling functioned such that Japanese people themselves performed the drama of "being Japanese." Ultimately, "while Kim Shin-rak from Korea became Momota Mitsuhiro and passionately played the role of 'the Japanese hero Rikidōzan,' the audience also passionately played the role of 'the Japanese shocked by defeat and suffering from a pent-up complex toward foreigners.'"[5]

The point that I would like to add to Kawamura's argument is that it was precisely street TV that made this double performance possible. In the mid-1950s, TVs for home use were still few and far between. Around the time that NHK began broadcasting in 1953, the number of households that had reception contracts was only 866, and although this number had reached as many as 50,000 households by 1955, watching TV at home with the family was certainly not the prevailing style of TV viewing, at least until the end of the 1950s. According to a field survey by NTV from September 7 to 18, 1953, the average number of viewers in a fixed time frame around street TVs in twenty-six locations around the capital was 9,200, so the estimated number of viewers in one day was calculated at more than 100,000 people.[6]

THE THEATRE OF STREET TV

So, where were these street TVs placed, who was viewing them, and in what way? In fact, we know the details for the fifty-five locations of TVs installed by NTV as well as for the 278 locations installed after the station opened. The fifty-five locations included major sites such as Tokyo Station Meitengai, Ginza Owarichō, Hibiya Park, in front of Shinjuku Station and in Shinjuku Nishiguchi Hiroba, in front of the head offices of the newspapers the *Asahi shinbun*, *Mainichi shinbun*, and *Yomiuri shinbun*, as well as in temple and shrine grounds such as Asakusa Kannon, Suitengū Shrine, Sugamo Togenuki Jizō, and Kagurazaka Bishamonten. In addition to the sites already noted, the 278 locations where TVs were set up after the TV station opened covered a comprehensive area including station fronts, shopping areas, and temple and shrine grounds, as well as facilities and establishments such as Tokyo Bowling Center and Shinjuku Skating Rink. Multiple TVs were set up in areas like Ueno and Asakusa, making these areas into "TV city"–type zones. At this point, TV installations were also spreading out to Gunma Prefecture, Tochigi Prefecture, Ibaraki Prefecture, and Shizuoka Prefecture; but in these prefectures TVs were mainly installed in front of city halls, in major shopping districts, and in temple and shrine grounds.[7]

When considering the locations in which street TVs were installed, the first thing that becomes clear is how carefully these locations were chosen according to where people in Tokyo would be most likely to congregate. According to Sano Shin'ichi, the mogul Shōriki Matsutarō "made it obligatory to produce a 'daily street TV report' for every single TV. As he looked over these reports each day, he would take meticulous charge, yelling, 'There aren't a lot of viewers around here. It's a bad location. Hurry up and move it somewhere else'; and if any of the TVs broke down, steam would come out of his ears and he would shout, 'What do you mean, broken down? Hurry up and go fix it!'"[8] Then, staff who had received Shōriki's strict orders would "arrive at a proposed installation site, alight from the train, make a rough sketch [of the area], find someone who seemed willing to manage a TV, and then negotiate. Since agreements were never made right away, they would withdraw at a suitable moment and then dash off to the next place. From inside the train, too, they would stare outside, searching like hawks for available land or sites with wide pedestrian streets. They were repeatedly mistaken for land brokers."[9] If an agreement could not be reached with a shop, the NTV staff would negotiate with the local officials to find an installation site and caretaker in that way. Since managing a TV really only meant "locking and unlocking it, and turning the power on and off," they said—no remuneration was paid to caretakers. Documents from NTV state that "at many places, [NTV] did not even pay for the electricity fees."[10]

Although NTV's street TVs had an overwhelming impact around Tokyo, in other areas of the country the general public's first experiences with TV was more likely to be with the televisions installed at electrical goods shops than with NTV's street televisions. The daughter of an electrical shop owner who displayed a TV that he made himself looks back on those days:

> At the time my father was running a small electrical shop; he would design his own radios and TVs and things, buy the parts like the vacuum tubes and picture tubes and then put them together . . . but even for a child like me, the TV he made was not really all that cool. There were fat glass rods around these thick bulky picture tubes, vacuum tubes mounted on the chassis, transformers, and condensers. Since there was no case covering these parts, everything looked so exposed, and I was always afraid that someone would get an electrical shock. But my father looked so happy. He set that TV up in front of a small window so that the screen faced outside. At that time TVs were not very common, so people passing by would stop and stand there to watch it. When children's programs came on, the kids from the neighborhood would all gather around. When popular programs came on, people would bring chairs and congregate there, and I would take a chair from the shop and go sit out there together with them and watch TV. It was good business for my father to have crowds of people gather in front of his shop, and for me, too; it made me happy to sit there next to someone who was usually a bully, being all quiet and well-behaved.[11]

So how many of these electrical shops were there around Japan that installed TVs in front of their shops, and how did they go about it? In 1953, the year that television broadcasting began, there were more than 20,000 electrical goods shops around the country; 30,000 shops in 1958, as TV sales began to boom; and more than 40,000 in 1964, the year of the Tokyo Olympics. If many of these stores were also setting up TVs in front of their shops at this initial stage, this means that massive numbers of "street TVs," far exceeding the number installed by NTV, were making their way onto street corners in every nook and cranny of the country. Iida Takao has analyzed the promotional magazine *National Shop,* which Matsushita Electric distributed to its affiliated stores, and made some very interesting findings about this period. According to Iida, in the case of one shop owner who had built his own TV and made it available to the public in May 1954, "so many people gathered inside the store and on the street outside that there was literally no room to breathe; finally there was a commotion trying to get the window closed, and ultimately, the owner received a warning from the police for obstructing traffic." With no other options, the owner used the empty shop next door to display his TV, and "for popular programs like professional wrestling he would borrow the rooftop of a nearby apartment building, and every time more than a hundred people gathered there."[12] So if a considerable number of shops like this existed all over the country, that means that in the mid-1950s perhaps more than one million people were simultaneously and enthusiastically watching what was happening in professional wrestling and baseball games, on both NTV's street TVs and also on televisions in front of various electrical goods shops.

However, the connection between the street TVs that I have been discussing and the crowds on the streets was not "invented" by NTV and electrical shops. In fact, this connection goes back at least to the 1920s, when radio first appeared in Japanese cities. Yamaguchi Makoto, focusing on midday baseball broadcasts in the early stages of radio broadcasting, reveals that at the time "the style in which 'family members would all spend some time together sitting around the radio' was neither primary nor typical." As Yamaguchi convincingly shows, in the late 1920s when radio was beginning to spread rapidly, even in major cities like Osaka the vast majority of ordinary households had fixed-rate contracts with electric companies and did not receive electric power during the daytime; so even if they did own a radio, the number of households that could actually listen to it in the daytime was very small. Rather, in cities like Osaka and Tokyo, extremely large numbers of retail radio stores would set up radios with speakers in front of their shops, and audiences would flock to listen. When a game was on, "no matter how busy you were, you would manage to make the time to go to a radio shop or any other shop where a radio was set up in front, and you'd rub shoulders with the people gathered there, and for this short period of time, you would chat with the other people there like friends, waiting for the broadcast to start." As demonstrated by Yamaguchi, then, crowd-like audiences, like those that surrounded street TVs later, were already present in large cities in the 1920s.[13]

As Iida Yutaka points out, the direct predecessors to NTV's street TVs were experiments in which televisions were publicly exhibited at fairs and at all kinds of special events. From the late 1920s, radio dealers and amateur wireless receivers were presenting prototype televisions at fairs and exhibitions. Before long, NHK and the research institute of the Ministry of Communications and Transportation became involved in these exhibitions and experimental public displays; and as the country faced war, crowds increasingly gathered around televisions.[14]At this experimental stage, people likely were already well accustomed to the crowds, since, as Yamaguchi has shown, it was already an everyday occurrence with street radio. In other words, in the modern city of the 1920s, various types of spaces were already being created in which crowds of people and new media were coming into contact on the streets, and people's everyday sensibilities were increasingly bound up with this city/media environment. According to Sano Shin'ichi, Shōriki repeatedly stressed that street TVs were his own "original idea," despite the fact that it was the American electrical engineer William Halstead who taught him how to increase advertising profits by aiming for as large an audience as possible.[15] By emphasizing this, Shōriki not only concealed the origin of his own ideas but also the most important background for understanding how street TVs in the 1950s were so widely supported by the Japanese general public.

FROM KARATE CHOPS TO MITCHI'S SMILE

By the end of the 1950s, with the popularity of Rikidōzan's professional wrestling still undiminished, the relative importance of street TVs and home TVs had started to reverse. Judging from the success of street TVs, restaurants, bars, and all kinds of shops realized how effective TVs were for bringing in customers and soon started installing TVs inside their stores and in their shop windows. Television thus slowly began to move from the streets and into shops and homes. With the shift in "the places where TV was watched," the social meanings of television media also began to change. On October 9, 1955, the *Asahi shinbun* reported that street television had already passed its peak in popularity and that television had begun to move "from street corners to living rooms." This article predicted that, as the location of TVs changed, programming content was also bound to change. In fact, "the reason that

> WITH THE SHIFT IN "THE PLACES WHERE TV WAS WATCHED," THE SOCIAL MEANINGS OF TELEVISION MEDIA ALSO BEGAN TO CHANGE.

sports broadcasts have occupied a privileged position is precisely because it has been an age of street television. While this period has not ended, studio programs more suited for viewing in a relaxed atmosphere at home are gaining more and more popularity. Even at private TV stations, regular programming that has been ignored by sponsors until now is doing very well." If this trend continued, programs aimed at home viewing would become the mainstream, and new types of sponsors would flood to the stations. It is true that even after television had begun to spread to ordinary households, professional wrestling broadcasts still boasted viewing rates overwhelmingly higher than other programs. For example, in October 1960 a large gap can be seen in viewing rates between professional wrestling, at 50.3 percent, and second-place *Lassie,* at 36.7 percent. By May of the following year, the rate for professional wrestling broadcasts had gone up to 57.4 percent.[16] At the same time, however, in surveys conducted by private television stations, viewers consistently named professional wrestling broadcasts first for programs that were "boring" or "inappropriate for viewing at home."[17]

In other words, while professional wrestling was as popular as ever in terms of ratings, for home television viewing it was criticized as inappropriate and aberrant. Also around this time, some negative incidents caused professional wrestling to be seen as a bad influence on the public. For example, a widely circulated report in April 1962 stated that two elderly people who were watching a Rikidōzan match "died of shock from the brutality." In fact, they had chronic diseases like cardiac asthma, and a causal relationship between the contents of the show and the heart attacks cannot be substantiated. However, in the press, the "brutality" of professional wrestling in particular was emphasized. A month after this incident, the Osaka Prefectural Police submitted a request to TV stations that broadcasts of professional wrestling matches be suspended. Between this and frequent reporting about incidents of violence involving wrestlers, professional wrestling gradually came to acquire a dark image. When Rikidōzan was stabbed to death by a gangster in December 1963, the nationwide treatment by newspapers of the death of this postwar "hero" was unnaturally cool, considering his prior national popularity.

Until the mid-1950s, Rikidōzan was the center of mass television consumption on the streets. However, as television later began to move from the streets to people's living rooms, Rikidōzan could no longer be a "national" hero. So with this shift in the social space of television, did a new image for consumption appear? The obvious answer to this question is the 1959 wedding parade of the Crown Prince and the smile of the Crown Princess, "Mitchi," displayed there. NHK and the NTV and KRT (now TBS) conglomerate networks vied for the best wedding parade broadcasting.

Of course, this transformation of the "royal wedding" into a media event did not stop at simply broadcasting the parade. Although that was certainly the climax, the romance between "the Imperial household" and "the people" (*kokumin*) was uniformly produced by all the TV stations through the composition of TV programs starting several days before. For example, NTV, which had been the most important station in broadcasting professional wrestling on street TVs, planned a series of "special programs from April 5 to April 12 celebrating" the wedding, programs that would "thoroughly capture the appearance of the Crown Prince and Michiko-san as the happy day approaches and the joy of the people on the streets; furthermore [NTV would] incorporate the happy expressions on people's faces all over the country by relay through Sapporo TV, Yomiuri TV, and Nishi Nippon TV, thus unfolding the momentous picture scroll of the century." Then, on the day of the wedding itself, various programs were to be shown that would "combine images of Shōda Michiko-san as she begins this happy day in front of the Shōda residence, as well as images taken with cameras placed at various locations, to present a picture of her facial expressions."[18] It is important to note here that the focus of the camera in this series of programs was clearly on "Michiko-san" rather than the Crown Prince himself.

NATIONAL TIME, NATIONAL NARRATIVE

Through the programs it broadcasts, television forms a part of our world of meaning, and broadcasting itself functions to construct our lives. Television's biggest effect at this time was to introduce "national time" into the home. Until then, "in everyday life, time and media did not exist in a closely linked relationship." However, with the penetration first of radio into society, "precise time came to acquire the status of a shared social standard of behavior." The transmitter was thus able to become the object of "a consciousness [on the part of viewers] that did not exist in previous types of media, a consciousness in which people's lifestyles were thought of in terms of time."[19] Sada Kazuhiko summarizes this point as follows:

> In order to continue to broadcast a large number of programs every day, programs were lined up based on a certain way of thinking; as a result,

> delimitations were applied to the passage of "time," and so-called "time" came to be articulated. Furthermore, the relationship between program contents and time slots was carefully considered, contributing to the meanings given to everyday "time" . . . It was not only direct methods such as time announcements but the process of broadcasting a large number of programs itself that resulted in the articulation of "time."[20]

Eventually, television would inherit this function of time scheduling from radio and bring it to a much deeper level. Through viewing times, a large number of channels, and the formation of many programs, television functioned to create a uniform sense of national time all over the country.

The time-scheduling function of television was seen most strikingly in the construction of the so-called "golden hour," "morning hour," and "afternoon hour" time slots. "Golden hour" in particular, which was generally the three-hour period from seven until ten in the evening, represented the highest concentration of TV viewing in Japan from the 1960s to the 1980s. For many households, this time frame was experienced in largely homogenous ways. That is, in many cases, families would begin by watching the 7:00 news, then a program that targeted children, such as cartoons or a family quiz show. After 8:00, dramas or variety shows were the main attraction, and after 9:00 dramas took center stage. Otherwise, professional baseball was almost permanently on the air between seven and nine at night, so it was also common for fathers in particular to be watching. In Japanese society since the high-growth period, this basic viewing pattern has been firmly maintained.[21]

Of course, the "golden hour" was not the only "national time slot" developed for television. From the 1960s through the 1970s, television produced at least two others. One of these was from about seven to nine in the morning. For an urban salaried (*sarariiman*) household, this corresponds to the busy time of the morning when family members are getting ready for work and school. Since the 1960s, NHK's morning serial dramas (*asa no renzoku terebi shōsetsu*) and commercial broadcasters' "morning shows" provided meanings to this time slot that were complementary to the "golden hour." TV functioned in place of a clock to ensure that people would not be late, and we must not forget that through this type of viewing, people's actual daily time at home overlapped with a particular historical consciousness of time circulating in the postwar. The third time slot that was developed was from about eleven in the morning until two in the afternoon, occupied by melodramas and "wide shows" (talk and variety shows). While the other two time slots functioned to align the rhythm of family life with a consciousness of national time, the audience for this slot was primarily housewives, and it produced images of a gendered reality linked with the sphere of women's weekly magazines. Thus, since the 1960s Japanese TV broadcasting has been organized around the three characteristically different national time slots of "morning," "afternoon," and "evening"; the time slots in between have been peripheral, without a distinct character.[22]

What is important here is that through the creation of these three time slots, the meaning of those times was experienced in relation to television, and forms of social gathering were thus also reorganized. For example, according to the NHK survey *Zenkoku seikatsu jikan chōsa,* there was a remarkable correlation between the time flows of "people watching TV" and "people eating," but this did not simply mean that people had started watching TV at mealtimes. People also started having meals at TV time. A similar situation can be seen in the way that people experienced time itself; for example, it is uncertain whether people would start watching NHK news when 7:00 pm rolled around, or whether the time "7:00 pm" itself existed as the experience of watching NHK news. Thus, the flow of television is never just an external factor that conditions our experiences of time and our lifestyle habits; rather, it is the moment of organization that makes those experiences and habits possible.

Therefore, in postwar Japan, television was not some strange object that infiltrated a previously closed home space. On the contrary, the postwar sense of the intimate sphere of the home itself (pleasant time spent with the family [*ikka danran*]) was produced through the medium of television. With regard to this point, Fujitake Akira notes that "it is not just a matter of the simple fact that television was being viewed in the home, but that the home itself was being organized as a sacred space for people at the time, the place where family members could most easily secure privacy, and where they could go for refuge from the pressures of outside society."[23] In a survey conducted from 1979 to 1980 by NHK's *hōsō yoron chōsajo,* there was a positive correlation between television viewing time and the frequency of family communication. The rate of people who answered that television had increased opportunities for the family to talk together (50 percent) far surpassed the rate of people who answered that it had decreased such opportunities (19 percent). In response to the question of whether television was necessary to family time (*ikka danran*), 46 percent of respondents from Tokyo and 61 percent of respondents from rural areas answered that it was "more necessary than not," a significantly higher number than those that answered that TV was "more of an intrusion" (15 percent in Tokyo and 10 percent in rural areas). Furthermore, in response to the question of whether the TV was turned on during

MEDIA IS NOT SIMPLY AN INFORMATION MEDIUM; IT IS A MEDIATING AGENT THAT ORGANIZES SOCIAL RELATIONSHIPS.

family time, 77 percent of respondents in rural areas and 67 percent of respondents in Tokyo answered that "it is usually turned on."[24] To state it broadly, family time in the space of the postwar family was created through and has operated via the medium of television.[25]

Radio had already been functioning as a medium for family relationships in characteristic ways. For example, shortly after the war, one housewife had this to say about the radio in her house:

> For housewives who were often holed up inside, radio was the only real enjoyment, and I think it was also a way to absorb culture and learning. But I felt hesitant with my mother-in-law there, so I didn't listen to the programs that I wanted to as often as I would have liked. But for news or women's programs that I really wanted to listen to, I would turn the radio on and invite her to listen, too. At first she wouldn't listen with me, but eventually she started to, and then she found that she was able to chat more with my husband at night, too. So she started listening happily to the radio, which she had just thought was noisy before. This is a really small thing, but from this experience, my life and my mother-in-law's life were able to blend together, and I was also able to have some free time.[26]

These examples teach us that media is not simply an information medium; it is a mediating agent that organizes social relationships.

Since the mid-1960s, people have thus consumed countless groups of image texts that have established their own styles as genres, such as family dramas (*hōmu dorama*), period dramas, quiz shows, singing shows, documentaries, variety shows, and talk shows (*waido shō*). This consumption, furthermore, has occurred within the time structures of daily broadcasting that had been formed up until the early 1960s, and within the family relationships that had been mediated by this construction of time. In recent years, detailed semiotic analyses of each genre have become an especially productive field within new research on television culture.[27] The rise of this trend is good news, but to avoid an analysis that remains bound up in the image text of television, it is important to be conscious of the fact that television is fundamentally a temporal medium. Not only does each image text get constructed temporally but the "time" of these texts is positioned within the temporal structure of daily broadcasting and is consumed within the temporality of social relations that are mediated by this construction. If we continue to broaden our perspective in this way, it is likely that a central question that will arise in television research is the relationship between the "time" of families' ordinary lives and life histories, and the fictional "time" that is related through television.

CONCLUSION

Ever since television started to spread widely to ordinary postwar Japanese homes in the 1960s, countless multilayered relationships, including amplification and resistance, twists and slippages, adjustments and collisions, have been played out between the "time" being related on the TV and the "time" of the receiving viewers. Especially since the 1960s in Japan, television has taken root in ordinary life as national media. Therefore, perhaps the most important question to explore is in what ways national time recounted to viewers through various program genres has been entwined with the "time" of each family's life history as consumers of TV. Although space does not permit me to adequately address this question here, I would like to end with a simple reference to NHK's morning serial dramas (*asa no renzoku terebi shōsetsu*) and Sunday night historical dramas (*taiga dorama*), in order to suggest some possibilities for worthwhile future research.

NHK's morning serial dramas began in 1961 with an adaptation of Shishi Bunroku's *Musume to watashi* (My daughter and me). The original story, serialized in *Shufu no tomo* magazine from 1953 to 1956, portrays the history of the author's family from the end of the Taishō period (1912–26), throughout the war period, and up to when the "daughter" crosses over into Europe after the war. To create a series that ran from April 1961 to March the following year, the scriptwriter Yamashita Yoshikazu decided to "recreate Japanese people's most difficult memories of having been born during wartime."[28] The history of NHK's morning serial dramas (*ren dora*) began here, and the prototypical style of these programs was already evident in this very first series. Other major hits such as *Ohana-han* (1966) and *Oshin* (1983) all portray the biographies of women who survived a national context of prewar and wartime hardship to find happiness.

On the other hand, when NHK's *taiga dorama* began in 1963 with *Hana no shōgai,* the intention of the creators was not so much just to produce historical dramas but to create "large-scale wholesome amusement productions." Therefore, many of the works proposed for adaptation were popular historical novels such as Nakazato Kaizan's *Daibosatsu tōge* (1913–41, Bodhisattva pass; movie, 1966, *The Sword of Doom*) and Naoki Sanjūgo's *Nangoku taiheiki* (1931,

Record of the peaceful southern countries). "The creators were thus made to believe" that in order for this type of TV adaptation to succeed, and for this particular series to succeed, the protagonists of the drama must be "national heroes" based on actual history.[29]

Questions that remain to be explored are how such time structures of national storytelling, including their gendered organization, have connected with the "time" of the lives and memories of the people who welcomed television into their homes, and what the role of broadcasts, as technologies of time, has been. Clearly, an analysis of this sort must also link together questions such as where televisions were placed and how the social groupings of audiences changed. An analysis of television as media must not simply stop at a structural analysis of images, nor simply examine the history and function of broadcasting. Even a detailed examination of the social history of the purchasing of TVs as "consumer electronics" would only be considering one aspect of television. In order to grasp the cultural dynamics of the television medium, we must concretely and theoretically reconsider the processes by which its various aspects intertwine. We must consider television as an apparatus that is positioned in some kind of social space, and its symbolic meaning (television = apparatus); broadcasting as schedule and its relationship with the rhythms of daily life (television = time); and TV as a text in which the interpretations of subjects confront each other in multilayered ways and in which stories are told based on a specific consciousness of time and construction of memory (television = program).

This is an abridged translation of "Terebi ga ie ni yatte kita: Terebi no kūkan, terebi no jikan," originally published in "Terebijon saikō (TV Reconsidered)," a volume of the journal Shisō (no. 956, [2003]).

Notes

1. NHK Hōsō Bunka Kenkyūjo Yoron Chōsabu, *Shichōsha kara mita "terebi 50 nen"* (Fifty years of television seen from the audience) (Tokyo: NHK Broadcasting Culture Research Institute, 2002), 13, 29.

2. Ibid., 19.

3. Inose Naoki, *Yokubō no media* (Media of desire) (Tokyo: Shōgakukan, 1990), 268–88.

4. Shimazaki Toshiki, "Puroresu o miru shinri" (The truth the press sees), *Asahi shinbun,* May 1, 1962, 13.

5. Kawamura Takashi, "Enjirareta 'Rikidōzan,' enjirareta 'Nihonjin'" (The 'Rikidōzan' who could play a part, the 'Japanese' who were played), in *Rikidōzan to Nihonjin* (Rikidōzan and the Japanese), ed. Okamura Masashi (Tokyo: Seikyūsha, 2002), 48–60.

6. Hōsō Bangumi Iinkai, "Terebi 50 nen o kangaeru" (Thinking about fifty years of TV); Sankō shiryō, "'Gaitō terebi' ni kansuru Nihon terebi no chōsa kekka" (Results of a research study on Japanese TV starting with "street TV"), *Hōsō Bangumi Kōjō Kyōgikai geppō*, February 2003, 28.

7. Ibid., 29–31.

8. Sano Shin'ichi, *Kyokaiden* (Legends of great wonders) (Tokyo: Bungei Shunjū, 1994), 474.

9. *NTV junpō* 5, August 15, 1956.

10. Hōsō Bangumi Iinkai, "Terebi 50 nen o kangaeru," 28.

11. "Watashi to terebijon: Omoide no deai," (Television and I: Meeting with memories), in *Jinsei tokuhon: Terebi* (Guidebook to life: TV) (Tokyo: Kawade Shobō Shinsha, 1983), 42.

12. Iida Takao, "Mono = shōhin" toshite no media: Terebijon juzōki no shakaiteki juyōshi" (Media as "things = goods": The history of social demand for television sets) (Master's thesis, Tokyo University Jinbun Shakaikei Kenkyūka, 2001), 69.

13. Yamaguchi Makoto, "'Kiku shūkan,' sono jōken: Gaitō rajio to ōdiensu no furumai" ("Listening to customs," those conditions: The conduct of street radio and its audience), in *Masu komyunikeeshon kenkyū* 63 (2003): 144–61.

14. Iida Yutaka, *1930-nendai Nihon ni okeru terebijon no gijutsu shakaishiteki kenkyū: Hakurankai jigyō to no kakawari o chūshin ni* (Research on the social history of television technology in 1930s Japan: Focusing on matters relating to the expo project) (Master's thesis, Tokyo University Gakusai Jōhōgakubu, 2004).

15. Sano, *Kyokaiden*, 470–72.

16. Minpō Gosha Chōsa Kenkyūkai, ed., *Nihon no shichōsha* (The Japanese television audience) (Tokyo: Seibundō Shinkōsha, 1969), 22. At the time, although *Lassie*'s popularity rate was high overall, it was extremely low only among the working classes. In a survey conducted in 1957 by the Public Opinion Research Center (Yoron Kagaku Kyōkai), among the working classes this program had a viewing rate of only 18 percent and a very low support rate, while with other classes it enjoyed a viewing rate of over 30 percent and high support ratings. "Dono bangumi ga omoshiroku mirarete iru ka: Kansai-hen" (Which programs are seen as interesting? Kansai), *Shijō chōsa* 79: 10–13.

17. For example, see Kokumin Seiji Kenkyūkai, *Shufu wa terebi o dō miru ka* (How do housewives watch TV?) (April 1964), 11. Here, we see opinions such as "In professional wrestling, a lot of the scenes are staged, and some scenes are grotesque and brutal; you can't say it's a healthy sport. I wouldn't want to show it to a child, who has little sense of judgment."

18. *Kōtaishi goseikon hōshuku tokubetsu bangumi* (Special programming for the Crown Prince's wedding celebration) (Tokyo: Nihon Terebi Hōsōmō Kabushiki-gaisha, 1959).

19. Takeyama Akiko, *Rajio no jidai* (The radio age) (Tokyo: Sekai Shisōsha, 2002), 44–45.

20. Sada Kazuhiko, *Hōsō to jikan* (Broadcasting and time) (Tokyo: Bun'ichi Sōgō Shuppan, 1988).

21. "Golden hour" was a Japanese-made English word; in English this period of time was only referred to as "prime time." Attaching an adjective like "golden" to this time frame, and naming it as though it were actually "English," and furthermore having it

spread into common use, seems to project the special consciousness that Japanese people had toward TV during the high growth period.

22. In general, television viewing other than during the three major time slots was probably not a focused activity from the beginning. One housewife had this to say about watching TV in the early 1960s: "Housewives are essentially not suited to constantly referring to the program guide in newspapers, or to properly sitting down to watch and listen. You just kind of think to yourself that you would like to listen to music while ironing or something, so you turn the dial, and if the program that comes on after that song happens to be good, then you just forget to turn it off. My children often do their homework in front of the TV, or they try to talk with my husband about social issues that they learned about from daytime broadcasts. But in any case the TV is always singing or talking in the background." Sakai Ayako, "Shufu to hōsō" (Housewives and broadcasting), *Hōsō asahi*, June 1962.

23. Fujitake, *Terebi media no shakairyoku*, 99.

24. NHK Hōsō Yoron Chōsajo, *Kazoku to terebi* (Family and television) (Tokyo: Nihon Hōsō Shuppan Kyōkai, 1981), 108–19.

25. In terms of living space, it has been generally thought that TV viewing was more strongly linked to people living in apartment complexes (*danchi*) than to lifestyles in ordinary residences. Around 1960, 61 percent of housewives living in apartment complexes said that the way they spend their free time is by watching TV—a rate almost 20 percent higher than wives living in shopping areas, at 42.9 percent, and almost 15 percent higher than ordinary residences, at 48.5 percent. Rōdōsōhō Fujin Shōnen Kyoku, *Seikatsu jikan hakusho* (Tokyo: Ōkurashō Insatsukyoku, 1961). Wives living in apartment complexes show a much higher rate of engaging not only with TV but also with newspapers and other kinds of reading than women from shopping areas or ordinary residences, and an increase in media contact that correlated with a new kind of lifestyle in apartment complexes has been generally acknowledged. However, perhaps this correlative relationship between the type of residence and media contact is a false correlation, and it is not the case that people started watching a lot of TV because they were living in apartment complexes but rather that a lot of people who lived in apartment complexes had the kind of income and lifestyle that allowed for a lot of TV watching.

26. Ibid., 21–22.

27. See for example, the excellent work by media researchers such as Fujita Mafumi for period dramas, Ishida Saeko for quiz shows, Ishida Hidetaka for detective shows, Niwa Yoshiyuki for documentaries, and Muramatsu Yasuko and Sakamoto Kazue for home dramas.

28. Yamashita Yoshikazu, "Konnichiteki igi no aru kyakushoku" (Dramatizations with Significance for Today), *Hōsō bunka,* July 1962, 15–18.

29. Mikuni Ichirō, "'*Hana no shōgai*' kara '*Kunitori monogatari*' made" (From "Flamboyant and Ephemeral Life" to "A Tale of Acquiring Provinces"), in *Taishū bunka no sōzō* (Tokyo: Kenkyūsha Shuppan[?], 1973).

KUKHEE CHOO

Hyperbolic Nationalism: South Korea's Shadow Animation Industry

South Korean popular culture has become an integral part of the global media flow, from the popularity of K-Drama, K-Pop, and films over the past decade to the explosive circulation of "Gangnam Style" around the world in 2012. But as critics have pointed out, South Korean popular culture has mostly been represented abroad by its live-action films and television drama, as well as by its attractive entertainers.[1] What remains largely unexamined is the production, since 1950, of animated series and movies for South Korean audiences, most of which were developed by South Korean animation studios that were used by Japanese anime companies.

The Japanese animation industry is built on its vast subcontracting networks, which include many international companies. Currently there are approximately 700 animation studios in Japan, with sixty-five major companies that belong to the larger animation production organization called the Association of Japanese Animations (*Nihon dōga kyōkai*).[2] Those that are not a part of this organization are mostly small studios—sometimes as small as a room with a handful of employees—that work as subcontractors to larger ones. Therefore, major animation studios often subcontract to foreign production houses that can complete work more quickly.

Currently, Japanese animation companies rely heavily on subcontractors in China, the Philippines, Thailand, and Taiwan; however, Japan's earliest major outsourcing country was South Korea. Beginning in the mid-1960s, South Korea became an essential part of Japanese animation production. In fact, subcontracting for Japanese animation studios (as well as for U.S. and European cartoons) not only made animation production a viable industry in South Korea but also contributed to South Korea's position as the third-largest animation producer in the world until the end of the 1990s.[3] As Thomas Lamarre points out, the fact that Japanese animation studios outsourced so much of their production to other countries complicates the "Japaneseness" of the finished animation.[4]

In a similar vein, I argue that the very notion of "Japanese" anime becomes more complex and nuanced when viewed from within the larger history of animation in Asia, and that often the outsourced animation work of the "other" has been overlooked by global audiences due to the dominance of the Japanese anime industry. In this article, I will map the historical development of South Korean animation, tracing its origins back to the 1950s and focusing particularly on titles with conspicuously hybridized narratives and visual qualities. By doing so, I aim to bring to light the various modalities and praxes that allowed South Korea to come out from the shadow of the Japanese anime industry.

It was on HLKZ Television (*Daehan Bangsong*), South Korea's first private television station established in 1956, that animation became an integral part of the emerging media industry in postwar South Korea.[5] A few short advertisements and experimental animations appeared throughout the late 1950s and early 1960s, and in 1967 South Korea saw its first animated theatrical film, *Hong Gil-dong*, produced by Shin Dong-heon. Since then there have been five to ten animated films released annually, but production has dwindled as viewership of South Korean animation has decreased over the years. Recent South Korean media has asked questions such as why South Korea, a country with an animation production infrastructure similar to Japan's, and a country that has been actively creating Korean-language animation for years, has not produced a figure such as Tezuka Osamu. Some analyses suggest that South Korean audiences do not accept animation.[6] Nevertheless, owing to decades of active production, South Korea's animation industry eventually attracted the government's attention, which led to official recognition and promotion of digital animation in 1999.[7] This influenced the Japanese government to push for its own "Content Industry" promotion policy in 2004.[8]

Despite this official acceptance, there have been few studies of Korean animation compared to the scholarly work on Japanese anime: John A. Lent and Yu Kie-Un present a brief history, and Yoon Ae-ri explores how South Korean animators are situated "in-between" the demands of globalization and their traditional ideologies.[9] Yet, there are virtually no studies that look into the history of South Korean animation, especially to examine titles that purportedly "plagiarized" Japanese animations. These so-called copies constituted the majority of animation production in South Korea from the 1960s to the 1980s. Plagiarism is defined as "an act or instance of using or closely imitating the language and thoughts of another author without authorization and the representation of that author's work as one's own, as by not crediting the original author."[10] However, as Marilyn Randall notes in her analysis of plagiarism in literature, "Plagiarism . . . cannot be found in the text, or even in the intertext. It exists only in the space circumscribed by texts, readers, and their cultural presuppositions, that is, in the pragmatic space of the literary context."[11]

In other words, plagiarism is not defined by the simple act of reproducing the original without acknowledgement, but, according to Randall, "plagiarism expresses structures of and struggles for power that implicate far more than the individual agents or victims."[12] Similarly, it may be difficult to categorize South Korean animation as plagiaristic products because the companies were created to reproduce (or copy) Japanese animation. That is to say, if South Korean animation originated from the continuous practice of duplicating Japanese anime cels, the definition of plagiarism is inadequate because it does not capture the processes and intricacies at the very origin of South Korean animation. Furthermore, although South Korean children grew up watching Japanese television anime without knowing its country of origin, there needs to be a more comprehensive understanding of how South Korea's nationalistic animation also contributed to this "unawareness," as the boundaries between Japanese and South Korean animation were blurred by hybrid visual representations. In this way, analyzing the development of South Korea's prolific, yet globally invisible, domestic animation production provides a new perspective on Japan's globally popular anime enterprise.

EARLY YEARS

The first animation in South Korea was long thought to be the Lucky Brand toothpaste commercial created by Mun Dal-bu in 1956.[13] Mun was the art director of HLKZ Television, and he completed the entire production by himself, including drawing, tracing, and filming. The black-and-white commercial was shot cel by cel with a still camera, because no animation cameras existed in South Korea yet.[14] However, in 2006 it was found that another CM animation by Mun, an advertisement for OB Shinalko, preceded the Lucky Brand commercial by two months. According to Kim Dae-hong, this new discovery altered the history of South Korean animation and provided more insight into how animation was closely tied to film culture; these advertisements were shown in movie theaters during the golden era of Korean cinema.[15] Unlike Japan, whose anime industry began in 1962 with Tezuka Osamu's Mushi Production and relied mainly on television sponsorship, South Korea's animation originated from tie-ins with commercial enterprises and relied on the theater networks. The first theatrical animation director Shin Dong-heon, who created *Hong Gil-dong* in 1967, also started out as a creator of animated commercials. Success with both *Jinro soju* (Jinro vodka, 1960) and *Jinro-paradise* (1962) gave Shin the confidence to venture into full-length theatrical animation.

However, it was the development of the Japanese animation industry that truly ignited South Korean animation production. Although there was no direct connection to Tezuka's Mushi Production, the spillover effect of his studio's success in Japan stimulated animation production in South Korea throughout the 1960s. After South Korea and Japan established diplomatic ties in 1965, Samsung Mulsan (Samsung Group) contracted with the animation company Jeil Donghwa (Jeil Moving Pictures) and began to subcontract for Japan's Tōei Animation.[16] The storylines and scripts were delivered from Japan, but everything else, including drawing, tracing, and filming, was executed in South Korea. Samsung began to hire full-time staff and invited Japanese animator Morikawa Nobuhide to educate a new generation of Korean animators. The two animations that emerged from this effort were *Golden Bat* (1967, *Hwanggeum bakjui*) and *Phantom Human* (1968, *Yogwae ingan*). Both series were produced during Morikawa's four-year stay in Korea. Because the first broadcast of *Golden Bat* was in 1967 for Japan and 1968 in South Korea, it was long thought that the series was a Japanese animation imported into South Korea (and the same goes for *Phantom Human*). However, according to Morikawa, both series were actually produced in South Korea and then exported to Japan.[17]

After the production of these two series, South Korean television animation became more or less limited to subcontracting for Japanese studios. The formal broadcast of Japanese animation in South Korea began in 1970 with *Marine Boy* (1966, *Kaitei shōnen Marin*), which was featured on Munhwa Bangsong (MBC). In the same year, *Tetsuwan Atomu* (1963, *Astro Boy*) was also broadcast on Dongyang Bangsong (TBC) under the Korean title *Uju sonyeon Atom* (Space boy Atom). Most of the animated television programs that appeared on South Korean television over the years were Japanese anime titles that were outsourced to South Korean companies and then purchased by the television stations at low cost. However, it was through this subcontracting and coproduction that South Korea was first introduced to Japanese animation, rather than through purchasing television animation series directly from Japan. In this sense, South Korea's position is unique in that it was not a passive consumer but rather an active participant in the production process of Japanese animation, which led to its booming domestic industry.

Around the same time *Golden Bat* was produced, there were other animations being made in South Korea. In 1967 the first full-color theatrical animation, *Hong Gil-dong,* was released, as well as *Hopi wa Chadol bawui* (Hopi and Chadol stone), both by Shin Dong-heon. The first stop-motion animation, *Heungbu wa Nolbu* (Heungbu and Nolbu), was also produced that year using doll-like puppets. All three animations were based on traditional Korean folklore that emphasized moral values such as bravery, modesty, and kindness. None of the films resembled Japanese animation, with its often large-eyed characters and prominent science fiction narratives.

The year 1968 saw not only more folktale animations, such as *Seonhwa gongju wa Son oh-gong* (Princess Seonhwa and Monkey King), but also the first "science fiction" title, *Hwanggeum Cheolin* (Golden Ironman), both of which were produced by Pak Yeong-il. What is more, *Golden Ironman* was also the first official South Korean animation exported to Japan, in 1969. Also in that year, a sequel to *Hong Gil-dong* (dir. Yong Yu-su) was produced, and the Western children's story *Bomulseom* (*Treasure Island*, dir. Pak Yeong-il) became the first Korean animation to feature anthropomorphized animal characters.

After a year without any domestic releases in 1970, 1971 saw three productions, *Wangja Hodong gwa Nakrang gongju* (1971, Prince Hodong and Princess Nakrang), another traditional Korean myth, as well as *Beongae Ateom* (1971, Lightning Atum), produced by Yong Yu-su. As Japan's *Tetsuwan Atomu* was first introduced to South Korean audiences in 1970, it is not difficult to notice the similarity between it and Yong's film.

When *Lightning Atum* was released in theaters in 1971, the boy character named Atum (instead of Atom) registered as similar to *Tetsuwan Atomu* and attracted a young audience. The popularity of *Tetsuwan Atomu* was such that there was a nation-wide rerelease of *Lightning Atum* in 1975 under the different title *Dolaon Beongae Atom* (1971, Return of Lightning Atom). From the posters (Figures 2 and 3), Yong's *Lightning Atum* and *Return of Lightning Atom*

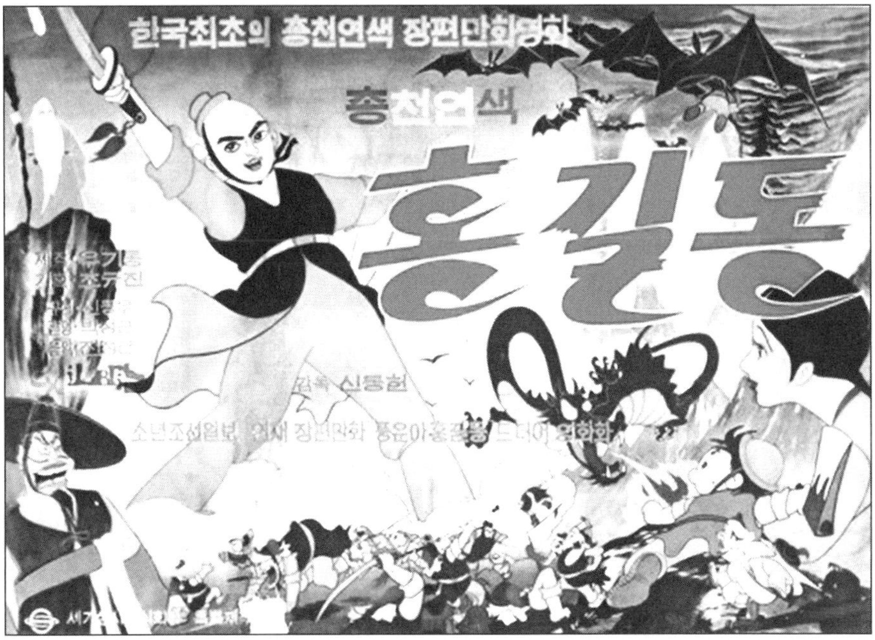

FIGURE 1. Shin Dong-heon's *Hong Gil-dong* (1967), a tale about a thief who steals from the rich to help the poor.

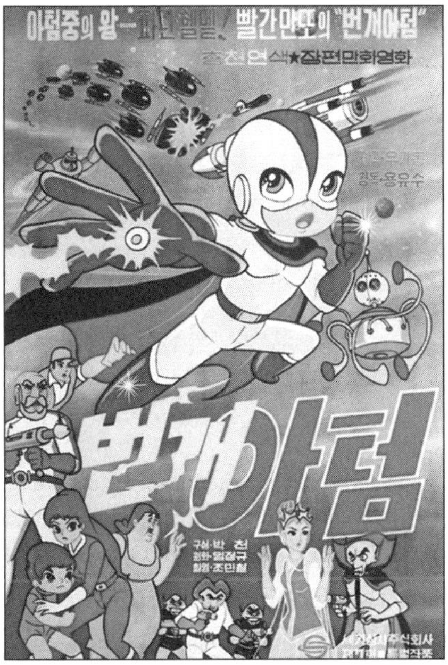

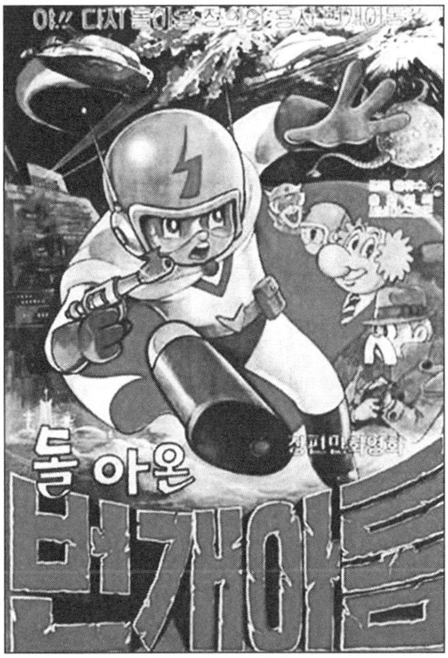

FIGURE 2 (LEFT). Yong Yu-su's *Beongae Ateom* (1971, Lightning Atum). **FIGURE 3 (RIGHT).** Yong Yu-su's *Dolaon Beongae Atom* (1971, Return of Lightning Atom).

appear to be two distinctly different animations. The original film poster is faithful to the character designs in the film, which appears to be influenced more by U.S. cartoons and Disney animation. On the other hand, the 1975 poster for the film's rerelease shows the clear influence of *Tetsuwan Atomu* both in terms of character depiction and pronunciation of the protagonist's name. Rereleasing the film in 1975 under the old title *Lightning Atum* may have been deemed inadequate, as South Korean children already knew the *Tetsuwan Atomu* anime by its Korean name *Uju sonyeon Atom*. In the 1971 film poster, the protagonist's name "Atum" is pronounced as "Ah-t-uhm," while the 1975 version uses the same name as Tezuka's "Atom," which sounds like "Ah-t-ohm." The one vowel difference renders the 1971 "Atum" an awkward mimicry, yet at the same time evokes nostalgia among contemporary South Korean audiences, who view *Lightning Atum* as one of the early *original* animations produced in South Korea, with a narrative completely independent from *Tetsuwan Atomu*.[18] Moreover, throughout the film we witness blatant national branding, with "ROK" (Republic of Korea) written on technological devices, asserting the creators' strong nationalistic sentiments. In short, although *Lightning Atum*'s imitation of *Tetsuwan Atomu* ends with its title and the 1975 rerelease poster, this weak, yet distinct, linkage to a popular Japanese title of the time makes it possible to consider it the beginning of South Korea's ostensible copying of Japanese anime.

After *Lightning Atum*, director Yong Yu-su also created *Gwaesu daejeonjaeng* (Great monster war), the only animation produced in 1972.[19] There was no another domestic production until 1976, as subcontracting for Japanese animation became the sole focus of South Korean animation studios. Overall, South Korean animation produced from the late 1960s to the early 1970s consisted of traditional Korean stories and Japanese-inspired narratives; however, the proportions changed drastically during the second half of the 1970s.

ROBOTORAMA: KOREA'S NATIONAL ANIMATIONS

In the decade from 1976 to 1986, South Korean animation generated a strong domestic following. Up to ten theatrical animation films were produced annually during the peak years between 1979 and 1983, surpassing the number of Japanese animation films produced during the same time. This period could be viewed as the golden age of Korean animation. Most of these animations were science fiction narratives, which were shown either as Children's Day specials on May 5, or as summer vacation specials at local theaters and culture centers. Children—mostly boys—waited in anticipation all year for these films. Most showed strong parallels to Japanese animation of the time. Some titles, including *Roboteu taegweon V* (1976, Robot Taekwon V), *Dalryeora Majinga X* (1978, Run Mazinga X), *Mujeok yongsa hwanggeum nalgae* (1978, Invincible warrior golden wing), *Uju heukgisa* (1979, Space black knight), *Heukseong roboteu sseondeo A* (1981, Black planet robot Thunder A), *Solla won tu sseuri* (1982, Solar one two three), *Seupaeiseu Gandam V* (1984, Space Gandam V), as well as many other films, used visuals and narratives reminiscent of popular Japanese anime series. As evident from the titles and film posters, most of the influences came from anime such as *Mazinger Z* (1972–74, Majingaa zetto) and *Grendizer* (1975–77, UFO robo gurendaizaa).

Starting with *Robot Taekwon V,* Kim Cheong-gi emerged as a visionary science fiction animation director. He made more than thirty animated films in fifteen years, including five *Taekwon V* sequels as well as the famous *Ddori* boy-adventure series. Kim began as a comic book artist in the early 1960s, drawing storylines inspired by U.S. film narratives.[20] He worked as an animator on *Princess Seonhwa and Monkey King* (1968), but after establishing his own company, Seonjin Munhwa (Advanced Culture) in 1971, he mostly worked with Dongyang Bangsong (TBC) creating animated commercials. Kim

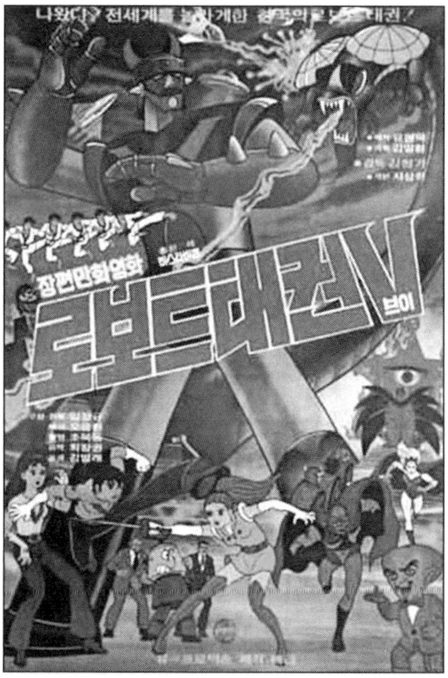

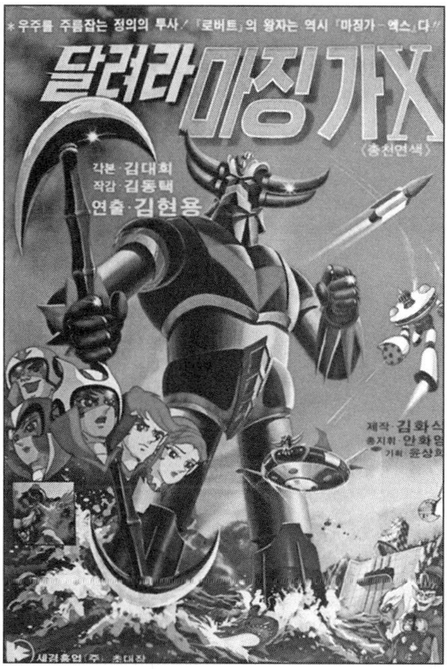

FIGURE 4 (LEFT). *Roboteu Taegweon V* (1976, Robot Taekwon V). **FIGURE 5 (RIGHT).** *Dalryeora Majinga X* (1978, Run Mazinga X).

was known to be dissatisfied with South Korea's position as a subcontractor to Japanese animation houses.[21] He opened his animation studio Seoul Donghwa (Seoul Moving Pictures) in 1975, and his dream to create autonomous local animation began with *Robot Taekwon V,* which generated a huge following in South Korea.[22] Kim wanted to differentiate his films from Japanese anime, and he asserted their Korean-ness by incorporating the national martial art Taekwondo in order to "reimagine" and "reinvent" Korea's identity after the consecutive national traumas of Japanese colonialism (1910–45), Korean War (1950–53), and the subsequent division into two Koreas.[23] Kim produced similar films over subsequent years, but none rivaled the success of his first film. In fact, the repetitious production of similar narratives seemed to damage his reputation.

Kim's *Roboteu gundan gwa meka 3* (1985, Robot corps and mecha 3) was a hodgepodge, cut and pasted together from separate films that Kim had previously directed—*Solar one two three, Space Gandam V,* and *Robot Taekwon V.* Due to the patchwork editing, the robots and human characters never appear in the same scene together, as they are originally from separate animations. Therefore, the entire film consists of long robot battle scenes with nondiegetic theme songs for each robot playing whenever they appear. The film suddenly cuts between different battle scenes without any continuity, resulting in bizarre lapses in character interaction as well as discontinuities in the narrative structure; a comical effect for some audiences but completely distasteful for others. For example, characters whose body parts had been cut off reappear intact later in the film. Also, the text "to be continued in the second part" appears randomly midway through the film without any break in the scene or narrative, indicating that the hour-long film may have been a two-part television series sutured together.[24] The battle scenes and reaction shots of both protagonists and enemies are all mixed to the point that even the children viewing the film in 1985 felt a sense of "betrayal," especially those who had been anticipating new entertainment.

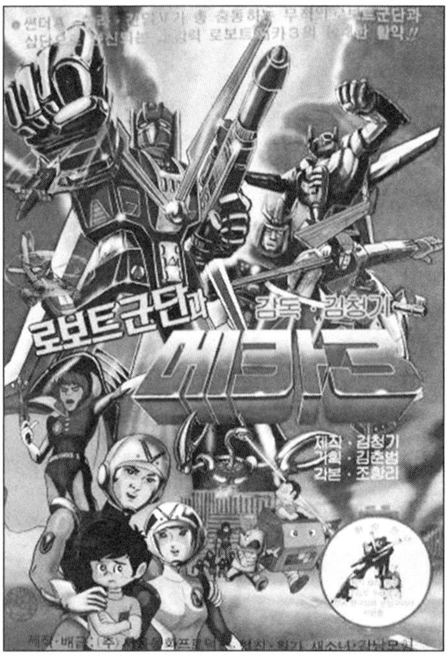

FIGURE 6. Kim Cheong-gi's *Roboteu gundan gwa meka 3* (1985, Robot corps and mecha 3).

However, this type of rushed production was not uncommon in South Korea at the time. In the South Korean *manhwa* industry, copying and borrowing characters from Japanese manga and collaging them together into a new narrative under a Korean name (what I have termed "patchwork" *manhwa*) was widespread and popular throughout the 1980s,[25] so Kim's appropriation of such a method was not unusual at the time. But in retrospect (especially after the explosive popularity of Japanese anime around the world), Kim's "patchwork" practice and the resemblance to Japanese characters may be viewed as wounding Korean national pride. Kim has come to represent South Korea's vigorous animation production of the past. For example, recent South Korean bloggers appear to be split about Kim: they either accept him as a product of his time or condemn him for blatantly copying Japanese anime.

These two reactions to Kim's work correspond to Marilyn Randall's two discourses about plagiarism, "apology and condemnation." One camp argues that most human activity consists of constant repetition, and therefore plagiarism is "inevitable," whereas the second honors "intellectual property, originality, and individual authenticity."[26] Randall notes that plagiarism is viewed as bad "only when it is not good."[27] However, I would argue that Kim's "bad" animations might be interpreted as a parody of his own films as well as an effort to toy with, or bring attention to, the fact that most Japanese robot anime were produced in Korea at the time. By overtly and *hyperbolically Koreanizing* the Japanese anime subcontracted to Korea, Kim was undermining the authenticity of these Japanese works. Years of experience as Japanese anime subcontractors enabled South Korean animators to feel confident in creating their own narratives. In a sense, being subcontractors to their former colonizer instilled a stronger sense of nationalism among the South Korean animators because they were driven by the desire to produce South Korean–brand animation similar to the subcontracted animation consumed by Japanese audiences. In other words, the motivation to create animations featuring robots that resembled Japanese anime was driven by a strong sense of competition, resulting in what I term "hyperbolic nationalism" and "unapologetic mimicry."[28] These phenomena were only accelerated by the rising economic position that Japan enjoyed during the 1970s and 1980s.

The South Korean animators' "unapologetic" nationalism was not limited to animation produced for their domestic audiences. The former board director of the Association of Japanese Animations (AJA) Yamaguchi Yasuo told me in an interview that South Korean animators had a strong sense of pride as artists, which sometimes led to problems for Japanese animation companies.[29] Yamaguchi had to deal with South Korean animators on a regular basis as the producer of the popular television series *Candy Candy* (1976–79), based on the well-known girls' comic book series by Mizuki Kyōko and Igarashi Yumiko. He explained that numerous times he had to return cel drawings to South Korea via mail (which sometimes took up to a month) because artists had tried to leave their "stamps" on the animation cels. One particular artist repeatedly put small Korean temples in the background, even though the narrative of *Candy Candy* was set in the United States and Europe. In other words, through these "stamps" or "signature marks," the cel artists asserted that they were not mere subcontract laborers to Japanese animation companies but Korean artists who could intentionally sabotage, undermine, and subvert the authentic "Japaneseness" of anime. Although Yamaguchi light-heartedly reminisced about his experience thirty years later, he said that it was one of the most difficult things about dealing with South Korean animators, because these attempts sometimes delayed production of the weekly series, which spanned 115 episodes.[30]

In a similar vein, it could be argued that Kim Cheong-gi's robot animations, which appeared to be insipid copies of Japanese mecha anime, were also nationalistic attempts to break away from the confines of being Japan's invisible labor force. Other examples include the way *Gundam* was transformed into *Uju heukgisa* (1979, Space black knight, dir. Pak Jong-hi) and the way *Space Battleship Yamato* (1977, Uchū senkan Yamato) was appropriated for *Nalara! Uju jeonham geobukseon* (1979, Fly! Space battleship turtle ship, dir. Song Jeong-ryul).

This last title was an especially potent historical symbol of Korean identity. Turtle ships defeated Japanese forces during Toyotomi Hideyoshi's invasions of Korea during the sixteenth century. By taking Japan's nationalism in *Space Battleship Yamato* and reconstructing it as a Korean modality, the film constituted a postmodern *hyperbolic mimicry,* which differs from Homi Bhabha's postulation of postcolonial mimicry.[31] Bhabha argued that the colonized used mimicry to emulate and "become" the colonizer. However, in the case of *Fly! Space Battleship Turtle Ship* (1979, *Nalara! Uju jeonham geobukseon*), the reappropriation was to "overcome" rather than to "become." The in/visible gaze of the colonizer and its associated anxieties, ambiguities, and ambivalence were here circumvented by the fact that the praxis of mimicry in South Korean animations were unknown to both the Japanese and South Korean audiences at the time. Unlike Bhabha's "almost the same but not quite/not white" relation, the South Korean animators' overdetermined and unapologetic appropriation of Japanese anime created a hyperbolic mode of mimicry—"not only the same, but *actually* Korean"—that existed for the gratification of South Koreans only.[32]

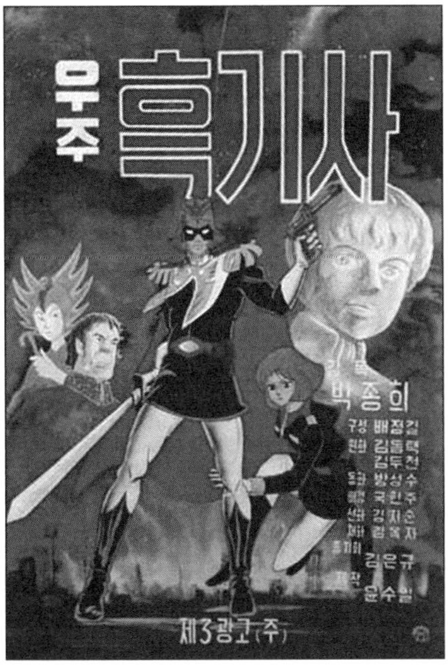

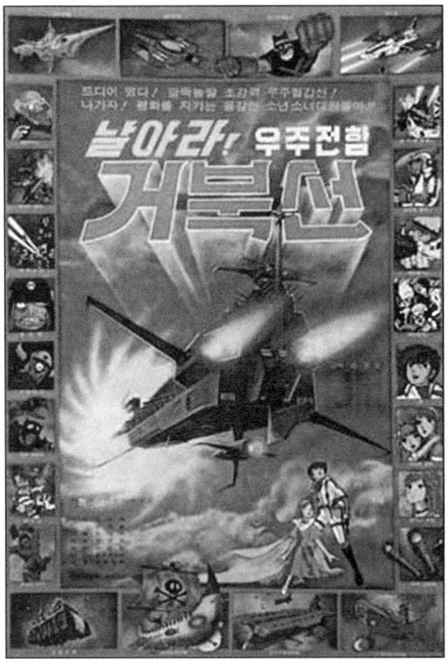

FIGURE 7 (LEFT). *Uju heukgisa* (1979, Space black knight). **FIGURE 8 (RIGHT).** *Nalara! Uju jeonham geobukseon* (1979, Fly! Space battleship turtle ship). The turtle ship was the traditional warship of the Joseon Dynasty (fifteenth to nineteenth century), which aided in the defeat of Toyotomi Hideyoshi's attacks on Joseon during the sixteenth century.

DISLOCATED YET SHARED IDENTITIES

Another unique case study in South Korean animation is the *Kagaku ninjatai Gatchaman* (*Science ninja team Gatchaman*) franchise. *Gatchaman* was first broadcast on Fuji TV in 1972, and the theatrical film and second television series were released in 1978, followed by another television series in 1979. The 1972 *Gatchaman* was broadcast on Korea's TBC in 1979 under the title *Doksuri 5 hyeongjae* (Eagle 5 brothers) and rerun on the national broadcast station KBS in 1990 and 1996.

There are three distinct South Korean animations that share the *Gatchaman* lineage. In *Cheolin 007* (1976, Iron man 007), directed by Han Ha-rim, the five characters were decreased to four, but dressed the same as the *Gatchaman* characters. Another related film, Kim Tae-jong's *Taegeuk sonyeon huindoksuri* (1979, Taegeuk boy white eagle), was the world's first 3D animation feature. It required the audience to wear special blue and red cellophane glasses. The copy line on the poster read "Wow! Exciting! Completely three-dimensional full-length animation film that only *our country's* children will get to see for the first time

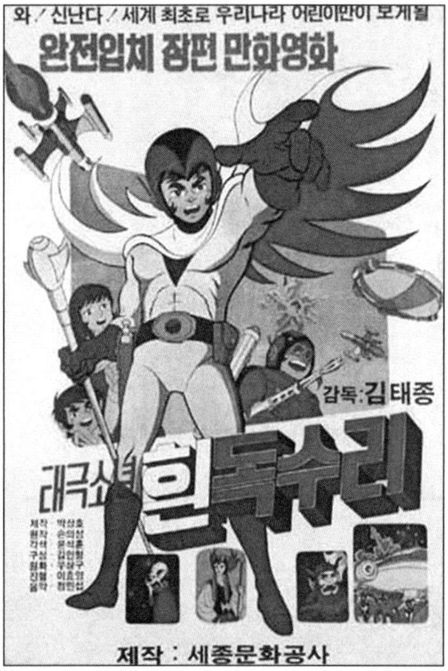

FIGURE 9. The first 3D animation film *Taegeuk sonyeon huindoksuri* (Taegeuk boy white eagle), produced by Kim Tae-jong in 1979.

in the world" (emphasis added, Figure 9). Here, we observe a solicitation of national sentiment directed not only toward the potential viewers, the children, but also toward the parents who would be taking them to the theaters.

The word *uri nara* (our country) is a common term that South Koreans use whenever speaking about their country *among themselves*.[33] In combination with the title, the "Taegeuk" symbol from the South Korean flag, and a reference to the ancient traditions of Korean spirit, the poster emphasizes that *only* "uri nara" children would be able to view and understand the animation. This appeal spoke to both the children and their parents' sense of nationalistic identity.[34]

Japanese animation companies outsourced animation to South Korean studios due to their ability to create works with high production values at efficient speeds. Therefore, many Japanese companies turned a blind eye to the explicit copying practices carried out by their South Korean counterparts.[35] When Samjeong Production, the South Korean subcontractor for Tatsunoko Production's *Gatchaman* series, saw that the Korean broadcast of the series in 1979 had become popular, they requested permission from Tatsunoko Production to create a South Korean version for domestic audiences.[36] Possibly to maintain a good relationship, Tatsunoko Production consented to this plan.

This rare event resulted in *Doksuri 5 hyeongjae,* produced in 1980 by the newcomer filmmaker Lee Gyu-hong.[37] What is unique about *Doksuri* is the fact that the entire production consisted of animators who were already working on the *Gatchaman* series, enabling them to immediately use the resources at hand. With a few tweaks in characters, scenes, and narratives, the South Korean version of *Doksuri* became a new spin on the previous television series and the 1978 theatrical film. Furthermore, the nationalist desire to create a "better" version of the same narrative was actualized through *Doksuri*: the South Korean artists paid more attention to details and artistry in producing the film (Figure 11). Since Tatsunoko Production granted permission for the production of *Doksuri,* this film can be considered a legitimate sequel to the famous *Gatchaman* franchise. But because many regarded the film as simple plagiarism, it has yet to be remastered and receive its due recognition.[38]

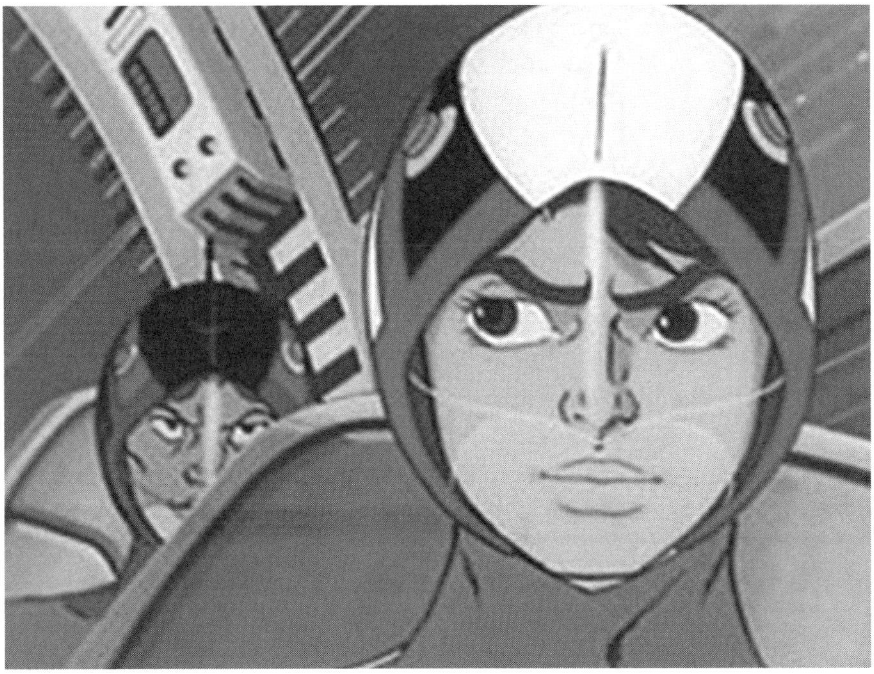

FIGURE 10. Japanese *Gatchaman*.

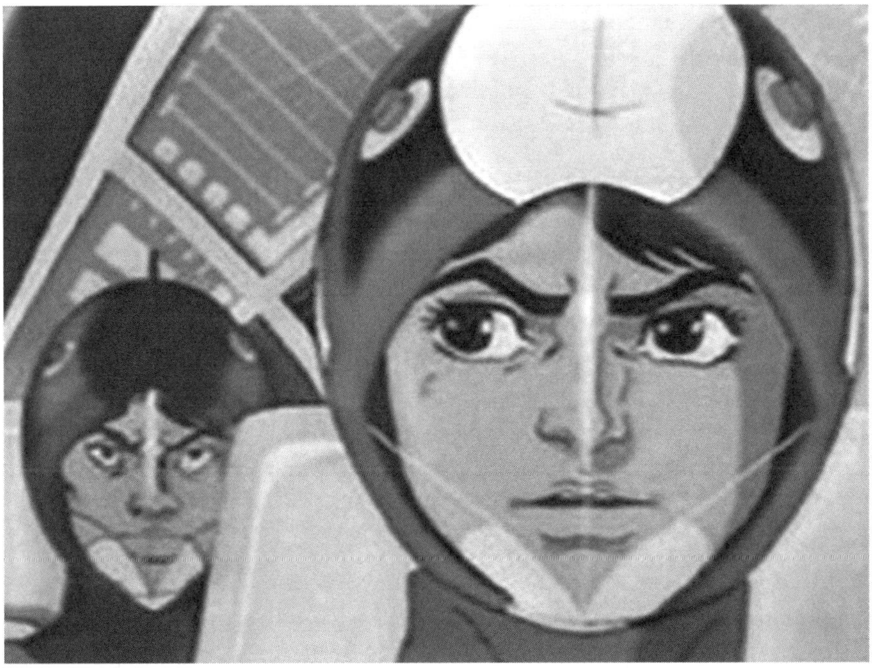

FIGURE 11. South Korean *Doksuri*.

Similar practices exposed South Korean audiences to animation narratives that were parallel but altered versions of Japanese counterparts. This parallelism may be one of the primary reasons behind South Korea's "oblivious" consumption of early Japanese television anime, rather than, as some scholars have argued, an inherent "nationless" or "odorless" quality of anime that disconnects it from its country of origin. It also complicates criticisms leveled against so-called South Korean plagiarism of Japanese anime. Such criticisms fail to take into account the multiple processes, layers, and directions of globalization which produce media that transcend spatial, textual, and cultural boundaries.

The South Korean–produced animations functioned as nationalist media for domestic youth audiences. Furthermore, they were virtually no different from Japanese anime in terms of narratives and character design, paradoxically creating a dislocated yet shared animation identity. Other similar phenomena include the recent development of Bucheon's *manhwa* and animation cluster center and the creation of Robot Land in Incheon, both closely tied to South Korea's present nation-branding strategy.[39] With the 1988 Seoul Olympics in mind, South Korean animation began to create local narratives that were less influenced by Japanese productions, mostly adapted from domestic *manhwa* titles. Most of the science fiction robot animations disappeared from the South Korean landscape starting in 1987.[40] Without a "rival" to mimic and overcome, South Korean animation lost its direction and entered a transitional period in its search for an identity. Nonetheless, some domestic titles that tried to assert Korean-ness still bore a strong resemblance to popular Japanese titles. The first "adult" animation, *Blue Seagull* (1994, *Beullu sigeol*) corresponds to *City Hunter* (1987–88), and the adventure feature *Jeonsa Raian* (1997, Warrior Raian) calls to mind various Japanese saga anime.

The quest for something more local resulted in a decrease in popularity. What failed the industry was not a lack of talent but the perception by the South Korean public that South Korean animation was childish, even shameful, low-quality plagiarism. Ironically, it was these "imitations" that the South Korean animation industry was built upon and which audiences enjoyed for decades. To reiterate, South Korea's seemingly gratuitous reappropriation of Japanese animation functioned as a tool to move beyond Japanese works; the manner in which the South Korean animators imagined they could overcome their positions as "shadow labor" for Japanese anime was, ironically, to create similar products. In a sense, it was not the lack of resources or talent but rather the limited nationalistic mindset of South Korean animators that may have restricted their creative potential.

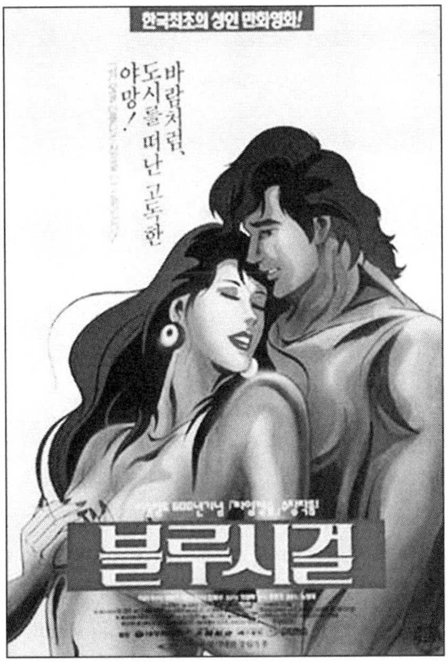

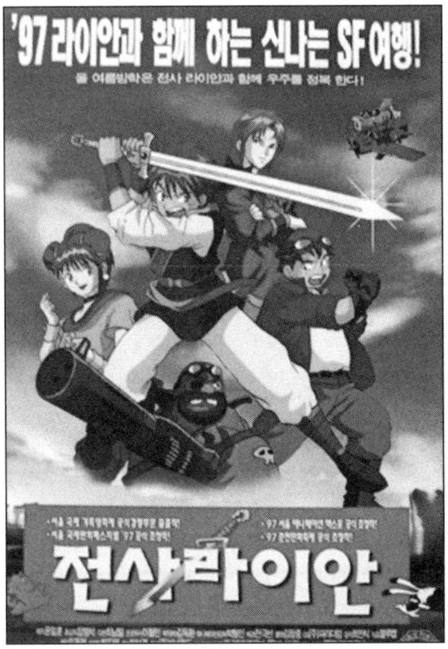

FIGURE 12 (LEFT). *Blue Seagull* (1994, *Beullu sigeol*). **FIGURE 13 (RIGHT).** *Jeonsa Raian* (1997, Warrior Raian).

What stands out in the contemporary discourse on South Korean animation is the fact that the two decades of robot animation titles that dominated the industry were considered a disgrace and were erased, only to resurface when the "nation" deemed it necessary. South Korea's 2013 development of Incheon Robot Land, a $5.6 billion theme park filled with robots from animation and live-action films, is planned to open in 2016.[41] The proposed design features a giant *Robot Taekwon V* statue towering over the entire theme park. Another robot-themed park is to be developed in Masan, in the southeast region of South Korea. The urge to envision and assert South Korea's competitiveness in a digital/robotic technological future is being manifested in the vigorous development of these robot-related theme parks across the country. It is only natural that South Korea looked to *Robot Taekwon V* when searching for the "origin" of its national robot imagination.

In sum, South Korean animation appears to have been caught in a mire: trying to escape, yet continuously mimicking Japanese anime, engaging in a reactionary hyperbolic nationalism in order to "overcome" the rival within. However, the latest movement to eliminate *Robot taekweon V* as a national symbol from the Incheon Robot Land is another confirmation that South Korea has yet to overcome and embrace its complicated animation history vis-à-vis Japan.

Notes

1. Sun Jung describes the rising phenomena of attractive Korean male entertainers as "Kkonminam" (Flower boy) syndrome in her article "*Chogukjeok* Pan-East Asian Soft Masculinity," in *Complicated Currents: Media Flows, Soft Power, and East Asia,* ed. Daniel Black, Stephen Epstein, and Alison Tokita (Victoria, Australia: Monash University ePress, 2010), 8.1–8.16.

2. "The Association of Japanese Animations" website, http://www.aja.gr.jp/english/.

3. Kim Ho-rim, "Study on Animation Industry of Korea in the Process of Cultural Industry" (Masters thesis, Jungang University, 2002).

4. Thomas Lamarre, *The Anime Machine: A Media Theory of Animation* (Minneapolis: University of Minnesota Press, 2009), 90.

5. HLKZ Television was also the fourth broadcast station established in Asia and the fifteenth in the world. It became the public Korea Broadcast Station (KBS) in 1961. Jang-soon Park, http://www.ibcm.tv/skin/board/register/daily_example.html.

6. Jujak, "We hangukpan dejuka osamu neun tanseng mothana?" (Why can't there be a Korean version of Tezuka Osamu?), December 14, 2010, *Sesang modeun geot eui ribyu* website, http://zazak.tistory.com/1320.

7. See South Korea's Digital Media Promotion Policy.

8. Kukhee Choo, "Nationalizing 'Cool': Japan's Global Promotion of the Content Industry," in *Popular Culture and the State in East and Southeast Asia,* ed. Nissim Otmazgin and Eyal Ben-Ari, 83–103 (London: Routledge, 2011).

9. John A. Lent and Kie-Un Yu, "Korean Animation: A Short but Robust Life, " in *Animation in Asia and the Pacific*, ed. John A. Lent, 89–100 (Bloomington: Indiana University Press, 2001); Ae-Ri Yoon, "In Between the Values of the Global and the National: The Korean Animation Industry," in *Cultural Studies and Cultural Industries in Northeast Asia*, ed. Chris Berry, Nicola Liscutin, and Jonathan D. Mackintosh, 103–16 (Hong Kong: Hong Kong University Press, 2009).

10. Dictionary.com, http://dictionary.reference.com/browse/plagiarism.

11. Marilyn Randall, *Pragmatic Plagiarism: Authorship, Profit, and Power* (Toronto: University of Toronto Press, 2001), 190.

12. Ibid.

13. The first animation in the Korean peninsula was "Gae Ggum" (Dog Dream), reported in *Choseon Ilbo* on November 25, 1936, http://www.ohmynews.com/NWS_Web/view/at_pg.aspx?CNTN_CD=A0000253320.

14. Jang Sang-yong, "Pilleum/poseuteo deung enimeisheonbakmulgwan gaegwan" (Film/poster, animation museum opens), *Ilgan seupotseu* (Daily Sports), October 6 2003.

15. Kim Dae-hong, "Presenting 'OB Shinalko,' the first Korean animation," *OhmyNews*, May 5, 2006, http://www.ohmynews.com/NWS_Web/Articleview/article_print.aspx?cntn_cd=A0000328588.

16. See the *Treaty on Basic Relations between Japan and the Republic of Korea*, available at http://en.wikisource.org/wiki/Treaty_on_Basic_Relations_between_Japan_and_the_Republic_of_Korea.

17. "Morikawa Nobuhide no sekai" website, http://www.k2.dion.ne.jp/~nersury/page007.html#lcn002.

18. *Lightning Atum* is about an alien prince who comes to Earth, where he regains his superpowers to fight against a galactic dictator.

19. *Gwaesu Daejeonjaeng* is a cel animation featuring characters similar to Japan's Godzilla and Ultraman.

20. Kim Chang-deok, "'Taekweonbeui' abeoji Gim Cheong-gi 'Il Majinga bogo . . .'" (Father of *Taekwon V,* after seeing Japan's *Mazinga* . . .), January 26, 2013, Donga Ilbo website, http://news.donga.com/3/all/20130125/52591732/1.

21. Jenka, "Gim Cheong-gi gamdok e daehan dareun saenggak" (Other thoughts on Kim Cheong-gi), June 17, 2004, Egloos website, http://taeppo.egloos.com/96199.

22. According to Kim Chang-deok, the film attracted audiences of approximately 300,000 people in Seoul alone during its first three weeks in theaters.

23. Aaron Han Joon Magnan-Park, "Technologized Tae Kwon Do Millennialism: *Robot Taekwon V* and the Assertion of a Triumphant South Korean National Identity," *Journal of Japanese and Korean Cinema* 2, no. 2 (2010): 109–30.

24. It is unclear whether the text "to be continued in the second part" appeared on the screen when the film was first released in the theaters in 1985. However, in the videocassette released in 1993, the text is embedded in the animation.

25. Kukhee Choo, "Consuming Japan: Early Korean Girls Comic Book Artists' Resistance and Empowerment," in *Complicated Currents: Media Flows, Soft Power, and East Asia,* ed. Daniel Black, Stephen Epstein, and Alison Tokita (Melbourne: University of Monash ePress, 2010), 6.1–6.16.

26. Randall, *Pragmatic Plagiarism,* 3.

27. Ibid.

28. The terms "hyperbolic mimicry" and "unapologetic nationalism" may be used interchangeably. The term "unapologetic" has been inspired by Kyung Hyun Kim's analysis of "apologetic" South Korean men depicted in Lee Chang-dong's films *Peppermint Candy* (1999) and *Poetry* (2010). According to Kim, generations of South Korean men have assumed the historical and psychological burden of consecutive military dictatorships and the Kwangju Massacre, producing "apologetic" masculinity in Lee's films (working paper presented at Tulane University, February 19, 2013).

29. Author's interview, March 18, 2008.

30. Ibid.

31. Homi K. Bhabha, *The Location of Culture* (London: Routledge, 1994).

32. Ibid., 86–92.

33. It is a term that presupposes imaginary bonds among South Koreans as well as creating an invisible shackle that limits global mobility. Even though the term carries a nuance that "all Koreans" are included, in fact it excludes North Korea.

34. The South Korean flag is called "Taegeuk-gi," which means "Taegeuk flag." The protagonist's belt in the animation poster has an engraved Taegeuk mark. The film begins with the male protagonist gaining supernatural power after receiving a ginseng root from Korea's founding God, Dangun, and after the space aliens are defeated, Jesus appears to bless the protagonists, creating a postmodern blurring of Eastern and Western elements.

35. Yamaguchi Yasuo, author's interview, March 18, 2008.

36. Pennyway, "Gweajak yeoljeon No. 119" (Encyclopedic list of strange films), Pennyway.net website, http://pennyway.net/1773.

37. Lee's only other work was *Shupeo teukgeup Majinga 7* (Super ultra Majinga 7), produced in 1983, which was another film influenced by *Mazinger Z*.

38. Pennyway, "Gweajak yeoljeon No. 119."

39. The 364-foot Robot taekweon V statue planned to be built in Robot Land is six times taller than the 59-foot Gundam Statue built in Odaiba, Tokyo, in 2009. Jeong Ji-seon, "Robot Taekweon V Is Coming to Incheon?" *Seoul Munhwa Today*, Feb 12, 2010, http://www.sctoday.co.kr/news/articleView.html?idxno=4117.

40. Examples of South Korean animation from this time included stories about an insolent baby dinosaur (1987, *Agi gongryong Duli* [Baby dinosaur Duli]); a rebellious girl marathoner (1988, *Dalryeora Hani* [Run Hani]); and an updated version of the Monkey King narrative (1990, *Nalara supa bodeu* [Fly! Superboard]), which was an overt imitation of Toriyama Akira's *Dragon Ball* (1986).

41. Bang Eun-ju, "Incheon Robot Reandeu 3 weol cheot sap ddeunda" (Inchon Robot Land starts its project in March), January 2, 2013, ET News website, http://www.etnews.com/news/device/device/2700526_1479.html.

起源

BRIAN RUH

Conceptualizing Anime and the Database Fantasyscape

In spite of the growing body of literature on anime, very few people have examined what the term denotes. Most simply equate "anime" with "Japanese animation"; this is a relatively easy "out" in order to get past tricky questions of definition, and one to which I must admit engaging in on occasion. For example, in *Stray Dog of Anime: The Films of Mamoru Oshii,* I wrote that "'anime' does not denote any particular style or content; it simply means animation from Japan."[1] Carl Silvio has rightly criticized me for this overly simplistic statement, asserting that "Ruh offers us a definition [of anime] that is virtually invulnerable to refutation."[2] This definition presents something of a problem because many fans would not consider all animation from Japan as anime. For example, when Yamamura Kōji's *Mt. Head* (2002, *Atamayama*) was nominated for an Academy Award for best animated short film in 2003, it was relatively ignored by "anime" fans. The film's entry in the online encyclopedia on the Anime News Network website even states "Some people would not consider this as Anime [sic], but rather 'Alternative Japanese Animation.'"[3] This entry goes into no further detail and does not explain how "Alternative Japanese Animation" differs from "anime," but it seems clear that some fans have drawn a line around the concept of "anime" that does not include all animation from Japan.

A useful tool for examining the definitional limbo of the term "anime" is Matt Hills's study of fan cultures. In his book's preface, Hills explicitly states that he is taking a "suspensionist" position in which he is "approaching the contradictions of fan cultures and cult media as essential cultural negotiations that can only be closed down at the cost of ignoring fandom's cultural dynamics."[4] Like Hills, it is not my intention to arrive at a singular "expert" definition of anime but to pursue how anime is discussed within English-language fan and academic circles in order to explore how the meanings of such terms may change over time, sometimes taking on and discarding new connotations.[5] However, even within this suspensionist viewpoint, "anime" cannot mean just anything. In order for the term to be meaningful, it needs to be given structure, even if this structure does not point in the end to a singular definition.

Before the term "anime" came into widespread use in the late 1980s and early 1990s, such animation had often been called "Japanimation" in English. Anime historian Fred Patten traces the first use of the word "Japanimation" to around 1978, shortly after anime fandom became formalized with the establishment of the first U.S. anime fan club, called the Cartoon/Fantasy Organization (CFO), in May 1977.[6] The term "Japanimation" began to fall from popularity nearly a decade later—one reason was that it got too easily twisted into a racially derogatory term by detractors (e.g. "Jap animation"). Most people now writing use the term "anime," save a few. Japanese media scholar Ueno Toshiya, for instance, defends his use of the term "Japanimation," saying, "I use this term to emphasize both geography and the particularity of its characteristic styles, for these are quite different from animations in the general sense."[7] In this way, such animation becomes territorially marked by the term "Japanimation"; "anime," on the other hand, does not necessarily carry such connotations and seems to have the potential to be a much more fluid marker.

Some books on anime have introduced their topic of discussion in these ways: "Japanese cartoons (more properly, anime, which simply means 'animation')"; "anime (Japanese animation)"; and "Japanese animation, or 'anime,' as it is now usually referred to in both Japan and the West."[8] Other writers take a different approach to examining anime. In his introduction to the edited collection *Cinema Anime,* Steven T. Brown writes, "What is anime? Anime is so multifarious in its forms and genres, its styles and audiences, that one needs to pose the question differently: Where is the anime screen?"[9] Brown's reformulated question suggests that the meaning of anime comes about through the process of viewing anime onscreen, wherever that may be, and, as such, the term "anime" is situationally dependent. In this way, anime may not necessarily denote animation from a specific country but rather indicates a way of positioning images and information onscreen and how viewers interact with them.

One might notice that all of these definitions of anime are relatively recent. This is due to the fact that academics did not begin paying serious attention to it until the mid-1990s. For example, of the 814 entries in the Online Bibliography of Anime and Manga Research in 2010, only 84 (or 10.3 percent of the total) were published before 2000, and only one of those was published before 1990.[10] Thus, the English-language study of Japanese comics and animation is a relatively recent field, with the vast majority of the work published in the past ten years. This growth coincides with the development and popularity of anime in the United States. This popularity began to increase in the early 1990s because of the international success of Ōtomo Katsuhiro's *Akira* (1988), the growth of fansubs (which began to be technically feasible in the late 1980s), the founding of U.S. distribution companies like AnimEigo and AD Vision (which were essentially founded by anime fans who became professionals) that increased anime's presence in retail stores and on rental shelves, and the expansion in communication on the Internet, which enabled anime fans who did not live in Japan to be more aware of the latest developments in anime programs, films, and culture.

That such previously debased media forms began to receive serious scholarly attention in the 1990s was indicative not only of a change in how media scholars constructed objects of study but also of a new kind of Japanese power that was seen as cultural rather than military or economic.[11] There were almost no scholarly studies of Japanese animation before the 1990s, and the first in-depth book in English to look at Japanese animation was not published until 1993.[12] Other works that came out around this time also took Japanese popular culture as a site of serious academic inquiry, trying to figure out the reasons for its growing popularity. Some like Ron Tanner used discourse that explicitly tied such pop culture imports directly to the events of World War II ("How Japan Really Won the War"), couching the popularity of such products in terms of a Japanese "victory" over the United States.[13] This rhetorical metaphor of popular culture flows as conflict is a device that continues to be employed in writing about anime. Others scholars like Annalee Newitz postulate that the content of Japanese pop culture is relatively conservative, and that U.S. consumers have turned to Japanese products because they could not find such entertainment in their own "politically correct" culture.[14]

Subsequent articles on anime have touched on other issues related to the form, from textual analyses to discussions of its global popularity. However, as Rayna Denison points out in her examination of the anime markets in Japan, France, and the United States with regard to Miyazaki Hayao's film *Spirited Away* (2001, *Sen to Chihiro no kamikakushi*), "Where studies of anime as a global phenomenon do exist, they tend to understand the globalization of anime as its Americanization."[15] Denison's criticism is a reminder that anime has traveled to many countries outside of Japan and has relatively long histories in East Asia, Australia, and Europe.[16] At the same time, though, we need to be aware that, as Azuma Hiroki puts it, "the history of otaku culture is one of adaptation—of how to 'domesticate' American culture."[17] Therefore, although anime is global, it is important to pay particular attention to the cultural and economic exchanges between Japan and the United States in order to understand the form's development.

ANIME IN A GLOBAL FRAMEWORK

It is the intersection of U.S. and Japanese popular culture that seems to be driving much of anime's popularity. A related term that often comes up in discussions of anime is *mukokuseki*. Both Susan J. Napier and Koichi Iwabuchi reference the term in their respective studies of how Japanese popular culture flows transnationally, although each gives a slightly different interpretation of its meaning. Napier describes the term as "meaning 'stateless' or essentially without national identity," while Iwabuchi writes that the term is used "to suggest the mixing of elements of multiple cultural origins, and to imply the erasure of visible ethnic and cultural characteristics."[18] Probably the most salient reference point for anime's *mukokuseki* nature is the physical appearance of many anime characters. Even when an anime series is supposed to take place in Japan, often many of the characters do not look "Japanese." This leads some critics to assert that anime is symptomatic of a general Japanese cultural inferiority vis-à-vis the United States.[19] Although it is true that such anime characters do not necessarily adhere to the usual Japanese phenotype, it would be false to infer that, because of this, such characters look "Western" or "Caucasian." Rather, the characters look nationless and are drawn as representations of the human body that can be more or less abstracted depending on the creator as well as narrative and genre tropes. For example, Mizuki Takahashi chronicles the development of style in Japanese girls' comics and asserts that the large eyes found in such manga are used to portray emotion and to elicit an emotional response from the reader.[20] The use of such *mukokuseki* characters has two main results. One, according to Napier, is that *mukokuseki*-ness is a way for contemporary Japanese to playfully escape their own concepts of Japan and their own feelings of Japaneseness. That is to say, fantasized *mukokuseki* anime bodies can be free from the cultural and societal baggage of physical bodies; this characteristic works not only for Japanese consumers who wish to "try on" different identities but also for non-Japanese viewers as well—some of whom may very well wish to play with the idea of having a Japanese identity. The second result is that such programs in which the characters appear nationally and culturally unmarked are much easier to export to other countries, where they can be relocalized by the importer.

This brings up one of the main ironies regarding anime's *mukokuseki* nature: its style allows it to travel transnationally with relative ease, while at the same time such "stateless" anime has become to represent Japan and has attracted international fans to the study of Japanese language and culture. Iwabuchi sees Japan's *mukokuseki* popular culture to have been stripped of elements identifying such products as Japanese. Because of this, he wonders if the newfound global appreciation of Japanese popular culture is in fact a yearning for "an animated, race-less and culture-less, virtual version of 'Japan'" and theorizes that "what is experienced through Japanese popular culture is actually a highly materialistic Japanese version of the American 'original.'"[21] Because, according to Iwabuchi, such popular culture goods lack a strong "cultural odor" marking them as Japanese, the current discourse in Japan and elsewhere celebrating Japan's increasing global cultural power is somewhat misguided. However, returning to my introduction of Matt Hills's "suspensionist" approach to fan studies, I think holding the contradictions inherent in *mukokuseki* anime in suspension without trying to make them resolve into a singular conclusion is a useful approach. Anime may not necessarily carry with it markers of an "authentic" Japan (however this may be construed), but in practice many people now associate these "stateless" anime programs with ideas of Japan, and in this way the culturally "unmarked" anime becomes "marked" as Japanese not because of necessary elements within the text, but because of how anime has become a part of popular discourse.

In order to see how anime became a hybrid *mukokuseki* media product, it is necessary to briefly examine the historical roots of animation in Japan. Daisuke Miyao gives an account of anime's early antecedents, which are located in the Pure Film Movement, an effort in Japan in the 1910s that tried to establish film as its own medium, as distinct from literature and live theatrical drama.[22] This move was a rejection of previous "theatrical" methods of

> ITS STYLE ALLOWS IT TO TRAVEL TRANSNATIONALLY WITH RELATIVE EASE, WHILE AT THE SAME TIME SUCH "STATELESS" ANIME HAS BECOME TO REPRESENT JAPAN AND HAS ATTRACTED INTERNATIONAL FANS TO THE STUDY OF JAPANESE LANGUAGE AND CULTURE.

Japanese cinematic communication in favor of American and European techniques. Much of the imported animation first shown in Japan in 1909 was from France and served as a model for subsequent Japanese experiments. Since efforts in animation were inherently nontheatrical, Miyao suggests that the early Japanese animators may have fulfilled the goals of the Pure Film Movement better than many of the live-action filmmakers.[23] However, there were debates over the form and content of animation among some in the movement due to the fact that one of its intended results was to bring Japanese film into line with other global cinema. Miyao writes that although some in the movement "insisted on the necessity of Japanese stories and landscapes in order to differentiate the Japanese product for the foreign market, many opted nonetheless for subjects and stories that would be comprehensible to audiences accustomed to Western films."[24] One can see even at this early stage of animation in Japan the tension between making a recognizably Japanese product and an easily exportable global one. This is because in order to be recognized as a Japanese film by the rest of the world, early Japanese cinema had to become less "Japanese," or as Darrell William Davis puts it, "To become Japanese, Japanese cinema had to make overtures to foreign recognition as a prelude to the seduction of foreign markets. The films had to shed their provincial trappings and put on the 'high class' garb . . . of the universal commodity."[25] That is to say, Japanese cinema had to become more familiar and commodifiable to a global audience by incorporating the increasingly standardized language of cinema in order to be perceived as Japanese. In some ways this is exactly what happened with anime—in order to create a space for Japanese animation to thrive, it needed to secure its own marketplace niche by first becoming less Japanese and more "global." It was only after that that the form could be recognized as Japanese.

THE DATABASE FANTASYSCAPE

As we can see from the previous discussion of anime, to a certain extent it is relatively futile to force a singular definition of "anime." We can analyze the discourse surrounding the term, as above, which can bring us toward an understanding of how anime has been conceptualized, but this still gets us no closer to a discussion of how something like anime moves transnationally. This is the main question on which I want to focus—the "how" rather than the "what" of media globalization.

As mentioned above, the idea of *mukokuseki* explains in part how certain aspects of anime could cross national boundaries by seeming culturally unspecific. However, the biggest problem with this way of thinking about global media is that it ignores the fact that nothing can ever really be nationless since, as mentioned above, nothing really has pure national characteristics. Thinking about a media product like anime in such a way sets the stage for our discussion of what enables the products of popular culture, like anime, to flow and flourish outside of their native (and ostensibly intended) viewing community. The framework I have developed for analyzing this transnational media movement is called the "database fantasyscape." This framework melds two different ideas, by Azuma Hiroki and Susan J. Napier respectively, into an overall way of thinking about the flow of contemporary media. My analysis of anime is an example of a general trend in contemporary media that blurs the boundaries between different forms.

The "database" part of this concept comes from the writings of media theorist Azuma Hiroki on otaku media, in which he postulates a "shift from the supremacy of narrative to the supremacy of characters."[26] This focus on "characters" does not, however, mean more attention is being paid to characterization. In fact, it is just the opposite—instead of complex, well-rounded characters in stories, this shift toward "characters" signals an increased emphasis on affective elements such as characters' looks, personality traits, and other archetypes that can be easily recognized and transferred from medium to medium. As Azuma writes, "many of the otaku characters created in recent years are connected to many characters across individual works, rather than emerging from a single author or work."[27] Therefore, Azuma formulates the concept of what he calls "database consumption," since to consume a modern anime product "is not simply to consume a work (a small narrative) or a worldview behind it (a grand narrative), nor to consume characters and settings (a grand non-narrative). Rather, it is linked to consuming the database of otaku culture as a whole."[28] This type of consumption also influences how one reads contemporary anime texts. Thomas Lamarre has written that "limited animation [of the type commonly associate with anime] . . . shaped a new kind of viewing and consuming, one that entails scanning, re-reading, searching information, discerning technical innovation, and so forth. In other words, one might say that anime generated a viewer experience that was very much like an experience of informatization itself."[29] Thus, in Lamarre's perspective, how we view and process media like anime have strongly influenced how we interact with and evaluate information in general. This is a powerful assertion and indicates the degree to which anime can give rise to the "anime-ic," a term that can be used to describe the tendency toward anime or anime-like characteristics. My concept of the anime-ic derives strongly from Thomas Looser's work, in which he writes of anime, "the insistence on multiple layers, consisting of mixed styles and mixed media each with their own particular orientations, brought together on a single plane without any one point of origin that would fix the relations between them . . . this, I think, is a productive approach to anime and, more generally, to an understanding of the everyday in the latter part of the twentieth century."[30] In other words, an anime-ic space is a space containing multiple (not unified) points of view that lacks a fixed perspective. The term anime-ic can be used to describe off-screen spaces as well as onscreen ones and does not necessarily dictate that such spaces be animated. In this way, anime not only becomes something to view onscreen but a way of organizing and conceptualizing the world around us and the information it contains. Thinking of spaces as anime-ic is a potentially useful way to describe the diffusion of animated spaces away from the screen and into interactions with off-screen spaces. To describe a certain space as "anime-ic" is not necessarily to ascribe some inherent quality to the space as much as it is to describe a way of thinking about and experiencing that space.

The "fantasyscape" part of the "database fantasyscape" comes from Susan J. Napier's discussion of the development and transnational flow of anime.[31] In her formulation, what she calls the "fantasyscape" can be seen as a useful addition to Arjun Appadurai's idea of the five global flows—the ethnoscape, financescape, technoscape, mediascape, and ideoscape.[32] However, although Napier originated the concept of the fantasyscape, her book does not fully unpack the term. However, it is a useful tool that fits into Appadurai's model and allows us to envision global flows in ways that might help us to see clearly things that may have been otherwise opaque.

The absence of a specific fantasy dimension to Appadurai's theoretical framework is very interesting because he begins the personal narrative in the first chapter of *Modernity at Large* by sketching out the fantasies of his youth. These fantasies came to Appadurai in various forms, including magazines, films, clothing, and even deodorant. In this short narrative, the reader can begin to sense the multifaceted ways in which a young Appadurai was confronted and enticed by these small things, none of which had critical importance in themselves but which all contributed to feeling "modernity as embodied sensation."[33] Appadurai goes on to state the importance that imagination has in his work. Indeed, as in the imagined communities of Benedict Anderson, Appadurai places a great deal of emphasis on the functioning of what he calls the "work of the imagination," which is "neither purely emancipatory nor entirely disciplined but is a space of contestation in which individuals and groups seek to annex the global into their own practices of the modern."[34]

However, one of the reasons there may not be a specific fantasyscape in Appadurai's formulation is that he seems to take a relatively dim view of fantasy as compared to the imagination, and he makes distinctions between the functions of the two. He seems to consider fantasy as essentially impotent and inward looking, while imagination is a catalyst for action and outward looking. He writes that "the idea of fantasy carries with it the inescapable connotation of thought divorced from projects and actions, and it also has a private, even individualistic sound about it . . . [it] can dissipate (because its logic is often so autotelic), but the imagination, especially when collective, can become the fuel for action."[35] In other words, the purpose of fantasy is fantasy itself, while the purpose of imagination is to conceive of how things could be better.

I am not going to dispute Appadurai's division of mental labor between the fantasy and the imagination, but I do want to argue with the duties he extracts from them. Even if fantasy is inherently directed toward one's self, that certainly does not mean it can be divorced from outward behaviors. I would argue that it was fantasy, not imagination, that provided Appadurai's "embodied sensation" of modernity. In many cases it is the pull of fantasy that spurs people to action; in the case of anime fans, this might include buying DVDs, reading manga, downloading programs online, learning Japanese, attending conventions, and even traveling to Japan. Even though fantasy may be directed inward, it does have very real outward results that can be felt in social and economic ways. Therefore, how these fantasies travel around the world is an important consideration when thinking about Appadurai's theory of global flows.

Merging Azuma's database concept and Napier's fantasyscape concept to examine the flow of media provides a useful way of thinking about how a media phenomenon like anime spreads. It is transmedia storytelling in a global context. If we can stretch the database metaphor, we might be able to think about the flow of anime, even within Japan, as similar to how data is transmitted via the Internet. Just as a Web page or an e-mail is broken into simpler parts, transmitted, and reconstituted at its endpoint (a drastic oversimplification, of course), an anime series is broken into smaller elements both textual and extratextual—characters, dialogue, scenes, episodes, DVDs, and so on—in order to make the journey. However, the reconstitution process for cultural products is much more variable than that of an e-mail because these different parts do not necessarily all flow at the same rate, and, due to reasons both commercial and cultural, the final product often does not look the same as its initial formulation. The reason some of the database elements flow and others do not depends to a significant degree on certain cultural norms, ideals, and fantasies, and how these individual and collective fantasies play out on multiple levels.

> MERGING AZUMA'S DATABASE CONCEPT AND NAPIER'S FANTASYSCAPE CONCEPT TO EXAMINE THE FLOW OF MEDIA PROVIDES A USEFUL WAY OF THINKING ABOUT HOW A MEDIA PHENOMENON LIKE ANIME SPREADS.

Fantasyscape is how the database travels. It is both the conduit that conducts certain of the database elements as well as how the pieces are understood. Database provides an immediate apprehension that may directly influence how we choose what we watch and how we watch it.

Bringing my own experience to bear, there are many anime series and films that I do not watch because I can tell immediately from the art (character designs, backgrounds, style of animation, and so on) that it will not be to my taste. This is not simply a bias against a type of design or animation. The elements of animated art serve as stylistic shorthand that can communicate to the viewer certain aspects of what the show might be like and allows for a more successful navigation of animated "waters." Of course, as with any form of shorthand, mistakes can be made and elements can be misread. But, in general, what happens when someone creates a new anime series or film is that one is not only trying to create something new but is also engaging many decades of animated history that have given rise to certain taste formations within the anime-watching community. This large amount of history is the database that can be selectively referenced. The database is inescapable; even if a creator is not trying to reference previous anime or manga, the viewers may bring these database assumptions with them when engaging the works of the creator.

The database fantasyscape engages with Henry Jenkins's idea of media convergence, which, he writes, "represents a cultural shift as consumers are encouraged to seek out new information and make connections among dispersed media content."[36] In other words, Jenkins argues that contemporary media convergence owes in part to consumers taking in diverse media sources and piecing them together based on their own personal experiences.

One might rightly wonder, though, how such "dispersed media content" came about in the first place. For example, in the case of an anime film or television program, why are viewers encouraged to read the manga and light novels (which may or may not have preceded the animation), play the video games, purchase the supplementary DVDs, and collect the figurines? I believe the answer lies in the idea of the database fantasyscape and that ability of both producers and consumers to apportion a work into its component pieces, which are then available for reuse and movement into other media and across national borders.

Notes

1. Brian Ruh, *Stray Dog of Anime: The Films of Mamoru Oshii* (New York: Palgrave Macmillan, 2004), 1.

2. Carl Silvio, "Animated Bodies and Cybernetic Selves: The Animatrix and the Question of Posthumanity," in *Cinema Anime: Critical Engagements with Japanese Animation,* ed. Steven T. Brown (New York: Palgrave Macmillan), 135.

3. "Mt. Head," *Anime News Network,* http://www.animenewsnetwork.com/encyclopedia/anime.php?id=2275.

4. Matt Hills, *Fan Cultures* (New York: Routledge, 2002), xiii (emphasis in original).

5. A discussion of the boundaries of "anime" in the Japanese-language context is unfortunately beyond the scope of this article.

6. Fred Patten, *Watching Anime, Reading Manga: 25 Years of Essays and Reviews* (Berkeley, Calif.: Stone Bridge Press, 2004), 24–25.

7. Toshiya Ueno, "Techno-Orientalism and Media-Tribalism: On Japanese Animation and Rave Culture," *Third Text* 47 (1999): 97.

8. Patrick Drazen, *Anime Explosion! The What? Why? & Wow! of Japanese Animation* (Berkeley, Calif.: Stone Bridge Press, 2003), vii; Antonia Levi, *Samurai from Outer Space: Understanding Japanese Animation*, (Chicago: Open Court, 1996), ix; Susan J. Napier, *Anime from* Akira *to* Howl's Moving Castle: *Experiencing Contemporary Japanese Animation* (New York: Palgrave Macmillan, 2005), 3.

9. Steven T. Brown, "Screening Anime," in *Cinema Anime: Critical Engagements with Japanese Animation,* ed. Steven T. Brown (New York: Palgrave Macmillan), 2.

10. Mikhail Koulikov, "Online Bibliography of Anime and Manga Research," http://www.corneredangel.com/amwess/acad_1.html.

11. Douglas McGray, "Japan's Gross National Cool," *Foreign Policy* (June/July 2002): 44–54.

12. Helen McCarthy, *Anime! A Beginner's Guide to Japanese Animation* (London: Titan Books, 1993).

13. Ron Tanner, "Toy Robots in America, 1955–75: How Japan Really Won the War," *Journal of Popular Culture* 28, no. 3 (1994): 125–54.

14. Annalee Newitz, "Magical Girls and Atomic Bomb Sperm: Japanese Animation in America," *Film Quarterly* 49 no. 1 (1995): 2–15. Newitz's article was written before a turn

in the late 1990s to more "politically incorrect" entertainment; in the case of U.S. animation, probably best represented by shows like *South Park* (1997–present) and *Family Guy* (1999–2002, 2005–present).

15. Rayna Denison, "The Global Markets for Anime: Miyazaki Hayao's Spirited Away (2001)," in *Japanese Cinema: Texts and Contexts,* eds. Alastair Philips and Julian Stringer (Routledge: New York, 2007), 308.

16. See Marco Pellitteri, *The Dragon and the Dazzle: Models, Strategies, and Identities of Japanese Imagination: A European Perspective* (Latina, Italy: Tunue, 2010).

17. Hiroki Azuma, *Otaku: Japan's Database Animals,* trans. Jonathan E. Abel and Shion Kono (Minneapolis: University of Minnesota Press, 2009), 13.

18. Napier, *Anime from* Akira *to* Howl's Moving Castle, 24. Koichi Iwabuchi, *Recentering Globalization: Popular Culture and Japanese Transnationalism* (Durham, N.C.: Duke University Press, 2002), 71.

19. Sato Kenji, "More Animated Than Life: Ethnic Bleaching in Japanese Anime," *Kyoto Journal* 41 (1999): 22–27.

20. Mizuki Takahashi, "Opening the Closed World of Shōjo Manga," in *Japanese Visual Culture: Explorations in the World of Manga and Anime,* ed. Mark W. MacWilliams (Armonk, N.Y.: M.E. Sharpe, 2008): 114–36; Iwabuchi, *Recentering Globalization,* 33.

21. Iwabuchi, *Recentering Globalization*, 33, 35.

22. Daisuke Miyao, "Before Anime: Animation and the Pure Film Movement in Pre-war Japan," *Japan Forum* 14, no. 2 (2002): 191–209.

23. Ibid., 197–98.

24. Ibid., 200.

25. Darrell William Davis, *Picturing Japaneseness: Monumental Style, National Identity, Japanese Film* (New York: Columbia University Press, 1996), 28.

26. Hiroki Azuma, "The Animalization of Otaku Culture," trans. Yuriko Furuhata and Marc Steinberg, *Mechademia* 2 (2007): 181.

27. Azuma, *Otaku,* 49.

28. Ibid., 54.

29. Thomas Lamarre, "From Animation to Anime: Drawing Movements and Moving Drawings," *Japan Forum* 14, no. 2 (2002): 337.

30. Thomas Looser, "From Edogawa to Miyazaki: Cinematic and Anime-ic Architectures of Early and Late Twentieth-Century Japan," *Japan Forum* 14, no. 2 (2002): 310.

31. Susan J. Napier, *From Impressionism to Anime: Japan as Fantasy and Fan Cult in the Mind of the West* (New York: Palgrave Macmillan, 2007).

32. Arjun Appadurai, *Modernity at Large: Cultural Dimensions of Globalization* (Minneapolis: University of Minnesota Press, 1996).

33. Ibid., 2.

34. Benedict Anderson, *Imagined Communities: Reflections on the Origin and Spread of Nationalism* (London: Verso, 1983); Appadurai, *Modernity at Large,* 4.

35. Appadurai, *Modernity at Large,* 7.

36. Henry Jenkins, *Convergence Culture: Where Old and New Media Collide* (New York: New York University Press, 2006), 3.

Rescripting History

起源

LAURA MILLER

Rebranding Himiko, the Shaman Queen of Ancient History

While doing fieldwork on the divination industry in Tokyo, I discovered a place where a specialist offered tarot card readings using the famed 1889 Tarot de Marseille deck. In order to get an interview I went to her place of business, located in a decrepit office building in Shibuya. She greeted me at the entryway together with her officemate, a woman named Yasuko. Yasuko was also in the divination business and told me she was carrying on a tradition established by the first great Japanese shaman, Himiko, a third-century CE ruler described only briefly by Chinese historians. Why does a contemporary divination professional feel the need to link divination entrepreneurship to an ancient sovereign? Yasuko is not alone in her fascination with Himiko, and it is this interest in a historical figure about whom we know very little that I wish to explore in this essay.

Other visions of Himiko's persona are less inspiring than Yasuko's. Some manga and anime creators portray Himiko as a presumptuous tyrant, promiscuous sorceress, or vain hag unworthy of power. At first glance these disparate perceptions seem to have no relationship to each other. Was Himiko a diabolical dictator, a talented witch, or an adorable shrine attendant? Do people see in Himiko a sexy manipulator or a spiritual mastermind? Interpretations

REPRESENTATIONS OF HIMIKO ARE RARELY NEUTRAL, AS MOST ENTAIL ENCODING OF SELECTED ASSUMPTIONS ABOUT ANCIENT HISTORY AND FEMALE AUTHORITY.

vary depending on the goals and attitudes held by creators of her image, particularly their ideas about female power. Women such as Yasuko view Himiko as a metaphor for female agency and innate occult abilities. Other popular culture producers see in Himiko an aberrant and unwise attribution of political authority to women. As Laurel Thatcher Ulrich pointed out, the figure of Joan of Arc has been many things across the years, including witch, virgin, heretic, whore, transvestite, peasant, and saint.[1] A woman demonized in one era might be venerated in another. Himiko also reflects this type of shifting assessment, often holding contrasting personas within the same time period.

My aim is not to engage in recuperation of Himiko as a positive origin symbol but rather to survey the diversity in uses of her image. She is put to service for civic boosterism, national-identity construction, and to legitimize the divination enterprise. Some of the more interesting images of Himiko are also the most challenging to understand. Representations of Himiko are rarely neutral, as most entail encoding of selected assumptions about ancient history and female authority. This essay will review some ways she is depicted in literary treatments and in visual culture, where she appears as shaman priestess, alluring ruler, and dangerous witch. I draw on history and popular culture texts to trace how the hazy yet tantalizing aspects of her story make her an appealing icon easily available to serve a range of interests. The iconography depends on who is looking at Himiko and for what purposes they include her in their project.

HIMIKO'S ORIGIN STORY

Himiko might be the subject of more media than any other woman in Japanese history. She fascinates not only scholars but anyone interested in Japanese history and identity. She was described in ethnographic chronicles about Japan written by third-century Chinese, yet is not named in the earliest Japanese mythological histories, the *Kojiki* (712, Record of ancient matters) and the *Nihongi* (720, Chronicles of Japan, alternate title *Nihon shoki*). Because the Japanese compilers of these mytho-histories consulted much earlier Chinese sources that contained details about Himiko, it is clear they intentionally excised her name. No doubt, acknowledging Himiko's role would have interfered with their ideological project to establish a patrilineal kinship group as the divinely ordained rulers. One outcome of this discrepancy, however, is that Himiko's biography has been the subject of extremely broad interpretation.

In one of the early Chinese histories, the *Wei zhi* (Records of Wei) book of the *Sanguozhi* (Records of the Three Kingdoms), compiled by historian Chen Shou (233–97), there is a section on Japan entitled "Account of the Eastern Barbarians" that describes Himiko with some intriguing information.[2] She was the ruler of a confederation of chiefdoms, was the recipient of a return gift of one hundred Chinese bronze mirrors from the Wei court, was mature in age yet remained unmarried, and was a shaman who was buried in a lavish tomb. There have been centuries of speculation and theorizing about Himiko and the polity she ruled, which the *Wei zhi* called Yamatai. The people of Himiko's time spoke an unknown proto-Japanese language that was transliterated by Chinese scribes using a third-century form of classical Chinese. I use the modern version of her name as a placeholder for what her actual name may have been.

Himiko assumed leadership of the Yamatai confederation in 190 CE, when she was a young woman, and ruled until her death in 248. Current scholarship is a hotbed of debate, but one camp supports the theory that she was a royal princess known as Yamato-totohi-momoso-hime-no-mikoto.[3] She may be buried in the Hashihaka Kofun (Chopstick Tomb), located in Sakurai city in Nara Prefecture, evidently the oldest tomb of its type and size. This time frame provides another reason the representations of Himiko can be so diverse. Himiko lived during a transitional period between the Yayoi (usually 300 BCE–250 CE, but may be earlier) and Kofun (250–538) eras. The evolution from late Yayoi to early Kofun is generally based on the presence of huge mounded tombs in a distinctive keyhole shape, of which Hashihaka Kofun is the earliest. However, clothing styles and other forms of material culture changed gradually over the nearly six-hundred-year span of the Yayoi and Kofun periods, so artists and illustrators of Himiko often conflate these periods in their representations.

HIMIKO'S MAGIC AND RULERSHIP

The precise nature of Himiko's power and her status in the court hierarchy of her Yamatai kinsmen is the subject of conflicting conjecture. The majority of scholars accept the *Wei zhi* account that she was selected by her people to be their ruler and that her reign initiated a new cultural era. Images of Himiko often include objects from archeological sites and tombs of the Kofun period. Her principal ritual accoutrements most likely included items found in the archeological record, such as Chinese bronze mirrors, swords, distinctive comma-shaped beads known as *magatama*, and a special type of bronze bell, called a *dōtaku*, which characterized Yayoi sites but which was not included in the Kofun-era repertoire of ritual objects.[4] As Ishino Hironobu has discussed, it is right after Himiko's accession to power that *dōtaku* begin to be discarded, broken, and burned; thus they "tell a tale of rejection" of the ritual objects associated with rulers who preceded her.[5] Nevertheless, manga, anime, museum exhibits, and book illustrations often depict Himiko with *dōtaku*. For example, in the Osaka Prefectural Museum of Yayoi Culture, a painting by the artist Einaga Dajirō shows Himiko as a young woman wearing a simple white *kosode* (the basic unisex robe form) with a red sash and underskirt, embellished with two strands of green *magatama* and holding both a Chinese bronze mirror and a rod of office. Next to her are two large *dōtaku* bells.[6]

The Chinese bronze mirrors associated with Himiko were part of her ritual set and not simply precious exchange goods. These round cast-metal objects had a polished reflecting surface on one side and an intricately decorated back with ridged rims and a protuberant knob in the middle. The mirrors were held in the hand by the knob or a cord drawn through it. If we find an image of a woman wearing ancient clothing and holding a bronze mirror, it is safe to assume that we might be looking at an image of Himiko. An example of this framing of Himiko is found in a manga history series of fifty notable Japanese figures (Figure 1).[7] Himiko inaugurates the series, and although she is shown wearing clothing that seems more like that from the Jōmon era (13,000–300 BCE), she has a bronze mirror clasped to her chest.[8] Her hair is in the looped fashion called *mizura*, seen in Kofun-era imagery and described in the *Wei zhi* as being for men. She wears an elaborate diadem with a sunburst motif.

The descriptions of Himiko in the *Wei zhi* indicate that she was a shaman, a ritual specialist able to communicate with the supernatural realm after achieving an altered state of consciousness. There are various techniques for arriving at this trance state, including ascetic practices, ingesting drugs, and ecstatic dancing. Accounts of ancient history written in Japan occasionally lack a comparative perspective, ignoring the fact that the shaman role is rather common in the global ethnographic record, and that female shamans are the norm in East Asia.[9] We know from history and ethnography that female shamans in Japan received great respect from their local communities.[10] In regards to Himiko's form of shamanship, the *Wei zhi* described it as *guidao* (Japanese *kidō*), a term generally used to mean Daoist folk practices. The literal translation, "way of demons," refers to the shaman's ability to make contact with dead spirits. Contemporary image creators often interpret this term negatively as "black magic" practiced by a calculating witch, but not always: a recent book entitled *Gakkō de oshiete kurenai: Hontō no Nihonshi* (2012, You aren't taught this in school: The real history of Japan), makes the point that *kidō* is merely shamanism that involves serving as an oracle. Himiko, a smart cookie and a "charisma queen," is illustrated in the book as a racially ambiguous woman with long hair encircled by an ornate crown and holding an evergreen *sakaki* branch.[11] This positive image of Himiko practicing "good" magic, however, is balanced by equally negative imagery of her entanglement in murky and mysterious forms of *kidō*.

In Himiko's case, some scholars also see a close association between her and snake cults and deities, as well as the imported Chinese cult of the Queen Mother of the West.[12] Interestingly, few manga or anime make reference to these themes. When the illustrator of Himiko wants to emphasize her nature as a religious leader, she is most often shown holding a bronze mirror or a *sakaki* branch (Figure 2). Within Shintō, *sakaki* is one of the trees associated with ritual and practice. The thick-leaved, dark evergreen branches are used to adorn shrines and sacred spaces, as purification tools, and as props in ritual

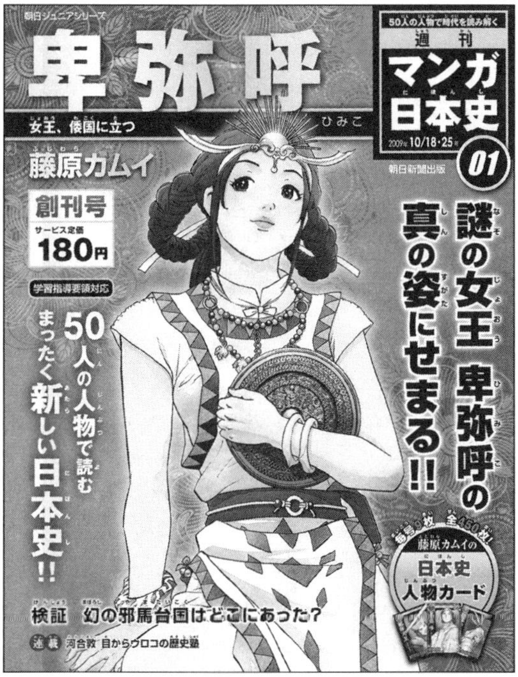

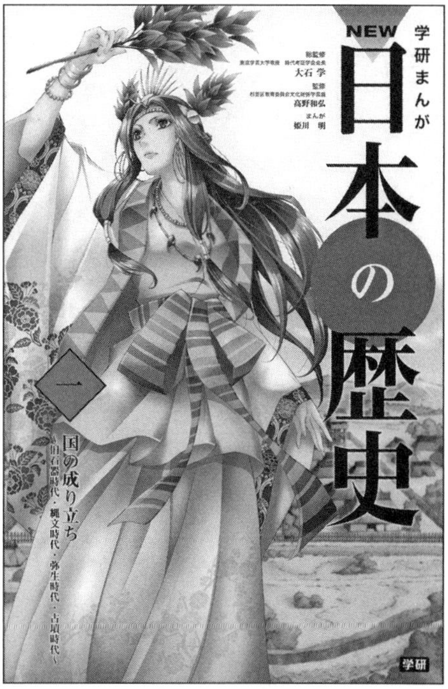

FIGURE 1 (LEFT). Cover of Fujiwara Kamui's *Himiko: Shūkan manga Nihonshi* (2009, Himiko: Weekly manga history of Japan). **FIGURE 2 (RIGHT).** Cover of *Gakken manga new Nihon no rekishi* (2012, Gakken's new manga history of Japan), by Ōishi Manabu, Takano Kazuhiro, and Himekawa Akira.

dancing. A wonderful example is a fan drawing of Himiko submitted to the website sponsored by Nico Nico Seiga, where amateurs share illustrations. On the pages tagged with the name Himiko, there is one that represents a typical manga schoolgirl with huge eyes and long hair embellished with an enormous puffy red bow. Over a cushiony red skirt she is wearing a robe edged with Yayoi-style geometric designs, and she is waving a healthy branch of *sakaki*.[13] Himiko is also the subject of numerous other fan art websites, where she gets similarly "cutified" and infantilized.

WHAT DID HIMIKO REALLY LOOK LIKE?

In popular depictions of Himiko like the one described above, how much has a basis in the historical record, and how much is simply imagined? In Himiko iconography there are many productive elements that manga artists, illustrators, museum curators, and costume designers have available to draw on for creative expression. One can imagine her wardrobe, her hairstyle, and also the possible ritual paraphernalia she held or owned. As noted above, the great diversity in Himiko styles reflects her position as a transitional figure between two eras. Even so, as a late Yayoi queen who ushered in the new Kofun cultural milieu, she probably wore continental-inspired fashion, most likely a one-piece, wide-sleeved *kosode,* under a vest-like garment, as well as a skirt, a belt, and a sash. The sash is seen on female shamans depicted on *haniwa* (clay cylinders with figures of people, animals, and objects on them, implanted around the burial mound). Most illustrators depict Himiko bejeweled with strands of beads, especially *magatama.* But her hairstyle seems to pose a special problem for the imagination. Did she wear it straight and long or tied up in the *mizura* fashion? *Haniwa* figures of female shamans show them with hair tied up and topped with flat hats.

There are archeological remains of looms, shuttles, and spindle whorls from the Yayoi era, so we know people made interesting textiles. Some of the cloth was made of hemp, flax, ramie, and silk. Immigrants from the Korean peninsula entered the Japanese islands in waves during the Yayoi and Kofun eras, armed with the latest weaving technology. Himiko, according to the *Wei zhi,* sent gift textiles as part of her tribute to the Wei court, and in return she received crimson brocade, white silk, and dark blue brocade. She may have had a bronze mirror hanging from her belt, as well as jingle bells. There is no way to tell whether Himiko wore a simple cloth headband or an elaborate diadem. Both are found in manga, anime, and historical illustrations.

Many of the precise illustrations and museum displays of what Himiko might have worn reproduce inferences made by costume historians such as Takeda Sachiko, a professor at Osaka University, who based her reconstructions on late Kofun *haniwa,* and Asuka-era (538–710) textiles and paintings. Her reconstructions are among the most widely known and show Himiko wearing an elaborate "treasure crown." Historical painter Yasuda Yukihiro contributed another popular Himiko image in 1968. His modern painting is part of the collection in the Museum of Modern Art, Shiga, and depicts a fleshy, mature Himiko in a headdress decorated with a gold phoenix and rays, wearing a small bead necklace with *magatama,* and holding a rod of office. Her deep orange robes are decorated with a design of paired fish.

POSITIVE IMAGES OF HIMIKO AND POSTWAR CIVIC IDENTITY

Beyond (but related to) her appearance, the other interesting thing to look at in depictions of Himiko, is the characterization of her political authority, which connects in an interesting way with Himiko's role as a symbol of local civic engagement.

A popular depiction of Himiko that emphasizes her authority is Ishinomori Shōtarō's 1997 manga history of Japan. His story of Himiko begins when she is a serious young woman intensely lobbied by male elders to take on leadership of their warring chiefdoms. She wears a simple *kosode* covered by a long-sleeved white tunic tied in the front with a white sash. Her white headband is knotted into bows on either side of her head. Around her neck is a strand of *magatama* beads, while in her hand is a *sakaki* branch. In the scene where she assumes queenship, she announces to the crowd standing below her elevated Yayoi-style palace: "From now on all the chiefdoms will cease fighting. My heart will reflect the mind of the deities."[14] Ishinomori's Himiko is given the mandate to rule because of her great spiritual authority. He uses the term *matsurigoto,* an ancient word for governance, to reinforce that Himiko was both a secular and religious leader.

Another powerful image of Himiko appears in a surprising context, a manga by the ultraconservative manga artist Kobayashi Yoshinori. His political manga *Shin tennōron* (2010, A new theory of the emperor) contains drawings of a sober, commanding Himiko.[15] She looks intent as she stands near a blazing fire and brandishes a tortoise plastron above her head, indicating a type of divination called *scapulamancy.* Scapulamancy is the interpretation of cracks on charred shoulder bones of deer and wild boar, a term generally extended to include turtle shells. Unlike the corresponding practice in China there was no writing on them.

Departing from the right wing's usual fierce support for a male-only imperial line, Kobayashi makes a case that Japan should change its succession law to allow a female Emperor. He mentions her as an early shaman, writing that although her female power is "primitive," it is close to the gods.

The issue of Himiko's political authority and her role as a unifier maps intriguingly onto the landscape of postwar Japan's local politics and gender politics. To examine this we first need to ask where Himiko was from. One of the thorniest issues surrounding Himiko is the location of her realm. Over the centuries, two different theories locating Yamatai have vied for prominence—one placing it in north Kyūshū and another locating it in the Kinki region near present-day Kyoto, Osaka, Nara, and Kobe. Archaeological discoveries since the end of the Pacific War have contributed to the dispute. The discovery of a late Yayoi site in Yoshinogari, Saga Prefecture (Kyūshū), in 1986 generated renewed interest in Himiko. For example, the famous literary figure Saegusa Kazuko claims in the afterward to her novel about Himiko that she was inspired by the discovery of the Yoshinogari ruins to tackle this subject. In her story, Himiko is a rustic Yayoi-era shaman who eventually goes blind.[16]

Yoshinogari archeologists unearthed fabulous Korean-style daggers, molds, weapons, and tools in what was a vast settlement with massive elevated stockades. A bestselling 1967 book *Maboroshi no Yamataikoku* (1967, The illusive country of Yamatai), about a retired man's fanatical hunt for Himiko, supported the Kyūshū theory.[17] In the film version of the book, released in 2008, the beloved actress Yoshinaga Sayuri played the part of a dignified Queen Himiko. Yoshinaga's intelligent, calm visage and Juno-esque appearance has become an enduring model of Himiko.[18] According to one source, Yoshinaga herself contributed ideas to the design of the costume, which required a team of twenty to create.[19] Yoshinaga's hair is worn long, covered by a headband with attached jewels dangling to her shoulders, and draped around her neck is a strand of beads interspersed with green *magatama*. Her white *kosode* with pale dusky rose details cost ten million yen to create. Yoshinaga's performance as Himiko has a staying power akin to Elizabeth Taylor's role as Cleopatra. This image is so endearing it was selected for a set of commemorative stamps released in 2008. It also appears on many Kyūshū goods and products, such as Sun Brewing's special release of Kagoshima *shōchū* named "Himiko Fantasia" (Figure 3).

Himiko is a rich resource for regional groups in need of a city mascot,

HIMIKO IS A RICH RESOURCE FOR REGIONAL GROUPS IN NEED OF A CITY MASCOT, BEAUTY CONTEST THEME, OR TOURISTIC MOTIF.

beauty contest theme, or touristic motif. The debate over the location of Yamatai provides an opening for several cities to claim her as their very own icon that represents both local identity and historical authenticity. She fulfills this civic duty in multiple ways. She is featured in parades and floats and her statue is placed in prominent positions.[20] Cities continue to jockey for recognition as the birthplace of Himiko, even though the newest archaeology supports a Nara basin location for her capital. One of the loudest claims emanates from the city of Yoshinogari in Kyūshū. The city hosts an annual Fire Festival that climaxes with a dramatic ritual bonfire, set ablaze by a woman dressed up as Himiko. She wears colorful garb and a headdress that looks rather like something associated with Native Americans. The Yoshinogari City Hall also sponsors costume exhibitions of Kofun-esque garments of the sort that might have been worn by Himiko. Promoters also worked with Sanrio to create a Himiko-themed Hello Kitty keychain. Kitty-chan as Himiko wears a pink *kosode* with a bright red sash, blue beads, and a red headband with her ubiquitous bow attached.

Not to be outdone, Sakurai city in Nara Prefecture began vigorously promoting Himiko following news reports that Hashihaka Kofun may be where she is buried. Signs around town feature "Himiko-chan," the town's cute

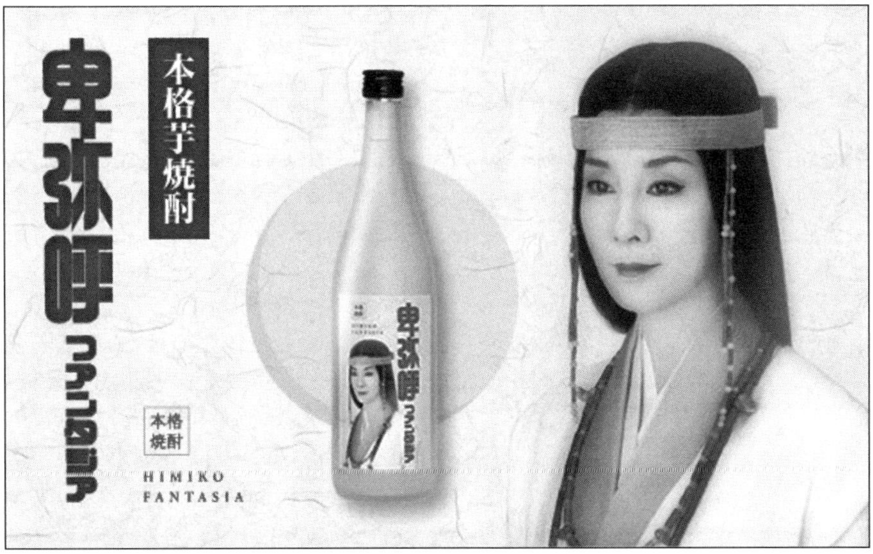

FIGURE 3. Advertisement for Sun Brewing Company's special release of Kagoshima *shōchū* named "Himiko-Fantasia."

character mascot, with the words "Welcome to Himiko country!" City leaders created some comical Himiko-chan anime that are posted online. A few feature Old Lady Himiko, a humorous battle-ax version of the queen.[21]

A popular method to celebrate regional roots and civic pride is to sponsor Queen Himiko Contests in which young women compete on the basis of charm and appearance. For most of the Himiko contests, the queen slot is open to any woman over eighteen. There are usually large cash prizes given to the winners. One of the earliest was created by the smallish town of Yamatokōriyama in the Nara area (Figure 4). Their Queen Himiko contest was established in 1982, based on an author's contention that this town is the origin site.[22] A competing thesis was published in 2010, proposing that Yamatai was located in Ōmi, present-day Shiga Prefecture.[23] This claim sent the city of Moriyama into high gear to advocate their version of the Miss Queen Himiko Contest, fondly nicknamed "Himikon."

The Moriyama Himikon explicitly promotes the "Ōmi Theory" as justification for its first contest, held in 2011. The costuming of Queen Himiko was of great interest to the men in the Moriyama city office. The unveiling of the official Himiko costume was itself a media event, and officials held numerous press conferences highlighted in newspapers. Photos show them posing with the outfit that the selected winner would eventually wear. Oddly, there were never any women included in these photos of the disembodied dress. The costume, with a gauzy mud-red top layer, was created by a local designer named Mama Riina, whose blog describes the difficulties she had obtaining materials and constructing this fantastical ensemble.[24]

A third Himiko contest is held in Asakura, in Kyūshū's Fukuoka Prefecture, as part of the local Yamataikoku Festival of Flowers. The Himiko images in their contest posters construct notions of cute girlhood and a form of costume play. Most of the posters feature two young women dressed in would-be

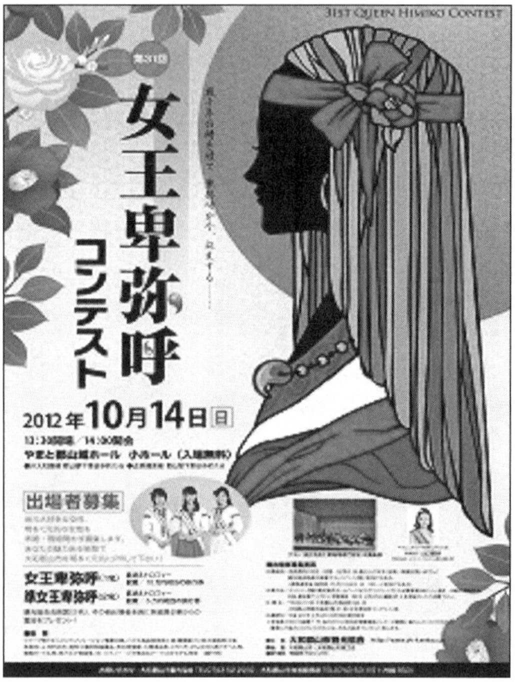

FIGURE 4. Poster for the Yamatokōriyama Queen Himiko contest.

Himiko garb (Figure 5). These posters of two Himiko queens shift focus away from the Yamatai ruler and toward the community service activity of dressing up as a historic figure purportedly from one's hometown.

In announcements, books, and manga seen widely in Japan, Himiko is put forth as a role model for all age groups, from children to adult women. A popular campaign targeting school children urges them to chew their food well, just as Himiko did, with the slogan "Himiko's teeth are great!" (Figure 6). Created by the Gakkō Shokuji Kenkyūkai (School Meals Study Group), the movement was based on the idea that ancient Japanese ate less processed food, so remained healthy. According to the posters, chewing well prevents obesity, tooth decay, and cancer, develops taste, aids pronunciation and the digestive system, contributes to brain development, and promotes physical strength.

For the older set, the founder of the new religious group Kōfuku no Kagaku (Happy Science) published a book entitled *Josei riidaa nyūmon: Himiko, Kōmyō Kōgō ga okuru, genzai joseitachi e no adobaisu* (2011, Introduction to female leaders: Advice for contemporary women given by Himiko and Empress Kōmyō).[25] Empress Kōmyō (701–60) was a politically astute ruler who supported Buddhism and philanthropic projects. The book coaches readers on how they can combine their intuitive spiritual capacities and pragmatic skills in order to achieve life goals.

But in contrast to instances in which Himiko is held up as a paragon of female capability, there are also intriguing images of her that ignore the inconveniently mature and powerful queen of history in favor of something altogether different.

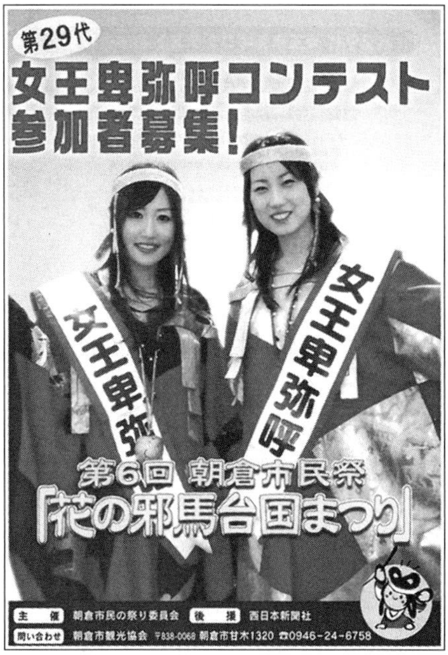

FIGURE 5. Poster for the "Yamataikoku Festival of Flowers" Himiko contest in Asakura, Kyūshū.

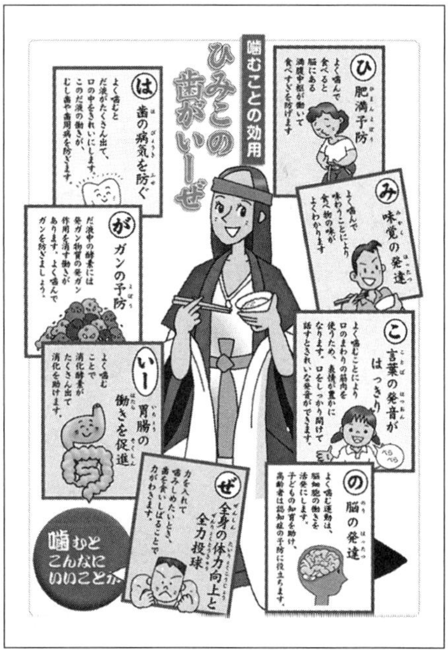

FIGURE 6. "Himiko's teeth are great!" Public service poster for the Campaign for Better Chewing, promoted by the Gakkō Shokuji Kenkyūkai (School Meals Study Group).

THE BAD, SAD, AND NAUGHTY HIMIKO

Not all artists and illustrators depict Himiko's power as located in superior spiritual and leadership skills. Often she is seen as manipulative, tyrannical, or downright wicked. In much contemporary culture, the experienced religious leader who united warring clans into a petty kingdom becomes a slutty babe with attitude. Himiko appeals particularly to the otaku dreams of game creators and card illustrators. Perhaps some culture producers believe that only an eroticized (or erotically infantilized) woman is capable of projecting enough convincing authority to usurp male privilege. These images of Himiko include sexy witches with hitched up skirts, plunging corsets, and enormous bosoms. In the Atlantica Online role-playing game, produced in Korea, she is just such a figure, the "Mercenary Empress Himiko."[26] Her wardrobe is neo-Renaissance steampunk streetwalker with hints of dominatrix.

In an erotic manga series aimed at women, Taniguchi Chika depicts Himiko as a raunchy queen who manages to rule while also spending much of her time engaged in interesting sexual adventures (Figure 7).[27] Another version of a sexpot Himiko is found in the Marvel comic series *The Savage Sword of Conan The Barbarian*.[28] The 1992 *Witch Queen of Yamatai* places Conan in the Far East, where he battles a cunning Queen of Yamatai, renamed Nojingo, who has kidnapped the Chinese Emperor. This vipress ruler wears a stripper's black plunging thong monokini with decorated tights. She is served by a troupe of samurai-attired Amazonian women. Similarly, Shinoda Masahiro's 1975 softcore film entitled *Himiko* used her persona in order to show lots of vivid writhing (Figure 8).[29] Here Himiko is a lascivious and conniving seductress who wants to have sex with her half brother. She is content to serve as a symbolic leader while the men around her hold the real authority. Eventually, she is justly executed by male kinsmen due to her depravity.

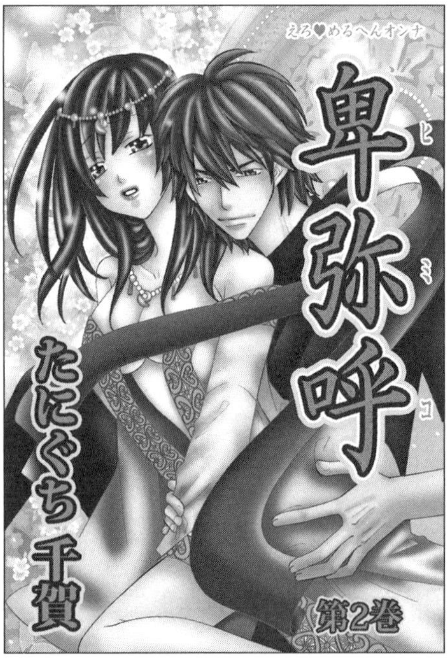

FIGURE 7. Cover image from volume 2 of Taniguchi Chika's manga *Ero meruhen onna Himiko* (2012, Adult fairytale Himiko), from the 2013 Sekirara Bunko digital edition.

Tezuka Osamu's much lauded *Phoenix* series, which stretches from the origins of civilization into the far future, includes Himiko in the first volume. In *The Phoenix: Dawn* (1967, *Hi no tori: Reimei hen*), Himiko is a ridiculous, brawling scold consumed with vanity.[30] From the *Wei zhi* we know she was savvy enough to begin diplomatic relations with the Chinese court, yet Tezuka presents her as narrowly obsessed with appearance and with finding the Phoenix who will restore eternal life and youthful beauty. When a solar eclipse occurs, Himiko cowers inside a cave, calling into question the shamanistic abilities that were part of her status. Scholars such as Rachael Hutchinson believe that Tezuka represented Himiko as an evil shrew because he was interested in discrediting the *Nihongi* and *Kojiki* through their portrayal of the *kami* (deity) Amaterasu. In other words, Himiko was a "mad shamaness that later became the tale of Amaterasu."[31] Tezuka's cave scene was meant to evoke the story of Amaterasu hiding in a cave after she was bullied by her brother. Most manga scholars and fans similarly hold an affirmative interpretation of Tezuka's portrayal, emphasizing that he was engaged in debunking mainstream historical discourse. It is indeed clear from the rest of the *Hi no tori* series that Tezuka uniformly draws authoritarian

IN MUCH CONTEMPORARY CULTURE, THE EXPERIENCED RELIGIOUS LEADER WHO UNITED WARRING CLANS INTO A PETTY KINGDOM BECOMES A SLUTTY BABE WITH ATTITUDE.

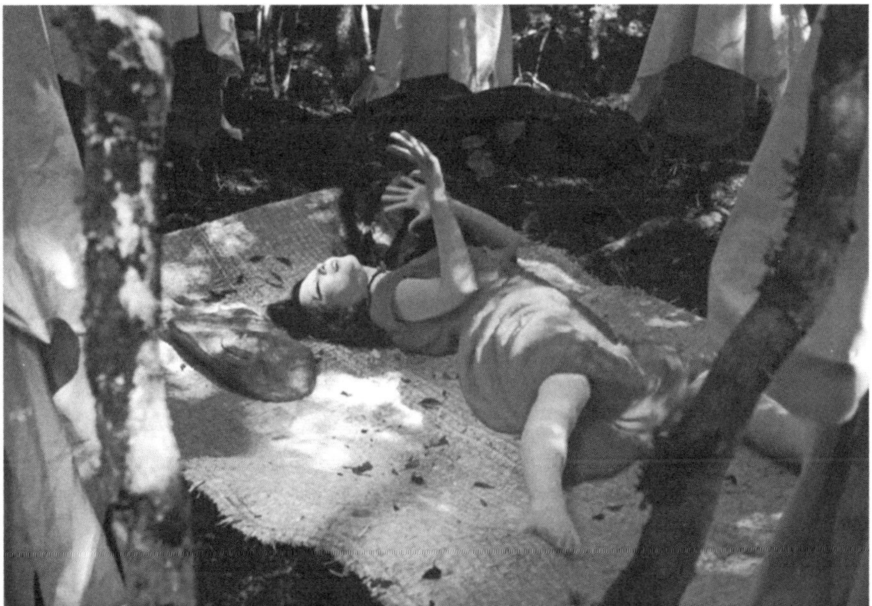

FIGURE 8. An image from the opening of Shinoda Masahiro's 1975 film *Himiko*.

rulers as venal and corrupt. But my criticism of how he uses Himiko for this critique rests on the manner in which he goes about demonizing her. There are many ways to illustrate women as wicked rulers without having to resort to sexist imagery. It is odd that, if this was Tezuka's intended critique, he would feel it important to include so many scenes of her yelling "My face! My face!" A female leader can certainly be symbolic of totalitarian excess without having to paint her as a presumptuous and unhappy virago.

Furthermore, the "Himiko became Amaterasu" theory is neither obvious or established. For centuries Himiko has been identified with various female characters mentioned in the *Kojiki* and the *Nihongi,* including Empress Jingū and two different Yamato princesses. Amaterasu was the clan deity (*ujigami*) for the Yamato lineage, and this is why she is featured in the Yamato mytho-histories. If we seek Himiko in these chronicles, she is most likely the person identified as the shaman aunt of Emperor Sujin, stripped of any political power. I find Patricia Tsurumi's discussion of early female rulers useful because she notes that women rulers were not necessarily intermediaries or exceptions, as many historians seem to assume.[32]

Scholars do not need to conflate different historical and mythological women in order to make sense of them. Female shamans were important figures in ancient Japan, and thus were not anomalies usurping male prerogative. Yet Tezuka depicted Himiko as ruling through bullying and fear, rather than the religious respect history indicates was accorded to her. Tezuka is often said to have been a great fan of Disney animation, and certainly his Himiko bears some slight resemblance to both Snow White's awful stepmother and Cruella De Vil. Among the anime adaptations of *Phoenix* is a 2004 TV series directed by Takahashi Ryōsuke (Figure 9).[33] Like the manga, the TV series does not recognize Himiko's power and authority as legitimate, and instead of a wise auntie queen's melody, her grating voice continuously delivers unreasonable demands. Rob Vollmer, in his review of this anime, states that Himiko is "the least ambiguous villain in a piece populated by heartless bastards all around."[34]

In other manga Himiko might be less vicious, yet remains a vehicle for expressing current cultural and political issues. In Mutsuki Nozomi's manga *Hakoniwa kigeki 1* (2012, Comedy garden 1), Himiko is a depressed young woman who feels trapped and frustrated by life's circumstances.[35] Mutsuki's melancholy Himiko grumbles about her gloomy life shut indoors with her handmaidens. When Himiko has a tantrum and bawls, "I want a boyfriend!" her assistants remind her that such a thing is impossible for a *miko* and instead find a pet gorilla to keep her company. She ends up liking the gorilla a bit

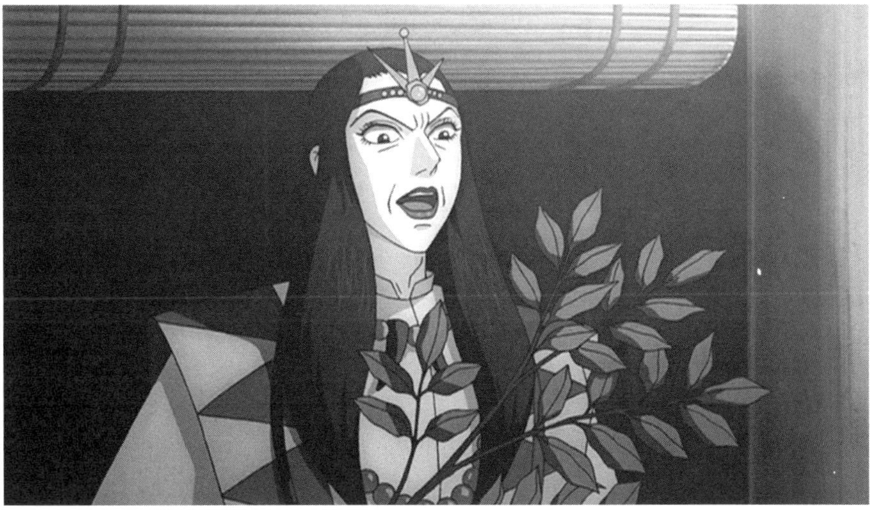

FIGURE 9. An image of Himiko from episode two of the *Phoenix* TV series, directed by Takahashi Ryōsuke.

too much. Instead of a great queen, she is an impaired and conflicted twenty-something who lacks magical talent and no longer performs at ritual events.

HIMIKO PARADOXES

Yasuko, the Shibuya divination provider introduced at the beginning of this essay, told me she was carrying on the knowledge passed down from the original queen shaman. In saying this, she was joining a larger discourse found in contemporary girl culture. Himiko appears in divination products and advertising to denote female power and ethnic spirituality. Himiko can be imagined as a symbol of female supernatural power today because creators of her image are not concerned with the same issues that obsessed illustrators in the past, such as her place in the imperial line. Yet even in the divination domain, Himiko reflects odd inconsistencies.

In *Akujo uranai* (2011, Evil woman divination), an ironic spin on divination types, the authors point out that the so-called evil woman of today is not what she was in the past.[36] Although rebellious and nonconforming, these bad girls might be an instructive way to gauge one's own character and future possibilities. "Evil women don't have such a bad meaning," they say, and offer a collection of types from world history, including Abe Sada, Murasaki Shikibu, Queen Elizabeth I, Joan of Arc, Mary Stuart, Cleopatra, and Himiko. The reader uses her own birthday to determine which of the evil woman categories corresponds to her own destiny. The "Villainess Type Himiko" is a divination maniac, self-centered and totally unrealistic. Neurotic and prone to emotional instability, she cares nothing for the opinions of others. So in this case, even though the text starts out to validate women previously labeled as troublemakers, Himiko's association with *kidō* has effectively erased any of her positive attributes.

But other contemporary divination-related images of Himiko are more positive. Hieda On Mayura is a divination provider and popular author of divination books and articles in most of the major weekly women's magazines, and claims to be the present-day reincarnation of Himiko.[37] She uses various methods, including tarot cards, a crystal ball, and a form of *kidō*. Hieda wears Chinese-style clothing, but her dangling earrings have tiny *magatama* on them. In her advertising profiles she presents a rather stern face to her prospective clients.

One fascinating development is the manner in which Himiko has become a motif on Japan-made tarot cards (Figure 10).[38] On these decks she replaces the High Priestess (the Papess or female Pope) to symbolize female religious authority. Many artists who make new tarot decks in Japan reject the Christian iconography found on early decks, and instead replace figures from European feudal times with those from ancient Japanese history and mythology. Because the original card was meant to depict a woman with a potent religious mandate, replacing the High Priestess with Himiko is common. On some of the Himiko High Priestess cards, she is depicted with *magatama* beads, a Chinese bronze mirror, a sword, or *sakaki* branch. She is often eroticized, and appears nude on at least one card.

These divination-related examples illustrate the oddity and diversity of narrative views that inform constructions of Himiko. Her images are symbolic of

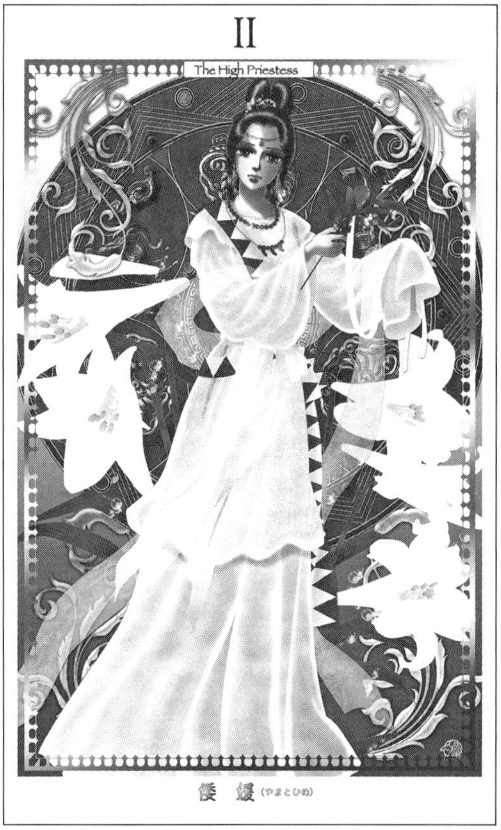

FIGURE 10. A tarot card design showing Himiko as the High Priestess, by Haru Usagi, originally published at http://albireo-haru.sakura.ne.jp/t.1saiguu.html. Courtesy of the artist.

tussles going on in gender politics. Sometimes she is part of a general effort to redeem seemingly rebellious women.[39] Control of Himiko images no longer resides in the hands of elite scribes or historians. Anyone—manga artists, fans, filmmakers, and others—may play with her story, persona, and image, which they freely imagine and promote in more widespread ways. Culture producers like to speak for her. “Kill that woman!” shrieks a jealous and hysterical Himiko in Tezuka’s manga, while a calmer woman addresses her willing subjects in Ishinomori’s version with “I do this for the sake of the people’s happiness and the preservation of the country of Yamatai.”[40] Knowledge of Kofun-era clothing styles has not prevented anyone from putting Himiko into a revealing bustier and stiletto boots. Knowing that she was the unifying ruler of warring chiefdoms has not stopped anyone from refashioning her as an ineffectual schoolgirl, or as a ditzy gal attired in a Jōmon-era tunic paired with Heisei-era Kogal boots.[41] She is a wicked necromancer in many media, but a shaman hero among divination specialists. These iterations have less to do with her origin story than with postwar anxieties about status and dominance. The threatening possibility of female power is contained by rescripting Himiko as an adorable yet weak maiden, an unhinged and ill-tempered dictator, or a wanton intriguer. Her role as a capable ruler appears to be beyond the imagination of modern audiences and producers.

THE THREATENING POSSIBILITY OF FEMALE POWER IS CONTAINED BY RESCRIPTING HIMIKO AS AN ADORABLE YET WEAK MAIDEN, AN UNHINGED AND ILL-TEMPERED DICTATOR, OR A WANTON INTRIGUER.

In the case of other resurrected historical figures, we may be able to trace their reemergence to specific cultural developments. Medieval wizard Abeno Seimei’s sudden celebrity status in popular culture followed the publication of a series of popular novels and manga.[42] The interest in Himiko, however, is much more diffuse. It is obviously linked to a relaxation in older imperial ideology that reified patrilineal kinship, yet her postwar uses among pornographers, filmmakers, manga artists, game creators, divination card illustrators, and novelists reflects many issues beyond this. Current Himiko branding allows the viewer to place her in a known constellation of female slots that either buttress or challenge existing stereotypes. What we know about Himiko is so provocative, so murky, and so far in the distant past that it provides much room for creative intervention. In a cultural field populated with women warriors, avatars, and continued debate over how to locate women’s power in Japan, Himiko’s own elastic story makes her image ripe for ideological work in the twenty-first century.

Notes

I would like to thank participants at the Symposium on Pop Heroines and Female Icons of Japan, hosted by the University of Missouri–Saint Louis, where I initially presented this essay. Gratitude for generous funding is also extended to the Japan–United States Friendship Commission and the Northeast Asia Council of the Association for Asian Studies. Jan Bardsley and Christopher Bolton gave me especially helpful feedback. Rebecca Copeland, Jennifer Robertson, and others also contributed suggestions.

1. Laurel Thatcher Ulrich, *Well-Behaved Women Seldom Make History* (New York: Alfred A. Knopf, 2007).

2. For a recent English translation of this section of the *Wei zhi,* see Edward J. Kidder, *Himiko and Japan's Elusive Chiefdom of Yamatai: Archaeology, History, and Mythology* (Honolulu: University of Hawai'i Press, 2007).

3. Some of the most recent English language scholarship is found in Kidder, *Himiko,* and Gina L. Barnes, *State Formation in Japan: Emergence of a Fourth-Century Ruling Elite* (London: Routledge, 2007). See also Walter Edwards, "In Pursuit of Himiko: Postwar Archaeology and the Location of Yamatai," *Monumenta Nipponica* 51, no.1 (1996): 53–79.

4. *Magatama,* because of their long association with ancient Japan and Himiko, have become a faddish charm in girl culture, and are featured in magazine articles and sold in bead shops.

5. Ishino Hironobu, "Rites and Rituals of the Kofun Period," *Japanese Journal of Religious Studies* 19, no. 2–3 (1992): 191–216.

6. The confusion about Himiko's era is widespread. Esther Friesner produced two novels featuring Himiko as a child and shaman warrior. In interviews Friesner claims she consulted reliable histories, yet details in the books suggest an early Yayoi milieu. Oddly, the covers depict Himiko wearing later kimono-style clothing. Esther Friesner, *Spirit's Princess* (New York: Random House, 2012); Esther Friesner, *Spirit's Chosen* (New York: Random House, 2013); Matt Staggs, "An Interview with Esther Friesner, Author, *Spirit's Princess*," http://suvudu.com/2012/04/an-interview-with-esther-friesner-author-spirits-princess.html.

7. Fujiwara Kamui, *Himiko: Shūkan manga Nihon shi 1-gō* (Himiko: Weekly manga history of Japan, issue 1) (Tokyo: Asahi Shinbunsha, 2009).

8. One wonders if the Jōmon-era clothing was an attempt to make Himiko appear to be more natively Japanese and less like the Korea-derived culture and people that characterize the Kofun era.

9. Carmen Blacker, *The Catalpa Bow: A Study of Shamanistic Practices in Japan* (London: Allen and Unwin, 1975).

10. Blacker, *The Catalpa Bow,* chapters 6, 7, and 8.

11. Rekishi no Shinsō Kenkyūkai, *Gakkō de oshiete kurenai: Hontō no Nihonshi* (You aren't taught this in school: The real history of Japan) (Tokyo: Asahi Shinbunsha, 2012), 302.

12. See Kidder, *Himiko,* for snake cult, and Barnes, *State Formation,* for Queen Mother of the West.

13. Iio posting to "Tagu Himiko o fukumu irasuto" (Illustrations with tags that include Himiko), http://seiga.nicovideo.jp/seiga/im752459?track=seiga_illust_keyword.

14. Ishinomori Shōtarō, *Manga Nihon no rekishi vol. 2: Yamataikoku to Himiko no matsurigoto* (The country of Yamatai and Himiko's governance) (Tokyo: Chūō Kōronsha, 1997), 18.

15. Kobayashi Yoshinori, *Gōmanizumu sengen special: Shin tennōron* (A special arrogant manifesto: A new theory of the emperor) (Tokyo: Shōgakukan, 2010).

16. Saegusa Kazuko, *Joō no Himiko* (The Empress Himiko) (Tokyo: Kōdansha, 1991).

17. Miyazaki Kōhei, *Maboroshi no Yamataikoku* (The illusive country of Yamatai) (Tokyo: Kōdansha, 1967).

18. *Maboroshi no Yamataikoku* (The illusive country of Yamatai), dir. Tsutsumi Yukihiko, DVD (Tōei, 2009).

19. "Yoshinaga Sayuri Is Queen Himiko," *Japan Zone Entertainment News,* http://www.japan-zone.com/news/2008/08/22/yoshinaga_sayuri_is_queen_himiko.shtml).

20. Himiko statues are found all over Kyūshū: outside Kanzaki Station, near Miyazaki Takachiho Gorge, and on the grounds of Himiko Shrine in Hayato.

21. Sakurai City, "Himiko-chan no peeji" (Miss Himiko's page) http://www.city.sakurai.nara.jp/himiko/index.html.

22. Torigoe Kenzaburō, *Oinaru Yamataikoku* (Great country of Yamatai) (Tokyo: Kōdansha 1975).

23. Sawai Ryūsuke, *Yamataikoku Ōmi setsu: Kodai Ōmi no ten to sen* (Yamataikoku Ōmi theory: Points and lines to ancient Ōmi) (Tokyo: Gentōsha Renaissance, 2010).

24. Mama Riina, "Kuiin Himiko ishō" (Queen Himiko's costume), http://ameblo.jp/ri-namama/theme-10038768211.html.

25. Okawa Ryūhō, *Josei riidaa nyūmon: Himiko, Kōmyō Kōgō ga okuru, genzai joseitachi e no adobaisu* (Introduction to female leaders: Advice for contemporary women given by Himiko and Empress Kōmyō) (Tokyo: Kōfuku no Kagaku Shuppan, 2011). The idea of Himiko as a leader is also seen in Takemoto Novala's novel *Shimotsuma monogatari,* in which the mythical embroiderer and head of the Ibaragi group of girl bikers was named Himiko. Takemoto Novala, *Shimotsuma monogatari* (Tokyo: Shōgakukan, 2002); translated by Masumi Washington as *Kamikaze Girls* (San Francisco: Viz, 2008).

26. *Atlantica Online*, free computer game (NDOORS/Nexon Corporation, 2008).

27. Taniguchi Chika, *Otona: Meruhen onna Himiko* (Adult: Fairytale woman Himiko) (Tokyo: Takarazuka Wandaanetto, 2012).

28. Roy Thomas, John Buscema, and Ernie Chen, *The Savage Sword of Conan The Barbarian: The Witch Queen of Yamatai,* no. 194: 1–45 (New York: Marvel Comics, 1992).

29. *Himiko,* dir. Shinoda Masahiro, DVD (Art Theatre Guild, 1975).

30. Tezuka Osamu, *Hi no tori: Reimei hen,* vol. 1 (Tokyo: Kadokawa Shoten, 1967); translated by Dadakai as *Phoenix, vol. 1: Dawn* (San Francisco: Viz, 2003).

31. Rachael Hutchinson, "Sabotaging the Rising Sun: Representing History in Tezuka Osamu's *Phoenix,*" in *Manga and the Representation of Japanese History,* ed. Roman Rosenbaum (New York: Routledge 2012), 27.

32. Patricia Tsurumi makes the point in regard to a later string of female sovereigns, of which there were eight between 592 and 770. Patricia Tsurumi, "The Male Present versus the Female Past: Historians and Japan's Female Emperors," *Bulletin of Concerned Asian Scholars* 14 (1982): 71–75.

33. *Hi no tori,* dir. Takahashi Ryōsuke, TV series, 13 episodes (2004); translated as *Phoenix: Perfect Collection,* 3-DVD box set (Anime Works, 2010). For the early episodes that feature Himiko, see volume 1 (2004, *The Persistence of Time*).

34. Rob Vollmar, "Phoenix Volume One: Dawn-Recommended," *Manga Reviews,* http://comicsworthreading.com/2007/06/01/phoenix-volume-one-dawn-recommended/.

35. Mutsuki Nozomi, *Hakoniwa kigeki 1* (Comedy garden 1), (Tokyo: Entaaburein, 2012).

36. Fumiki and Noguchi Kōshin, *Akujo uranai* (Evil woman divination) (Tokyo: Futami Shobō, 2011).

37. Hieda Onmayura, "Genzai ni yomigaeshi Himiko Hieda Onmayura," http://www.nifty.com/onmayura.

38. Laura Miller, "Tantalizing Tarot and Cute Cartomancy in Japan," *Japanese Studies* 31, no. 1 (2011): 73–91.

39. See Rekishi no Shinsō Kenkyūkai, *Jidai o yurugashita dokufu no shinjitsu* (The truth about poison women who rocked the ages: The enigma of ninety-nine evil women from Japanese history) (Tokyo: Takarajima-sha, 2009).

40. Tezuka, *Hi no tori,* 224; Ishinomori, *Manga Nihon no rekishi,* 146.

41. *Warriors Orochi 2,* Playstation 2 video game (Koei, 2008). Her weapons are anachronistic Jōmon-derived *dogū* figurines that fire laser pellets.

42. Laura Miller, "Extreme Makeover for a Heian-Era Wizard," *Mechademia* 3: 30–45.

CHRISTOPHER BOLTON

Tezuka's *Buddha* at the Tokyo National Museum: An Interview with Matsumoto Nobuyuki

In the summer of 2011, the Tokyo National Museum held an unprecedented exhibition titled *Buddha: The Story in* Manga *and Art,* featuring Tezuka Osamu's landmark *Buddha* manga (1972–83).[1] This was the first exhibition to include manga in the 140-year history of the museum, the flagship cultural institution that anchors museum row in Tokyo's Ueno Park. But what was most remarkable was the visual and cultural context in which it placed Tezuka, by juxtaposing pages from the manga with twenty examples of premodern Buddhist sculpture, ranging from second-century Pakistani stone reliefs to medieval Japanese statuary.

The exhibition demonstrated something that has been argued several times in the pages of *Mechademia*: that we can discover a great deal about manga and anime as media by examining how they have been translated for display, study, or consumption in the space of the museum.[2] To learn more about the *Buddha* exhibition, I spoke with its curator Matsumoto Nobuyuki, director of the Curatorial Planning Department at the museum and head curator in Asian Art. I have translated our conversation, which took place two weeks after the opening in early May of 2011. It was also just two months after the earthquake and tidal wave in eastern Japan, and in the midst of the ongoing nuclear disaster at the Fukushima power plants 150 miles north of Tokyo. I had threaded my way through darkened streets to the museum for the interview: many streetlights and neon signs still remained eerily extinguished at night, to conserve electricity and observe a respectful austerity. As discussed at the end of the interview, this provided both a poignant and a pointed context for the exhibition.

In addition to revealing how the show came together, Matsumoto's comments shed light on several senses of "origin" that are taken up in this volume: the connections between premodern and contemporary art, the status of an original artwork in the context of mass media like manga and anime, and the issues of historical and artistic biography that inevitably seem to dominate our thinking about a work like Tezuka's *Buddha*.

CHRISTOPHER BOLTON: I saw the exhibition this week, and I thought it was wonderful. The individual artworks are striking in their own right, but the way they are juxtaposed is also very thought provoking. My own work centers very much on media comparisons, and what we can tell about anime and manga by contrasting them with other media. Comparing Tezuka's *Buddha* manga with Buddhist statuary is an inspired idea. What was the initial impulse for this show, and where did the idea for that comparison come from?

MATSUMOTO NOBUYUKI: I'm delighted you liked the exhibition. As you know the anime film based on Tezuka Osamu's *Buddha* manga is due out later this month. Tōei Company contacted us last fall to say they were making this film and asked us if we would consider an exhibition related to Tezuka's *Buddha*. But because this museum deals with traditional Japanese and Asian culture (basically pre-nineteenth-century materials), a show just on Tezuka falls outside our purview. So at first I suggested that Tōei approach one of the modern art museums in Tokyo; the National Museum of Modern Art had a large-scale Tezuka exhibition several years ago. But they were very interested in doing something with us, and I was interested myself—I read the manga when it came out and I'm a fan. So I started to think about how to combine contemporary manga and anime with traditional culture.

The hero of Tezuka's manga is obviously the historical figure of the Buddha, so I thought if we brought it together with Buddhist statuary, one could see the manga in a historical context, and we could get fans of anime and manga interested in traditional culture. And since most of our usual visitors are interested in traditional culture or history, I thought with this exhibition

BY COMPARING TWO-DIMENSIONAL AND THREE-DIMENSIONAL MEDIA, WE WANTED TO ENCOURAGE PEOPLE TO EXPAND THE IMAGE THEY HAD OF THIS FIGURE.

we could also show them the merits of manga and anime. That was the origin of the idea.

CB: That's very interesting. But if you wanted to juxtapose the manga with traditional or historical images of the Buddha, you could have chosen Buddhist painting for example, or something in a similar medium. Why did you choose Buddhist sculpture?

MN: Comparing different two-dimensional media does not provide a very interesting contrast. And I think it is three-dimensional art, like reliefs and statuary, that provides the strongest image (*imeeji*) of the historical Buddha, of Shakyamuni. It lets you picture him. By comparing two-dimensional and three-dimensional media, we wanted to encourage people to expand the image they had of this figure.

CB: And Tezuka's *Buddha* manga is represented by hand-drawn and -inked page art. Can you say something about that?

MN: All manga is printed from these hand-drawn, camera-ready originals called *genga*. But the *genga* and the final printed version of the manga are not at all the same. The size, the color, the touch of the pen—everything is different. I think it's the *genga* that more closely convey Tezuka's original idea (*orijinaru na omoi*), so I thought that's what we should display. After all, the sculptures are all original artworks, too. We wanted to emphasize that original quality.

There really are all sorts of things you can't see once the *genga* are printed and published as manga—like the way Tezuka traces the design, drawing one layer over another, or the texture of the ink. We have some color drawings in the exhibition that appeared on the covers of the manga volumes, and the actual drawings are completely different from the printed covers—the way the paint is applied, the detail, and the three-dimensional quality that emerges even in a two-dimensional medium. Again, this is a museum, so as far as possible we want visitors to see original works.

CB: In many of those color images, Tezuka draws the Buddha against a background that simulates a relief carving or a three-dimensional surface (Figure 1). It's a flat medium, but there is definitely a three-dimensional quality.

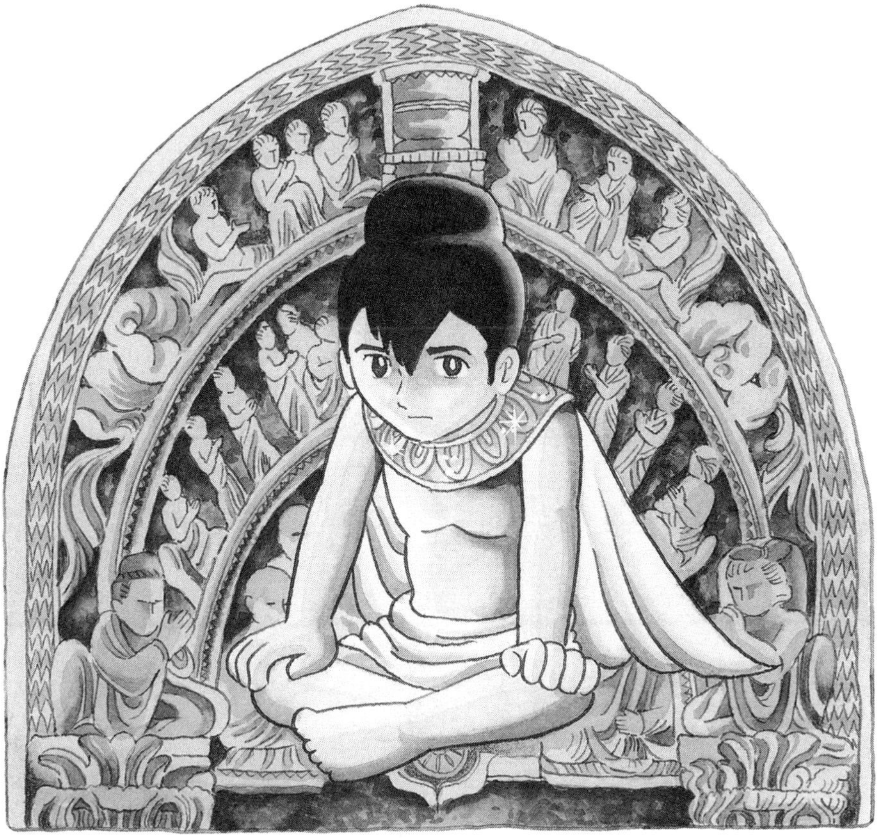

FIGURE 1. A watercolor *genga* (camera-ready artwork) for the cover of *Buddha*, volume 3, in the *Osamu Tezuka manga zenshū* edition (Kōdansha, 1983–84). Copyright Tezuka Productions. Images 1–7 are reproduced from the exhibition catalog, *Tezuka Osamu no Budda ten / Buddha: The Story in* Manga *and Art*, ed. Tokyo National Museum and TŌEI Company Ltd., trans. Maiko Behr (Tokyo National Museum, 2011).

MN: Yes, exactly. This show is a rare chance to see so many of Tezuka's color *genga*. There's a real beauty to these, in the color and in the level of detail. These are drawn with much more care than his black-and-white pages. For Tezuka, I think these color *genga* were works of art that go above and beyond his manga. This was his work as a fine artist. And again, you can only see that in the original *genga*. That's why we chose to put them in frames so you could get close to them. As much as possible we also avoided putting the sculptures in cases, so you can see them up close as well. Even just doing away with the glass lets us have visitors get near the art, and reduces that feeling of separation (*iwakan*).

CB: But as you said, I noticed you can see some of those details and even that three-dimensional quality in *genga* for the regular manga pages as well. There, too, I noticed the layers created by pieces of paper pasted over revisions or mistakes (Figures 2 and 4).

MN: Yes, and some areas are painted over with white out.

CB: But those corrected areas become fewer and fewer as the series goes on. The scene of the Buddha's death, from the end of the final volume, is pristine, with no corrections whatsoever.

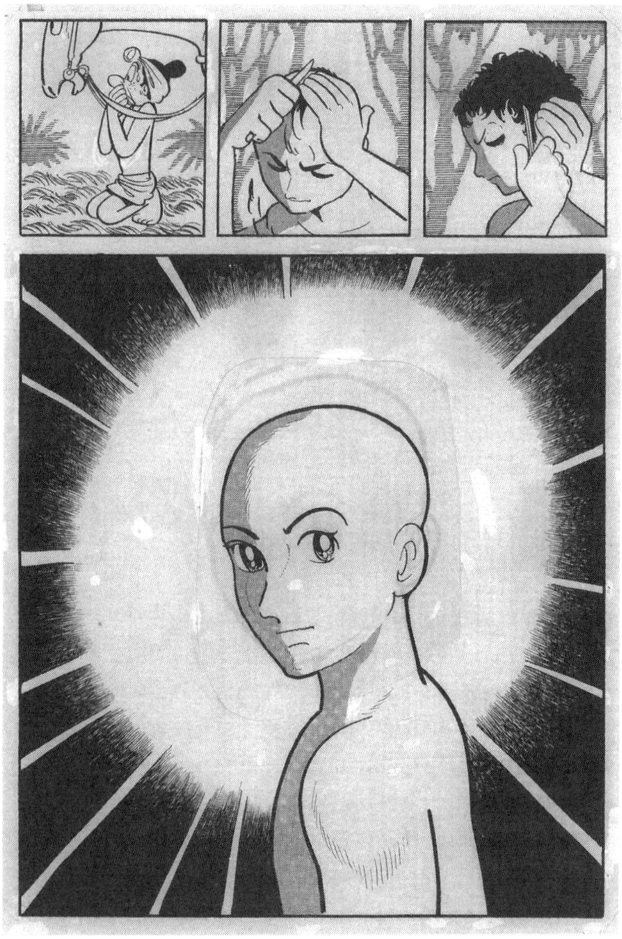

FIGURE 2. The head-shaving scene that signifies renunciation of the world, from Tezuka's *Buddha*. This hand-drawn *genga* has a layer of paper pasted over the center area, showing where Tezuka redrew the head with slightly different proportions. In the original serialization, this page appeared in the August 1974 issue of *Kibō no tomo*. Copyright Tezuka Productions.

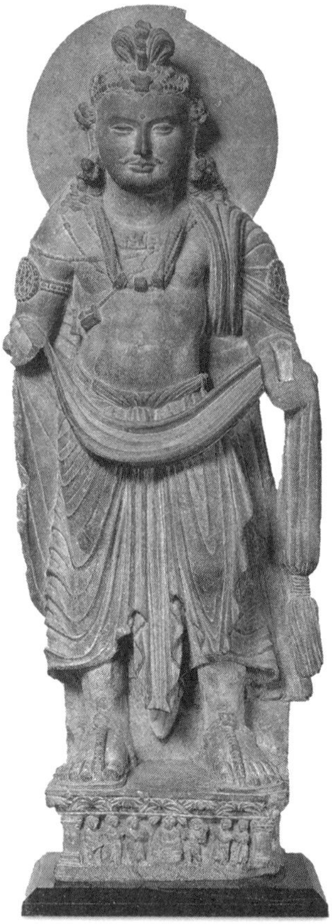

FIGURE 3. Standing Bodhisattva. This second- or third-century stone image from Gandhara, Pakistan, shows the same kind of halo depicted in Tezuka's drawing (Figure 2). 100 cm. Collection of the Tokyo National Museum. Copyright Tokyo National Museum.

MN: Yes. It seems Tezuka became very practiced at drawing these images as time went by.

CB: So the exhibition is organized around the biography of the historical Buddha, but the drawings become a record of the artist's life as well.

MN: Exactly. And you can only see that in the *genga*.

POINTS OF COMPARISON

CB: I was interested in your essay in the exhibition catalog. You write that Tezuka's manga and the sculptures are all interpretations of the Buddha's life, each informed by its own place and time, and you suggest that visitors can construct their own vision of the Buddha. You also mention that there are faithful or historical parts to Tezuka's depiction but also more creative parts.[3] Comparing the manga with the sculpture, what are the contrasts that stand out most for you?

MN: Before I actually put them side-by-side, when we were still in the planning stage imagining what the gallery would look like, I was worried that the sculpture and the manga would present themselves as completely different things. So I wanted to try to blend them in such a way that there would be no disjunction between them, so that visitors could look at each separately but also see them as a whole and create an image of the Buddha's life. But when we actually put them side-by-side, they blended (*tokeatta*) much more naturally than I had thought. So it's not the contrast but this unexpected similarity or harmony that stands out for me.

CB: Yet the sculpture has been carefully chosen to present a wide variety of images of the Buddha at different stages of his life, and the manga adds even more variety.

MN: Yes, but they're not just lined up together; they supplement one another. The manga captures one part, and what's not in the manga is captured by the sculpture. I believe in the gallery they achieve a kind of interdependence (*sōkan kankei*).

CB: The portions from the manga that you selected match the sculptures perfectly (Figures 2, 3, 4, and 5). But the manga must have offered a wide range of scenes that would resemble any given sculpture. How did you select the manga scenes that you would exhibit?

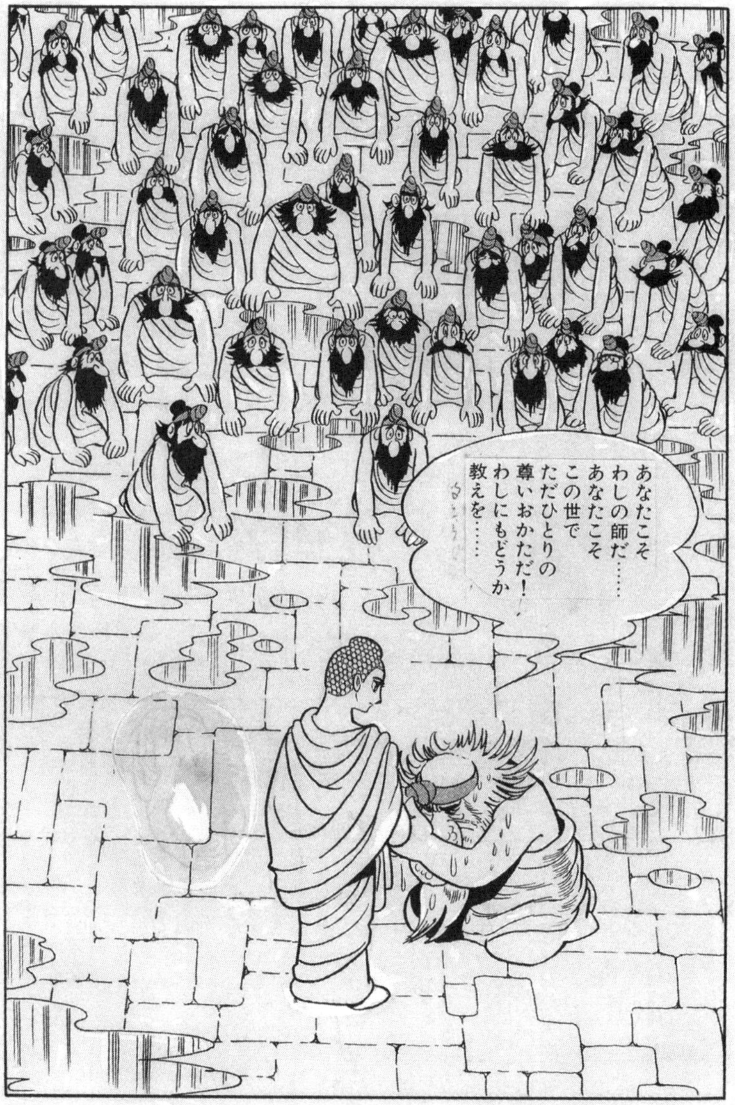

FIGURE 4. Buddha converts the Kasyapa brothers. In the original *genga*, one can see that an additional figure just to the Buddha's left has been pasted over, giving more prominence to the two figures in the foreground. Originally published in *Kibō no tomo* in July 1980. Copyright Tezuka Productions.

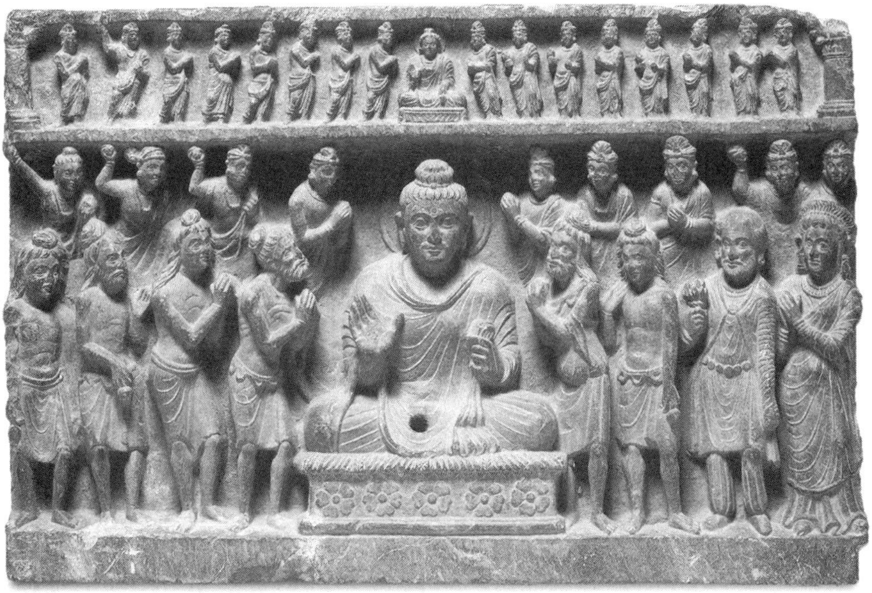

FIGURE 5. "Kasyapa Brothers Worshipping Buddha," from Illustrated Scenes of the Life of Buddha. A second- or third-century stone relief from Afghanistan. 59 × 88 cm. Copyright The Japanese Committee for the Protection from Dispersement of Cultural Properties.

MN: That was the most challenging part. *Buddha* is fourteen volumes, over a thousand pages in all, with several frames on each page. And there's an endless amount of Buddhist sculpture out there, from India, Pakistan, China, Korea, Southeast Asia, and Japan, dating from the second century down to today. The hardest thing was deciding which sculpture to combine with which image from the manga. But we didn't just match things that resembled one another; we deliberately paired things that were a little bit different, to produce that mutual supplementarity I mentioned. The result is that you see both, and then you start to construct a story from them.

CB: But the point of departure was the idea to trace the Buddha's life chronologically, in both media?

MN: Yes, that was the starting point, and we chose the materials from there. Tezuka only portrayed the life of Shakyamuni from birth to death, but actually in Buddhism there's also the story of his previous incarnations. So we chose to include two reliefs depicting the Buddha's previous existence and the time after his death, when he is placed in the coffin—things not in the manga. Then we picked the highlights from his life that we wanted to portray, for example his birth, his marriage, his leaving the palace. Finally we thought about which sculpture would go with a specific event, for example, and which page in the manga would fit that sculpture.

TIME AND THE STORY UNFOLD FROM ONE WORK TO THE OTHER. THIS IS HOW WE PUT THE EXHIBITION TOGETHER.

CB: So you chose the sculptures first, and then selected the manga scenes to match?

MN: No, it went both ways. There were some powerful scenes from the manga that I knew I wanted to use, for example the scene where he shaves his head (Figure 2).

CB: Were there any other scenes you particularly wanted to include?

MN: The scene of the Buddha as a baby. Also the marriage scene. There's not a single example of the marriage depicted in sculpture, but it's an important moment, and the language in that section of the manga shows Tezuka's sense of humor, a trademark of this work. If you look only at sculpture, you'll never be able to picture this scene and its humanity (*ningensei*).

As for sculpture, there was one particular statue from the Nara National Museum that I definitely wanted to include. It's a rare opportunity to see this work; it hasn't been exhibited in Tokyo in decades. It shows the Buddha after he has emerged from the mountains at the end of a period of ascetic practice. The subject is a common one—there would be no real point in comparing it with the same scene from the manga. So we chose these scenes from the manga where he's in the midst of these austerities (Figures 6 and 7). Time and the story unfold from one work to the other. This is how we put the exhibition together.

CB: It's striking how the different pieces work together in the gallery. The atmosphere of the exhibition space itself was also very innovative. The high ceiling, and up on the walls, the green lighting that outlined those leafy silhouettes—it was like being in a jungle, or in one of Tezuka's primeval worlds (Figure 8).

MN: I was thinking if one were to represent the image of the Buddha, Shakyamuni, with a color, what would it be? Buddhism is a religion centered on freedom from struggle: learning peace, escaping suffering, helping others. For me the color that matches that image is green. And Nepal, where the Buddha was active, is a lush green place. So the image of the environment when the Buddha was alive was probably forests, groves, grasslands. That's how we chose green for the background color. Did you notice the shadows were moving?

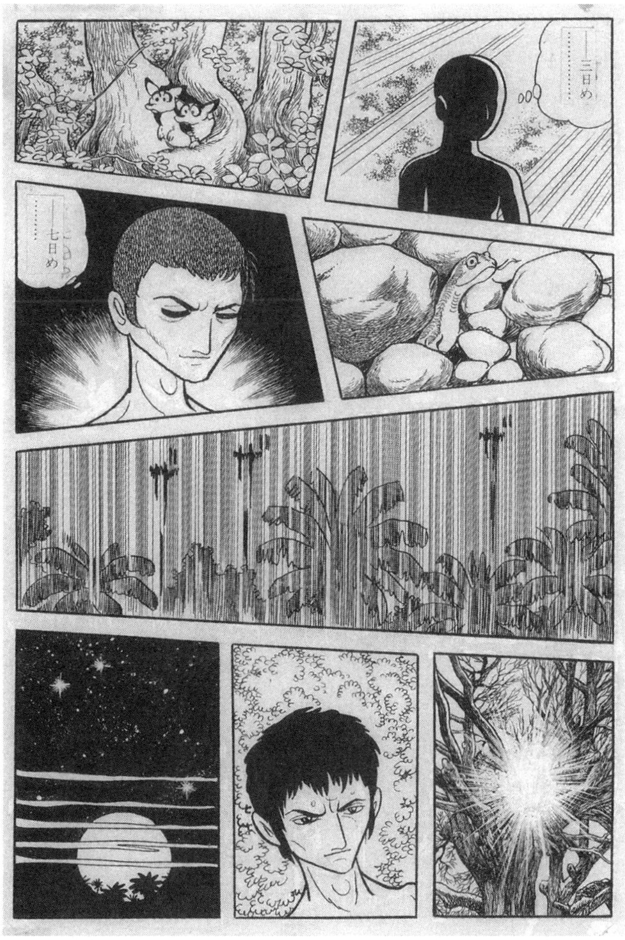

FIGURE 6. The Buddha practicing austerities. *Genga* for a page originally published in *Kibō no tomo* in November 1975. Copyright Tezuka Productions.

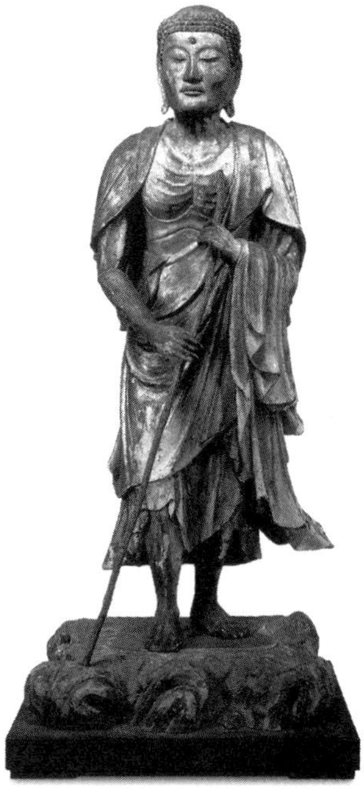

FIGURE 7. Shakya Emerging from the Mountains. This fourteenth-century Japanese sculpture depicts Buddha at the completion of his austerities. Wood with gold overlay. 96.3 cm. Collection of the Nara National Museum. Copyright Nara National Museum.

CB: Yes, that was very effective!

MN: We used small fans to move the leaves and projected the shadows on the wall. The manga and statuary don't move, so to enrich the image visitors would have, we wanted to introduce some movement separate from the art. Even if you don't look up at the moving shadows, you notice them at the edge of your vision when you are in the gallery. It affects you without your realizing it.

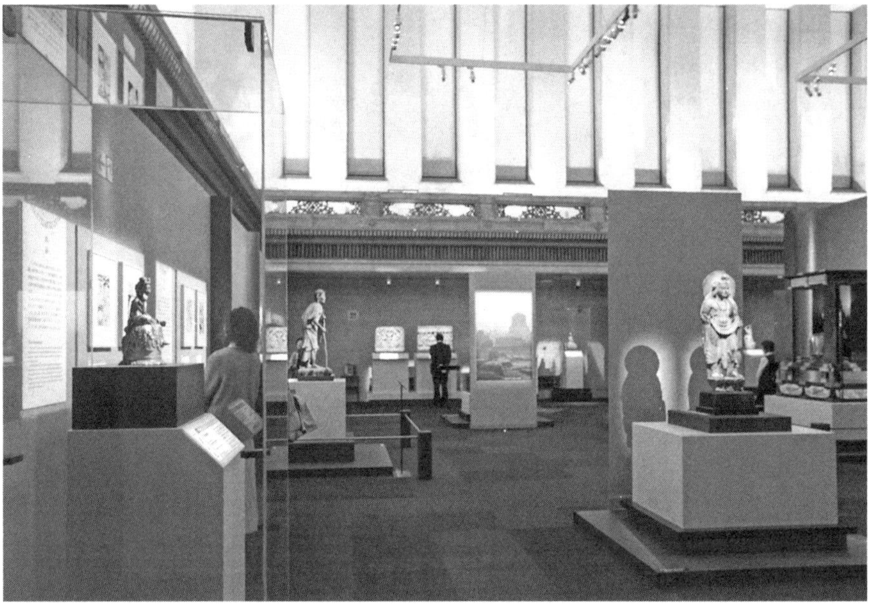

FIGURE 8. The exhibition space was characterized by its innovative arrangement and display of materials, as well as a subtle sense of movement generated by lighting effects projected on the upper walls. Photograph courtesy of the Tokyo National Museum. Copyright Tokyo National Museum.

YOUNG AND OLD, OLD AND NEW

CB: So this is the first exhibition at the Tokyo National Museum to incorporate manga?

MN: Yes, the first one.

CB: It has been open for two weeks now. What has the response been like so far?

MN: The majority of the people who come to the museum are in their forties, fifties, or sixties. But for this exhibition, the largest category of visitors has been people in their thirties, then teenagers, then people in their twenties. That includes a number of people who are coming to the museum for the first time.

CB: There was quite a variety of visitors when I was there, and different people definitely seemed to be looking at the art in different ways. How many people have seen the exhibition?

MN: We have had about 1,800 people a day on average, which is surprisingly good for something this size. The proposal came just last fall, so we put it together in six months, a very short time, and we could only allot about 500 square meters of gallery space. (In comparison, we're now doing a major show of the eighteenth-century woodblock print artist Sharaku, and that gets 4,000–5,000 people a day, but it occupies about six times the floor space.) Ideally I would have liked to make the *Buddha* exhibition somewhat larger, with a greater variety of materials, but given the restrictions I'm happy with the result. This time was a kind of experiment. We wanted to have as many people as possible see the exhibition and get as much feedback as we could.

CB: It's impressive that at a museum specializing in pre-twentieth-century material, Tezuka can compete with Sharaku. He is among the most well-known artists in a popular genre, *ukiyoe* woodblock prints.

MN: Yes, and the Sharaku exhibition is a major event. It has been five years in the making, and it brings the best Sharaku prints from around the world. It's conceived of as a definitive show.

CB: The first time I visited this museum was in the 1980s, and my memory is that there were not many woodblock prints exhibited. For me things like manga, graphic design, and *ukiyoe* prints like Sharaku's all share some of the same aesthetic qualities. Manga has certainly become more and more popular. Have exhibits of things like *ukiyoe* increased in the last three decades?

MN: The status of *ukiyoe* as art has not changed so much. What has changed a little bit is that Japanese themselves have attained a more global perspective and become conscious of the judgments of people abroad. For example, woodblock artists like Sharaku and Hokusai are very popular in the United States and Europe. It's true that to some extent museums have begun to exhibit more of this work. But for Japanese, *ukiyoe* is just one part of Japanese culture, so even now we don't have many large exhibits focusing exclusively on *ukiyoe*.

CB: Manga and anime are also popular abroad, and the Japanese government has become conscious of these as cultural exports. There's the Cool Japan campaign, for example. Do you think museum practices will change in connection with this?

THE DESIGN OF THE EXHIBITION POSTER INCORPORATED SOME THINGS THAT WERE NEW FOR US, BOTH IN THE GRAPHICS AND THE TEXT. THAT BRIGHT PINK TEXT AGAINST THE GREEN BACKGROUND—WE'VE NEVER USED A COLOR QUITE LIKE THAT BEFORE.

MN: Yes, to some extent. But for Japanese (and others), manga and anime were rooted in everyday life long before the government did any of this. Even people in my generation think the government's idea to incorporate anime and manga into national policy is coming rather late [*laughs*].

CB: But when something is familiar from everyday life, doesn't that make it hard to start thinking of it as fine art?

MN: It's true, it does. When something is always so intimately present, often people are less likely to think of it as part of art or tradition. But just as in the case of woodblock prints, when manga and anime became popular in other places, then Japanese realized there might be more to these things than they had thought, and began to think of them as fine art or as an extension of traditional culture. In a way it's a case of reverse importation.

CB: That's very interesting. Was there anything that was particularly challenging about organizing the *Buddha* exhibition?

MN: We changed the publicity activities significantly from the way we've traditionally done things at this museum. The design of the exhibition poster incorporated some things that were new for us, both in the graphics and the text. That bright pink text against the green background—we've never used a color quite like that before.

And the Sharaku exhibition poster was influenced by that. It is also very different from previous posters. For example, the image of the Sharaku print on the poster is cropped—we cut out the center of the image to bring the top and bottom parts together. We had never done that. At this museum one of our first principles is to exhibit the thing *as is*; so as far as possible we avoid manipulating the original. But this time we aimed for visual interest (Figures 9 and 10).

To appeal to a young audience we also used blogging and Twitter much more actively than for other exhibitions. Mizuki Nana, a voice actress from the anime, recorded the audio guide and attended the opening. We had some interesting guests there, the kind of people we don't usually see at the museum, who came to see her [*laughs*].

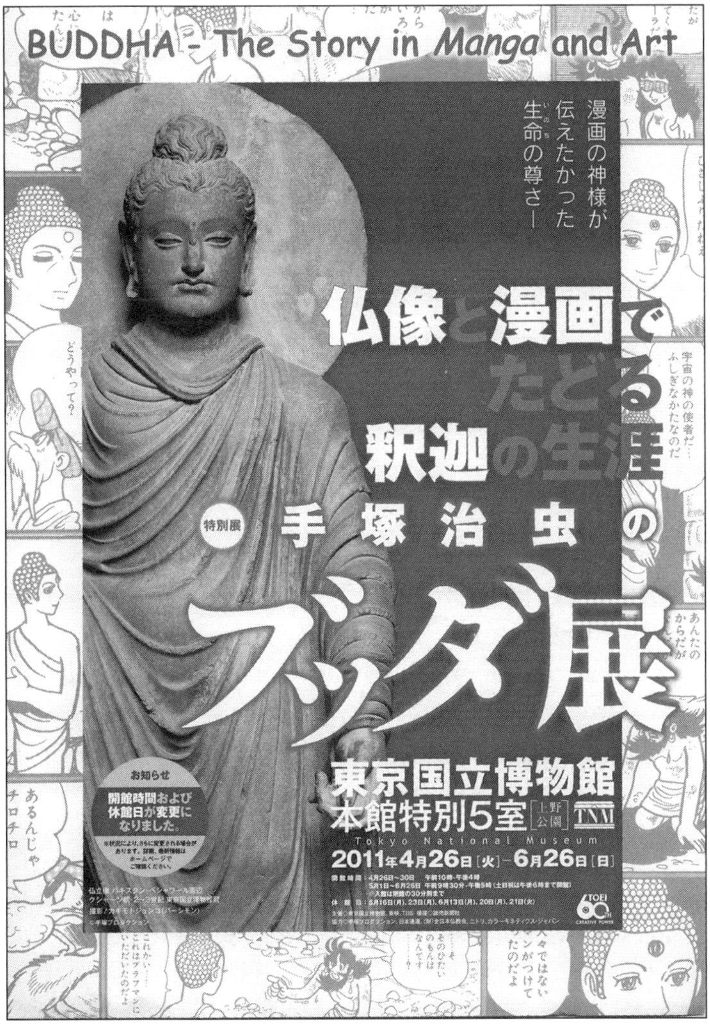

FIGURE 9. The exhibit flyer's novel design. The text says in part: "The sanctity of life, as expressed by the god of manga." Copyright Tokyo National Museum.

FIGURE 10 (BELOW). A sign outside the museum advertising the Buddha and Sharaku exhibitions together. Like the flyer in figure 9, the Buddha sign has a bright green background with text in white and hot pink, which is carried over into a pink, black, white, and yellow scheme on the strikingly cropped Sharaku poster. Copyright Tokyo National Museum. Photograph by Christopher Bolton.

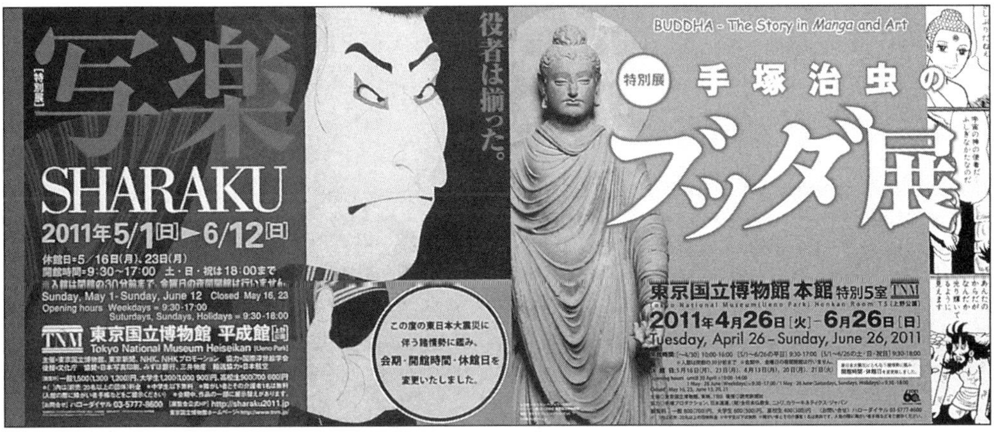

CB: I've been to some conferences like that! But that's part of the fun.

MN: Yes, certainly. As a museum, unless we change, if we think only of tradition, tradition, tradition, and nothing else, we'll quickly become a stale place. We have to be as creative as possible.

CB: That's exciting—I'm very excited to see what you come up with in the future.

MN: Thank you.

CB: Before we end, is there anything we didn't touch on that you wanted visitors to know about the exhibition?

MN: One hidden message of the exhibition relates to the recent earthquake and disasters in eastern Japan. As I mentioned, when we were first planning the exhibition, the themes we wanted to include through Tezuka's *Buddha* included things like peace, or helping others, or escaping suffering. Then the earthquake happened, and now all of Japan is suffering. So we're hoping people can enjoy the exhibition but also take away that message of aiding others, of peace.

CB: In the wake of the earthquake, certainly some of us who write about these things are asking how art, literature, or popular culture can respond to it, and how we can respond in our own writing.

MN: It does make you think. From that perspective, I've felt anew that Tezuka's manga, including *Buddha,* has a universality to it. Among manga, Tezuka's style is not at all new; he probably falls under the category of classic manga. But because of that, I think maybe it's a form that will always be with us.

Notes

1. Tezuka Osamu, *Budda,* vols. 288–300 of *Tezuka Osamu manga zenshū* (Tezuka Osamu's complete manga) (Tokyo: Kōdansha, 1983–84); translated by Yuji Oniki, Maya Rosewood [et al.?] as *Buddha,* 8 vols. (New York: Vertical, 2003–2005).

2. For example, see Michael Foster's travelogue comparing the treatment of war and remembrance at the Mugonkan and the Mizuki Shigeru Kinenkan, in volume 4 (2009): 164–81, as well as my articles discussing the MAK museum in Vienna, the Kyoto Manga

Museum, and the Art Mecho Museum in Second Life, in *Mechademia,* volume 2 (2007): 298–99; volume 3 (2008): 191–98; and volume 4 (2009): 198–210.

3. Tokyo National Museum and TŌEI Company Ltd., eds., *Tezuka Osamu no Budda ten / Buddha: The Story in* Manga *and Art,* trans. Maiko Behr (Tokyo: Tokyo National Museum, 2011), 13. Matsumoto pointed out that most of the text in the catalog appears in both Japanese and English—a conscious effort to make the catalog accessible to readers from outside Japan.

起源

DALE K. ANDREWS

Genesis at the Shrine: The Votive Art of an Anime Pilgrimage

In 2002 a *dōjin* group known as 07th Expansion produced a sound novel (visual novel) format game called *Higurashi no naku koro ni* ("When they cry," hereafter referred to as *Higurashi*).[1] Over the next several years, anime, manga, light novels, films, and other *Higurashi* products swept into the marketplace for an ever-expanding fan base. *Higurashi* is a mystery story that follows six central characters who are haunted by a series of murders. Much of the action of the narrative takes place in the rural community of Hinamizawa in June 1983. Besides one male protagonist, Maebara Kei'ichi, the main characters are all female and include Furude Rika, Hōjō Satoko, Ryūgū Rena, and the Shinozaki sisters, Mion and Shion. Additionally, there is one more character of interest: Rika's ancestor, Hanyū, who happens to be the deity worshipped in the local shrine in Hinamizawa.

All of this, of course, is standard enough for an anime. But there is a twist—not with the story itself but rather with how fans reacted to it. Particularly stimulated by the television airing of *Higurashi* in 2006, fans set off on a quest, driven by Japan's popular culture and accented by artistic intention, to enshrine their beloved *Higurashi* anime characters at the crossroads of the two-dimensional and three-dimensional worlds. They traveled to the site of the genesis of the anime.

THE HIGURASHI PILGRIMAGE

In the same way that motion pictures, TV dramas, and commercials are filmed on location, anime productions regularly incorporate backdrops adopted from real places; in recent years, more and more anime fans are choosing to actually embark on trips to these places, journeys that bring the two-dimensional world of the anime to the three-dimensional setting on which it is modeled. Fans have adopted the term *seichi junrei,* a compound meaning "sacred site" (*seichi*) and "pilgrimage" (*junrei*), for this spiritual enterprise.[2] Within Japan's otaku culture, *seichi* are not limited to the settings of anime and games but also include thriving maid cafes, the homes and workplaces of anime or manga artists, factories manufacturing otaku-valued commodities, and Tokyo's Akihabara shopping district, a mecca for assorted hobbyists.[3] In this way, the term *seichi* is pervasively used by otaku in general, but it is anime fans in particular who tend to use the expression *seichi junrei,* which further emphasizes the pilgrimage aspect and the act of actually journeying to the sacred site in question.

Although *seichi junrei* remain largely unknown outside the fan community, such pilgrimages first started in the 1990s when fans began to seek out sites connected with specific anime. One of the earliest known pilgrimages occurred when fans inspired by the series *Sailor Moon* (1992–97, *Bishōjo senshi Seeraamūn*) gathered at the Hikawa Shrine in Tokyo's urban neighborhood of Motoazabu.[4] Since that time, the cultural phenomenon of anime *seichi junrei* has grown, and today there is an emerging genre of books listing pilgrimage sites throughout the country.[5] Although academic research into anime pilgrimage is in its infancy, studies of pilgrimage as a form of tourism are more and more common, and one can even find a handbook instructing municipalities how to use pilgrimages to invigorate their local economies.[6]

In the case of *Higurashi,* fans perform the pilgrimage in order to spiritually connect with other fans, with the production of the anime, with its creators, and above all, with the characters. Although Hinamizawa is a fictitious village created for the narrative, it is based on an actual site: Shirakawagō, a village in Gifu Prefecture famous as a tourist showpiece of nostalgic rural Japan. Some *Higurashi* fans make the pilgrimage to Shirakawagō only once, some several times, and those enraptured by *Higurashi* visit repeatedly.

To facilitate the pilgrimage, fans have appropriated a tourist map of the real site of Shirakawagō and transformed it into a downloadable map of Hinamizawa, overwriting the original locations with those in the *Higurashi* story.[7] Fans carry these maps in order to find, for example, a building that serves as a model for a character's home depicted in the anime. Methodically capturing a photographic image of a building from the same angle as in *Higurashi,* fans will then post the photo on their blogs and homepages along with an account of their journey.[8] This coincides with what John Urry calls the "hermeneutic circle," which entails "travellers demonstrating that they really have been there by showing their version of the images that they had seen before they set off."[9] Furthermore, such images not only commemorate their trip, but also monumentalize the site as a sacred place of pilgrimage.[10] Fans, who begin their journey by viewing the two-dimensional *Higurashi,* travel through the three-dimensional space of Shirakawagō and then proceed to document this categorically "analog" activity in a digital space online. The fans' engagement with *Higurashi* moves full circle, further cementing the two-dimensional and three-dimensional worlds together.

FANS, WHO BEGIN THEIR JOURNEY BY VIEWING THE TWO-DIMENSIONAL *HIGURASHI,* TRAVEL THROUGH THE THREE-DIMENSIONAL SPACE OF SHIRAKAWAGŌ AND THEN PROCEED TO DOCUMENT THIS CATEGORICALLY "ANALOG" ACTIVITY IN A DIGITAL SPACE ONLINE.

THE SHRINE WITHIN THE SHRINE

One major reason that fans are increasingly interested in pilgrimage is the associated *ema* (votive tablet). An *ema* is a small wooden tablet or plaque on which visitors write their wishes or prayers; these are often left at a shrine with the hope that their prayers will be fulfilled by the resident deity. The word *ema* literally means "picture-horse," because the tradition developed out of an old custom of dedicating horses to the gods. Over time the horse came to be embodied in painted form on a wooden tablet, the three-dimensional living creature transformed into a two-dimensional representation. The pictures on *ema* expanded beyond just horses to encompass a myriad of symbolic imagery including other animals, religious objects, and the deities themselves. The Japanese continue to use *ema* to petition deities or to express gratitude for their divine grace, but nowadays the practice has become primarily text centered, and drawing or painting on *ema* by worshippers is more the exception than the rule. Generally shrines and temples market *ema* with preprinted designs; supplicants personalize these by simply writing in their prayers.[11]

The anime fan on pilgrimage goes against this trend and often draws a picture of his or her own design. If a shrine that appears in an anime actually exists, then fans are certain to visit. And if they find an *emakake* (the rack used to hang *ema*) they may offer *ema* adorned with their own illustrations of anime characters. They may also write in a comment about the pilgrimage experience, express appreciation for the anime production or pilgrimage location, or jot down a character's set phrases and the argotic language of anime fans and Internet users. But more than the writing itself, it is the illustrations, the visual portrayal of characters, that represent the most distinctive characteristic of fan-generated *ema*.

If most people who offer *ema* refrain from illustrating them, what then compels anime fans to make this effort? This is a critical question, for certainly a copious amount of thought, energy, and skill go into composing what the fans call an *itaema,* which translates roughly as "painful votive tablet." The naming alludes to the pain of being socially stigmatized for bringing one's private obsession with anime out into the open and subjecting it to public scrutiny, perhaps even ridicule.[12] If the "medium is the message," as Marshall McLuhan long ago suggested, then it is deeply meaningful that these fans choose to express themselves through the physical object of the *ema* and that they do it through images, not just words.[13] By drawing their own versions of the anime characters, they not only replicate the actions of the illustrators of the original text, but they also make that text their own, personalizing it, animating it, and indeed, *creating* it themselves.

Despite their creative and collective participation in the pilgrimage and their shared interest in the *itaema,* however, fans tend to refrain from entering into face-to-face conversation with each other. From the fans' perspective, then, the *emakake* is not only a hallowed space within the shrine but also a site of communication. Through personal observation at the Shirakawagō Hachiman Shrine, I estimate that although only a small minority of fans actually produces *ema,* all the fans making the *Higurashi* pilgrimage circuit of Hinamizawa (Shirakawagō) stop by to check out the *emakake.* Communication between fans is neither face-to-face nor virtual, but it is vital and real, anchored in the material plane through the medium of the *ema.* The *emakake* serves as the solitary place in Shirakawagō where fans communicate with each other, albeit indirectly. The *itaema* on display signify the fans' "public show of labor" and commitment to the *Higurashi* community.[14]

Communicative exchange among fans in this way is in constant flux as new *ema* are dedicated at the *emakake.* The rack has rows of pins on which visitors hang *ema* by a fastened string, usually placing new *ema* in front of older ones. Fans will often lift up or push aside *ema* to get a look at those hidden from view. And some visitors, on finding a well-drawn *ema,* will physically move it into the front row to be better viewed by all. In a reflection of their social media literacy, fans curate this physical forum as they might an Internet site, contributing postings (*ema*) to a message board (*emakake*). At times, written comments directed at surrounding *ema* even mirror a threaded discussion online. And just as with an online discussion, nonfans may find themselves at a loss when confronted by unfamiliar language and imagery.

It is plausible that without an *emakake,* the fan experience, both on and off the pilgrimage, would be significantly altered. On other anime pilgrimages fans employ communicative strategies, such as writing in notebooks, but the visual allure and the open, public quality of the *emakake* cannot be matched.[15] Fans appreciate and anticipate fan-made renditions of the characters that are artistically, intellectually, and even emotionally stimulating. The visual conspicuousness of the *itaema* is what sets the fans' work apart from other *ema*. In essence, fans have taken the languishing craft of illustrating *ema* and reinvigorated it with a vibrant, contemporary aesthetic.

THE ART OF PRAYER

At the Shirakawagō Hachiman shrine, the raw color emanating from the *itaema* immediately grabs one's attention. Volant in the wind, the *ema* signal their presence with an unrhythmical click-clacking sound. At most shrines the *ema's* bidding, more often than not, goes unheeded by the passerby. But even for people familiar with seeing *ema* at shrines, the in-your-face compositions distinctive of an anime pilgrimage are unusual and attract attention.

I conducted a field survey of the *ema* at the Shirakawagō Hachiman Shrine on November 11, 2007. In total I found 577 *ema.* Of these, 511 (almost 90 percent) contained textual or image references to anime or the Internet, and inferably can be associated with fan pilgrims.[16] A total of 469 (about 80 percent) made direct reference to *Higurashi.* All together 303 (just over 50 percent) contained artwork, most with *Higurashi* characters.[17] The *ema* included in this survey represent this originating period of the pilgrimage, from 2005 to 2007. Some, but not all, *ema* have dates inscribed on them; the three earliest *ema* date back to 2005, which predates the television release of the anime but is presumably when the shrine first started selling *ema.*[18] One of these three was an *itaema.* In 2006, after the broadcast of the anime series, we witness a sharp increase in the number of *itaema,* and an even greater proliferation as we move into 2007.[19]

Fans produce votive art according to their own tastes and abilities. Drawn by male and female fans alike, female character illustrations predominate. A machete-like hatchet and a baseball bat, weapons in *Higurashi*'s murderous storyline, appear repeatedly as motif objects. Some fans create extemporaneous works, ranging from a quick sketch to a detailed drawing. Others prepare ahead, bringing graphics or stickers that they affix to the *ema*. Still others purchase an *ema*, take it elsewhere, and bring it back when it is completed, presumably to produce votive art of higher quality. And a devoted few manufacture the *ema* themselves, crafting it from a cut of wood.

CREATING PRESENCE

Fan art springs from mundane fan-life activities, such as watching animations or playing games, much of which entails appreciation of and interaction with images.[20] Indeed, Japanese culture has long placed emphasis on the visual, particularly within the arts.[21] But in and of itself, this immersion in visual culture does not explain why fans would go through the effort to illustrate *ema* with anime images.

Based on Azuma Hiroki's work and with reference to the *Higurashi* pilgrimage, Maruta Hajime explains that because anime are often modeled on actual places, fans can physically retrace the footsteps of fictional characters in the three-dimensional landscape within a "manga/anime realism." But ultimately fans recognize that an anime is fiction and that their own experience is limited to physically being in the place where characters stand; they do not actually experience the place as the characters would.[22] He further posits that an alternative way of processing experience is present in what is known as "game realism," in which a character comes down into the three-dimensional world the fan inhabits.

It has been suggested that *itaema* represent an attempt to transcend the limitations of "manga/anime realism" in accordance with "game realism." In studying the *Sengoku Basara* (2005, Sengoku BASARA) game pilgrimage, Satō Yoshiyuki notes the overriding significance of *itaema*. Through creating and offering an *itaema*, he argues, fans can imagine that the characters overcome the restrictions of the two-dimensional anime and enter into the three-dimensional world where the fans themselves exist. Manifested on the *itaema*, the characters literally become part of the living world of the pilgrims. The fans are no longer just experiencing the places characters have been; rather it is as if they are playing a game in the three-dimensional world, where they are both creating the characters through their art and also observing themselves as reflected in the characters they have produced.[23] While Satō's conclusion gestures to the general importance of the visual images on *itaema,* I would argue that in order to better understand the dynamics of fan interaction with the anime and with each other, it is critical to closely examine the actual artwork found on the *itaema.* If, as Satō suggests, fans are actively engaging with characters at the pilgrimage site, then details of the illustrations will shed light on the nature of this engagement.

The first *Higurashi itaema* I will use to exemplify anime votive art is an anonymously drawn and brilliantly illustrated piece featuring a female character in a fit of psychotic laughter (Figure 1). The face, the central element, seems to overflow the 14 cm wide by 10 cm high, elongated diamond shape of the *ema,* creating a close-up that gives an impression of movement toward the viewer. A tilting of the head further contributes to the animated effect. Opened wide, with retinas like those of a snake, her eyes peer out and gaze down on the viewer. An elongated mouth reveals a thin, white line of small, jagged, razor-like teeth running from corner to corner. Under this row of teeth the tautly stretched mouth is a dark pit from which an eerie laugh emerges. The laugh is the only script on this particular *ema*: the *hiragana* characters translate as an echoing "ha-ha-ha." The letters encircling the face float off

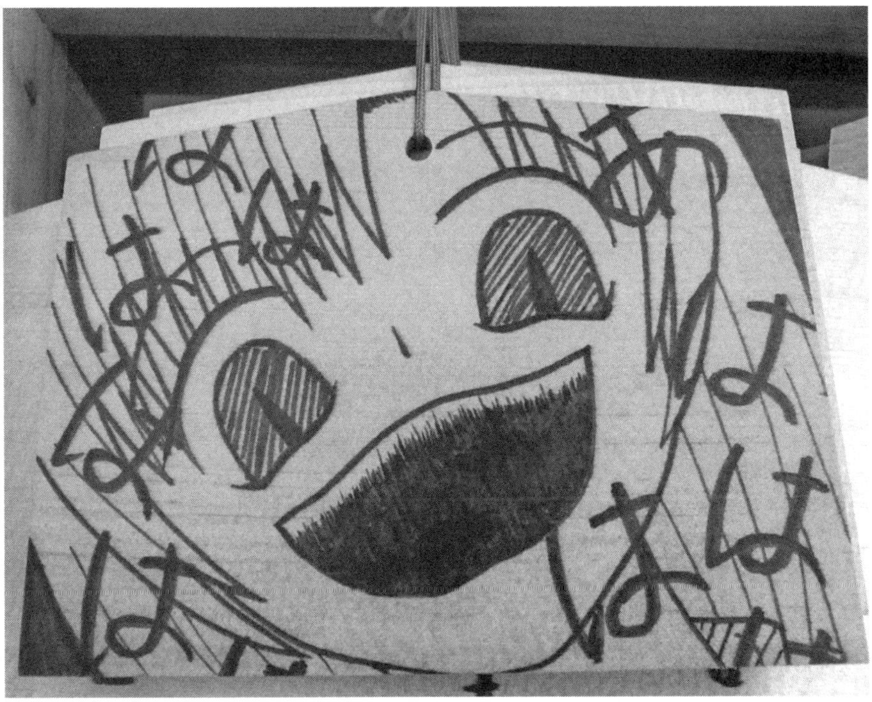

FIGURE 1. A *Higurashi* character laughs eerily. Photograph by the author.

haphazardly in all directions, conveying a demonic energy. This *ema* is an example of the artwork's capacity to visually communicate an animated presence. Even for a viewer with no firsthand knowledge of the storyline, the impression delivered by this image is unsettling. Folklorist Simon J. Bronner has recognized that "a key characteristic of the Internet that distinguishes it from face-to-face talking is how visual it is."[24] Although the *emakake* is a pointedly nondigital space of communication, here, too, visuality is key to a form of communication that is not face to face.

An *ema* with Hanyū (Figure 2) provides insight into another critical aspect of *itaema,* namely the opening of interplay between characters and fans. On the *ema,* the demon-goddess Hanyū has raised her right-hand level with her face to forcibly point an index finger at the viewer. Boldface in red, and positioned vertically along both sides of her head, are the ominous words: "If you do not offer (an *ema*), a curse on you." Because her mouth itself is drawn as a miniscule triangle, this threat bellows forth as if telepathically transmitted, penetrating into the viewer's inner psyche.

On the one hand, the prayer is a comical plea from one fan to another to make an appreciable contribution to the pilgrimage experience, thereby intensifying it for everyone. On the other hand, in complying with Hanyū's decree to offer a votive tablet, fans engage in a dialog with the characters as well as

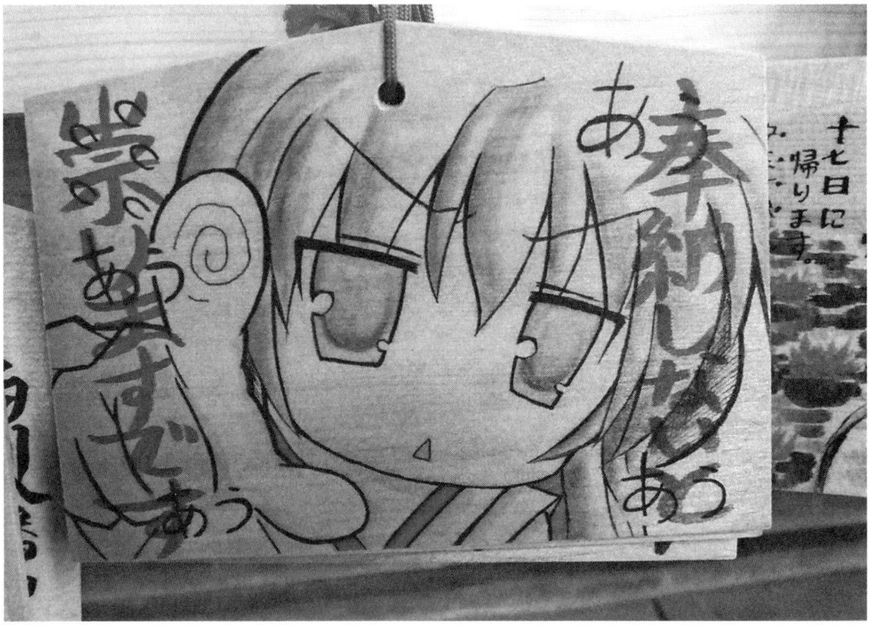

FIGURE 2. The demon-goddess Hanyū threatens fans. Photograph by the author.

with other fans. Through (re)producing and displaying a visual representation in this way, fans transfer the narratives of the characters from the screen of a television or video monitor to the physical setting of the pilgrimage site. Both the image and the accompanying text, in the form of dialog, allow the illustrated characters to interact with pilgrims and vice versa. In a sense, Hanyū serves as a conduit, voicing a message from one pilgrim to others who follow.

When Donald H. Holly Jr. and Casey E. Cordy investigated present-day activities surrounding the gravesites of alleged vampires in Rhode Island, they commented that they learned little if anything about the motivations of the people who left objects (coins, candles, and so on) at the graves.[25] Unlike the material record in their research, however, *itaema* contain explicit illustrations and therefore provide a plethora of information about *Higurashi* fans and offer insight into why they invest so much time and energy on the pilgrimage. One example contains a large figure of Hanyū backed by a smaller Shion (Figure 3). Looking straight forward, Hanyū wears a matter-of-fact expression as she instructs fans on how to make a petition. Her rounded mouth is opened to suggest that she is uttering the written text. She informs us that we should offer her favorite food, cream puffs.[26] At first glance we see that fans entertain each other with tantalizing references to the *Higurashi* story; shared knowledge is continuously communicated by both text and visual image on

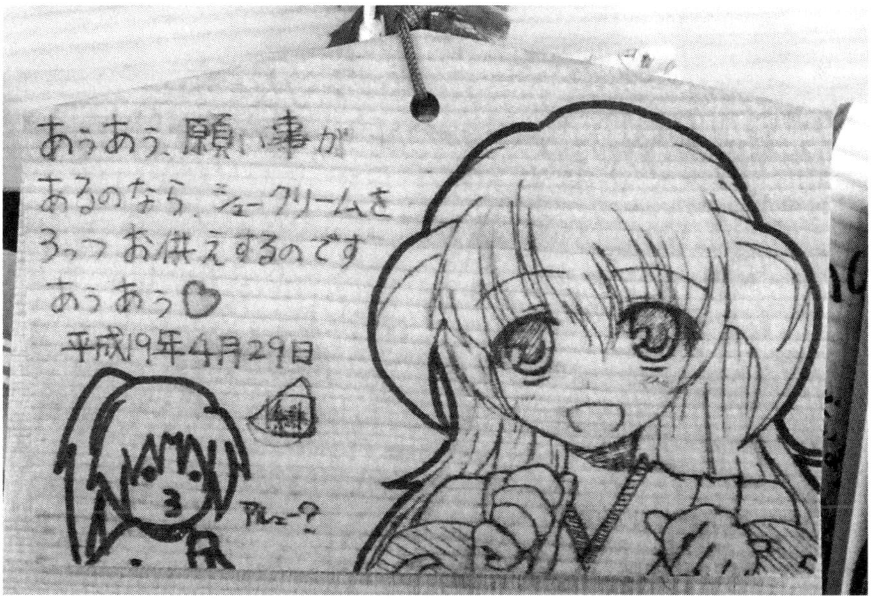

FIGURE 3. Hanyū instructs fans how to petition her by offering cream puffs. Photograph by the author.

BY COLLECTIVELY SUPERIMPOSING HINAMIZAWA ON THE THREE-DIMENSIONAL SPACE OF SHIRA-KAWAGŌ, FANS BRING THEIR BELOVED ANIME CHARACTERS INTO A MATERIAL REALM.

the *itaema*. Yet we also witness the establishment of a relationship with the characters that is a step beyond what is ordinarily expected. In this example, although presented as inside humor, fans overtly sanction the petitioning of the *Higurashi* characters.

Fans use the *ema* to restructure their surroundings in order to bring themselves and the characters to the source of the *Higurashi* world. On one side of the *ema* sold by the shrine is the shrine name printed with a scene of the local traditional lion dance, animals connected with birth years, and other such auspicious images. The other side is left blank to provide space to write a prayer. Of the *ema* I examined, I found that eight fans elected to write Hinamizawa's shrine's fictional name, Furude Shrine, on the *ema*. Two *ema* had the name of Shirakawagō Hachiman Shrine crossed out and rewritten with the fictional shrine's name. A third was blackened over with a marker so that the scene was completely indiscernible. We can interpret these actions as the fans actively working to imagine that Shirakawagō is the fictional Hinamizawa; that is, by overwriting the name in this way, fans transform Shirakawagō Hachiman Shrine, where Ōjin Tennō (Emperor Ōjin, reign circa 270–310) is enshrined, into Furude Shrine, where Oyashiro-sama is worshipped. In a sense, they are also questioning which is the original: was Furude inspired by Hachiman, or is it actually the other way around? Through their active participation the pilgrims blur the lines between the two-dimensional and three-dimensional worlds, between fiction and reality.

Moreover, by collectively superimposing Hinamizawa on the three-dimensional space of Shirakawagō, fans bring their beloved anime characters into a material realm. For them, Hanyū, the deity who is worshipped at Furude Shrine, replaces Shirakawagō Hachiman Shrine's deity not just in name but in practice. In her work on the modern popularity among Japanese schoolgirls of the tenth-century sorcerer Abe no Seimei (921–1005), Laura Miller has noted that worshippers offer *ema* so the enshrined deities can read them, which is standard practice at shrines and temples throughout Japan.[27] A review of all of the *ema* at Shirakawagō Hachiman Shrine shows that on numerous occasions the fans directly petitioned Hanyū and other characters to grant their wishes.[28] In 2007, out of 511 *itaema,* 231 (45 percent) were inscribed with prayers and petitions. For all practical purposes, the anime characters have become the deities.

Media and technology scholar Sherry Turkle has posited that Internet users are akin to “dwellers on the threshold between the real and virtual,” an observation that certainly applies meaningfully to anime pilgrims as well.[29] Indeed, some pilgrims demonstrate a vivid awareness of the fact that they are enacting a link between the real and the virtual, between the three-dimensional world and the two-. One example that explicitly comments on this point is an *ema* (Figure 4) with multiple characters: Satoko, Rika, and Rena (from left to right) with a smallish figure on top of Rika’s head, possibly Hanyū. The figures are drawn in a more childlike style than most other votive illustrations in the survey, and the low placement of the characters on the tablet contributes to the effect of short stature. Moreover, because their rounded eyes are expressed rather flatly, lacking lucidness, the three main figures exude a sense of innocence. Consequently, the image attains an added quality of sincerity that complements a thought-provoking supplication: Satoko prays for more people to be able to distinguish between reality and the two-dimensional world. Here the separation between the two worlds becomes all the more blurred, as fans turn to the two-dimensional world of the anime to communicate with each other in the three-dimensional world.

The image also raises some important questions. Is Satoko’s wish simply tongue-in-cheek commentary about the perceived mental state of *Higurashi*

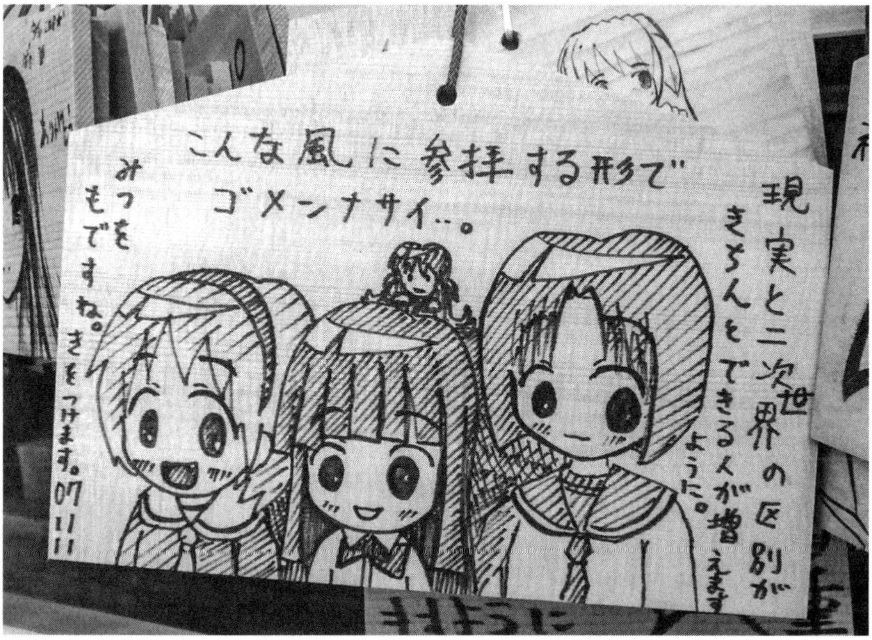

FIGURE 4. Satoko prays for people to be able to distinguish between reality and fiction. Photograph by the author.

fans, or does it, more profoundly, reveal a philosophical outlook that could help explain the need to produce *ema* illustrated with anime characters? Satoko advocates for people to distinguish between reality and fantasy, an ironic request of course, considering that it is being made by an anime character. But if we read between the lines, this irony reveals that the fans are, as Satō seems to suggest, able to transcend the paradox of their liminal condition. The votive art is central to connecting the three-dimensional (human/real) with the two-dimensional (divine/fictional).[30]

> WHEN THEY TRAVEL TO THE THREE-DIMENSIONAL HINAMIZAWA, THEY SENSE AN EMPTINESS, AN INCOMPLETENESS, WITHOUT THE ANIMATING PRESENCE OF THE CHARACTERS WHO ARE INSEPARABLE FROM HINAMIZAWA. SO, FANS UNDERTAKE TO COMPLETE THE PICTURE, AS IT WERE, TO DRAW THE *HIGURASHI* CHARACTERS INTO THE THREE-DIMENSIONAL HINAMIZAWA AS ILLUSTRATIONS ON *EMA*.

One final example (Figure 5) presents an image reminiscent of a traditional *ema* motif of a worshipper in prayer.[31] We find Satoko with head slightly lowered, eyes gently closed, hands raised with palms pressed against each other. Her mouth is hidden from view by her hands. The high positioning accentuates the act of worship while simulating the manner in which Japanese customarily pray at shrines and temples. The image is simple enough, but the accompanying text presents a puzzle that once more blurs the lines between the real and the virtual. In *Higurashi,* the main characters of the story organized themselves into a club, and the text of this *ema* reads, "(I pray) that I can make a scenario in which I am doing the club (activities) with my big brothers and sisters." The words are straightforward, but because of the site and context of its articulation, the meaning is ambiguous. Is the *ema* referencing the artist's desire to interact with other pilgrims, the desire of Satoko to play with the other members of the club, or is Satoko expressing a desire to have the pilgrims become a part of her world?

Such "pictorial and narrative polysemy," as Jennifer Robertson has noted about *ema* in other contexts, is characteristic of many of the *ema* found at the Shirakawagō Hachiman Shrine.[32] It is up to the viewers to interpret the meaning of text and image. Moreover, it is the viewers who ultimately decide who is speaking: the character, the fan who offered up the *ema,* or both. Had fans refrained from adding art and simply followed the general custom of only inscribing text on their votive offerings, then the *ema* would not have become so readily observable (visual), and the relation with the characters would not have become as lively and interactive.

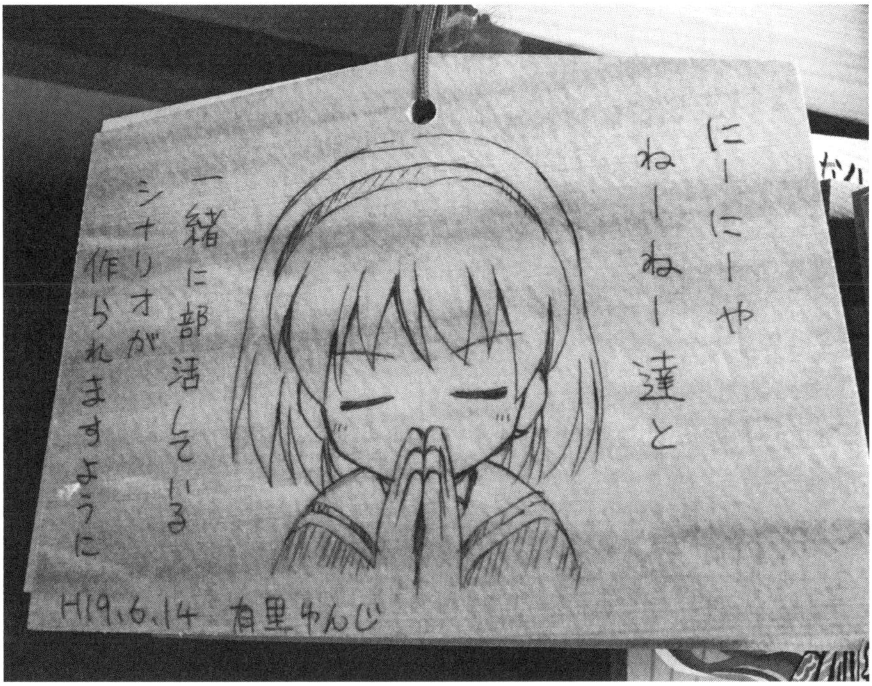

FIGURE 5. Satoko in prayer. Photograph by the author.

In fact, I would argue that it is the *illustrations* that constitute the vehicle for this transference of characters from the flat world of anime into the three-dimensional pilgrimage terrain. Despite being recognizable as material products, the characters on the *ema* are "in the status of persons."[33] It has been noted that in contemporary Japan, the anthropomorphizing of objects is now part and parcel of everyday life, and many people express an emotional attachment to fictional characters.[34] On an *ema* featuring a drawing of Rika one fan wrote, "Rika, I love you, I love you! So please raise my grades."[35] In such instances, we see fans pursuing intimate interaction with *Higurashi* characters as well as treating them as if they were deities to be petitioned.

In describing how a person receives an amulet from a shrine or temple, H. Bryon Earhart explains that the shrine or temple contains more power and sacrality than the home.[36] Extending this train of thought to our subject, the movement of the characters out of the private and into the public sphere—more specifically off the TV or computer screen in the home to the *emakake* at the pilgrimage site—is a sacralizing action that imbues the characters, embodied on the fans' *ema,* with ubiety in the three-dimensional world. The *Higurashi* world arose from the scenery found in Shirakawagō; fans recognize that Shirakawagō is the origin of Hinamizawa. But when they travel to the three-dimensional Hinamizawa, they sense an emptiness, an incompleteness, without the animating presence of the characters who are inseparable from Hinamizawa. So, fans undertake to complete the picture, as it were, to draw the *Higurashi* characters into the three-dimensional Hinamizawa as illustrations on *ema*.

Bronner has suggested that people tend to doubt the realness of what they see on the screen because of an object's intangibility.[37] Accordingly, by situating the image of characters within the three-dimensional world, fans invest them with an added, real-world authenticity. They make them tangible. The materialization of the characters' presence within the physical landscape of the pilgrimage is an act of genesis that simultaneously animates the instrumentality of the *Higurashi* characters and also makes real a place called Hinamizawa. McLuhan defined "medium" as "any extension of ourselves": by extending themselves through *itaema* imagery in the sacred space of the shrine, *Higurashi* fans literally make themselves part of the story, and part of the place where it occurs.[38] Through this act of creation, fans give birth to their own world.

Notes

Thanks to *Mechademia*'s anonymous reviewers, and thanks to Michael Dylan Foster. His editorial attentiveness to both the author's and the readers' needs is inspirational. Finally, I extend my deepest gratitude to Suzuki Iwayumi, professor of religious folklore, for years of untiring tutelage.

1. A *dōjin* circle is a group of people with shared interests, i.e. in making fan-created works. *Higurashi no naku koro ni*, PC (07th Expansion, 2002).

2. *Seichi junrei* commonly refers to a pilgrimage to a traditional religious setting; however, the parameters of the term are expanding to reflect current social attitudes regarding spirituality. For an overview of contemporary pilgrimage sites both in and out of Japan, see *Seichi junrei tsūrizumu* (Pilgrimage tourism), ed. Hoshino Eiki, Yamanaka Hiroshi, and Okamoto Ryōsuke (Tokyo: Kōbundō, 2012).

3. Nomura Sōgō Kenkyūjo, *Otaku shijō no kenkyū* (Otaku marketing) (Tokyo: Tōyō Keizai Shinpōsha, 2005), 34.

4. Ishii Kenji, *Terebi to shūkyō: Oumu igo o toi naosu* (Television and religion: A new inquiry in the wake of Aum Shinrikyo) (Tokyo: Chūō Kōron Shinsha, 2008), 214–15.

5. Dorirupurojekuto, *Seichi junrei navi: Anime & komikku* (Pilgrimage navigation: Anime and comics) (Tokyo: Asuka Shinsha, 2010); Kakizaki Shundō, *Seichi junrei: Anime manga 12 kasho meguri* (Sacred site pilgrimages: A tour of 12 anime and manga locations) (Tokyo: Kirutaimu Comyunikeeshon, 2005). There are also manga-based pilgrimages: Ofusaido Bukkusu Henshūbu, *Manga no arukikata* (How to find manga settings) (Tokyo: Sairyūsha, 1999).

6. Imai Nobuharu, “Fan ga nichijō o ‘seika’ suru: Ema ni kakerareta negai” (Fans sacralize the everyday: The prayers written on votive tablets), in *Shūkyō to tsūrizumu: Sei naru mono no henyō to jizoku* (Religion and tourism: The change and continuity of sacred things), ed. Yamanaka Hiroshi, 170–89 (Kyoto: Seikai Shisōsha, 2012); Okamoto Takeshi, “Rakisuta seichi ‘Washimiya’ junrei to jōhōka shakai” (The pilgrimage to the Lucky Star sacred site ‘Washimiya’ and the information society), in *Kankō no kūkan: Shiten to apurōchi* (The space of tourism: Viewpoint and approach), ed. Kanda Kōji, 133–44 (Tokyo: Nakanishiya, 2009); Yamamura Takayoshi, *Anime/manga de chiiki shinkō: Machi no fan o umu kontentsu tsūrizumu kaihatsuhō* (Local development by means of anime/manga: A content tourism developmental method to create fans of the local community) (Tokyo: Tōkyō Hōrei, 2011).

7. “Hinamizawa kankō annai chizu” (Hinamizawa tourist map), http://outdoor.geocities.jp/hinamy2006.

8. A parallel can be drawn with the Edo-period pilgrim as explained by Akinori Kato, who would take back a souvenir for those who could not join the pilgrimage. The *Higurashi* fan’s souvenir is a posted image on a blog, for example, that she or he can share with friends. Akinori Kato, “Package Tours, Pilgrimages, and Pleasure Trips,” in *The Electric Geisha: Exploring Japan’s Popular Culture,* ed. Atsushi Ueda, trans. Miriam Eguchi (Tokyo: Kodansha International, 1994), 54.

9. John Urry and Jonas Larsen, *The Tourist Gaze 3.0* (Los Angeles: Sage, 2011), 179.

10. E. Frances King points out that the act of taking home souvenirs (material culture) from a pilgrimage is invaluable in communicating the experience to others. E. Frances King, *Material Religion and Popular Culture* (New York: Routledge, 2010), 97.

11. Ian Reader provides a comprehensive explanation of *ema.* Ian Reader, “Letters to the Gods: The Form and Meaning of *Ema,*” *Japanese Journal of Religious Studies* 18, no. 1 (1991): 23–50.

12. This interpretation of *itaema* is based on conversations with numerous fans at various venues, including gatherings of *itasha* (anime-decorated automobiles) enthusiasts.

13. Marshall McLuhan, *Understanding Media: The Extensions of Man* (New York: McGraw-Hill, 1965), 7.

14. Simon J. Bronner, *Grasping Things: Folk Material Culture and Mass Society in America* (Lexington: University Press of Kentucky, 2005), 130.

15. I documented a *Kamichu!* fan-made spiral notebook at the *emakake* of Misode Tenmangū Shrine in Onomichi, Hiroshima Prefecture in April 2008. Multiple fans added comments, prayers, and illustrations.

16. The remainder (roughly ten percent) may also include fans.

17. In a March 2012 survey this number had risen to just under 64 percent.

18. The shrine’s caretakers did not disclose the exact year they began selling *ema.*

19. From 2008 onward, the shrine’s caretakers began to periodically remove many of the *ema,* presumably to make space available for new *ema* to be dedicated. Periodic removal is common practice at many shrines and temples; see Reader, “Letter to the Gods,” 35.

20. Henry Jenkins, “‘Strangers No More, We Sing’: Filking and the Social Construction of the Science Fiction Fan Community,” in *The Adoring Audience: Fan Culture and Popular Media,* ed. Lisa A. Lewis (London: Routledge, 1992), 210.

21. Richard Chalfen and Mai Murui, “Print Club Photography in Japan: Framing

Social Relationships," in *Photographs Objects Histories: On the Materiality of Images,* ed. Elizabeth Edwards and Janice Hart (New York: Routledge, 2010), 175.

22. Maruta Hajime, *Bashoron: Webu no riarizumu chiiki no romanchishizumu* (Theory of location in the information society) (Tokyo: NTT Shuppan, 2008), 109–11; Maruta references Azuma Hiroki, *Geemuteki riarizumu no tanjō: Dōbutsuka suru posutomodan* (The birth of game realism: Japan's database animals 2) (Tokyo: Kōdansha, 2007).

23. Satō Yoshiyuki, "Otaku ema to wa nani ka: Miyagi-ken gokoku jinja no ema chōsa kekka to sono bunseki" (What are otaku votive tablets? The survey results and analysis of the votive tablets at Gokoku Shrine, Miyagi Prefecture), in *Community Development and Tourism for the Next Generation,* ed. Yamamura Takayoshi and Okamoto Takeshi (Sapporo: Hokkaido University, 2010), 125. For other articles concerning *itaema,* see Imai Nobuharu, "Anime 'seichi junrei' jissensha no kōdō ni miru dentōteki junrei to kankō katsudō no kakyō kanōsei: Saitama-ken Washinomiya jinja hōnō ema bunseki o chūshin ni" (The traditional pilgrimage and the connective potential of tourist activities as seen in the actions of anime pilgrimage participants: A focus on the analysis of votive tablets dedicated at the Washinomiya shrine in Saitama Prefecture), in *Media Contents and Tourism: An Experience of Washimiya Town and Neon Genesis of Tourism,* ed. Cultural Resource Management Research Team, CATS, Hokkaido University (Sapporo: Center for Advanced Tourism Studies Hokkaido University, 2009), 85–111; Imai Nobuharu, "Fan ga nichijō o 'seika'suru"; Satō Yoshiyuki, "Ika ni shite jinja wa seichi to natta ka: Kōkyōsei to hinichijōsei ga umidasu seichi no hatten" (How did a shrine become a sacred site? The public and extraordinary give birth to the development of a sacred site), in *Media Contents and Tourism,* 71–84.

24. Simon J. Bronner, "Digitizing and Virtualizing Folklore," in *Folklore and the Internet: Vernacular Expression in a Digital World,* ed. Trevor J. Blank (Logan: Utah State University Press, 2009), 29.

25. Donald H. Holly Jr. and Casey E. Cordy, "What's in a Coin? Reading the Material Culture of Legend Tripping and Other Activities," *Journal of American Folklore* 120, no. 477 (2007): 346.

26. Another *ema* displayed three months later shows Hanyū eating cream puffs while restating that pilgrims should offer some to get their wishes granted.

27. Laura Miller, "Extreme Makeover for a Heian-Era Wizard," *Mechademia* 3 (Minneapolis: University of Minnesota Press, 2008): 37.

28. Many fans petition to Oyashiro-sama, Hanyū's alter ego, whose name means roughly "Master (of the) Shrine."

29. Sherry Turkle, *Life on the Screen: Identity in the Age of the Internet* (New York: Touchstone, 1997), 10.

30. Colleen McDannell, *Material Christianity: Religion and Popular Culture in America* (New Haven, Conn.: Yale University Press, 1995), 39.

31. For excellent visual examples, see Kondō Masaki's publication on votive offerings. Kondō Masaki, ed., *Negai, uranai, omajinai: Yokubō no zōkei kikakuten* (Prayer, divination, incantation: Exhibition on the form of desire) (Mito, Japan: Ibaraki Kenritsu Hakubutsukan, 2000), 9–11.

32. Jennifer Robertson, "*Ema*-gined Community: Votive Tablets (*Ema*) and Strategic Ambivalence in Wartime Japan," *Asian Ethnology* 67, no. 1 (2008): 46.

33. Michael Ashkenazi and John Clammer, "Introduction: The Japanese and the Goods," in *Consumption and Material Culture in Contemporary Japan,* ed. Michael Ashkenazi and John Clammer (London: Kegan Paul International, 2000), 17.

34. Yoshimasa Kijima, "Why Make E-*moe*-tional Attachments to Fictional Characters? The Cultural Sociology of the Post-Modern," in *Pop Culture and the Everyday in Japan: Sociological Perspectives,* ed. Katsuya Minamida and Izumi Tsuji, trans. Leonie R. Stickland (Melbourne: Trans Pacific Press, 2012), 153–55.

35. This adoration for characters is reflected in a questionnaire I administered to sixty-eight Tohoku Gakuin University students who participated in my lecture class on October 10, 2012. In response to the question "Do you think it is possible to have an emotional feeling close to love for anime/game characters?" 47 percent answered in the affirmative.

36. H. Byron Earhart, "Mechanisms and Process in the Study of Japanese Amulets," in *Nihon shūkyō e no shikaku* (Approaches to Japanese religion), ed. Okada Shigekiyo (Osaka: Tōhō Shuppan, 1994), 618.

37. Bronner, "Digitizing and Virtualizing," 29.

38. McLuhan, *Understanding Media,* 7.

Repetition,
Remediation,
Adaptation

起源

FORREST GREENWOOD

The Girl at the Center of the World: Gender, Genre, and Remediation in *Bishōjo* Media Works

In the sculpture garden at Minneapolis's Walker Art Center stands a most curious piece. Deborah Butterfield's *Woodrow* (1988), a sculpture cast in bronze, depicts a skeletal horse-like figure constructed entirely out of what appears to be wooden sticks, logs, and branches. The statue catches the eye with its arresting appearance, but what truly holds the attention is its accompanying inscription. In it, the sculptor describes her early experiences making "horses out of real mud and sticks . . . to reflect how much a horse is part of his environment." This statement is interesting for the way that it reflects a common perception about animals: that they lack sufficient distance from their environment and thus do not have access to the world as such, in the manner of human beings. As Martin Heidegger argues, "a stone is worldless. Plant and animal likewise have no world; but they belong to the covert throng of a surrounding into which they are linked."[1] The environment that plants and animals inhabit is not a *world*, with the full expanse of possibility and potentiality implied by the term. Or perhaps, as Akira Mizuta Lippit puts it, animals *do* inhabit a world of sorts, "but this world is not their own: it is another's world."[2] It is our world, humanity's world: a world secured for our benefit by means of our faculty of language. We speak and listen in the abstract thoughts

THE SHŌJO REACHES OUT INTO THE WORLD THROUGH HER GAZE, REEMERGING FROM THE PAGE OR THE SCREEN TO ADDRESS THE VIEWER, TO MAKE DEMANDS, TO PROMISE POTENTIALITIES AND FUTURES UNTOLD.

enabled by language, thus affording us the ability to conceive of the future: to anticipate, to fear, to hope, to dream.[3]

This essay seeks to address the topic of origins by analyzing the agency of the shōjo, the ever-cute emblem of femininity who circulates through multiple spheres of anime and manga fandom. Like the animal, the shōjo finds herself cast as an integral part of her environment, lacking distance from it. Here, however, the environment in question is not that of "nature"—the environment of rocks, plants, and animals. Rather, it is a *mediated* environment, an environment constructed from media. When we differentiate the shōjo as a concept (characters in media) from the shōjo as a class of human beings (girls, or women in a more general sense), we do so on the basis of the signifiers of her mediation: the quality of a line that forms a portion of a facsimile of a face (or a particular arrangement of lines), the layout in which she presents herself on a page (surrounded by bouquets of lilies and halftone), the manner in which she operates through narratives, or the presence of a generic signifier. When we speak of the shōjo as a concept, then, we implicitly reference what Thomas Lamarre refers to as "a gap between girl and image."[4]

But though the shōjo remains as enmeshed within her environment as the animal does within its own, she may not entirely lack agency because of it. For while the animal may lack access to language, it does not sacrifice the ability to reemerge in the world because of that. Rather, the animal privileges other forms of communication, other modes of knowledge, other means of accessing the world and the future. "Animals," Lippit writes, "and their capacity for instinctive, almost telepathic communication . . . put into question the primacy of human language and consciousness as optimal modes of communication."[5] They invite consideration of the potential of the unconscious and, by extension, the cinema.[6]

Similarly, the shōjo reaches out into the world through her gaze, reemerging from the page or the screen to address the viewer, to make demands, to promise potentialities and futures untold. She speaks across the boundaries of language and culture, unveiling with each glance something of the structure of the hypermediated world we humans choose to construct and inhabit.

To explore this unveiling, this paper will examine the mechanisms through which the shōjo's gaze operates in *The Garden of Sinners* (2008–11, *Kara no kyōkai*)—a media saga comprising seven theatrical films and one direct-to-video episode. Produced by the animation studio ufotable and the independent game developer Notes (better known to their fans as TYPE-MOON), *The Garden of Sinners* follows its murderous protagonist, Shiki Ryōgi, as she adopts agency by learning to direct and interpret her quite unique gaze. In so doing, these films reveal how the shōjo does much the same.

Perhaps the films' most interesting aspect, however, is the manner in which they complicate the prevailing gender norms for works within the *bishōjo* media sphere—those sub-genres of media, like *bishōjo* games, *bishōjo* anime, *bishōjo* manga, and related light novels and *dōjinshi,* and their attendant fan cultures, which primarily focus on the activities of young female characters and which share certain representational and aesthetic norms. *The Garden of Sinners* films achieve this complication principally through the character of Shiki. Positioned unsteadily within the gender binary, she reveals herself as neither entirely female nor entirely male. Rather, she oscillates in and out of the shōjo paradigm, challenging viewer preconceptions and resisting reading strategies that seek to contain and categorize.

This ambiguity mirrors what Frenchy Lunning identifies as the almost uncanny power of the shōjo: simultaneously sexualized yet desexualized, feminine yet not entirely female, a shōjo "secures her identity as a desirable female yet keeps the abject content of mature feminine sexuality at bay."[7] Similarly, Brian Bergstrom identifies a theoretical dialogue that "posits a definition of *shōjo* that ostensibly distinguishes it from femininity, sometimes calling it a separate gender altogether."[8]

Laden with meaning and seeming contradiction, while being all image and no body, the shōjo wields a special sort of power. She freely navigates the labyrinthine commercial flows of the transmedia age, representing "the origin of the feverish proliferation and manic repetition of objects . . . a complex of concepts, conditions, and commodities."[9] This inherent multiplicity, according to Anne Allison, makes the shōjo a particularly potent vehicle for the consumerist imperatives of post-Fordist culture, "mak[ing] play and identification a pursuit ever more linked to consumerism"; the shōjo's inherent ambiguity and malleability yields "a plethora of body and character types" reminiscent of the variety of goods on sale in a shopping mall.[10]

Given ethereal form through evocative character design, she easily becomes one of Thomas Lamarre's "soulful bodies"—figures able to survive and communicate expression even under the conditions of restrained movement found in limited animation, as commonly practiced in the anime/manga media sphere—and she slips easily between the cycles of remediation that form the core of creative activity within this space.[11]

VISUAL NOVELS AND ANIME'S REMEDIATION FEEDBACK LOOP

In their book, *Remediation: Understanding New Media,* Jay David Bolter and Richard Grusin argue that media in Western cultures operate according to two logics: *immediacy* and *hypermediacy.* The logic of immediacy holds when media aim for perfect transparency in representation; as Bolter and Grusin put it, "the medium itself should disappear and leave us in the presence of the thing represented."[12] Media operating under the logic of immediacy aim to reveal their representational content in the manner of an Albertian window, providing a clear, unobstructed view.[13] At their most opaque, immediate works aim to frame the view, directing our gaze but never blocking or occluding it.

The logic of hypermediacy, however, aims for perfect opacity, placing the medium itself, and not its represented subject, at the center of attention. Hypermediacy "acknowledges multiple acts of representation and makes them visible . . . and in this way tries to reproduce the rich sensorium of the human experience . . . In every manifestation, hypermediacy makes us aware of the medium or media."[14] In works operating under the logic of hypermediacy, "the artist (or multimedia programmer or web designer) strives to make the viewer acknowledge the medium as a medium and to delight in that acknowledgement."[15]

These logics combine in the process of *remediation,* which Bolter and Grusin define as "the representation of one medium in another," and which they note as being "a defining characteristic of the new digital media."[16] Some remediations primarily adhere to the logic of immediacy, as in digitally scanned documents, digital video telecined from a film source, or digital photographs of paintings. These all remediate an older medium (print, film, or paint-on-canvas) through a newer one (digital imaging, digital video, or digital imaging again), but they aim to do so with minimal intrusion and maximum transparency; ideally, the viewer should "stand in the same relationship to the content as she would if she were confronting the original medium."[17]

Other mediations, including *bishōjo* games, emphasize hypermediacy. These games, also known as *galge* or *gyaruge* (short for "gal games"), task the player with managing potentially romantic relationships with one or more characters by navigating dense text-based narratives with multiple branching story paths.[18] Often, such games cast the player as a male avatar pursuing female characters, and commonly present the player with a dual-window interface similar to that found in a modern personal computer operating system.[19]

Here, the lower third of the screen displays a text-based menu system that serves as the player's primary means of interaction with the game world, while the upper two-thirds of the screen displays still or motion graphics that provide a visual reference for the menu-screen text.

Different sub-genres of *bishōjo* games employ these windows in different, but superficially similar, ways. Some games, often referred to colloquially as "dating sims," revel in their hypermediacy, compelling the player to manipulate stat bars as in a MMORPG [massively multiplayer online role-playing game]; when the player raises one or more bars to a sufficient level by performing repetitive tasks, romance paths open up with one or more of the game's characters. Other games invoke the relative transparency of the novel, presenting the player with lengthy first-person textual narratives that require minimal input to navigate.

In either case, several layers of remediation operate within most *bishōjo* games. The menu windows remediate printed novels, if the game focuses on narrative, or accounting ledgers, if the game focuses on statistics. Meanwhile, the image-display windows remediate painting or photography, often with a particular emphasis on naturalistic detail and linear perspective, at least in the case of background art. Taken in total, the compartmentalized, windowed interface of the *bishōjo* game (Figure 1) is hypermediated in much the same manner as the graphical user interface of a modern computer operating system, where the user "oscillates between manipulating the windows and examining their contents."[20]

Yet, as Patrick Galbraith notes, *bishōjo* games do strive for a sort of immediacy. This, however, is an immediacy born not of naturalistic representation—for, backgrounds aside, *bishōjo* games generally employ an art style that is profoundly abstract and stylized—but of "intensity, in the sense of affect."[21] Such games, in other words, strive for an immediacy of feeling—yet they do so seemingly in defiance of their remediations. One notable characteristic of *bishōjo* games is their use of the first-person perspective. Textual elements, particularly in the visual novel sub-genre, often assume the form of first-person narratives, with the player-controlled character serving as the narrator. Meanwhile, visual elements often assume a first-person linear perspective to visually represent the player character's view of the game world, though often this view takes the form of static digital imagery, rather than the volumetric, navigable environments of first-person shooter titles. From this perspective, environments unfold from a point of view at roughly eye height, and female characters directly address themselves to the viewer.

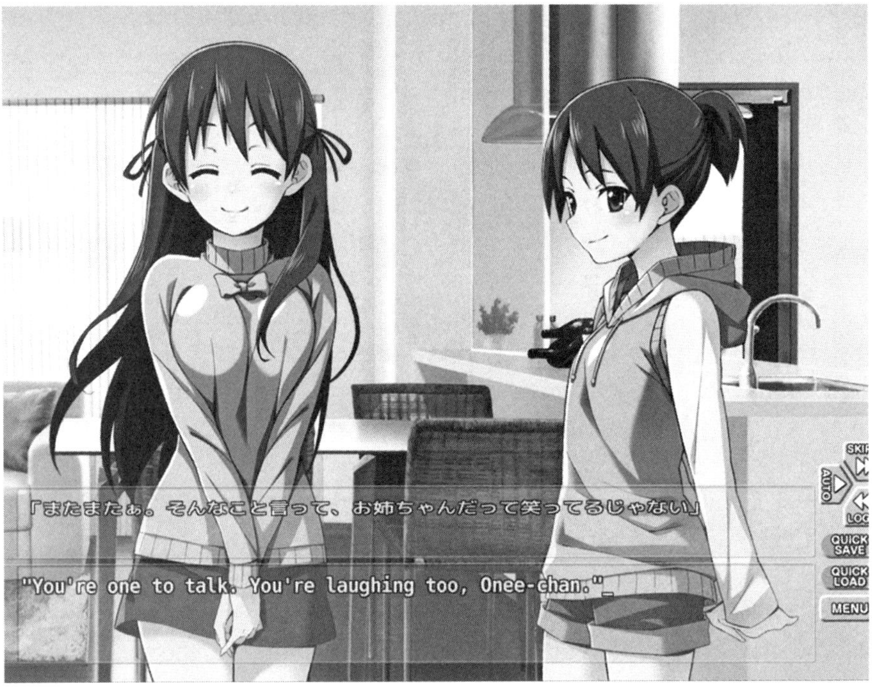

FIGURE 1. A screen image from OVERDRIVE's *Go! Go! Nippon! ~My First Trip to Japan~* (released as an English-language title through publisher MangaGamer), illustrating the sort of windowed, hypermediated interface commonly found in most *bishōjo* games.

SIGHTS AND SPECTACLE

Bishōjo games would thus seem to perfectly articulate the male gaze identified by Laura Mulvey. Indeed, Mulvey's description of how "women are simultaneously looked at and displayed, with their appearance coded for strong visual and erotic impact so that they can be said to connote *to-be-looked-at-ness*," could well apply to the visual and thematic setup of any number of titles in this genre.[22] In an early article on the *bishōjo* game genre, Emily Taylor reaches nearly this exact conclusion, albeit without reference to Mulvey or gaze theory. Noting that narrative agency in these games seems to rest entirely with the male protagonist, Taylor argues that female characters either figure as "defenseless playthings for the male character or are reduced to such by the end of the game."[23]

Yet Patrick Galbraith argues that Taylor's analysis oversimplifies matters: although we assume the position of a male-gendered avatar, the game's emotional core lies not within that avatar but within the female characters.

Reflecting on how *bishōjo* games often focus intently on the emotions of female characters, Galbraith suggests that "this bias in expressivity encourages identification" with those same figures.[24] In other words, we may view the world through a male gaze, but that gaze lacks the ability to control and dominate the shōjo in the manner that Mulvey suggests it does within the Hollywood cinema. The shōjo, rather, adopts a controlling power all her own: bursting free of the games' narrative structure, she compels the viewer to become swept up in emotion and thus claims for herself a potent, if circumscribed, agency.

This issue of viewer-character positioning, however, proves arguably more nuanced than either Taylor's or Galbraith's analyses seem to indicate. In many *bishōjo* games, such as Capcom's *Ace Attorney* (2001–present, *Gyakuten saiban*) series, the shōjo only assumes agency in a few key scenes. *Ace Attorney* protagonist Phoenix Wright (Naruhodō Ryūichi) proves to be a power-fantasy vehicle straight out of central casting: a good-natured fool who gradually becomes the confident, near-miraculous litigator suggested by the series' English title.[25] His assistant, Maya Fey (Ayasato Mayoi), largely provides comic relief in the form of bizarre non sequiturs and spacey comments on narrative happenings. These create room for Phoenix, and by association the player, to distance himself from Maya, often through sardonic inner monologues that treat her as something akin to an interloper from another planet (Figure 2).

At such moments, the shōjo's excessiveness becomes a source of bewilderment or comic relief, and she is othered accordingly. Yet she retains a key power: a mediated tendency to return the player's gaze. Today's anime media mix explodes with a profusion of female characters who stare out at the viewer. The frequency and intensity of this eye contact is arguably without parallel in other media environments, spreading as it does across a limitless array of media and products. This tendency toward direct address calls to mind Tom Gunning's cinema of attractions, which proudly "displays its visibility, willing to rupture a self-enclosed fictional world for a chance to solicit the attention of the spectator."[26] The anime media mix, in fact, proves a quite capable successor to the cinema of attractions, with works consistently foregrounding ever more inventive ways of moving characters out from the diegetic world behind the screen and into the world of sense perception inhabited by the player/viewer.[27] While this movement often takes the form of personalization—many *bishōjo* games allow the player to choose a name for the protagonist, and some, like Konami's *LovePlus* games (2009–12), take advantage of the limited number of phonemes in the Japanese language to allow the heroines to speak aloud the player's chosen name—it occasionally goes much further. Sega's concerts featuring virtual idol Hatsune Miku, for

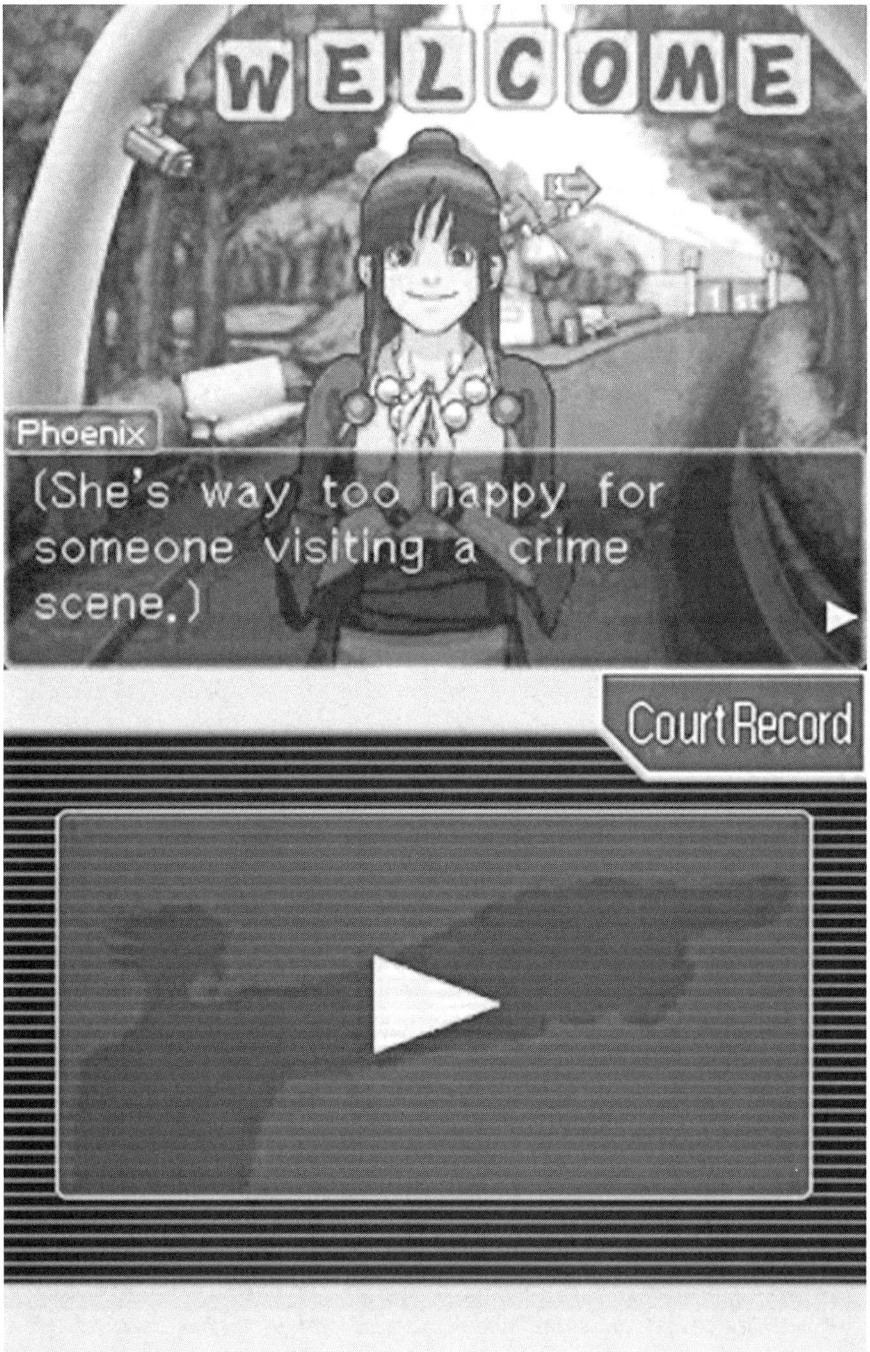

FIGURE 2. A screen image from Capcom's Nintendo DS adventure game, *Phoenix Wright: Ace Attorney* (*Gyakuten saiban*), illustrating an internal monologue of protagonist Phoenix Wright (Naruhodō Ryūichi) as he regards supporting character Maya Fey (Ayasato Mayoi, pictured).

example, pair a dual-projector setup with a transparent screen to create the illusion of a computer-animated Miku dancing live on stage alongside flesh-and-blood musicians. Most dramatically, Konami's *LovePlus* games employ the Nintendo DS's internal clock to synchronize their events with real-world time, allowing players to schedule dates with their virtual girlfriends according to a real-world calendar, with appropriately dire consequences for missed appointments.

BISHŌJO GAMES NEGOTIATE A COMPLEX INTERPLAY OF SPECTATORIAL POSITIONING: AT TIMES ADOPTING THE CONTROLLING, DOMINEERING MALE GAZE, WHILE AT OTHER TIMES CEDING GROUND TO THE SHŌJO'S EMOTIVE AGENCY.

The shōjo thus holds the potential—admittedly not always fully realized—for a uniquely mediated, almost cyborg agency. Even if the limitations of technology render her actions and yearnings as "trace communications, faint whispers of an ephemeral presence," she yet makes genuine emotional demands.[28] *Bishōjo* games thus negotiate a complex interplay of spectatorial positioning: at times adopting the controlling, domineering male gaze, while at other times ceding ground to the shōjo's emotive agency. This interplay extends into the realm of mediation; unlike the first-person cinema, *bishōjo* games do not convey their content in a transparent, immediate fashion. Rather, they compete for the viewer's attention with menu windows and gameplay icons. Meanwhile, their database-derived structure—in which the computer assembles the final mise-en-scéne from a combination of image, text, and audio files—foregrounds and calls attention to their hypermediated nature.[29] In this environment, players must choose where to direct their attention; no one element dominates the visual field.

Bolter and Grusin argue that this multiplicity of views fundamentally changes the position of the player, and the player's relation to the ludic diegesis. In contrast with the totalizing gaze of the film camera, which seeks to possess and control through its narrow intensity, the *bishōjo* game's hypermediated image field facilitates and encourages a different mode of viewing: a scanning across the image field. When we view in this way, "we do not look through the medium in linear perspective; rather, we look at the medium or at a multiplicity of media that may appear in windows on a computer screen . . . We do not gaze; rather, we *glance* here and there at the various manifestations of the media."[30] The numerous, overlapping media elements of the *bishōjo* game thus confuse and redirect the spectator's gaze, which may facilitate the movement between identification with the male avatar and identification with the *shōjo* posited by Galbraith.

GAZING UPON THE GARDEN

With its unique approach to *bishōjo* genre conventions, *The Garden of Sinners* film series provides a narrative and thematic elaboration of this movement, posing interesting challenges to the conventional spectatorial position. The films certainly boast a blue-ribbon generic pedigree, stemming as they do from the creative output of writer Nasu Kinoko and illustrator Takeuchi Takeshi, who, along with support staff, comprise the amateur group Type-Moon and the independent game developer Notes. Bursting onto the gaming scene in 2000, at the Fifty-ninth Comic Market in Tokyo, with the release of the PC-based visual novel game *Tsukihime,* Nasu and Takeuchi quickly made waves, with the title reportedly selling 65,000 copies.[31]

Fueled by the success of *Tsukihime,* Type-Moon formally incorporated in 2003 as the production company Notes, following up with 2004's *Fate/stay night,* a relative blockbuster whose success paved the way for a series of spin-offs, sequels, and derivative works, as well as a commercial revival of one of Nasu and Takeuchi's earliest works: *The Garden of Sinners.*[32] Originally published online as a serialized novella, the series evidently proved less than successful in its initial outing; in an interview, Nasu argues that "you can't get around the fact that print media doesn't fare well on the Internet," with Takeuchi describing the venture as "a bitter failure."[33] But the success of *Tsukihime* and *Fate/stay night* evidently prompted a public reassessment of *The Garden of Sinners,* as Nasu eventually finished the series, producing a proper print run of novels. Then, beginning in 2007, the animation studio ufotable adapted the series into seven films: one for each book.

At the level of their visual presentation, the films rely heavily on rich, evocatively composed scenic images, similar to those found in *bishōjo* games with relatively high production values. Furthermore, these images often foreground the traces of computer-graphics enhancement, sporting vivid, supersaturated colors that draw attention to the films' mediations. Meanwhile, in their discontinuous narrative structure, the films suggest database narratives in which the player is free to move between different story branches at will, by returning to a previous decision point and choosing a new option. *The Garden of Sinners* films challenge the spectator to divine the overarching narrative route of the series, as each film jumps forward or backward in time and space, sometimes returning to a previous point before jumping off again into uncharted territory. They present a varied cast of characters who blend the fantastic with the naturalistic, in much the same manner as in games: the films (and novels) follow the murderer Ryōgi Shiki, the investigator Kokutō Mikiya, the good magus Aozaki Tōko, and the magus-in-training Kokutō Azaka as they struggle to defuse the machinations and schemes of the demented Araya Sōren, a former colleague of Aozaki who employs a rather extreme ends-justify-the-means approach to his arcane research. But the interaction between protagonists Shiki and Mikiya constitutes the films' thematic core, where they hint at and toy with the complex interplay between player and shōjo that forms the core of the *bishōjo* game experience.

The first film, *Thanatos (Overlooking View)* (2007, *Fukan fūkei—Thanatos*), sets up this interaction quite vividly in its opening moments. We hear a doorbell ring, we see an eye looking out through what appears to be a door's security window, we hear a man's voice calling out for Shiki. As we soon learn, in this scene we share Mikiya's point of view as he calls at Shiki's apartment. Already a relatively bland character in the manner of most *bishōjo*-game avatars, Mikiya is thus presented as the lead character by default, and we prepare ourselves to see the films' narrative through his eyes. Yet, right away, Shiki aggressively returns Mikiya's (and our) gaze (Figure 3), suggesting that this apparent balance of power may not hold.

Indeed, Shiki quickly establishes her place as the true main character of the series when events render Mikiya comatose, forcing Shiki to investigate. Mikiya will never again wield ultimate narrative agency, though he does set certain events in motion. As the films progress, Shiki even takes Mikiya's place as the audience avatar: we begin to see directly through her point of view. This

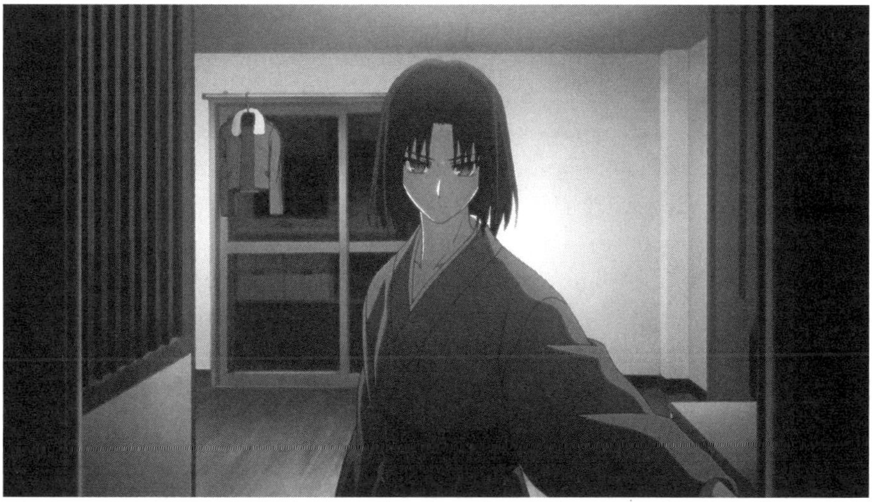

FIGURE 3. An image from the first *Kara no kyōkai* film, *Thanatos (Overlooking View)* (2007, *Fukan fūkei—Thanatos*). Here, we see through male lead Kokutō Mikiya's eyes as female lead Ryōgi Shiki pointedly returns his gaze.

shift in audience positioning turns out to serve an expository function: Shiki, we learn, possesses the ability to see the lines of life and death that sustain the existence of everything in the films' world. And if she can see them, she can cut them, which makes her an uncannily effective fighter and killer.

The Garden of Sinners filmmakers delight in showing the world as Shiki sees it, complete with glowing red lines of existence.[34] In addition to providing us with a physical point of view—and a nonmale gaze—Shiki also becomes the emotional center of the films' overarching narrative. Full of mystery and ambiguity, Shiki compels us to learn more about her, whereas Mikiya remains consistently droll, invariably the trusty sidekick to our murderous heroine. *The Garden of Sinners,* it turns out, is truly Shiki's story, and the films chronicle the path she walks toward assuming ultimate narrative agency. Yet the films never entirely commit to Shiki's agency; they oscillate between treating her as a proper agent, and treating her as an object to be gazed upon. While we may see through Shiki's eyes, we also see her undress (albeit in the first person), and the animators occasionally linger over third-person close-ups of Shiki adjusting her kimono.

> BY OWNING HER GAZE AND CHOOSING WHERE TO DIRECT IT, SHIKI JOINS THE GROWING THRONG OF SHŌJO CHARACTERS WHO TRANSGRESS THE BOUNDARY OF THE SCREEN IN ORDER TO DISRUPT THE PLAYER/VIEWER'S GAZE.

Just as the films remain slightly ambiguous about Shiki's subject position, they also openly raise questions about her gender identification, for Shiki possesses two unique personalities that exist simultaneously—and, most intriguingly, each half adopts a distinct gender. Shiki, the female personality, is taciturn, guarded, and severe (Figure 4), while Shiki-kun, the male, is bubbly, outgoing, and emotive (Figure 5).[35] In revealing this information to us, the films play with our understanding of how gender is constructed within *bishōjo* works; what we expect to be male turns out to be female, and vice versa.

Much as the interplay between the impotence of the male player and the emotive power of the female character forms the core of the character's agency in *bishōjo* games, so too is Shiki's ambiguous gender identity integral to her narrative quest for agency. In an arc that spans the second, fourth, and seventh films, Shiki ends up comatose after a car accident. When she wakes, she discovers to her horror that her Shiki-kun personality perished and will never return. Though nominally male, Shiki-kun displayed many of the outward signifiers of the shōjo, including a naive flirtatiousness and effervescent cheer, and the loss of this personality throws Shiki into a state of

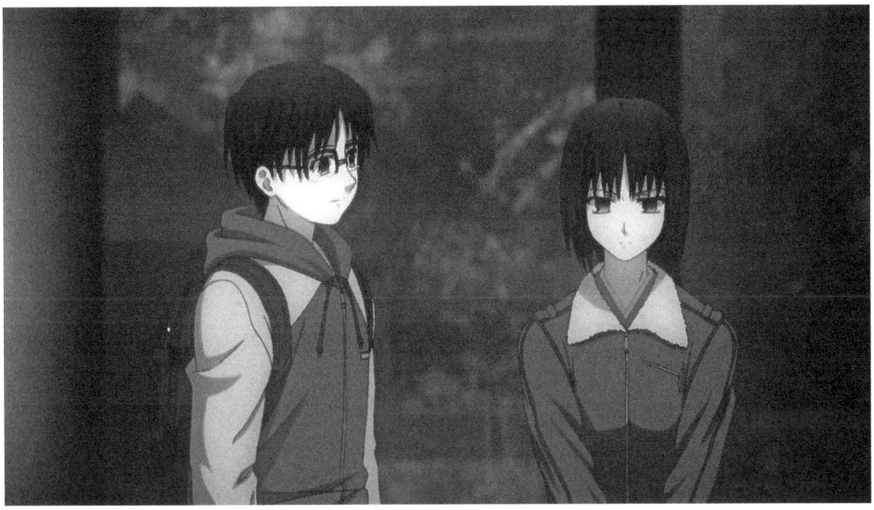

FIGURE 4. An image from the second *Kara no kyōkai* film, . . . *and nothing heart (Murder Speculation, Part One)* (2007, *Satsujin kōsatsu [zen]*). Here, we see Mikiya attempt to engage with Shiki's guarded, taciturn female persona.

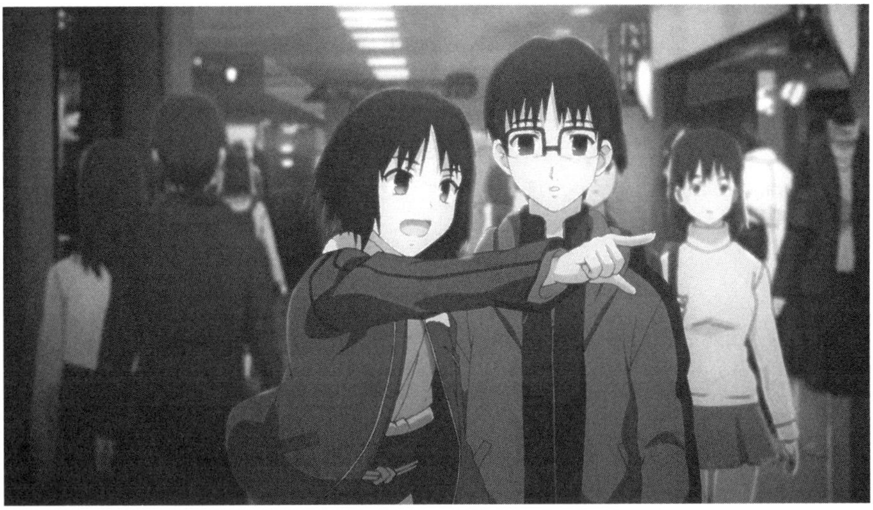

FIGURE 5. An image from the second *Kara no kyōkai* film, . . . *and nothing heart (Murder Speculation, Part One)* (2007, *Satsujin kōsatsu [zen]*). Here, Mikiya goes along for the ride as Shiki's bubbly, outgoing male persona, Shiki-kun, explores a shopping mall.

crisis. From this point onward, Shiki struggles to establish a stable sense of self. In so doing, she gradually grows comfortable expressing emotions and desires through her gruff female personality that she could previously express only by ceding control to Shiki-kun.

In a pat reversal of Miyadai Shinji's argument that otaku and other fans of *bishōjo* works retreat to their fictional goddesses in order to maintain "homeostasis of the self," Ryōgi Shiki sheds the outward trappings of shōjo-hood to achieve the same end.[36] At the same time, *The Garden of Sinners* films realign their narrative and visual structure to place Shiki both as the driving agent of the story and as the subject through whom the audience directs its gaze. By owning her gaze and choosing where to direct it, Shiki joins the growing throng of shōjo characters who transgress the boundary of the screen in order to disrupt the player/viewer's gaze, challenge it, or even reverse it to make actual demands. She counters her minimum safe distance from her mediated environment by adapting nonlinguistic forms of communication—forms that, like the communications of animals previously thought mute and dumb, enable her to move into states of knowledge and being previously thought beyond her grasp. She gains narrative agency, but more than that, she gains a future, a boundless expanse of potentiality that she may freely colonize in ways yet unimaginable.

This potential, of course, stands in contrast to the way in which we conventionally read fictional characters. When Derrida writes of the animal as being "naked without knowing it . . . not having knowledge of their nudity, in short, without consciousness of good and evil," he summarizes the line of philosophical thought, taken up by Heidegger, that argues that animals, without access to language, without sufficient distance from their environment, lack the capacity to comprehend abstract notions like death or shame.[37] The shōjo, seeming to also possess this lack, thus appears to be in a position of absolute exposure, naked before the eyes of the viewer, powerless to do naught but accede to his demands. In directing the shōjo's gaze out toward the viewer, however, the creators of *The Garden of Sinners,* and of many modern *bishōjo* games, disrupt this hierarchy, forcing the viewer to regard the shōjo as being something more than a mute, passive object. Unlike Butterfield's horse, the shōjo is not inseparable from the trappings of her environment; she shows flickerings of being more than mere ink and paint. She transcends her environmental origin, and opens herself to a world.

Notes

1. Martin Heidegger, "The Origin of the Work of Art," in *Basic Writings,* trans. David Farrell Krell (London: Harper Perennial, 2008), 170.

2. Akira Mizuta Lippit, *Electric Animal: Toward a Rhetoric of Wildlife* (Minneapolis: University of Minnesota Press, 2000), 57.

3. Ibid., 65.

4. Thomas Lamarre, *The Anime Machine: A Media Theory of Animation* (Minneapolis: University of Minnesota Press, 2009), 209.

5. Lippit, *Electric Animal,* 2.

6. Ibid., 24.

7. Frenchy Lunning, "Under the Ruffles: Shōjo and the Morphology of Power," *Mechademia* 6 (2011): 16.

8. Brian Bergstrom, "Girliness Next to Godliness: Lolita Fandom as Sacred Criminality in the Novels of Takemoto Novala," *Mechademia* 6 (2011): 34.

9. Lunning, "Under the Ruffles," 17.

10. Anne Allison, *Millennial Monsters: Japanese Toys and the Global Imagination* (Berkeley and Los Angeles: University of California Press, 2006), 160.

11. Lamarre, *The Anime Machine,* 201.

12. Jay David Bolter and Richard Grusin, *Remediation: Understanding New Media* (Cambridge, Mass.: MIT Press, 2000), 6.

13. Ibid., 25.

14. Ibid., 33–34.

15. Ibid., 41–42.

16. Ibid., 45.

17. Ibid.

18. Patrick W. Galbraith, *The Otaku Encyclopedia: An Insider's Guide to the Subculture of Cool Japan* (Tokyo: Kodansha International, 2009), 90.

19. Many games targeted at different audiences also employ a similar premise and format. *Hatoful Boyfriend* (2011, *Haatofuru kareshi*) and the *Tokimeki Memorial Girl's Side* series (2002–2010), for example, position the player as a female avatar pursuing attractive male characters. Many of the features, qualities, and implications of user-interface design for *bishōjo* games apply equally to these titles.

20. Bolter and Grusin, *Remediation,* 33.

21. Patrick W. Galbraith, "Bishōjo Games: 'Techno-Intimacy' and the Virtually Human in Japan," *Game Studies* 11, no. 2 (2011), http://gamestudies.org/1102/articles/galbraith.

22. Laura Mulvey, "Visual Pleasure and Narrative Cinema," in *Film Theory and Criticism,* 7th ed., ed. Leo Braudy and Marshall Cohen (New York: Oxford University Press, 2009), 715.

23. Emily Taylor, "Dating-Simulation Games: Leisure and Gaming of Japanese Youth Culture," *Southeast Review of Asian Studies* 29 (2007): 202.

24. Galbraith, "Bishōjo Games."

25. The games' main innovation in this regard, one might argue, is that they take their time building Phoenix up to that level, with plenty of setbacks along the way.

26. Tom Gunning, "The Cinema of Attraction[s]: Early Film, Its Spectator, and the Avant-Garde," in *The Cinema of Attractions Reloaded,* ed. Wanda Strauven (Amsterdam: Amsterdam University Press, 2006), 382.

27. See Marc Steinberg, *Anime's Media Mix: Franchising Toys and Characters in Japan* (Minneapolis: University of Minnesota Press, 2012).

28. Forrest Greenwood, "A Spectral Pop Star Takes the Stage: Hatsune Miku and the Materialization of the Ephemeral in Contemporary *Otaku* Culture," *Spectator* 33, no. 1 (2013): 10–17. See this article for a more thorough discussion of direct address and the boundary-crossing nature of the shōjo.

29. Azuma Hiroki, *Otaku: Japan's Database Animals,* trans. Jonathan E. Abel and Shion Kono (Minneapolis: University of Minnesota Press, 2009), 80.

30. Bolter and Grusin, *Remediation,* 81. My emphasis.

31. Fan-Yi Lam, "Comic Market: How the World's Biggest Amateur Comic Fair Shaped Japanese *Dōjinshi* Culture," *Mechademia* 5 (2009): 243.

32. Ibid., 242.

33. Nasu Kinoko, Takeuchi Takashi, and Sakamoto Maaya, "The Roots of the Garden of Sinners," in *The Garden of Sinners Visual Chronicle: English Translation* (Santa Monica, Calif.: Aniplex of America, 2011), 1.

34. Each film uses a different director, though the cast and many of the core creative staff remain the same throughout.

35. A shot in the second film, *. . . and nothing heart (Murder Speculation, Part One)* (2007, *Satsujin kōsatsu [zen]*), demonstrates that Shiki writes the name of each of her personalities using a different character. The—*kun* diminutive only appears in the films' spoken dialogue.

36. Miyadai Shinji, "Transformation of Semantics in the History of Japanese Subcultures since 1992," trans. Shion Kono, *Mechademia* 6 (2011): 240.

37. Jacques Derrida, *The Animal That Therefore I Am,* trans. David Wills, ed. Marie-Louise Mallet (New York: Fordham University Press, 2008), 5.

ALEXANDRA ROEDDER

The Localization of *Kiki's Delivery Service*

In 1997 when Buena Vista, working for the Walt Disney Company, was handed Miyazaki Hayao's *Kiki's Delivery Service* (1989, *Majo no takkyūbin*) to localize for United States distribution, they went beyond the usual requirements of translating and dubbing the script. They hired composer Paul Chihara to edit Hisaishi Joe's original score to, in Chihara's words, "make the film work" for U.S. audiences.[1] These edits are simple but powerful: music is shifted to hit points of audiovisual synchronization, extra music is added to scenes that were previously silent, and some scenes have their existing music supplemented with additional countermelodies. As a result, the initial English-language version of *Kiki* that U.S. audiences experienced on VHS was a very different film from the one experienced by Japanese audiences in 1989 in theaters. Instead of a quiet coming-of-age story about a young witch discovering the importance of believing in herself, Disney's localized *Kiki's Delivery Service* was a series of comic misadventures returning to the status quo—with a boyfriend in tow—at the end. In considering Studio Ghibli's reception in the United States, we must understand why the film's score was changed and the effect of those changes on the film. Examining the differences between the two scores is also essential to understanding the implications of the 2010 rerelease on DVD,

> DISNEY'S LOCALIZED *KIKI'S DELIVERY SERVICE* WAS A SERIES OF COMIC MISADVENTURES RETURNING TO THE STATUS QUO—WITH A BOYFRIEND IN TOW—AT THE END.

which reinstates Hisaishi's music, removes additional lines from the score, and attempts to erase any evidence that there had ever been a need to tinker with the film beyond translating it.[2]

Kiki's Delivery Service is based on the popular 1985 novel by Eiko Kadono. The titular Kiki is a thirteen-year-old witch who, following tradition, sets off to find a town of her own to live and work in for a year. In the novel, she encounters a series of challenges and adventures, and overcomes each in turn before returning home to visit her parents, with the clear intention of going back to her beloved new town just in time for book two. In the film, Kiki's character undergoes extensive development: she learns to see the good in all kinds of people, including herself. Midway through the film, Kiki loses her self-confidence and with it, her magic powers—the ability to fly and to understand her cat familiar, Jiji. Only a desperate need to rescue a friend in danger allows her to regain the ability to fly, though she has matured beyond needing to speak with Jiji. Due to small changes in dialogue and the edits to the music, the 1997 Disney version is quite different: not only can Kiki speak with Jiji again at the end, but the small adventures are emphasized in such a way that the large-scale arc of development is completely lost.

FROM THE BEGINNING

The changed score is evident from the beginning. As the film opens, the camera pans across an idyllic lakefront with wildflowers waving in the foreground and clouds skating through a windy sky. A radio can be heard giving the weather report. In Japanese, this report is strictly predictions and information; in English, the DJ is chatty, giving information about the airship which will figure heavily in the second half of the story, and, in saying that the weather will be clear that night, adds, "If you've been planning something special, tonight . . . might be the night!" which, like the chatter about the airship, foreshadows Kiki's leaving home.[3] Musically, the scenes employ the exact same segment of music (in film music terms, a "cue"), "Hareta hi ni" ("On a Sunny Day"). The cue uses a typical Hisaishi melody, regular in shape, in a gentle rolling waltz time.

Hisaishi's melodies are highly recognizable and are an important part of what defines his style. For that reason, it is necessary that I take a moment to explain how this melody is structured. Like most of his melodies, "Hareta hi ni" is in what music theorists call a *rounded binary* form: the entire piece can be split into three sections, with the final section a repeat of the first. Despite having three sections, it only has two segments, A and B—hence "binary." Because the final section is nearly identical to the first, it is called "rounded." Usually music theorists write the form as A-B-A or A-B-A′. Rounded binary form is one of the most common forms for music to take, and fits comfortably in our ears because of the balance of repetition and contrast: we come back at the end to something we recognize. (Think of a popular song you know which starts and ends with the chorus and only has one verse in between.) In the case of "Hareta hi ni," not only is the cue in large-scale rounded binary form, but also the A and B sections are themselves parsable into recognizable, repeating phrases, little a and a′ and b and b′ phrases, almost like a fractal or snowflake showing symmetrical splits continuously as one zooms further in. The effect is one of delicate balance between repetition and variation, and this balance has become part of Hisaishi's trademark melodies.

There are two small differences between Hisaishi's version and Chihara's version at the beginning: when and how each begins. Hisaishi's version has the cue beginning as Kiki gets up from the grass and begins running home, segmenting the scene into Kiki-at-rest versus Kiki-in-motion. The music starts with a firm tonic chord, unashamedly announcing its presence.[4] In contrast, Chihara's version begins some twenty-five seconds earlier, as a bee lands on a flower, and is preceded by a twinkly dominant seventh chord (or V^7 in traditional Roman numeral analysis) in synthesized chimes. In Western music, a dominant seventh chord is the chord with the strongest sense of wanting to resolve back to the home tonic. If on a piano you play a chord of G, B, D, and F, you will feel massively unsatisfied if you do not follow that with a chord of C, E, G. Chihara's use of this leading chord effectively softens the theme's entrance. As Claudia Gorbman points out, for over half a century, film composers have exhorted each other to write music that enters subtly, underneath the conscious listener.[5] The shift in starting time also enables Chihara to hit a number of small sync points aside from the bee's landing: for instance, as Kiki splashes through the mud on the other side of a fence, her three steps are synced with the three stepwise chords which link the aforementioned a and a' phrases of the A section.

The big changes to the opening sequence come as Kiki arrives at her home and tells Jiji to "Wake up! Tonight's the night!" (or, in Japanese, "*Kon'ya ni kimeta wa! Shuppatsu yo*!", literally, "I've decided on tonight! We're leaving!"). Hisaishi lets the theme play out at its full two-minute length. The only sync point is more of what Michel Chion would term a moment of "audiovisual phrasing" between the B section and the return of the A section: after Kiki has dropped the bombshell on her mother that she's leaving that night, the distracted mother's potion quietly explodes out of its test tube into her face.[6] The synchronization of this moment with the musical form cannot be coincidental; writing to match such a moment is common among Hisaishi's other film scores from the era.

Instead of presenting the scene as a single event, Chihara's score splits the scene into three distinct events: Kiki running home, Kiki talking to her mother, and then Kiki's mother talking with her customer. Each scene's music has a different emotional affect, setting it apart from the one before it and the one after it. Chihara's version does not even let the cue reach its B section. He cuts it off at the closure of the A section, which occurs at about the same time that Kiki pokes her head in through her mother's workshop window, interrupts a customer, and announces, "Hey Mom! It's gonna be clear tonight!" As Kiki's mother begins gently castigating her daughter for borrowing her father's radio and resigns herself to Kiki's sudden announcement that she's leaving, Chihara replaces Hisaishi's B section with a bouncy, jolly background non-melodic accompaniment in a key as distant from "On a Sunny Day" as possible: a tritone, or six half-steps, half an octave away (for example, the distance between C and F-sharp). The potion exploding marks the end of this new theme. After a pause in which Kiki's mother sighs, Chihara reintroduces Hisaishi's theme, again using a dominant fifth arpeggio to soften its entrance. Chihara ends in the middle of the A section as the customer begins reminiscing about the arrival of Kiki's mother to the town many years ago. The return of Hisaishi's music and its abrupt closure only highlights the bouncy accompaniment to Kiki's enthusiastic departure announcement. A final addition Chihara makes to the existing music is to introduce Jiji's theme, or *leitmotif,* at the cat's first appearance on the window ledge. Jiji's leitmotif is a sinuous little question mark of a motif, ambiguous and chromatic, shaped almost like the cat's tail itself. The leitmotif recurs throughout the film, particularly when Jiji is the focus of the action.

Thus we see how the rounded binary of Hisaishi's original cue is important in keeping the scene's sense of unity. When Chihara inserts original music, the rounded binary form is disrupted, and we understand the first few minutes of the film to be completely separate scenes instead of one scene split into multiple cuts.

Throughout the entire film Chihara's music frequently performs a similar function, breaking up Hisaishi's long stretches of melody into shorter phrases, usually never more than a minute long. As Marco Bellano has pointed out,

Hisaishi's use of these long melodies can be linked to the original production method of Ghibli films.[7] For each film, Hisaishi is given a bit of text, the "music memo," explaining the film and its characters, and from that information writes an "image album," which is usually released about a year in advance of the film, sometimes before even a trailer is out. The image album performs two functions. First, it allows Hisaishi and the studio to test musical material in advance, deciding on character themes and musical ideas. Second, it is a useful marketing tool, generating excitement about the film in advance. As Hisaishi has grown more and more famous over the years, his new album releases become much anticipated events. Hisaishi's long sweeping melodies are so closely associated with his name and style that, according to Kyoko Koizumi and my own ethnographic work, the term "Hisaishi melody" has become common parlance in Japan.[8]

In direct contrast to the way that Ghibli's films are made with the musical ideas first, U.S. film music composers since the earliest days of sound cinema have been exhorted to write music that can be easily chopped up and still be comprehensible. Function takes precedence over form. In U.S. animation this was—is—even more pronounced, resulting in frenetic action sequences to frenetic action music. The term "mickey-mousing" has come to refer to a one-to-one relationship between music and visuals because of this historical use of highly synchronous music. While Chihara's edits to the opening cue are hardly "mickey-mousing," being only the synchronization of a few footsteps and a cut-and-paste of existing ideas, he does employ the tactic elsewhere in the film to comic effect, as when Kiki is trying to use the outdoor bathroom without being seen by her landlords: Chihara provides an exactly isomorphic and isochronic accompaniment to each and every one of her movements, from getting up out of the bed to going down the stairs, to coming back up the stairs and sighing in relief.

The terms used above, "isomorphic" and "isochronic," should be self-explanatory. Michel Chion appropriated the term isomorphic, presumably from mathematics, to apply to audiovisual relationships that share shapes.[9] I have supplemented that with my own term, isochronic, to refer to the synchronicity in time: footsteps matching rhythm, for example, or a ship tossing in a storm to chaotic music that changes direction at the same time as the ship. It is possible for music to be isochronic without being isomorphic—"audiovisual phrasing" is an example of this, though on a large scale. And it is possible to be isomorphic without being isochronic, though in my experience this is a rare occurrence: an upwards melodic gesture in advance of a spaceship taking off, for instance, or a larger-scale movement in which smaller sync points are

MUSIC'S PRESENCE IMPOSES A SINGLE INTERPRETATION ON A SCENE.

ignored. It is my hope that these two terms will become more widely used, as they separate out the vague "synchronized" into separate axes of gesture and pacing.

The second important way Chihara's score changes the filmgoer's experience is by what I can only refer to as removing emotional autonomy and agency from the viewer. Scenes that had been silent—the "low-key enchantment" Roland Kelts so admires—instead have music.[10] The silence had allowed individual viewers to experience scenes differently, letting past experiences or expectations determine a scene's mood. Music's presence imposes a single interpretation on a scene, such as the comic effect mentioned above in connection with the use of highly isomorphic and isochronic music to accompany Kiki's anxious trip to the bathroom. When I watched that scene my first reaction was one of nostalgic embarrassment: as a child about Kiki's age I certainly hadn't wanted to be caught in my nightgown, much less coming out of a bathroom, by any adult, not even my parents. Other people may have different reactions, and when the scene is silent they are given the leeway to experience it as they choose.

An excellent example of this occurs just after Kiki settles with the friendly baker's wife, Osono, to borrow their storage room in exchange for help around the shop during Osono's pregnancy. Hisaishi leaves this scene silent: the only sounds are the dialogue between Kiki and Jiji:

JIJI: Covered in flour, isn't it.

KIKI: Mm.

JIJI: When tomorrow comes, I think I'll have turned into a white cat.

KIKI (opens window): Jiji, [one] can see the ocean.

JIJI: Tomorrow, [shall we] look for another town?

In the Japanese version, this is a moment of narrative closure. Kiki left her home the previous night, slept in a cattle train to escape a sudden downpour, and arrived in the new big town in the morning full of optimism. Her good mood, though, had been crumbling away bit by bit all day. She nearly collided with a bus, got into trouble with a policeman, was seemingly accosted by a boy who wanted to flirt with her, couldn't get a room at a hotel because she had no identification and no parents, and couldn't even sit quietly in a park without feeling hunted and out of place. The film is at an emotional low point when Kiki performs a random good deed for the baker Osono, flying on her broomstick to return a pacifier to a customer who'd left it in the shop. Upon meeting Osono, Kiki's troubles seem to be over. She's found a friend, she has a room to stay in, and she can move forward to the next step of self-discovery. Her tone of voice and her dialogue are neither optimistic nor depressed. The relative neutrality of this scene leads the viewer into a place of waiting: What will the morning bring?

The U.S. version is completely different. The changes—additional music and dialogue translation—combine to position the scene not as closure of a narrative arc but as a continuation of adventure and narrative tension. First, the dialogue is liberally translated to:

JIJI: This is . . . quaint.

KIKI: (exasperated) Jiji . . .

JIJI: (off frame) This isn't dust on the floor, you know, it's flour. (on frame) If you wake up tomorrow and find a white cat, it's me.

KIKI: (opens window): Ooh, Jiji, we can see the ocean from here! (Exclaims sounds of pleasure.)

JIJI: (disappointed, almost whining) Can we look for a new town? (When no answer, grumbles.)

The duo's fairly steady assessment of the situation evident in the Japanese lines has become a cynical, almost snide, judgment of the situation on Jiji's part, and a determined cheerfulness on Kiki's. The delivery of these lines is strikingly different from the almost neutral performance of Kiki's and Jiji's Japanese voice actors. Even though in both versions Jiji suggests looking for a new town, the Japanese *hoka no machi o sagasu?* ("Shall we look for a new town?") is more of a suggestion, request, or even a simple question rather than a complaint. Jiji's English lines encourage the viewer to be pessimistic about their situation and to juxtapose Kiki's optimism against negative odds.

The music Chihara uses for this scene is a solo piano rendition of "*Tabidachi*" (Setting off), which Hisaishi used to accompany the stretch of time between Kiki's affectionate cuddle with her father shortly before setting off and her actual departure. Again, as he did when editing the opening music, Chihara only uses a snippet of Hisaishi's extended melody. The music colors the scene with homesickness, not only because of its leitmotivic association with Kiki's parents and home but also because of its performance in a loose, slow-jazz affect that reminds me of the pianists one used to hear at upscale department stores. The performance is soulful and nostalgic without being sappy or dolorous. While certainly appropriate to an interpretation of the scene as one of homesickness, the question is whether the interpretation is needed. To Japanese audiences, it evidently wasn't: from the film producer to the composer to the audiences—whose support of the film skyrocketed Ghibli to its current fame—the scene apparently held up fine by itself. To the U.S. film professionals who localized *Kiki*, though, it was. Why?

There are two reasons. First, U.S. animated films, from the beginning with Disney's *Snow White* in 1937, have historically been musicals. In 1996 and 1997, when the Walt Disney Company and Studio Ghibli were negotiating the distribution agreement, Disney had recently released *Pocahontas* (1995), *The Hunchback of Notre Dame* (1996), and *Hercules* (1997), all of which are classic animated musicals. Suzuki Toshio mentioned in an interview in May 2012 that selling the films to the United States, particularly to Disney, had been difficult for this very reason: Ghibli films are not musicals.[11] To a viewer familiar with Japanese film and television, the silences of *Kiki's Delivery Service* are calming, charming, and comfortable. To an audience accustomed to the lively spectacle of Disney's films, *Kiki*'s soundtrack—not just the score but also pauses in dialogue and a low level of background noise—may easily have been awkward and uncomfortable.

In addition to the historical bias toward animated musicals, there is also the issue of what is now common knowledge to Americans exposed to anime: in the United States, cartoons are mostly "for kids," but Japanese animation had aimed at varying demographics for half a century. U.S. cartoons for adults certainly do exist now: *The Simpsons, Family Guy, King of the Hill,* and other shows that poke fun at our society. But these shows are aimed at adults, not at the discrete demographics of Japanese shōnen, shōjo, and other genres. Additionally, even now an animated film aimed at all ages (not "at families," which in the U.S. often means "at children") is rare. The way Chihara used and placed music in editing *Kiki* comes across as assisting an uncertain viewer in interpreting events. This is exactly the kind of helping hand a viewer new to the conventions of anime would want or, more important I believe, the kind of assistance children often get when processing new information. One of music's primary functions in narrative film is to provide emotional cues, and Chihara's score does this splendidly, often excessively. Although Chihara has said that aiming the film at an audience of children was not his intent, nevertheless his score positions the audience as a passive recipient of a predetermined interpretation of the film, rather than an active consumer of and semi-participant in Kiki's inner journey. This approach highlights a fundamental cultural difference in assumptions of what the experience of watching an animated film should be.

The edits to *Kiki's* score have largely passed under the radar of most viewers, although Andrew Osmond wrote:

> There are such extensive reorderings, additions and "enhancements"—such as Titanic-style wordless vocals—that the score is really a separate entity. Most obviously, the additions cover the deliberate silences that typify Miyazaki films (and much other anime). Elsewhere, passages are split into shorter pieces, with old or new music pushed in between. Whole sections of the film sound different. The sequence in which Kiki makes her first delivery, encountering geese and crows (accompanied in the dub by a cheesy "Mountain King") is almost entirely altered.
>
> For Hisaishi purists (myself included), these changes are often clumsy and ill-advised, leading to clashes and repetitions. (Indeed, there's a moment just before Osono appears when two tunes are heard fighting each other.)[12]

Most, though, don't seem to have cared too much. Helen McCarthy's assessment of the film is that nothing major was changed.[13] In Japan, the edited score is effectively unknown, despite being available as the English-language track on the 2001 Japanese DVD release. Even Suzuki Toshio, the film's producer, needed to be reminded of the fact that it was edited.[14] He then commented:

> Certainly there are passages where the details are different, but I don't think it's a problem. I think Hisaishi, were he to watch the movie properly, would have the same opinion.[15]

Suzuki is musically literate and holds his own in discussions of music with composers such as Sakamoto Ryūichi, and yet the changes to the score did not have a strong impact on him.[16] I sought Hisaishi's opinion on the subject during fieldwork in 2011–12 but was rebuffed by his formidable manager. She forbade me to ask him anything about Disney, was shocked that the edited score even existed, and seemed confident that Hisaishi didn't know either. As Hisaishi and Paul Chihara met in 1997 during the localization, it is probable that the manager simply didn't know Hisaishi's earlier history.

In 2010, Disney released a new DVD of *Kiki's Delivery Service* without Chihara's score and with almost none of the off-screen lines that are not present in the original script, most of which were comic asides by Jiji. Crucially gone is the line at the end where Jiji spoke to Kiki, which was essential in the 1997 version to bring the plot full circle back to Kiki as a witch who can speak with her cat, rather than progressing linearly as a journey into a mature state where she doesn't need to speak with Jiji.[17] It is the reinstatement of

Hisaishi's soundtrack that does the most to reclaim the quiet charm and enchanting silences of the original Japanese film, though only so much can be done to counteract the occasional poor voice acting and clumsy translations. The English-language version with Hisaishi's score retains large-scale narrative arcs instead of short ones, returns some emotional agency to the viewer, and avoids "mickey-mousing" jaunts up staircases or crashes with buses. The comic elements of Chihara's score have been largely removed, allowing the serious elements of Kiki's coming-of-age story to progress more obviously.

While Miyazaki purists and fans in search of "authentic" anime may rejoice over the reinstatement of the original soundtrack to the English-language version, there is a negative side to the 2010 rerelease. By reverting the film's soundtrack to Hisaishi's original and removing the extra dialogue, it is as if Disney is trying to rewrite history, to say that, no, we never needed anything other than a simple translation to make the film work for U.S. audiences. This was not the case at the time. Let us keep in mind that the edits to *Kiki* were not all that extreme when taken in context. In 1997, when Buena Vista/Disney decided that the film needed extra lines and music, edit-dubs such as Carl Macek's *Robotech* (1985) and DIC's *Sailor Moon* (1994) were considered the norm. Films were not immune, either: back in 1960, Tōei's *Saiyūki* (Journey to the west) was completely rescored as a Disney-style musical and released as *Alakazam the Great,* featuring the voice of Frankie Avalon. Fred Patten has written of the rocky road toward anime's current popularity and the varying successes of localization tactics.[18] Fred Ladd has likewise explained how his job in localizing shows such as *Astro Boy* was to completely disguise its Japanese origins.[19] Even into the 1990s, U.S. producers had doubts about distributing foreign Japanese films, even the excellent works of Studio Ghibli. Recall that *Nausicäa of the Valley of the Wind* (1984, *Kaze no tani no Naushika*) received its own edit-dub treatment to become *Warriors of the Wind* in 1985, a version that, according to Suzuki, Miyazaki "would like everyone to please forget."[20] If anything, recent releases of animated films with only a dubbed script are a revolutionary development in the U.S. reception of Japanese anime.

It is important in revealing this history not to forget that the many soundtracks of *Kiki's Delivery Service* involved hard work from many dedicated people. Hisaishi has worked to make his music into what he described in a 1987 as a "special brand," and it is safe to say that he has succeeded.[21] He is Japan's most popular film composer and has recently expanded his domain into film with directors in other parts of Asia. Young composers strive to become Hisaishi, whose minimalism-inspired melodic style has heavily influenced the sound of other Japanese live-action and animation film scores.[22] Since 1984 he has composed for each of Miyazaki's ten feature films, including Miyazaki's final film, *Kaze tachinu* (2013, The wind rises). What Hisaishi has written for the Ghibli films has, for mainstream Western audiences, become the sound of Japanese animation. Today, a Ghibli film without Hisaishi's music is not quite Ghibli.

In a 2011 interview, Chihara emphasized to me the difficulty of the entire Kiki project, and specifically of the frustrations of working with the material when they could not change a single frame. To Chihara, matching the lip-flap with a script that corresponded closely to the original Japanese was a major accomplishment. Chihara's music, similarly, had to be squeezed into the film to work with what was already there. To his ears at the time, his musical additions improved an otherwise unsellable product. The VHS national sales rankings show that the film did quite well, ranking eighth at its highest.[23] Chihara sees his score as a bridge between Japan and the United States, and is massively proud to have been the composer whose music was a part of the beginning of Ghibli's American popularity.[24]

It is highly likely that Paul Chihara's version of *Kiki* has influenced, even indirectly, how Hisaishi writes for animation. Hisaishi has said several times that American audiences need more music than Japanese ones, and that the Hollywood style of scoring, using character themes and isomorphic/isochronic writing, is very different from the Japanese way, which emphasizes mood and emotion.[25] In 1999, perhaps to avoid having someone else do it, Hisaishi specifically asked Suzuki for permission to rewrite the score for *Castle in the Sky*'s North American release himself, despite the amount of work it would take. That version, which was Hisaishi's first attempt at writing a Hollywood-style score for an animated film, edits the original score in many of the same ways that Chihara edited *Kiki*: adding more music, shifting cues to create sync points, and supplementing existing music with countermelodies, all for the sake of having music enter and exit more subtly and be more closely tied to the visual action on screen. Although there is no space here to detail my extensive studies of Hisaishi's evolving film score style, the 1999 *Castle in the Sky* score was Hisaishi's first attempt at writing in the Hollywood style, and the result sounds as if he used Chihara's edits for *Kiki* as a model for how American audiences wanted their cartoons. After *Castle in the Sky,* Hisaishi's next three scores for Studio Ghibli are all written in a grand symphonic style that borrows not only the sound but also the tactics of classic Hollywood film scores. Even if Hisaishi was not directly influenced by Chihara's *Kiki* score, he was definitely influenced by the knowledge that U.S. audiences want a particular kind of music.

IT IS NEVERTHELESS CLEAR THAT CHIHARA'S SCORE FOR *KIKI*, OR POSSIBLY JUST THE KNOWLEDGE THAT GHIBLI FILMS WERE BEING DISTRIBUTED GLOBALLY, INFLUENCED HOW HISAISHI PUT MUSIC TO FILM.

The history of artistic exchange between Japan and the United States has been reasonably well documented as to visual elements. However, as yet, the history of musical styles and practices is almost completely untouched. Above I mention the adaptation of *Astro Boy* and *Saiyūki* in the 1960s, but there is also the fascinating story of *Little Nemo: Adventures in Slumberland* (Japanese title *Nemo*, 1989; United States, 1992), a fully collaborative work between Japan and the United States. The production was huge and involved a number of people who either were important at the time or would later become important: Ray Bradbury worked on concept art; Chris Columbus of *Harry Potter* fame worked on the screenplay; Disney animation giants Ollie Johnston and Frank Thomas are credited as "story consultants," and all the characters look like Disney characters. In the music department there are the Academy Award–winning Sherman brothers of *Mary Poppins* fame writing the songs and Roy Prendergast, now a respected film music historian, as music editor. The rest of the score, by Thomas Chase and Steve Rucker, is a well-executed example of standard cartoon soundtrack writing. Despite the lavish production, *Little Nemo* was a commercial flop in both countries, and it is easy to see why Japanese audiences could have been put off by its overtly American artwork and soundtrack when they had distinctly Japanese films coming one after another out of Studio Ghibli around the same time. Fast forward fifteen years, however, and the same practices that were off-putting in *Little Nemo* were successful in *Howl's Moving Castle* (2004).

Therefore, this moment in history when someone at Disney decided that the score for *Kiki* was too silent was not just a moment of blank-minded cultural bias, as we "enlightened" anime fans and consumers of today could easily see. It was a very important moment in defining, first, that Ghibli's films would sell to North American audiences; second, that those North American audiences wanted a certain kind of music in their films; and third, a few years later, that Japanese audiences liked that kind of music, too. While it is overly simplistic to say that Hisaishi changed his compositional practices for the sake of reaching this North American audience, it is nevertheless clear that Chihara's score for *Kiki*, or possibly just the knowledge that Ghibli films were being distributed globally, influenced how Hisaishi put music to film. *Kiki*'s first localization and its edited score thus become intricately intertwined in not only one popular composer's personal development but also in the definition of what Studio Ghibli sounds like. And because Ghibli's films are so widely distributed, the sound of Ghibli is for many the sound of Japanese anime. Further, because Ghibli's films are so definitive as anime within Japan, and because so many young composers want to write like Hisaishi and become Hisaishi, it is Hisaishi's style and practices, as influenced by this history, that are defining contemporary anime music.

Scholars who write about the history of anime in America have a great advantage in that many of the creators we study are still alive and can give us their versions of this history. Therefore I would like to close not with a judgment of which version of *Kiki* is "better" but rather with an exhortation that, as historical documents, both are equally important. Instead of dismissing early edit-dubs as mistakes or embarrassments to be covered up, scholars need to understand these first attempts at localizing anime as exactly what they are: first attempts. Reinstating Hisaishi's score may have brought the English-language audio track closer to the Japanese version of the film, but in the end, watching a dub, no matter how good a translation, can never be exactly the same as the Japanese-language experience. Understanding the history of *Kiki*'s localization is not at all a question of which is right or which is better or which is more "authentic." It is a question of how *Kiki's* localization fits into the larger narrative of U.S. reception of anime as well as how Hisaishi's scoring style, and consequently the sound of Ghibli films—and anime soundtracks as a whole—have evolved.

Notes

1. Paul Chihara, personal interview, February 11, 2009.

2. To clarify, I am discussing the following releases: *Majo no takkyūbin,* dir. Miyazaki Hayao (1989), DVD (Buena Vista Home Entertainment, 2001); translated as *Kiki's Delivery Service,* dubbed VHS (Walt Disney Video, 1998); translated as *Kiki's Delivery Service,* DVD (Walt Disney Video, 2003); translated as *Kiki's Delivery Service,* DVD (Disney Presents Studio Ghibli, 2010). The second and third releases contain the same localized English audio track with Chihara's score.

3. Note to those who may be familiar with the film's English-language subtitles: the subtitles are not literal and are aimed at providing language appropriate to the situation if experienced in English ("pack up your picnic baskets!") rather than a translation ("warm weather"). These are often called "dubtitles," having often been taken from the dub script. In *Kiki,* the dubtitles and the dub script are not exactly the same—often the Japanese lines have a different timing than the dub—but they are very similar in meaning.

4. The tonic chord is the "home" chord of a piece of music. If a piece is in C major, the tonic chord is C major. If a piece is in D-flat minor, the tonic is D-flat minor.

5. Claudia Gorbman, *Unheard Melodies: Narrative Film Music* (Bloomington: Indiana University Press, 1987).

6. Michel Chion, *Film, A Sound Art,* trans. Claudia Gorbman (New York: Columbia University Press, 2009), 469.

7. Marco Bellano, "The Parts and the Whole: Audiovisual Strategies in the Cinema of Hayao Miyazaki and Joe Hisaishi," *Animation Journal* 18 (2010): 4–55.

8. Kyoko Koizumi, "An Animated Partnership: Joe Hisaishi's Musical Contributions to Hayao Miyazaki's Films," in *Drawn to Sound: Animation Film Music and Sonicity,* ed. Rebecca Coyle, 60–74 (London: Equinox, 2010).

9. Michel Chion, *Audio-Vision,* trans. Claudia Gorbman (New York: Columbia University Press, 1994), 121.

10. Roland Kelts, *Japanamerica: How Japanese Pop Culture Has Invaded the U.S.* (New York: Palgrave Macmillan, 2006), 56.

11. Suzuki Toshio, personal interview, May 16, 2012.

12. Andrew Osmond, "Will the Real Joe Hisaishi Stand Up?" *Animation World Magazine* 5.01 (April 2000), http://www.awn.com/mag/issue5.01/5.01pages/osmondhisaishi.php3.

13. Helen McCarthy, *Hayao Miyazaki, Master of Japanese Animation* (Berkeley, Calif.: Stone Bridge Press, 2002), 143.

14. Suzuki interview.

15. Suzuki Toshio, personal e-mail communication, June 11, 2012: "Ōki na henkō ga kuwaerareta to iu ninshiki wa motte imasen. Saibu ni kanshite wa, tashikani chigau kasho mo arimasu ga, mondai to wa omotte inai no desu. Chanto eiga o mireba, Hisaishi Jō-san mo onaji iken o motsu to omoimasu."

16. Suzuki Toshio, "*Sakamoto Ryūichi kanshū commons schola vol. 10 no happyō kinen tokubetsu tōku ibento ni ojama shite kimashita*" (Intruding on Sakamoto Ryūichi's *Commons Schola* vol. 10 special announcement talk event to commemorate the album release), podcast, May 24, 2012, http://podcasts.tfm.co.jp/podcasts/tokyo/rg/suzuki_vol226.mp3, listened to as advance copy on May 18, 2012.

17. Interestingly, in this respect the episodic nature of the 1997 Disney version is closer to the original novel.

18. Fred Patten, *Watching Anime, Reading Manga: 25 Years of Essays and Reviews* (Berkeley, Calif.: Stone Bridge Press, 2004).

19. Fred Ladd, *Astro Boy and Anime Come to the Americas: An Insider's View of the Birth of a Pop Culture Phenomenon* (Jefferson, N.C.: McFarland, 2008).

20. Suzuki, interview.

21. Hisaishi Joe, 1987, "Supesharu intabyū–Hisaishi Jō 'tsuneni supesharu burando de aritai,'" (Special interview: Hisaishi Joe "I want to always be a special brand"), *Kinema junpo* 973 (1987): 132–35.

22. Kuriyama Kazuki, personal interview, February 17, 2012.

23. The Hayao MIYAZAKI Web, "Ranking // Kiki's Delivery Service // Nausicaa.net," http://www.nausicaa.net/miyazaki/kiki/ranking.html.

24. Paul Chihara, personal interview, May 21, 2011.

25. Hisaishi Joe, interview with Miyazaki Mailing List, July 14, 1999, archived at *The Hayao Miyazaki Web,* http://www.nausicaa.net/miyazaki/laputa/interview.html; Hisaishi Joe, personal interview, June 9, 2012.

起源

RAYNA DENISON

Franchising and Failure: Discourses of Failure within the Japanese-American *Speed Racer* Franchise

Two texts are commonly cited by those recounting anime's early transnational history in the United States: Tezuka Osamu's *Astro Boy* (1963–66, *Tetsuwan Atomu*) and Tatsuo Yoshida's *Speed Racer* (1967–68, *Mahha go go go*).[1] However, where *Astro Boy* has been studied in some depth by academics, as a Tezuka creation and as the first anime to cross over to U.S. television, *Speed Racer* has received scant attention.[2] *Speed Racer*'s relative academic invisibility is contrasted by its recent renewal as a multimedia franchise. Starting in the 1990s, with the formation of Speed Racer Enterprises by John and Jim Rocknowski, *Speed Racer* has been rerun (initially on MTV), has been adapted multiple times for television and the cinema, and has been made available through a wide range of merchandise.[3] The franchise has also been augmented in Japan by its original creators, Tatsunoko Production Co., whose Mach Project Production Committee was created in 2003 to exploit the earliest incarnations of *Speed Racer*, especially the television anime *Mahha go go go*.[4] As these separate national approaches to *Speed Racer*'s continuing production suggest, the franchise is not a straightforwardly "Japanese" manga or anime property. This article examines the recent live-action *Speed Racer* film in order to investigate perceptions of its origins, as the franchise continues to be reproduced and repackaged across decades, continents, and cultures.

Beginning life as a moderate hit on Japanese television, *Mahha go go go* was only the second anime television series created by Tatsunoko Production Co. From its inception, *Mahha go go go* had transnational roots. Ippei Kuri (cocreator Toyoharu Yoshida's pen name) has stated that the series "was based strictly on our all-out adoration of America."[5] The Japanese version follows the adventures of race car driver Mifune Gō, whose family, girlfriend, and chimpanzee travel around the globe racing on futuristic tracks. The show was adapted for the American market by Peter Fernandez, who translated and redubbed *Mahha go go go* as *Speed Racer* for the Trans-Lux Television Corporation.[6] As with many of its anime contemporaries, therefore, the early transnational history of *Mahha go go go* was one of wholesale cultural reinterpretation and origin erasure.[7]

Like those earlier television productions, the *Speed Racer* (2008, dir. Lana and Andy Wachowski) film also has a transnational ethos at its heart: from the hybridized national locations invented for its diegesis; to the nationally specific car racing crews depicted within the film; to the mixture of European, Asian, and American stars who play its characters; to its partial European funding and production at Studio Babelsberg in Germany.[8] In these ways, the 2008 *Speed Racer* film heightens discourses about the places and origins of the *Speed Racer* franchise. The film also takes *Speed Racer* from cel animation into a new mixture of live action and CGI-effects filmmaking, making it a challenging example of remediation. Using Julian Stringer's approach to adaptation, which examines the discourses around adaptation in order to investigate how meanings are negotiated at specific historical-textual junctures, this article examines the industrial and reception discourses around the release of the *Speed Racer* film.[9] Through this analysis of American popular and industry reportage, it becomes possible to gauge how *Speed Racer* failed at the box office and what roles its transnational anime roots played in this failed experiment in blockbuster filmmaking.

Focusing on an unsuccessful adaptation also provides a rare opportunity to test the limits of manga and anime's global success. Its growing global profile over the last two to three decades has been noted. Henry Jenkins, for example, specifically cites anime and manga within his discussions of transnational pop cosmopolitanisms, and anime features strongly in Koichi Iwabuchi's contention that globalization should be conceptualized as a multidimensional process illustrated by Japanese media's spread to the rest of the world.[10] These challenges to American pop-cultural dominance offer

> THE EARLY TRANSNATIONAL HISTORY OF *MAHHA GO GO GO* WAS ONE OF WHOLESALE CULTURAL REINTERPRETATION AND ORIGIN ERASURE.

useful correctives to discussions of popular culture, but the risk is in overstating manga and anime's global popularity and reach. The failure of *Speed Racer* therefore provides an example of the kinds of "structuring absences" sought in reception studies: in order to understand the extent of anime's success, this study focuses on how an otherwise long-lived and successful manga-originated franchise can lead to "the costliest misfire of the year."[11]

Speed Racer's box office failure was widely reported as the worst of 2008. Commenting only a week after the film's initial release, Ben Fritz of *Daily Variety* baldly proclaimed, "Warner has a bomb on its hands."[12] The *New York Post*, meanwhile, quickly speculated on the implications of the film's failure, "Box-office bomb *Speed Racer*—which cost more than $120 million to make but raked in less than $20 million last weekend—is causing speed bumps for all involved," claiming that the film's perceived failure had thrown producer Joel Silver's relationship with Warner Bros. into question, and had caused the film's star, Emile Hirst, to fire his agents.[13] Estimates on the budget and box office for *Speed Racer* varied wildly in the months that followed, clarifying (and exaggerating) *Speed Racer*'s relative failure. Brooks Barnes of the *New York Times* estimated the total cost at "$250 million to produce and market," more than doubling initial budgetary estimates.[14] The escalating sense of calamity following the release of the *Speed Racer* film offers a good example of how high the stakes for anime adaptations can be, and why it is important to understand what explanations were given for its failure. This article therefore asks how initial critical disappointment with the *Speed Racer* film was couched in America and how those discourses connect to larger questions about the status of anime as an originating source for transnational, transmedia pop culture.

SPEED RACER'S FAILURE AND ITS TRANSNATIONAL ANIME ORIGINS

Thanks to the kinds of gloomy reporting noted above, *Speed Racer* quickly became synonymous with blockbuster failure. Even three years later, producer Joel Silver was still on the defensive, saying: "I tried to do [something similar to his new *Ben 10* film] with *Speed Racer* and failed miserably . . . You always learn more from the ones that don't work than the ones that do work."[15] However, one of the major differences between Silver's *Ben 10* cartoon adaptation and the adaptation of *Speed Racer* can be found in the latter's ambiguous national origins.

Speed Racer's complex transnationalism appears to have challenged critics, as they attempted to spot the "local" addressed in the film. At times, reviewers cited *Speed Racer*'s emphatic transnationalism as one of the problems with its narrative:

> The Wachowskis are unabashed; they want everything both ways, stuffing the cast with multinational actors . . . yet still supplying the hero with a pancake-flipping mother, a father who builds a winning car in his own garage, and a glass of cold milk on the victor's podium.[16] Vying signifiers of transnational and American cultures provide a source of tension for this reviewer, whereas, for others, a confused sense of generalized Asianness emerges.

Todd McCarthy, of *Daily Variety,* notes with some evident cynicism that *Speed Racer* includes "an Asian racing team (among them a driver played by Korean pop sensation Rain, who will boost B.O. [box office] in that part of the world)."[17] McCarthy's recognition of a hybridized Asianness in *Speed Racer* is taken further by the production staff's labeling of their car races as "Car Fu."[18] Kyle Smith is among those who responded negatively to this neologism, writing, "The Wachowski brothers call their movie's motorized kung fu—'car fu'—but the monkey makes it more like Jar Jar Fu. This is the costliest piece of camp ever manufactured."[19] Smith denies the producer's "car fu," associating *Speed Racer* with an earlier perceived special-effects failure, the *Star Wars* prequels' Jar Jar Binks character. Consequently, the transnational becomes ambivalent within *Speed Racer*'s reviews, revealing tensions around the filmmakers' appropriations of national signifiers, but specifically within the juxtaposition of American and Asian cultures. However, it is also in the palimpsest of Asian identities that the film becomes most clearly signaled as transnational—as having moved beyond a recognizable national origin point, offering instead regional, globalizing spectacle.

This does not mean that *Speed Racer*'s Japanese origins were unimportant. There was, however, considerable disparity about what, precisely, acted as the origin point for the live-action film. Kirk Honeycutt, for example, offers a complex reading of the film's origins, labeling *Speed Racer* "a Wachowski Brothers motion picture derived from a '60s Japanese cartoon television series that was itself inspired by a manga."[20] On this occasion, the American adaptation process of this anime into an Americanized cartoon is written out, in favor of a wholly Japanese set of media origins. This elision of Americanization is compounded by other reviews, as when Ann Hornaday in the *Washington Post* compares the "original" to its newest incarnation: "This frenetic adaptation of the beloved 1960s Japanese cartoon bears little resemblance to that anime classic of yore, unless you count Christina Ricci's saucer-like brown eyes."[21] The *Speed Racer* film, therefore, becomes associated with a number of "originals," from manga to anime to American cartoons. In this instability, the significance of *Speed Racer*'s origin point is drawn into question, even while a lingering sense of its cultural otherness remains.

A. O. Scott's review goes even further, claiming: "Many of us who grew up watching television in the 1960s and '70s have fond if vague memories of "Speed Racer." . . . Whether we knew it or not, the series was a primer in the aesthetics of Japanese animation, the love of which we could later pass along to our children."[22] In this example, the "forgotten" origins of *Speed Racer* in the United States are collapsed into the live-action film's pleasures, offering potential for a shared (re)discovery of the Japanese animated series, as well as the pleasure of sharing that nostalgically remembered text with a new generation of viewers. In contrast, some reviewers bypassed the film's Japanese roots altogether, focusing instead on North American comparators.

Describing the film's car races, one reviewer writes that, "the longest is a cross-country rally/demolition derby which seems indebted to another late '60s cartoon, 'The Wacky Racers' [*sic.*]."[23] Consequently, while there was some agreement about the importance of an original *Speed Racer* text, the origin of the adaptation remained a source of debate. Ambiguity about the origin points for the *Speed Racer* film, in combination with perceptions of its hybridized Asian–American content, suggest an emergent understanding of this live-action film as a transnational object located in Japanese *and* American roots. In these ways, the complexity of *Speed Racer*'s national origins and identity appear to have informed both sides of the divide in critical opinion, making the film easy to attack for its betrayal of a nostalgized precursor text, as much as it was lauded for its attempts to innovate around the transnational identity of the blockbuster family film.

ANIME AESTHETICS AND DISCOURSES OF EXCESS

Speed Racer's anime origins were read more deeply and ambivalently than this might suggest, however. Anime's influence on the aesthetic style of *Speed Racer* became another crucial factor in assessing the franchise's live-action incarnation. The *Boston Globe*'s review contends that the filmmakers were "aiming to replicate the experience of the anime on a metastasized scale, *Speed Racer* unsnaps the characters from the frame and lets them deliver their lines on floating multiple places of action, constantly wiping this way and that like cars playing chicken on a crowded freeway"[24] (Figure 1).

This idea, of an anime "experience" tied to excesses in *Speed Racer*'s visuals, is repeated elsewhere. Richard Corliss, in *Time* magazine, parrots the production team's language, stating that they "don't want to evoke feelings so much as visualize them. When young Speed first meets young Trixie, candy hearts and roses bloom around him, illuminating his innocent ardor"[25] (Figure 2). Therefore, whether as an embellishment or as a form of "metastasized" excess, anime's aesthetics became central to how critics discussed *Speed Racer.* Moreover, it is the filmmakers' interpretation of anime's aesthetic, not the aesthetic itself, that is deemed problematic and excessive.

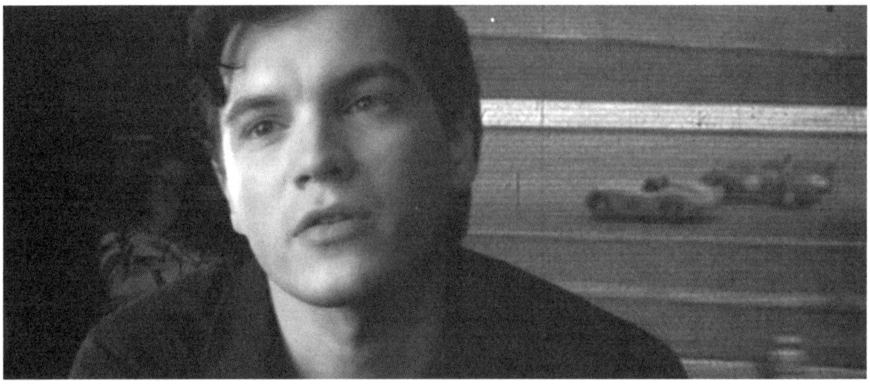

FIGURE 1. Speed Racer (Emile Hirsch) narrates his memories in front of a constantly panning set of matching images.

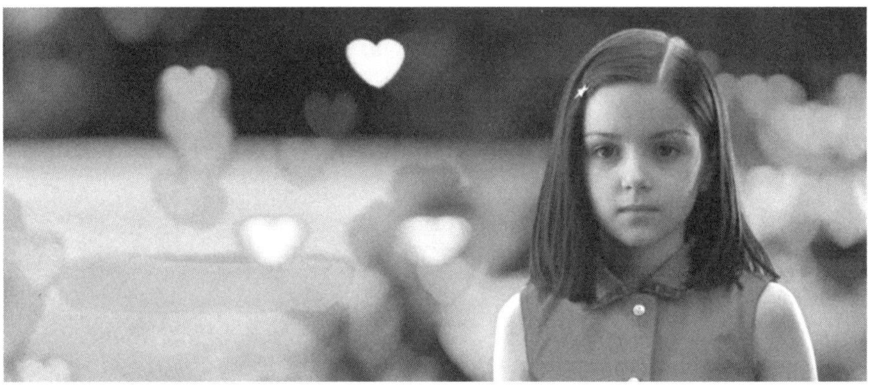

FIGURE 2. Young Trixie's love for Speed expressed through background heart-shaped defocusing.

By contrast, Kyle Smith writes that *Speed Racer* comes to us from the creators of *The Matrix,* and as my cerebral cortex was reeling from the onslaught of its jelly-belly colors and "Lucy in the Sky" graphics, I wondered if there was some parallel universe where it might be considered an entertaining experience. Maybe Japan?"[26] Smith's refusal of *Speed Racer*'s aesthetic excesses signals his sense of cultural dissonance with, and distance from, Japanese popular culture. Here, though, Japan itself becomes negatively construed as a space of aesthetic and cultural extremity. This denigration of Japanese culture may also attest to the lingering recognition of *Speed Racer*'s Japanese cultural origins.

Smith's assessment of the impact of anime origins on *Speed Racer*'s style was echoed across other reviews of the film. Tom Charity comments that "the movie integrates live action and kaleidoscopic digital effects to create a highly artificial, color-saturated fantasy world where race cars come equipped with retractable weaponry and battle it out like spinning tops (or the "beyblades" popularized by more recent manga)."[27] The marriage of older technologies (kaleidoscopes and spinning tops) with new digital technologies is a repeated reception theme here, with traditional technologies used to explain *Speed Racer*'s unusual aesthetics (Figure 3).

Additionally, Charity's comment about "beyblades" suggests that there was a tension around whom the film was aimed at: "*Speed Racer* proudly denies entry into its ultra-bright world to all but gamers, fanboys, and anime enthusiasts," Kirk Honeycutt similarly proclaims in a review for *The Hollywood Reporter.*[28] The assumed audiences for *Speed Racer*—young children raised on newer forms of Japanese culture, older audiences raised on Hanna-Barbera cartoons, and fan groups for specific media—provide a sense of niches but not a wider, general audience. Additionally, the fact that "anime enthusiasts"

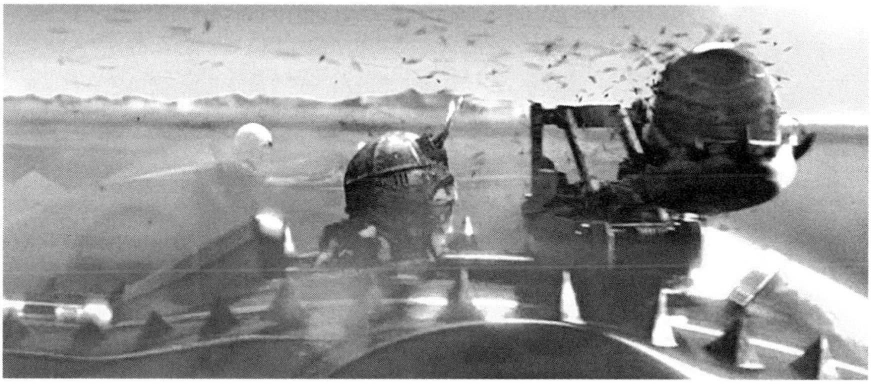

FIGURE 3. Car battles and gadgetry: Beehive catapult about to be thrown at Speed Racer.

form only one such group suggests that anime was not seen as the sole adaptation source for *Speed Racer.* That anime is bonded to notions of excess in many of these reviews also reveals a continuing understanding of anime as an extreme aesthetic, one perceived as separate from the aesthetics of the Hollywood blockbuster.

TECHNOLOGICAL HYBRIDIZATION: FAILURES OF THE OLD AND NEW

Within these discussions of anime's aesthetic influence on the *Speed Racer* film, critics were quick to assert links between its older, foreign cel animation origins and the new visual-effects technologies employed to update and adapt the *Speed Racer* concept. J. Hoberman calls this experiment a step toward the "cyborganization of the cinema," while David Ansen contends that "the narrowing line between live action and animation is obliterated spectacularly in *Speed Racer.*"[29] Both positions are responses to the remediation processes undertaken in the *Speed Racer* film, which marries studio filming and green screen work to extended sequences of computer-generated car races. However, the hyperbole in the critical language about *Speed Racer* offers a glimpse into the polarization of opinion that emerged regarding this experiment in live action–animation hybridization.

What is unusual about *Speed Racer*'s critical discourse is that both sets of technology, new and old, take the blame when the experiment is seen to fail. Jim Emerson, of the *Chicago Sun-Times,* states: "The Wachowski brothers (of the 'Matrix' movies) have spent $100 million on a mixture of photography and digital animation and called it *Speed Racer.* They have captured (almost) all the chintziness, inexpressiveness, and incoherence of the TV show in two hours and nine minutes, or about two hours too long."[30] Emerson lays the blame for *Speed Racer*'s failure squarely on the shoulders of both its anime ancestor and its mixing of new technologies. The production design also plays an important role in this hybridization debate: "Like so many other expensive, technologically elaborate big-screen adaptations of venerable pop-culture staples," claims A. O. Scott of the *New York Times,* "this movie sets out to honor and refresh a youthful enthusiasm from the past and winds up smothering the fun in self-conscious grandiosity."[31] Both of these commentators also pick up on the importance of size, found by Julian Stringer to be one of the core components of blockbuster discourse, using excessive scale and cost to criticize *Speed Racer*'s adaptation.[32] However, they differ about the importance of anime origins, with Emerson seeing them as a negative starting point, while Scott suggests *Speed Racer* is part of larger group of failed nostalgic adaptations. Critics' understandings of *Speed Racer*'s origins are reframed through the lens of the film's failure, with anime's value as source text (chintzy or venerated) put in doubt.

> WHAT IS UNUSUAL ABOUT *SPEED RACER'S* CRITICAL DISCOURSE IS THAT BOTH SETS OF TECHNOLOGY, NEW AND OLD, TAKE THE BLAME WHEN THE EXPERIMENT IS SEEN TO FAIL.

The extent of *Speed Racer*'s failure as a blockbuster is made clear by critical comparisons to *Tron* (1982, dir. Steven Lisberger), a much earlier filmic experiment in CGI and live-action hybridization. Mentioned in four of the reviews examined here, *Speed Racer* was lambasted for being worse than that earlier failure: "some of us would just rather re-rent *Tron* (1982), which was not only more immersive, dimensional, and original . . . but also funnier and more exciting."[33] Denying the importance of either film's technological experiments, *Tron*'s relative success comes instead from its more apparent depth, humor, and action. As such, *Tron*'s relative success is aligned with the failure of *Speed Racer* as a film adaptation.

Todd McCarthy asserts that the combined technologies augment "the desired spectacle. But it doesn't stimulate excitement or suspense, for the simple reason that you don't know what the rules are or what constitutes genuine jeopardy."[34] Mick LaSalle concurs, arguing that "cars fly, flip, drive up the side of icy mountains, do cartwheels, and burst into flames. These scenes come close to straight-up animation, but they're more like watching a video game—not like playing a video game, but like watching other people play, and for a very long time."[35] In this assessment, *Speed Racer*'s car races fail to engage because they fail to be filmic. Kirk Honeycutt goes so far as to argue that *Speed Racer* has the "sensation of being trapped inside a 3-D video game."[36] In these examples, instead of being reviewed as a hybridization of anime, CGI animation and live-action techniques, *Speed Racer*'s aesthetic experiments were critiqued for seeming to belong to another medium entirely. However, LaSalle argues that there are so many technical experiments contained within *Speed Racer* that "it soon becomes fun just to watch the ideas whiz by, even the bad ones. All the same, if this action extravaganza is the future of movies, it's going to be a sad, dead, and awful future."[37] Here, the origins of the franchise are displaced, with discourse circling around which aesthetic (CGI animation or videogame) offers the dominant inspiration for the new film incarnation of *Speed Racer*. As a consequence, the perceived failure of the film's aesthetic experiments commingle with discourses about the hierarchies in media production, and it is video game aesthetics, not anime's, that are seen to be the problem.

CONCLUSIONS: FAILURE AS A PLATFORM FOR EXPANDING FRANCHISES

Even as *Speed Racer* came out, and subsequently failed at the box office, *Variety* began reporting on the separate production of a new CG-animated television show.[38] Other new texts tangentially related to the film, like *Speed Racer* video games, also continued to be released in the months after the film's failure.[39] Additionally, despite its status as a "bomb," *Speed Racer*'s distributor, Warner Bros., made a point of continuing to use it when launching new distribution formats, such as its Chinese video-on-demand platform.[40] The continuation of the *Speed Racer* franchise in the wake of its failed live-action adaptation provides evidence for the resilience of anime- and manga-based intellectual properties within the global marketplace. However, the continual failure of anime film adaptations, including the CGI-animated *Astro Boy* (2009, dir. David Bowers) film, and the live-action adaptation of *Dragonball Evolution* (2009, dir. James Wong), suggests that there are significant challenges remaining in adapting Japanese texts across media forms and for the global marketplace.

In the case of *Speed Racer,* failure seems to have been generated out of a surfeit of adaptation strategies. Critics struggled to address the hybridity of remediation strategies used to shift *Speed Racer* from "limited" cel animation into high-definition digital filmmaking. Furthermore, even the producers struggled to articulate this shift. John Gaeta termed *Speed Racer*'s style "Photo Anime," going on to list the effects needed to generate this new style, including "designer shape de-focus, infinite depth-of-field, bling and super-bling flare enhancements, and candy-inspired 'Techno Color.'"[41] These new techniques became entangled in comparisons with other problematic adaptation types, from specific examples like *Tron* to general ones like videogames, compounding the impression of *Speed Racer* as a failed blockbuster film.[42] Consequently, instead of a new blockbuster cycle of "photo anime" films, we are left with questions about the extent of anime's cross-cultural adaptability.

Reviewers were quick to emphasize the mélange of national stereotypes and signifiers deployed in *Speed Racer,* and they were also acutely aware of its always already transnational status as an Americanized Japanese animation text. Some reviewers took issue with *Speed Racer*'s global aspirations. Highlighting the apparent tensions between its American and composite "Asian" elements, reviewers repeatedly noted that this "American" blockbuster film had not been made solely with American audiences in mind. The film's anime roots in Japan were therefore made more significant because the origin point's foreignness could be used to explain away the parts of the experimental filmmaking in *Speed Racer* that were difficult to understand or that seemed culturally distant for American reviewers.

Reviewers paid careful attention to *Speed Racer*'s manga and anime origins, highlighting points at which the hybridization of anime's aesthetics with blockbuster filmmaking practices became problematic and using anime to explain away disparities between *Speed Racer* and other blockbuster films. *Speed Racer*'s version of transnational film production, therefore, resides not simply in its aesthetics, or its casting, or its distribution, but also in its history; in the origins on which reviewers and filmmakers frequently drew to give meaning to the live-action film. These varied discussions of *Speed Racer*'s palimpsest of transnationalism and remediation encapsulate a significant historical moment wherein manga and anime were thrust to the forefront of global media cultures. Therefore, the *Speed Racer* was not just a "bomb," it was simultaneously a vehicle for relaunching the surrounding *Mahha go go go* and *Speed Racer* franchises, for creating new spaces for anime nostalgia, and for successfully shifting the discourse around anime adaptations.

Notes

The author would like to thank the UK Arts and Humanities Research Council for their generous support of this research project.

1. See, for examples, Anne Allison, "The Japan Fad in Global Youth Culture and Millennial Capitalism," *Mechademia* 1: 13; Sean Leonard, "Progress against the Law: Fan Distribution, Copyright, and the Explosive Growth of Japanese Animation," *MIT Working Papers* 04.02 (2004): 10, http://web.mit.edu/mit-Japan/outreach/working-papers/Sean%20Leonard.PDF; Mark W. MacWilliams, "Introduction," *Japanese Visual Culture: Explorations in the World of Manga and Anime,* ed. Mark W. MacWilliams (New York: M.E. Sharp, 2008), 14.

2. For examples of work detailing Tezuka Osamu's emergence as a key figure in Japanese manga and anime history, see Thomas Lamarre, "Speciesism, Part II: Tezuka Osamu and the Multispecies Ideal," *Mechademia* 5: 51–85; Susanne Phillips, "Characters, Themes, and Narrative Patterns in the Manga of Osamu Tezuka," *Japanese Visual Culture: Explorations in the World of Manga and Anime,* ed. Mark W. MacWilliams, 68–90 (New York: M.E. Sharp, 2008); Brian Ruh, "Early Japanese Animation in the United States: Changing Tetsuwan Atomu to Atom Boy," *The Japanification of Popular Culture: From Godzilla to Miyazaki,* ed. Mark I. West, 209–26 (Lanham, Md.: Scarecrow Press, 2009); Frederick L. Schodt, *The Astro Boy Essays: Osamu Tezuka, Mighty Atom, Manga/Anime Revolution* (Berkeley, Calif.: Stone Bridge Press, 2007); and Marc Steinberg, "Anytime, Anywhere: *Tetsuwan Atomu* Stickers and the Emergence of Character Merchandising," *Theory, Culture, and Society* 26, no. 2–3 (2009): 113–38.

3. More recently the original Japanese producers, Tatsunoko Productions, have been more aggressively and directly asserting their intellectual property rights. See "Tatsunoko Sues over Speed Racer Anime Licensing," http://www.animenewsnetwork.co.uk/news/2012–10–30/tatsunoko-sues-over-speed-racer-anime-licensing. For more on *Speed Racer*'s multimedia history, see Elizabeth Moran, *Speed Racer: The Official 30th Anniversary Guide* (New York: Hyperion, 1997); Ben Fritz, "WB Gears Up for 'Racer' Game," *Daily Variety,* August 8, 2007, 3; Michael Schneider, "'Speed' Races at Lionsgate," *Daily Variety,* June 20, 2007, 1.

4. Emiko Kishida, "Retro Characters Enjoying Rebirth," *Nikkei Weekly,* June 9, 2003.

5. Moran, *Speed Racer,* 26.

6. Ibid., 23–29.

7. Brian Ruh, "Transforming U.S. Anime in the 1980s: Localization and Longevity," in *Mechademia* 5: 31–49.

8. Martin Blaney, "Joel Silver Keen to Bring Future Projects to Babelsberg," *Screen International,* May 31, 2007.

9. Julian Stringer, "The Original and the Copy: Nakata Hideo's *The Ring* (1998)," *Japanese Cinema: Texts and Contexts,* eds. Julian Stringer and Alastair Phillips, 296–307 (Abingdon, UK: Routledge, 2007). The reception sources selected for this chapter represent a cross-section of U.S. print media, including newspapers, magazines, and trade presses, selected from across the political spectrum of American media news. All reception sources have been selected for their close proximity to *Speed Racer*'s release in the United States.

10. Henry Jenkins, *Fans, Bloggers, and Gamers: Exploring Participatory Cultures* (New York: New York University, 2006); Koichi Iwabuchi, *Recentering Globalization: Popular Culture and Japanese Transnationalism* (Durham, N.C.: Duke University Press, 2002).

11. Janet Staiger, "Taboos and Totems: Cultural Meanings of *Silence of the Lambs,*" *Film Theory Goes to the Movies*, eds. Jim Collins, Hilary Radner, and Ava Preacher Collins (New York: Routledge, 1993), 144; Pamela McClintock, "B.O. on Power Trip," *Daily Variety,* January 5, 2009, 1.

12. Ben Fritz, "'Iron' Pops Rivals' Rivets," *Daily Variety,* May 12, 2008, 1.

13. "Not So Fast, 'Speed'," *The New York Post,* May 14, 2008, 14.

14. Brooks Barnes, "At Movies, Fewer Eyes, Bigger Haul," *The New York Times,* September 2, 2008, 1.

15. Sam Thielman, "Big 'Ben' for Silver," *Daily Variety,* June 14, 2008, 1.

16. Anthony Lane, "Around the Bend," *The New Yorker,* May 12, 2008: http://www.newyorker.com/arts/critics/cinema/2008/05/12/080512crci_cinema_lane.

17. Todd McCarthy, "Speed Racer," *Daily Variety,* May 2, 2008, 2.

18. See, for example, John Gaeta, *Speed Racer*'s VFX supervisor, in Warner Bros. Entertainment, Inc., *The Art of Speed Racer* (New York: Universe, 2005), 5.

19. Kyle Smith, "No, *Speed Racer,* No!" *The New York Post,* May 9, 2008, 49.

20. Kirk Honeycutt, *"Speed Racer," The Hollywood Reporter,* May 2, 2008.

21. Ann Hornaday, "*Speed Racer* Is Stuck on a Fast Track to Nowhere," *The Washington Post,* May 9, 2008, http://www.washingtonpost.com/wp-dyn/content/article/2008/05/08/AR2008050803378.html.

22. A. O. Scott, "Gentlemen, Start Your Hot-Hued Engines," *The New York Times,* May 9, 2008, http://movies.nytimes.com/2008/05/09/movies/09spee.html?_r=0.

23. Charity is likely referring to the Hanna-Barbera show *The Wacky Races,* 1968–70. Tom Charity, "*Speed Racer* Rich in Color, Poor in Spirit," *CNN.com,* May 9, 2008, http://edition.cnn.com/2008/SHOWBIZ/Movies/05/09/review.speedracer/index.html .

24. Ty Burr, "'Racer' Tests Limits of Digital Overdrive," *The Boston Globe,* May 9, 2008), http://www.boston.com/ae/movies/articles/2008/05/09/racer_tests_limits_of_digital_overdrive/.

25. The positive tone of this review is not surprising, given the direct control of *Time* magazine by Time-Warner, the parent company of the film's producer, Warner Bros. Richard Corliss, "*Speed Racer*: The Future of Movies," *Time,* May 8, 2008, http://www.time.com/time/arts/article/0,8599,1738558,00.html. For comparison to production language, see Warner Entertainment, Inc., *The Art of Speed Racer* (New York: Universe, 2008).

26. Smith, "No *Speed Racer,* No!"

27. Charity, "*Speed Racer.*"

28. Kirk Honeycutt, "*Speed Racer,*" *The Hollywood Reporter*, May 2, 2008.

29. James Hoberman, "*Speed Racer* on a Fast Track to Nowhere," *Village Voice,* May 6, 2008 http://www.villagevoice.com/2008–05–06/film/speed-racer-on-a-fast-track-to-nowhere/; David Ansen, "Car and Driver, and Monkey," *Newsweek* 151, no. 20 (May 19, 2008): 50.

30. Jim Emerson, "*Speed Racer,*" *Chicago Sun-Times,* May 8, 2008, http://rogerebert.suntimes.com/apps/pbcs.dll/article?AID=/20080507/REVIEWS/115192456.

31. Scott, "Gentlemen, Start Your Hot-Hued Engines."

32. Julian Stringer, "Introduction," *Movie Blockbusters,* ed. Julian Stringer, 1–14 (New York: Routledge, 2003).

33. Emerson, "*Speed Racer.*"

34. McCarthy, "*Speed Racer.*"

35. Mick LaSalle, "*Speed Racer*: Not a Thrill Ride," *San Francisco Chronicle,* May 8, 2008, http://www.sfgate.com/movies/article/Movie-review-Speed-Racer-not-a-thrill-ride-3214610.php.

36. Honeycutt, "*Speed Racer.*"

37. LaSalle, "*Speed Racer*: Not a Thrill Ride."

38. Schneider, "'Speed' Races at Lionsgate."

39. Brian Crecente, "Speed Racer: The Videogame," *Daily Variety,* May 9, 2008, 14.

40. Patrick Frater, "Warner Bros. offers VOD Service in China," *Daily Variety,* November 5, 2008, 46.

41. Warner Bros. Entertainment, Inc., *The Art of Speed Racer,* 5.

42. Corliss, "*Speed Racer.*"

起源

ANDREU BALLÚS and
ALBA G. TORRENTS

Evangelion as Second Impact: Forever Changing That Which Never Was

Since the airing of the original series in 1995 and 1996, *Neon Genesis Evangelion* has acquired a quasi-mythical status for much of the otaku community in and out of Japan. There are many flourishing franchises in the world of anime, but the new installments and revisions of *Evangelion* that regularly appear are not just an indication of its commercial success but reflect the content of the series: the open, unstable nature of the fiction itself seems to propel the franchise forward through a process of incessant revision, keeping the interest of the audience alive. It is neither the first nor the most commercially successful product of the manga and anime culture, but this instability and repetition have made *Evangelion* a *primus inter pares,* an auratic and remarkable example of anime and of Japanese popular culture. And although the idea may pose a conundrum for the chronological history of anime, we will argue here that *Evangelion* has become a sort of absent point of origin, its own instability representing an archetypal and, at the same time, transformative force.

This is expressed in the way *Evangelion* coexists with itself as a fiction, filling two very different roles at the same time: it is simultaneously an ongoing series (with the original manga series and derivative material still in publication and the new reimagined episodes of the anime hitting the theaters every two or three years) and a classic, canonical work that serves as a point of reference to judge other manga and anime. This second role is evident in the persistent presence of the series in serious academic works on anime as well as in all kinds of rankings and top-ten lists produced by fans and experts in the Internet.[1] Like any other series, *Evangelion* has its detractors among fans but is invoked with a surprising frequency as a touchstone for almost any new anime that styles itself (or is proclaimed by the public) as "difficult," "dense," "philosophical," "groundbreaking," or any other of the adjectives that have become associated with *Evangelion* since its inception. This is true not only for anime of the mecha genre (within which, albeit with some justified reservations, most fans and academics locate the series) but also for other technological anime like *Serial Experiments Lain* (1998), and even titles from apparently unrelated genres, such as *Puella Magi Madoka Magica* (2011).[2]

This coexistence of the series with itself in different forms is relevant, of course, when trying to determine the meaning of its later instances or presentations: the recent films that constitute *Rebuild of Evangelion* (2007–) cannot be fully understood without comparison with the original series. But this same phenomenon of recurrence and reference also occurs in the "original" fiction considered by itself. In fact, even determining the exact boundaries of the original fiction is nontrivial: the series originally ended with its twenty-sixth episode (broadcast on television in 1996), and it can be interpreted as complete in this form, but most fans and critics include as part of the canonical work two theatrical films originally released in 1997: *Death and Rebirth* and *The End of Evangelion*.[3] The first is already a retelling of the first twenty-four episodes of the series, in condensed form and with significant narrative differences, while the second is an alternative ending (and clearly a very divergent one, despite sustained attempts at harmonization from the fan community). By accepting these addends as canonical, most interpretations of the original series present an unavoidable element of autoreferentiality and comparison. But even for those who attempt to approach to original twenty-six televised episodes by themselves, *Evangelion* still presents a very particular kind of duplication, as if it were acting simultaneously as original and copy, referent and reference.

That happens because, even if in its shortest form, *Evangelion* is an open work, not only in Eco's sense (a work not limited to one closed, linear, prescribed interpretation) but also in a more general sense: it is a fiction without clearly defined limits.[4] The beginning of the series presents us with all the classical elements of the mecha genre. There is a world under attack from inhuman enemies, the *shito* or angels. There is a teenage boy, Ikari Shinji, destined to save humanity by piloting a giant robot (the EVA), which his father created and only he can master, and so on.[5] The opening plays so clearly with the audience's knowledge of these conventions that it can be seen less as the start of a new series than as an exercise in repeating (or at the very least continuing) earlier referents. In more than one sense, then, the action starts *in media res*. However, a "phantom" apparition of the character Ayanami Rei—subtly located before her proper introduction in the story—connects this strangely "unoriginal" beginning with the story's final stages, those more clearly concerned with the "Genesis" idea already present in the title. In a scene from the beginning of the first episode, Shinji is standing at a public payphone when he looks onto an empty street, and just for a second, as in an optical illusion, he sees the figure of Rei, who is completely unknown to him at the time (Figure 1). This scene is especially interesting when compared with the final scenes of *The End of Evangelion,* where multiple instances of Rei approach every living person on the planet just before they explode and are "returned" to a (supposedly originary) state of indivision. In examples like this we can see something about the topology of the text and the story: it is not a line segment, starting on one point and traveling to another with no break in continuity, but something very

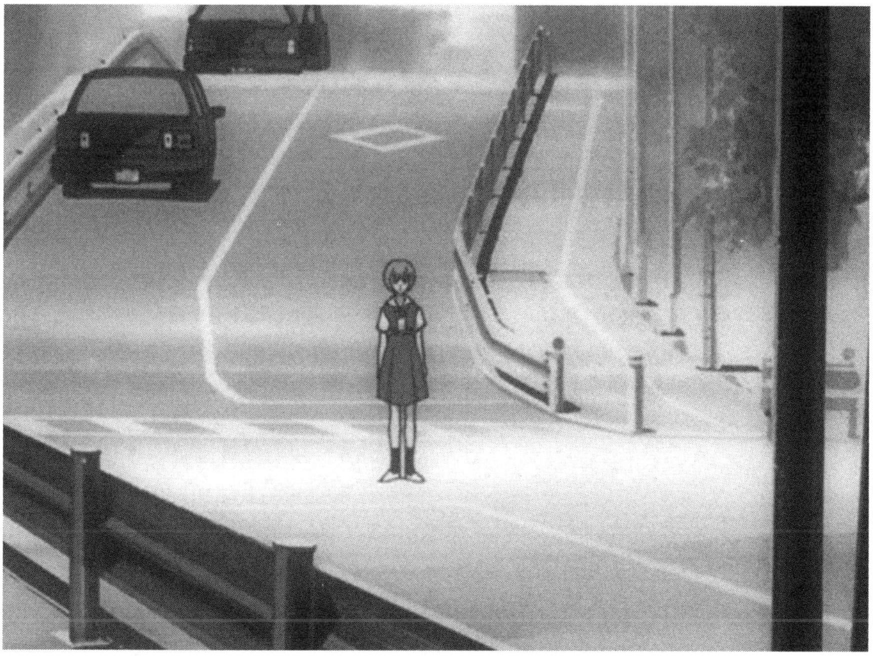

FIGURE 1. "Phantom" appearance of Ayanami Rei before she is formally introduced in the series. This scene is reminiscent of similar ones in the conclusion of the series, where instances of Rei appear to every person of Earth. All images captured from the series DVDs published as *Neon Genesis Evangelion: Platinum Collection* (ADV, 2005).

much like the real subjective experience of a period of time, with a past and a memory always implied and effective, and an expectation founded on that memory always extending into the future.

In this and other respects, we believe that Anno Hideaki's ongoing magnum opus can be understood in terms of some of the fundamental concepts in poststructuralist philosophy as developed by authors like Gilles Deleuze and Jacques Derrida. Of course, these are not the only intellectual points of reference in *Evangelion.* The clear references to various mystic traditions are deep and interesting.[6] And there are other philosophical references, including an episode name after Schopenhauer's "hedgehog dilemma" and compelling connections to Sartrean existentialism, Lacanian psychoanalysis, and other philosophical sources.[7] But the fundamental tropes or ideas of poststructuralist thinking correspond so closely to the structure, development, and impact of *Evangelion* that they shed particular light on this anime's ability to produce meaning.

CHARACTER REPETITION AND DELEUZEAN DIFFERENCE

One of the crucial poststructuralist principles represented in *Evangelion* is that it is difference, not identity, that is ontologically fundamental. While its most complete elaboration is probably Gilles Deleuze's *Difference and Repetition,* much of poststructuralist thinking is permeated by the general idea that self-consistent identity is not the ultimate basis for all existence, and that the more profound aspects of reality are themselves dynamic, unequal, and different.[8] The aforementioned features of *Evangelion* as a cultural product (its autoreferentiality, its tendency to reappear beside itself and to acquire new forms) might be taken to suggest that this fundamentally multiple character is an inherent part of the Japanese (and global) culture industry, a radicalization of Walter Benjamin's concept of reproducibility.[9] But we also find ideas of difference and repetition in the story itself, when narrative elements give way to nonnarrative, symbolic, and even "therapeutic" moments: it is not only that the story unfolds by betraying the expectations set by its stereotypical beginning but that the narration frequently breaks down, revealing that both the background/world and figure/story depend on a volatile set of narrative and imaginary choices, vague references, and simulations. This happens crucially in the two separate endings, discussed below, but also in many other scenes across the series, such as the beginning of episode 14 (labeled "Rei's poem"

> IT IS NOT ONLY THAT THE STORY UNFOLDS BY BETRAYING THE EXPECTATIONS SET BY ITS STEREOTYPICAL BEGINNING BUT THAT THE NARRATION FREQUENTLY BREAKS DOWN, REVEALING THAT BOTH THE BACKGROUND/WORLD AND FIGURE/STORY DEPEND ON A VOLATILE SET OF NARRATIVE AND IMAGINARY CHOICES, VAGUE REFERENCES, AND SIMULATIONS.

by fans because of its fragmentary, cryptic nature), or Shinji's "train monologue" in episode 16. When the Twelfth Angel, Leliel, attacks Earth and Shinji disappears inside the angel, we see him sitting in a train in front a younger version of himself. As the two Shinjis share a monologue/dialogue reminiscent of a psychoanalytic therapy session, abstract images of horizontal and vertical lines appear on the screen (apparently representing each of Shinji's "voices"); later we see images from earlier in the series, as other characters intervene in the "conversation." While resisting any definitive interpretation, scenes like these show that there is more to *Evangelion* than a fictional narrative and its imaginary background; they point directly to the problematic of difference and repetition and to the relationship between this issue and that of representation itself.

Deleuze's notions of simulation and simulacrum also suggest an interesting interpretation of *Evangelion*—both its content and its commercial history. Deleuze analyzed the platonic topic of the relation between the *original* or *authentic* and its *likenesses* or *copies* in a way that questions not only the dominant role of the former but also the supposedly primary ontological status of the relation itself. Following a line of thought initiated by Kierkegaard and Nietzsche, Deleuze asserts the positive role of simulacra:

> Hence, to overthrow Platonism means: to raise up simulacra, to assert their rights over icons or copies. The problem no longer concerns the distinction Essence/Appearance or Model/Copy. This whole distinction operates in the world of representation. The goal is the subversion of this world, "the twilight of the idols." The simulacrum is not degraded copy, rather it contains a power which negates *both original and copy, both model and reproduction.*[10]

This critique of originality and rethinking of simulation also plays an important part in defining Deleuze's project of a nonclassical, innovative *image of thought*. In the Deleuzian conception of life and philosophy, the rhizomatic, hyperconnected configuration of experiences, feelings, and thoughts that substitute for the Platonic order not only recalls Nietzschean masks but also describes *Evangelion*'s game of repetition without origin.

For example, consider Ayanami Rei. At first she appears to be just another of the teenage pilots who share the burden of protecting humanity from the attacks of the Angels. When she is introduced (already her second appearance, if we count her ghostly apparition in the payphone scene), she is shown injured, incapable of walking, but nonetheless willing to pilot an EVA unit and fight the Angels if Shinji refuses to do so himself. This scene and the first episodes seem to present Rei as an equal to Shinji, a companion, maybe a future love interest. As the story unfolds, however, we learn of the existence of several different incarnations of Rei; then we find out that Rei is a clone of Shinji's mother Ikari Yui; finally we realize that Rei is inhabited by the spirit of Lilith, mate of the primordial angel and mother of the entire human race. Rei is thus multiplied, incarnated in different bodies living separate lives, rediscovered at every turn as embodying a new meaning always more originary than the last, but never finally definitive (Figure 2). This situation is further complicated by the role she plays in the personal voyage of the antihero Shinji, whose relationships with Rei and the rest of the female characters represent a permanent test of his authenticity: "are these my friends, my family? How do they see me? Who am I?" As in the Deleuzian rhizome, this effort to define a stable personality seems doomed to fail, undermined by a never-ending game of deterritorializations and reterritoralizations.

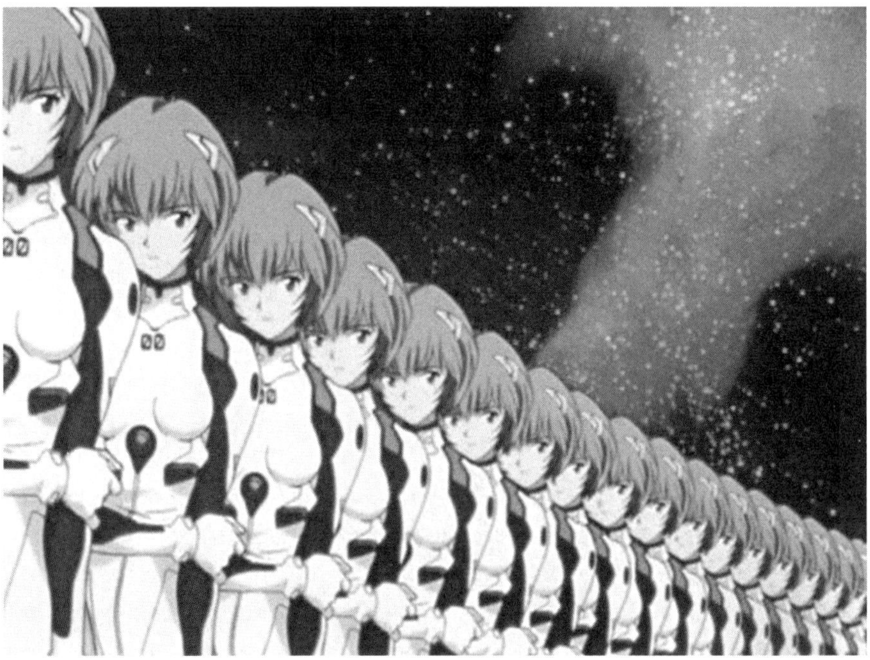

FIGURE 2. Image of multiple Reis in episode 14, popularly known as "Rei's poem."

ORIGIN STORIES AND DERRIDEAN DIFFÉRANCE

Even for those on the lookout for similarities, it is surprising how many elements of Deleuze's dense, groundbreaking onto-epistemology are mirrored in the narrative development of *Evangelion,* which is otherwise so difficult to interpret. We can also compare the content, form, and development of *Evangelion* with another great poststructuralist thinker, Jacques Derrida, who provides a complementary perspective on the Deleuzian ideas of ontological difference, simulation, and rhizome. Many of Derrida's works concern a particularly elusive relation of being with itself, a kind of relation we could describe as "hidden" or "failed," and marked by aspects that the history of philosophy has tended to confine to its margins, such as contradiction, ambiguity, and absence. This notion of a constitutive but inconsistent relation of being serves, like Deleuze's difference, as a starting point for Derrida's very particular style of hermeneutics, revealing the paradoxes of language, textuality, and signification.

Derrida develops his philosophical analyses using several strategies, which include a series of related coinages (trace, archi-writing, *pharmakós,* specter) that are used to critique or deconstruct fundamental binary relations that he says structure the history of ontology.[11] The most well known and arguably most important of these deconstructions are those the author undertakes in works like *Writing and Difference* and *Of Grammatology.*[12] In them, Derrida analyzes the complex historical relationships between the notions of voice and writing. He critiques the existence of an implicit order of being and thinking whereby the written form is always interpreted as dependent and secondary with respect to an "original text," generally thought of in terms of "inner voice" and pure presence of being to itself. Derrida attempts to revert this hierarchy, showing how the putatively "lesser" component of the opposition (in this case, writing) does in fact contain and produce the difference itself. This reversion, however, cannot be understood as a mere reintroduction of originality: on the contrary, it implies abandoning the idea of a pure origin from which representation spreads, and accepting the *dissemination* of meaning. In Derrida's words:

> Everything begins by referring-back (par le *renvoi*), that is to say, does not begin; and once this breaking open or this partition divides, from the very start, every *renvoi,* there is not a single *renvoi* but from then on, always, a multiplicity of *renvois,* so many different traces referring back to other traces and to traces of others.[13]

THIS IDEA OF A SORT OF "UNFOUNDED" FOUNDATIONAL GESTURE—AN EVER-DISTANT ORIGIN THAT HOLDS AT ITS VERY CORE A PASSING OF TIME THAT SEPARATES IT FROM ITSELF—PERMEATES THE CONCEPTION OF ORIGIN PRESENTED IN *EVANGELION*.

To clarify the meaning of this reversion or decentering of representation, it is helpful to consider Derrida's notion of *différance*. "*Différance*," Derrida writes, "is the non-full, non-simple, structured and differentiating origin of differences. Thus the name 'origin,' no longer suits it."[14] Derrida insists that *différance* is neither a concept nor simply a word; it refers both to the idea of *differing* (as in Deleuze's ontologically fundamental difference) and to the temporal sense of the English word *deferring*—leaving for later or postponing. It thus expresses the inherently temporal aspect of the original gesture, and also the lack of identity implied by the temporal dimension of being itself, and thus of any form of textuality or signification. This idea of a sort of "unfounded" foundational gesture—an ever-distant origin that holds at its very core a passing of time that separates it from itself—permeates the conception of origin presented in *Evangelion*. In a certain sense it also describes the function *Evangelion* has come to occupy in the world of anime: the revision and recreation of something that was not completely there until it was revised and recreated, through an operation that demands to be repeated again and again. In the fictional universe of *Evangelion*, this very structure is represented symbolically by the mysterious event known as the Second Impact—one of the quasi-mythological elements that constitute the "background" of the action, providing the illusion of a past within the story, the illusion of depth.

Information about the events that brought humanity to a conflict with the Angels is scarce, and the ending (in both versions) reveals more about *Evangelion*'s symbolism than about chronology and history. But the narrative does mention a few past events, the most important of which is the Second Impact that occurred in September 2001, fifteen years prior to the time of the series (Figure 3). This prior event involved an unknown, dangerous experiment performed on Adam, the First Angel; the experiment awakened Adam, caused a disaster that decimated humanity and the planet's ecosystem, marking the beginning of the Angel attacks. The Second Impact does more than rationalize the setting for the series: Seele (the same political organization that has concealed the original event with the cover story of a meteor impact and developed the EVAs to confront the angels) is planning to recreate the event in a controlled form. Ikari Gendo, the protagonist's father, leads this project with his own hidden agenda. This makes the Second Impact a constant premonition of what is to happen at the end of the series, the final encounter

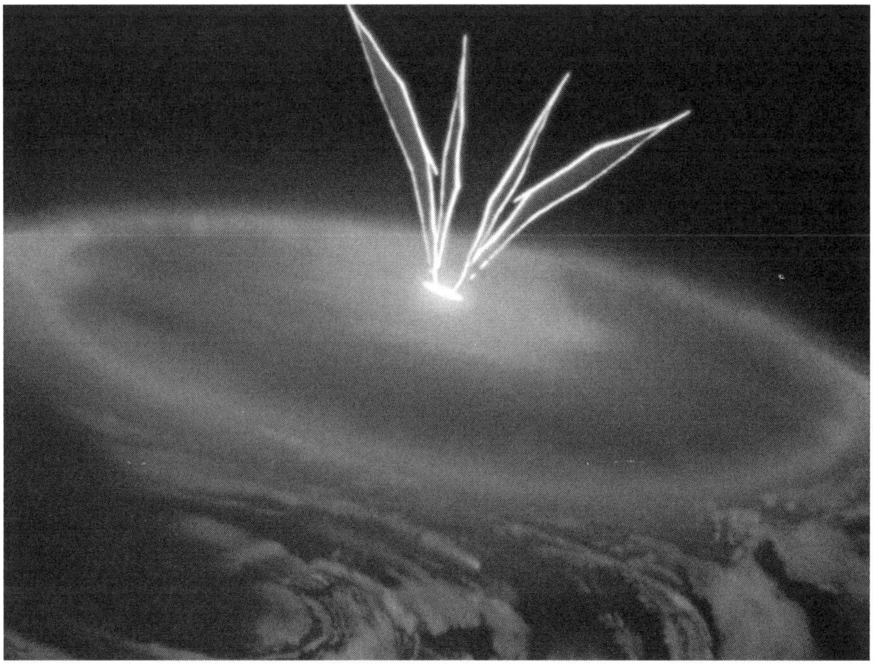

FIGURE 3. Image of the Second Impact appearing in episode 12, during a flashback to Misato's past.

between Angels and humanity. It is also the direct or indirect source of every expectation and project put forward in the series.

Even more significant, the Second Impact hints at the presence of a First Impact that is never narrated, described, or directly referred to in the series. Both we and the characters know it only through this vague reminiscence, a repetition in which we do not know exactly what is new and what is properly repeated. The relation of the Second Impact (and its projected echoes) to an unknown yet always present First Impact is one possible key to unpacking the complex notion of origin or genesis presented in *Evangelion*; it is also an almost perfect metaphor for the prominent position of the series itself.

Finally, does this interrogation of the origin by poststructuralism change our reading of *Evangelion*'s complex ending or endings? In a final turn that enraged some fans, the ending of the series abandons any clear narrative structure and undertakes what can be described as a therapeutic attempt: several of the characters address first Shinji and then the spectator, and invite them to stop hiding or cowering and to face real life with optimism. The second finale, presented in *The End of Evangelion,* provides more narrative resolution, but it also plays with breaking the fourth wall and pointing to the role of the spectator: we are shown, for instance, images of an empty stage and several of

AS IN THE MOST DARING TEXTS OF DERRIDA AND DELEUZE, WE ARE FORCED TO ABANDON OUR POSITION AS MERE INTERPRETER, SEARCHING FOR THE HIDDEN BUT INDEPENDENT TRUTH OF THE TEXT; INSTEAD WE MUST ASSUME FULL RESPONSIBILITY FOR THE MEANINGS WE PRODUCE.

the voice actresses. The film's final scene is also open to interpretation, with the spectator left to decide what Shinji and Asuka will attempt to do with the possibility of a "new genesis."

These endings are concerned not only with the matters of originality, difference, and repetition but also with the role of the reader. For critics like Deleuze and Derrida, the reader is fundamentally responsible for the meaning of any text or situation. *Evangelion* expresses this in an almost aggressive way: both at the end of the original series and after watching *The End of Evangelion,* we are left with the impression that the story of Shinji is a trap revealing our role as spectators, indicting us for being too passive or too comfortable in that role. What challenges Shinji is also a challenge to the spectator. As in the most daring texts of Derrida and Deleuze, we are forced to abandon our position as mere interpreter, searching for the hidden but independent truth of the text; instead we must assume full responsibility for the meanings we produce. In *Neon Genesis Evangelion,* as in some of the core texts of poststructuralism, the critique of the notion of origin serves as an instrument to force the reader to step out of his or her hiding place, confront the condition of being a reader, and decide what to do or make from that moment on.

Notes

1. For example, see the discussions of *Evangelion* in Susan Napier, *From Impressionism to Anime: Japan as Fantasy and Fan Cult in the Mind of the West* (New York: Palgrave Macmillan, 2007), and Thomas Lamarre, *The Anime Machine: A Media Theory of Animation* (Minneapolis: University of Minnesota Press, 2009).

2. These comparisons are made in academic criticism as well as in Internet forums. See Susan Napier, "When the Machines Stop: Fantasy, Reality, and Terminal Identity in *Neon Genesis Evangelion* and *Serial Experiments Lain,* in *Robot Ghosts and Wired Dreams: Japanese Science Fiction from Origins to Anime,* ed. Christopher Bolton, Istvan Csicsery-Ronay Jr., and Takayuki Tatsumi, 101–22 (Minneapolis: University of Minnesota Press, 2007).

3. The original series and the two 1997 films discussed here (all directed by Anno Hideaki), are available as *Neon Genesis Evangelion: Platinum Collection*, 6 subtitled DVDs (ADV, 2005); *Neon Genesis Evangelion: Death and Rebirth,* subtitled DVD (ADV, 2002); *Neon Genesis Evangelion: The End of Evangelion,* subtitled DVD (ADV, 2005).

4. Umberto Eco, *Opera aperta,* vol. 21 (Milan: Bompiani, 2000).

5. *Evangelion* draws heavily (to the point of metafiction) on previous mecha anime, both the original Super Robot tradition, represented by series like *Tetsujin-29* and *Mazinger Z,* and more realistic series such as *Mobile Suit Gundam* and *Super Dimension Fortress Macross.*

6. Mariana Ortega. "My Father, He Killed Me; My Mother, She Ate Me: Self, Desire, Engendering, and the Mother in *Neon Genesis Evangelion,*" *Mechademia* 2 (2007): 216–32.

7. For an analysis of *Evangelion* based in the philosophies of Hegel, Kierkegaard, Heidegger, and Sartre, see Manabu Tsuribe, "Prison of Self-Consciousness: An Essay on Evangelion," February 1999, http://www001.upp.so-net.ne.jp/tsuribe/anime/critique/evae.html. For connections to Sartre and Lacan, see Alba G. Torrents, "La relación con lo materno en el cuerpo robótico en Neon Genesis Evangelion," *Debats,* no. 119 (2013/2): 32–40.

8. Lawrence Grossberg, "Identity and Cultural Studies: Is That All There Is?" *Questions of Cultural Identity,* ed. Stuart Hall and Paul du Gay, 87–107 (London: Sage, 1996); Gilles Deleuze, *Difference and Repetition* (London: Continuum, 1994).

9. Walter Benjamin, *The Work of Art in the Age of Mechanical Reproduction* (London: Penguin, 2008).

10. Gilles Deleuze and Rosalind Krauss, "Plato and the Simulacrum," *October* 27 (1983): 52–53. Emphasis in the original.

11. Gayatri Spivak, Translator's Preface to *Of Grammatology* by Jacques Derrida (Baltimore: The Johns Hopkins University Press, 1980), ix–xc.

12. Jacques Derrida, *Writing and Difference* (Chicago: University of Chicago Press, 1980); Jacques Derrida. *Of Grammatology* (Baltimore: The Johns Hopkins University Press, 1998).

13. Jacques Derrida, "Sending: On Representation," trans. Peter and Mary Ann Caws, *Social Research* 49, no. 2 (1982): 324.

14. Jacques Derrida, "Différance," in *Margins of Philosophy,* trans. Alan Bass (Chicago: University of Chicago Press, 1982), 11.

起源

CHRISTOPHER BOLTON

From Ground Zero to Degree Zero: *Akira* from Origin to Oblivion

Let me begin with my own origin story. It was in March 1990 at the Music Box Theater in Chicago that I first saw *Akira*, and as the anime unfolded from its astonishing opening sequence, it set off a reaction in me. It was one of a series of encounters with Japanese film and fiction that year that propelled a software engineer improbably into graduate school in Japanese literature, as if the light coming off the theater screen had changed me in parallel with the film's story of psychic radiation, mutation, and transformation.[1]

And clearly I was not alone. For anyone seeking the origins of the anime boom in the United States, Ōtomo Katsuhiro's 1988 film is an irresistible starting point. One of the most lavishly produced anime to date, *Akira* brought anime from U.S. TV screens onto movie screens, a format suited to the epic physical scale of Ōtomo's story. Even its limited U.S. theatrical release in 1989 and 1990 attracted wide attention from audiences and critics. This has led many to identify *Akira* as the origin or ground zero for the explosion of anime's popularity in North America in the 1990s.[2]

In what follows I will examine *Akira*'s critical reception in the United States, to ask what was unique about this film at the time and what remains remarkable twenty-five years later. Paradoxically, *Akira* has been regarded both as a watershed moment in the history of anime and as an attempt to erase history itself, based primarily on its frenetic visuals and complex plot. I would like to look more concretely at the visual language of *Akira* by comparing it with a similar story in a different medium, the epic *Akira* manga that Ōtomo authored in parallel with the film. The comparison shows more specifically how the visual language of the film and the manga support or undermine the search for the kind of historical and political narratives we might associate with decisive origins or causes.

GROUND ZERO: *AKIRA*'S NUCLEAR ORIGINS

The characterization of *Akira* as a kind of bombshell that set off the anime boom is all the more tempting given the film's opening sequence, which is a literal explosion. The film fades in on an aerial view of a city, with the superimposed title "1988.7.16. Tokyo" (the date of the film's Japanese release). As the camera pans up to take in more and more of the distant city, there is the sound of wind on the otherwise silent soundtrack, and then a dome of alternating light and darkness appears at a distant point in the city's center. It illuminates the entire city in a harsh glare and then expands toward the viewer, sweeping away the city, until the light fills the frame (Figure 1). Slowly, an aerial view of a new, transformed city resolves itself out of this whiteness. An echoing drumbeat marks a transition to a more musical soundtrack, and a second title appears: "31 years after WW III. AD 2019 Neo Tokyo."

This ninety-second opening image—of a detonation that heralds violent change and renewal—became a metaphor for the influence of *Akira* on North American popular culture and anime's fortunes in the United States. As one popular guide to anime has it, "Just as the bubble of Japan's economy of the 1980s was about to burst, a bomb of a more positive nature detonated, with the premier of *Akira*."[3] But of course the more disturbing parallel is between this opening detonation and the atomic bombings of Japan. To see *Akira* in the United States in 1990 was to be transported back in history to the moment of Hiroshima at the very same instant one seemed to be lifted out of the story and out of the theater to see a flash of a new future for Japanese film (Figure 2).[4] In fact, these two senses of the explosion—as a celebratory, artistic, even metatextual one that seems to productively explode the rules or boundaries a whole genre or medium on the one hand, and the dark immersive or illusionistic historical reminder—seem to sum up the oscillation that is at the heart of *Akira*.

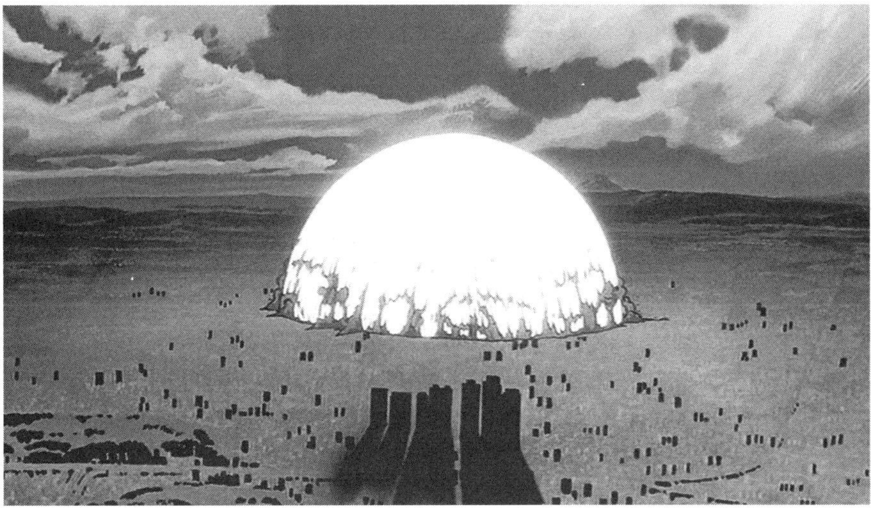

FIGURE 1. The opening sequence of the 1988 *Akira* anime, with an explosion that seemed to signify both a past war and a future media revolution. Images from the anime are captured from the 2001 Pioneer DVD.

English reviews and criticism of *Akira* have emphasized both sides of the film. In readings that emphasize the nuclear origins of *Akira,* it is said to represent a fixation on destruction that supposedly lies at the heart of Japanese popular culture, a legacy of the atomic bombings. This reading suggests Hiroshima and Nagasaki as original traumas that are then worked out and mastered through their repetition in popular culture. “It is easy to recognize the outlines of the Japanese A-bomb anxiety that has been embedded in their popular culture from *Godzilla* onward,” Dave Kehr writes in an early review of the film, and academic readings have often followed a similar tack.[5]

This thesis about the nuclear origins of Japanese popular culture has been sustained more recently by the Japanese visual artist Murakami Takashi. In 2005 Murakami curated a high profile exhibition titled “Little Boy” at the Japan Society in New York City,

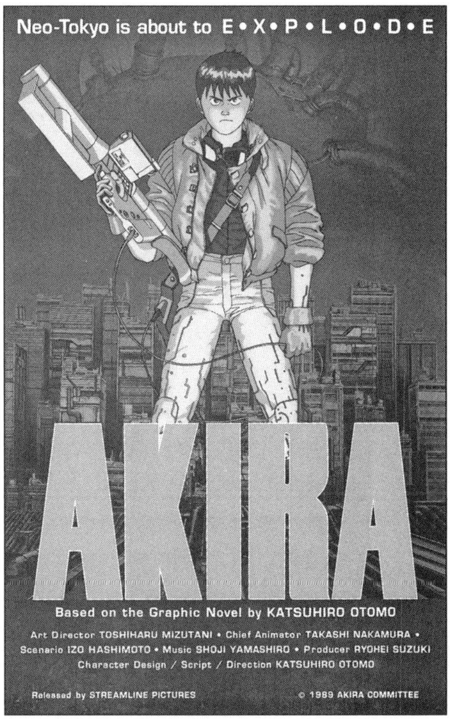

FIGURE 2. A movie poster used to advertise *Akira* for its American theatrical release, purchased at Chicago’s Music Box Theater in 1991. Note the focus on the trope of explosion.

> SO WHILE THEY TALK ABOUT ITS ATOMIC ORIGINS, ACADEMIC READINGS OF *AKIRA* HAVE ALSO BEEN INCLINED TO SEE IT AS A LOSS OR EFFACEMENT OF ORIGINS, A TEXT THAT UNDERMINES THE SEARCH FOR UNITARY MEANING OR INTERPRETATION AND INSTEAD PORTRAYS A WORLD IN WHICH THERE IS NO STABLE GROUND THAT COULD ANCHOR INTERPRETATION.

where he displayed anime, manga, monster films, and toys alongside his own paintings and sculptures and the work of his artistic circle. The exhibit drew a direct line from the Hiroshima bomb (code-named "Little Boy" by its inventors) to the *otaku* (the "little boys") who produce and consume the narratives of disaster, mutation, and invasion that figure so prominently in Japan's popular culture. "These images bespeak a profound psychological repression," wrote Sawaragi Noi in the exhibition catalog, suggesting that memories of defeat and later fears of Cold War nuclear annihilation "have never been channeled into a legitimate political consciousness. Instead, they have been transformed into the monstrous catastrophes and apocalyptic delusions depicted in the bizarre world of manga and anime." Significantly, Ōtomo's *Akira* manga occupied a central place in the exhibition catalog: Murakami's programmatic essay in the catalog referred to the anime as "an epic film that would define an era" and devoted more text to the manga than to any other single work in the exhibit.[6]

The popularity of the "Little Boy" show clearly owes much to the rhetorical power of this thesis, which is hard to refute and temptingly easy to understand and repeat. The idea of the nuclear explosions over Hiroshima and Nagasaki as the origins of Japanese popular culture, a big bang from which all else springs, satisfies our desire for origins or explanations. Faced with the bewildering variety of Japanese pop culture products and the disturbing mix of the familiar and alien that we find there, it is not surprising that we feel the desire for some kind of historical key that will unlock the meaning of these images, and this is precisely what Murakami provided.[7]

This is a powerful and plausible idea, but one with important political pitfalls: it can encourage a kind of victim consciousness that elides Japan's own wartime responsibilities, as well as a passive stance focused on past experience rather than future responsibilities. But here I would like to highlight a pitfall for *reading,* which is the reductionism of this interpretation, the way its sense of a decisive origin seems to close off more complex, more original, and potentially more productive interpretations.

For the last several decades at least, literary theory has struggled to reconcile its desire to connect literature to concrete, real-world events with its growing suspicion of unitary stable meanings for literary texts. There is a range of shorthand for the core or irreducible meaning these theories call into question, including "presence," "metaphysics," "transcendence," or "depth"; but "origin" will do as well as any other.[8] So while they talk about its atomic origins, academic readings of *Akira* have also been inclined to see it as a loss or effacement of origins, a text that undermines the search for unitary meaning or interpretation and instead portrays a world in which there is no stable ground that could anchor interpretation. This literary critical suspicion of origins arguably reached a peak in the early 1990s when *Akira* appeared, so it is not surprising that this approach suggested itself at the time, but even today many of these readings remain convincing in their core contention that *Akira* is a text about the unreliable function of language itself.

DEGREE ZERO: *AKIRA*'S POSTMODERNISM

Readings of the *Akira* anime as an effacement of origins have often invoked theories of the postmodern, theories that link the pace and flood of language in contemporary art and literature with an inability to construct meaningful political narratives. The term "postmodern" has been applied repeatedly to *Akira,* beginning with Susan Napier's influential 1993 article "Panic Sites," itself a kind of origin point for academic criticism of anime in North America.[9] These readings focus on the film's frantic visual pacing, which looks to some like a ceaseless rotation of vivid images unconnected by any coherent plot. Fredric Jameson identifies the postmodern closely with this kind of rapid but unstructured flow of language and imagery, which he relates to "the breakdown of the signifying chain . . . an experience of pure material signifiers, or, in other words, a series of pure and unrelated presents in time." The effect, says Jameson, is that the instantaneous present "suddenly engulfs the subject with undescribable vividness, a materiality of perception properly overwhelming, which effectively dramatizes the power of the material—or better still, the literal—signifier in isolation."[10] This is the erasure of deep meaning that Jean Baudrillard refers to as the "triumph of superficial form, of the smallest common denominator of all signification, degree zero of meaning."[11] For Jameson this loss of time and self not only erases our sense of historical narrative (historical cause and effect), it also undermines the kind of firm subjectivity that allows one to see oneself as an individual actor who can intervene to affect the future course of events. The resulting sense of freedom or lightness—exhilarating but disturbingly empty—is in some sense the essence of Jameson's postmodern aesthetic. Writing shortly after Napier, Freda Freiberg describes *Akira* as postmodern in precisely these terms: "In the absence of narrative coherence, the film grabs and grips the viewer by its visceral excitement, a constant bombardment and battering of the senses, a barrage of high intensity experiences."[12]

This reading of *Akira* is supported not only by the film's visuals but also by the confusion of its plot. Many initial reviews of *Akira* found the events of the film incomprehensible, and even later critics with the luxury of a DVD player have asserted that it somehow defies summary.[13] Although *Akira*'s politics are often confounding, the events of the story are fairly straightforward: one night while out riding with his motorcycle gang, the teenage Tetsuo crashes his bike into a young boy with prematurely aged features, who turns out to be a test subject escaped from a secret government project. The collision sets off a series of transformations in Tetsuo that give him psychic powers like those of the test subjects. As these powers grow, Tetsuo becomes increasingly unbalanced and destructive, first killing his fellow gang members and eventually battling the Japanese army through the streets of Tokyo. Tetsuo is following a series of clues toward the font of psychic power at the heart of the secret project, a force known to us only as "Akira." This psychic energy, we discover, is the source of the original explosion that touched off World War III at the start of the project, thirty-seven years ago. Throughout the film Tetsuo is pursued by his friend and rival in the gang, Kaneda, as well as the aged children who are the other test subjects, the shadowy "Colonel" (Taisa), who is now in charge of the project, and a group of guerrilla fighters, among other factions. All form shifting alliances with one another to try to possess, control, kill, or rescue Tetsuo before he locates Akira and risks reawakening its power. The chase scenes become increasingly frenetic and the combat increasingly kinetic until the film's climactic reveal, when Tetsuo locates Akira and exposes its true form, and all the forces converge for a final apocalyptic showdown.

Some of the factions in the film resemble real political actors and actions in Japanese history: the Colonel leads a coup that suggests Japan's prewar militarization or postwar remilitarization; graphic images of street demonstrations recall the massive public protests of the 1950s and 1960s, whose targets included Japan's support for U.S. military policy; and a vaguely defined group of "urban guerrillas" suggests the Japanese Red Army terrorism of the 1960s and 1970s. But the web of politics that connects these factions is tangled. Viewers experience the film from constantly shifting perspectives, as various characters take center stage one after another in a confusing rotation that continually fleshes out or complicates their motivations and their

> MANY INITIAL REVIEWS OF *AKIRA* FOUND THE EVENTS OF THE FILM INCOMPREHENSIBLE, AND EVEN LATER CRITICS WITH THE LUXURY OF A DVD PLAYER HAVE ASSERTED THAT IT SOMEHOW DEFIES SUMMARY.

relations to each other. Isolde Standish calls the film's politics a pastiche, Jameson's keyword for the postmodern accumulation of historical styles that robs those elements of any historical context or meaning and reduces them to free-floating signifiers. Standish suggests that Ōtomo's film quotes indiscriminately from the preceding fifty years of Japanese political struggle: the militarization of the 1930s, World War II, and Cold War politics are all intermixed in a way that collapses past, present, and future. For Standish, *Akira*'s images of strikes and street demonstrations become generic representations of "unrest" that neither provide nor require any understanding of Japanese politics or history.

Added to this is the hallucinogenic quality of Ōtomo's luminous cityscapes, the kinetic excitement of the motorcycle chase scenes, and the detailed scenes of the city's destruction that begin and end the film. All this contributes to the sense of an aggressive, even uncontrolled propagation of images that cannot be reined in by meaning. The culminating image comes in the climax of the film, when Tetsuo's psychic powers increase to the point where his body can no longer contain them, and he metamorphoses into a pulsating, pustulating mass of flesh and machinery that explodes outward, absorbing or consuming everything in its path. As Napier points out, the dissolution of bounded individual subjectivity (what Jameson traces on the level of language) is here enacted literally on the physical plane.[14]

The interpretation of *Akira* as a postmodern rejection of origins and decisive explanations seems to be at odds with the nuclear origin theory, the notion of a single traumatic historical event that forms the source of *Akira*'s imagery and anxiety. But the two readings have been combined by interpreters like Murakami Takashi into the idea that the atomic bombing represents the end of conventional history and representation, and the inauguration of a Japanese postmodern. Interpretations like Murakami's often identify a steady erosion of progressive political potential, beginning with the increasing conservatism of the U.S. occupation from 1946 to 1952 and continuing with Japan's support for U.S. Cold War military policy from the 1950s onward and the ostensibly failed public protests of the 1950s and 1960s, followed in the 1970s by the bloodily destructive and self-destructive violence of underground groups like the Japanese Red Army. Coupled with this political narrative is the postmodern idea that popular political activism was undermined by rising consumer culture: first the remarkable industrial and economic growth of the 1960s (displayed to the world at the 1964 Tokyo Olympics) and later the superheated bubble economy of the 1980s.[15]

In this narrative the events of the postwar, historically and symbolically concentrated into the single initiating event of the atomic bomb, somehow evacuate political and historical meaning from the present, in a way that is reflected by the frantic propagation of imagery in popular texts like *Akira*. This is how *Akira* comes to represent an origin and a lack of origins at the same time: the film's opening explosion blows away meaning along with everything else.[16]

Neither the origin nor the oblivion thesis by itself is intensely interesting or productive: each tends to close down meaning, by seeing *Akira*'s meaning as either overdefined by the atomic (not up for discussion) or completely indefinable (and undiscussable). And interpretations like Murakami's seem to do both. I would agree that *Akira* reflects both the impulse to locate origins and the impulse to efface them, but not in the way Murakami suggests. For me, *Akira* oscillates *productively* between these two positions, with a realism that provokes a shock of recognition, but also a presentation that makes spectators question how that reality can be represented to begin with. As I've argued in one way or another in most of my writing on anime, one of its chief strengths is this power to alternate rapidly between illusionistic realism that expresses some meaning or truth, and a kind of deconstruction of expression. In its best moments, that oscillation provides a sense of the real stakes involved in the slippery, often unreal project of representing the reality around us.

This oscillation manifests itself concretely in *Akira* in different ways: at the level of the plot, it is easy to see the film as torn between a desire for a law-and-justice resolution that would restore moral or political order and a visual or visceral celebration of destruction for its own sake. And in its tone, *Akira* often seems to drift frustratingly between juvenile and adult literature: many early reviews of *Akira* state that this is a not a children's cartoon, but it is also true that scenes of slapstick violence and romantic farce constantly intrude in a way that suggests the film has trouble staying on any one track.[17] But ultimately I would like to go beyond examining these tensions at the level of plot or tone and ask if there is not a way that the visuals of *Akira* and other anime reflect, address, or even resolve the tensions remarked above: the desire for historical perspective and political direction, juxtaposed with the utopian fantasy of a new visual mode that would permit us to move beyond the sometimes grim realities of Japan's postwar and start thinking or building anew.

How then do we begin to notice the specific visual details of *Akira* that are important, and how do we attach meaning to them? Here I would like to attempt that by comparing the anime with the manga drawn by Ōtomo.

Although the film was in some sense adapted from the manga, it is not my intent to treat the manga as a backstory or a better story that will answer all our questions about the anime. That would simply replace one origin with another, replacing *genbaku* (the nuclear bomb) with *gensaku* (the nucleus of the franchise, the original text). Instead, I want to use the comparison to focus our attention on the distinctive visual styles and devices these two texts employ, and reveal how the same author working in different media can accomplish very different effects and even reach very different destinations. This tells us something about the relative strengths and weaknesses of anime as a medium, the things it can and cannot depict, and the problems and solutions it can and cannot prompt us to think through.

AN INCONCLUSIVE CONCLUSION

Before it was a film, *Akira* was a publishing event in Japan, a long-running manga series drawn by Ōtomo that began serialization in *Young Magazine* in 1982.[18] Archie Goodwin argues that *Akira* represents the origin of Japan's manga boom in the 1980s, that it helped establish *Young Magazine,* driving its circulation over a million and paving the way for an entire genre of serial comic magazines aimed at young men. At intervals, these twenty-page biweekly installments were collected, sometimes revised again by Ōtomo, and published in thick, large-format paperback volumes (an innovation at the time, when collected volumes were typically published in smaller formats than the original magazine publication). Eventually the series ran to 120 installments, published from 1982 to 1990 and collected in six volumes totaling about 2200 pages. But the story became popular enough in its first few years to spur interest in making a film, which was started before the manga narrative was complete. In early 1987, about three quarters of the way through the story, Ōtomo stopped serialization for a year and a half to work on the film. The film follows the content of the first thirty episodes or so, but also carries the story forward to a kind of resolution. After the film was released, serialization of the manga resumed, and over the next year and a half it worked its way toward its own resolution that borrowed some elements from the film but changed others.[19]

While some aspects of the film's pacing clearly borrow from the episodic structure of the manga, ultimately the two works are organized visually in very different ways.[20] Consider the visual differences between the conclusions of the two texts.

In the film's climactic reveal, Tetsuo locates the force that has until now been identified by the cryptic term "Akira" and learns it was the name of a child, the most powerful of the military's original test subjects, whose psychic awakening generated the explosion that opens the film. Akira now exists only as a series of tissue samples in glass jars, housed in a supercooled vault beneath the old city, in the Colonel's secret base located under the explosion crater. (The base is concealed by a symbol of the reconstruction, a new Olympic stadium being built over the old ground zero.) As Tetsuo breaks open the vault, his rival Kaneda and the Colonel bring increasingly powerful weapons to bear on him, but to no avail. Growing stronger by the minute, Tetsuo begins to lose control of his growing power and transforms dramatically into an explosion of flesh that begins to consume the stadium, the other characters, and eventually the city itself. To stop him, the test subjects Masaru, Takashi, and Kiyoko intervene by using their own powers to reawaken Akira, who reassembles himself and reappears momentarily as an embodied child. Then almost immediately he turns into an expanding globe of light like the one in the opening scene, a widening sphere that destroys the surrounding city and engulfs Tetsuo, Kaneda, and the test subjects all at once.

This finale is full of light imagery. The glowing ball of light that emanates from Akira seems to absorb and reconcile everything and everyone. Swirling clouds and surging seas topple the surrounding buildings to the accompaniment of a dramatic organ fugue, but this ends relatively quickly, and the clouds are shown clearing as rays of light pierce them and shine down biblically on the city. Inside the sphere of light, Kaneda and/or Tetsuo recall their friendship in a series of flashbacks that seem to reconcile them, then Kaneda is transported back to the city. We see him crouched in the rubble, cupping a tiny light that is all that remains of the now contracting explosion, a personal illumination (memory, realization, enlightenment) that he takes into himself (Figure 3). Kaneda is reunited with Kei, and they ride off into the city on his motorcycle. The screen fades to white, and then there is a series of light/dark images—abstract flashing shapes, then stars and galaxies—accompanied by a voiceover saying "I am Tetsuo."

This imagery is distinctly spiritual, from the accompanying organ and choral music and biblical sky to Kaneda's entering the light and taking the light inside himself, and finally the suggestion that Tetsuo presides over the birth of a new universe. But this new-age transcendence fails to provide much closure. It certainly does not address or resolve any of the political issues that are in the background of the film. Consider the conflicted symbolism of Akira himself. If the film portrays a conflict between order and oblivion—between

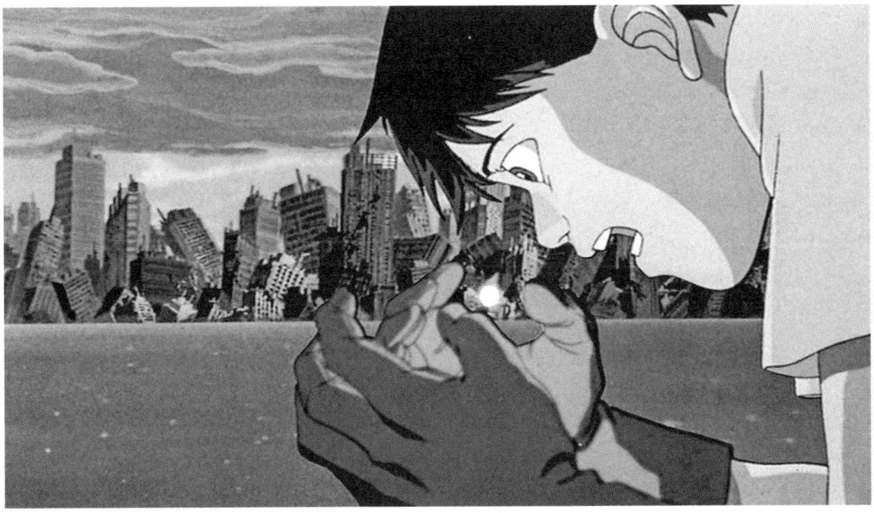

FIGURE 3. Near the end of the anime, Kaneda emerges from the giant sphere of light generated by Akira and then cups the shrinking ball of light in his hands, in a gesture that seems intended to signify growth and resolution. Both narratively and visually, this conclusion seems a little trite. Note, too, the relatively flat background, which contrasts with the volumetric portrayal of rubble in the manga.

the Colonel's militaristic order and memories of World War II (or III) on the one hand and the guerrillas' violent revolution or the bikers' blissful anarchy on the other—then Akira is the contradictory combination of both. He is memory and history: like the Colonel, he is the regrettable military past buried beneath a reconstructed Japan; with his fellow test subjects Masaru, Takashi, and Kiyoko, he is the victim of war—the blameless child, the fallen soldier, the buried casualty now disinterred. And yet with Tetsuo he is also youthful revolution personified, the hope of a future that is cut off from the sins of the past, an idealistic, violent cleansing that will wipe every slate clean. These tensions are resolved by having Akira, Tetsuo, and the rest of the test subjects disappear in a ball of light, leaving the film's multiple political threads hanging. The future seems to belong to Kaneda and Kei, a new Adam and Eve who survive and embrace in the wreckage; but politically, what does this domestic couple of biker and guerrilla now stand for?

Akira and the final explosion become a kind of new-age cheat, a divine light that resolves everything by magic. One could consider this ending a failure of narrative or political imagination. One could suggest that Otomo resorted to the abstractions of this final *deus ex machina* or *deus ex lumina* because he could not think of a way to resolve the plot. I would like to turn this around and point out that the light and dark imagery is the grammar that

Ōtomo uses throughout the whole film, starting with the opening explosion and the nighttime motorcycle chase. That language is optimized for depicting particular problems and finding particular solutions, but it is not really equipped to find a way out of the political and representational dilemmas we've been discussing. In other words the film is inconclusive not because Ōtomo could not think of a solution but because he could not animate it: his film does not possess the visual language to describe how the characters might navigate this maze of postmodern dilemmas.

ANOTHER CONCLUSION (AND ANOTHER AFTER THAT)

Let's compare this with the visual qualities of the manga, particularly its conclusion. About a third of the way through the manga Tetsuo awakens Akira from his thirty-seven-year sleep in the cryogenic vault, which causes a second explosion that wrecks a part of the city—just as in the film. But in the manga this explosion does not carry away Tetsuo or the psychic child test subjects. Instead, Tetsuo survives to form a gang and rule the ruins, holding United Nations aid workers at bay and keeping Tokyo effectively cut off from the world. All the main characters live on in the isolated city, scattered and forced to survive in the rubble. But many of them are transformed, as factions shift and old villains like the Colonel become new heroes. It is this struggle and transformation that make up the entire second half of the manga narrative.

Ōtomo is famous for his meticulous draftsmanship, and these ruins are unquestionably the manga's visual signature.[21] Accordingly, the manga lavishes much more attention on the city's destruction and transformation than the anime does: page after page is devoted to depictions of toppled buildings. These images resonate realistically and powerfully with scenes of devastation and reconstruction in the immediate postwar period, and they represent both destruction and survival. Many of the subnarratives revolve around characters' efforts to navigate the wreckage—to find a path, or a person, to fight through a barrier, and so on. In the last four volumes, characters struggle to restart from zero (or ground zero) and redefine their position, geographically, socially, and morally. This is figured not only in terms of the plot, which involves a lot of travel through the city on various quests, but also in terms of the concrete visuals, which depict the characters in long-distance views that display these symbolic and actual journeys through the ruins (Figures 4 and 5).

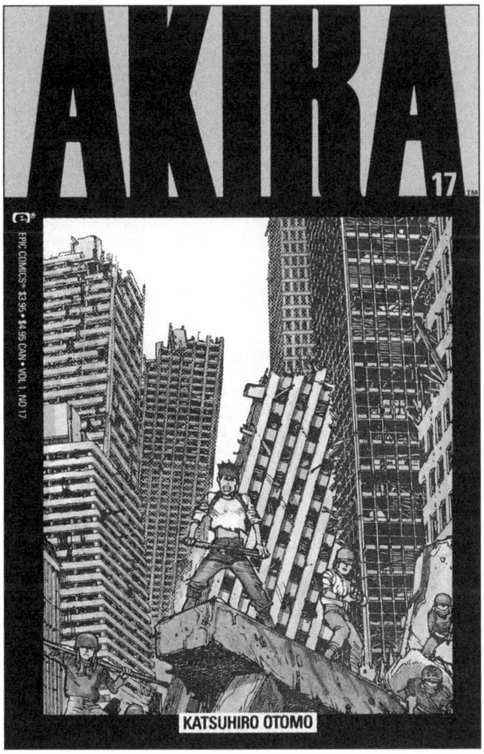

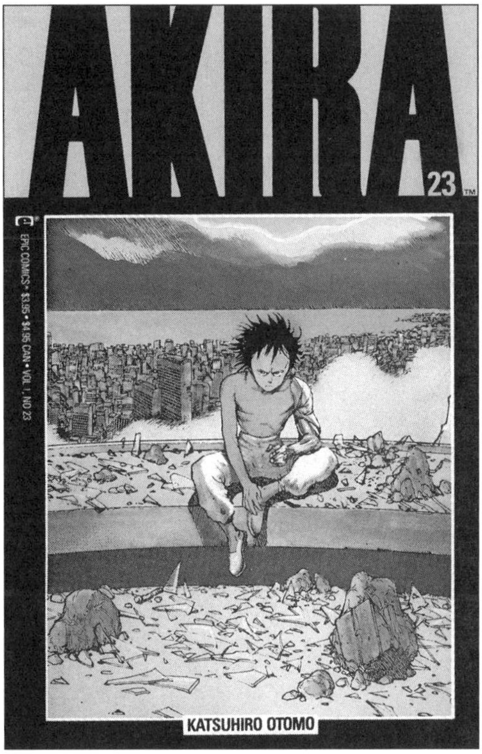

FIGURE 4 (LEFT). Much of the *Akira* manga is dominated by scenes of rubble, which characters navigate in a visual and narrative attempt to locate their place in the city. Cover image from the English color version of the manga, issued serially by Marvel's imprint Epic Comics (issue 23, 1990). **FIGURE 5 (RIGHT).** Tetsuo with the city spread out beneath him. The scene conveys his power, but with his back turned on the vista, he seems unable to locate himself or find his own place in this new world. Cover image from the Epic Comics serialized English version (issue 17, 1990).

There are also numerous sequences where we start with a view of a building in the distance and then zoom in frame by frame to a close-up of a previously invisible character in a window or doorway, locating the character in a geographical context. In one of the more symbolic images, Tetsuo's stone throne sits on a concrete island floating in the middle of a half flooded Olympic stadium—a visual riff on the imperial palace and moats in Tokyo, and the idea of Japan or the city as an independent, self-sufficient island empire. In other words, the manga's three-dimensional landscapes become metaphors for the political worlds that the characters are trying to build or locate themselves within.

For technical reasons, the anime cannot give the city this kind of volume: in the manga Ōtomo is able to draw still images of architecture and collapsing architecture in exquisite detail, but these kinds of images were impossible to animate even with *Akira*'s budget, and except for a brief sequence of crumbling buildings at the end, the film defaults to the typical animation pattern of moving the characters across relatively flat, stationary backgrounds (Figure 3). Even in the opening scenes where it is introduced, the city remains a backdrop of two-dimensional sliding layers. No matter how far or in what direction the characters ride in that opening scene, the buildings do not seem to get any nearer or further away, but exist as a kind of looming backdrop, like mountains, impossibly large and impossibly distant (Figure 6).[22]

The light/dark dynamic that characterizes the anime also flattens the film's third dimension and makes everyone seem lost in the darkness. The characters and their machines hurtle through night, struggling to light their own way, but these lights rarely seem to penetrate more than a few feet into the gloom. The result is that the characters seem trapped in a foreshortened space they cannot escape. By the time obstacles appear in their headlights (literally or figuratively), it is already too late to avoid a collision. This is a central motif of the opening sequence: the black screen that follows the title credit is revealed to be the inside of the bomb crater, but only after the camera manages to pull back and show the crater edges, and this is the last time for a while that the spectator or anyone in the anime will achieve that kind of perspective. After a shot of the flickering light outside the Harukiya bar, the motorcycles take off in a flash of sparking wheels, light trails, and glaring headlights, but as the characters shoot out of the brightly lit new city and into the darkness of the old city's ruins, their headlights illuminate only small patches of road ahead (Figure 7).

At the climax, the rival biker that Tetsuo is pursuing crashes when an obstacle looms up of the darkness directly in front of him, and then Takashi appears suddenly in Tetsuo's headlights, too close to avoid. Moments later, the Colonel's helicopters materialize in the darkness at point-blank range: magically the huge machines have remained undetected (unheard, unseen, unfelt) until their probing searchlights reveal them directly overhead. Several critics have commented on the play of light and darkness in the film.[23] In my reading, it is this device that makes the characters seem unable to gain a sense of distance or perspective, or place themselves in the wider world. The faster they drive, the less warning they have of what is ahead, so that the quicker they try to get somewhere, the more compressed or foreshortened their world becomes. The only way for the film to escape this regime is to light up everything, with the ball of illumination that reveals everything to Kaneda in the conclusion. But after the effective claustrophobia that has preceded it, that solution seems both too sudden and too trite. Unlike the manga, the visual

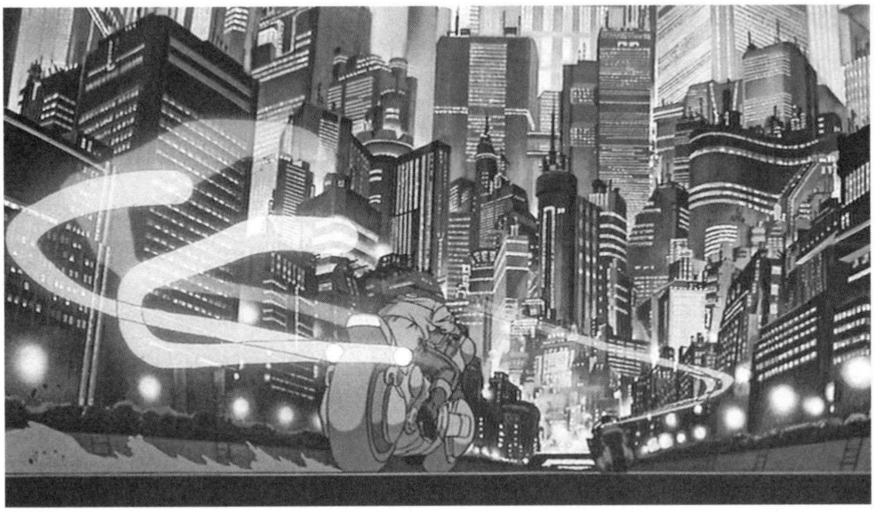

FIGURE 6. Distant, unmoving, and impossibly large, the skyline in the background of the anime's opening sequence obeys no laws of linear perspective.

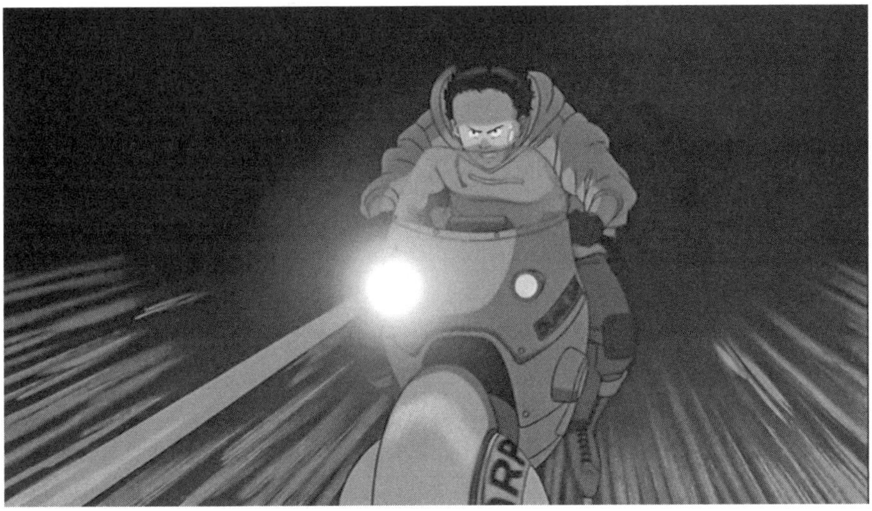

FIGURE 7. The bikers hurtling through the darkness near the beginning of the film can see only a few feet ahead, a visual figure for the postmodern world the film portrays.

dynamics of the anime are optimized for portraying the character's confusion or oblivion, the flattened world from which they cannot escape.[24]

All this marks the anime as much more postmodern than the manga. Jameson, for example, associates the postmodern strongly with a flatness or depthlessness, his central figure that connects the literally flat picture plane of artists like Warhol with all the symptoms of metaphorical depthlessness discussed above: the loss of deep meaning, historical perspective, and psychological interiority. This plays out dramatically in the work of Murakami Takashi, whose "Superflat" art borrows ideas like Jameson's. At the outset we discussed Murakami's thesis that Japanese fine art and political discourse have both been unable to capture the political meaning of the atomic bomb and occupation; only popular media like anime, manga, and character design have come close to portraying these issues, but always in a flattened (distorted, indirect, dimmer) way that corresponds to their two-dimensional visual aesthetic. Superflat art emulates that aesthetic deliberately, with very two-dimensional compositions that defeat any sense of perspective, and even sculptures that seem intended to mimic the flat images of anime. Not unlike Jameson, Murakami suggests that there is something simultaneously empty and liberating about this art.

But in the case of *Akira,* the manga seems to regain something that the anime has lost. The kind of three-dimensional representation we see in the manga represents the recovery of an origin that could orient the characters: it is now literally the origin coordinate or vanishing point of a linear geometric perspective.[25]

Consider the difference between the final images of the manga and the anime. In plot terms, the manga's finale is similar to the anime's, but with more factions (including, significantly, an invading contingent of U.S. special forces) battling Tetsuo and each other. The result is that the story's politics become more complex. But on the final pages, Akira again envelopes Tetsuo, Kaneda, and the child test subjects in a sphere of light, and the emphasis on friendship as a resolution is repeated. Kei calls Kaneda back from inside the light, and when the smoke clears, the two find themselves at the top of a ruined building looking out on a sunrise. That was the final image of the serialized version of Akira as it appeared in *Young Magazine*.[26]

This ending cannot resolve all the conflicts of the preceding 2200 pages. The final pages leading up to this image display a few frames of each main character to assure us that they have survived the explosion, but there is no explicit resolution to the political conflicts between them. Furthermore, while the sunrise seems intended to express optimism about the future, that visual metaphor falls flat on the manga page. It is not just that the manga is in black and white; it's also that its vistas are dominated by an evenly lit deep focus that reveals every detail of the cityscape, so that it has trouble harnessing contrast in the dramatic way the anime does. The result is that the sunrise in the serial's final image seems washed out, anticlimactic.

However, I would argue that for readers attuned to the use of perspective and the path-finding motif in the manga, the way Kaneda and Kei survey the city's wreckage from on high creates a kind of *visual closure* that is far more interesting than the trite sunrise metaphor: it is the panoramic quality of this final view that suggests they will be able to locate themselves in the world (individually, ethically, and politically) and move forward (even if it does not describe precisely how).

> THE KIND OF THREE-DIMENSIONAL REPRESENTATION WE SEE IN THE MANGA REPRESENTS THE RECOVERY OF AN ORIGIN THAT COULD ORIENT THE CHARACTERS: IT IS NOW LITERALLY THE ORIGIN COORDINATE OR VANISHING POINT OF A LINEAR GEOMETRIC PERSPECTIVE.

One might wish that the manga had concluded with that image and remained finished. But apparently either Ōtomo or his fans were dissatisfied with this ending. In a move that further complicates the question of which text is the original *Akira*, Ōtomo added a thirty-five-page epilogue when the serialized episodes were collected into the final paperback volume, a coda that renders the ending more blunt and more decisive, both in terms of its plot and its perspectival visuals.

In that epilogue, Tetsuo's gang collapses after his disappearance, and UN aid workers are finally able to enter Tokyo. But at this point the remaining bikers and guerrillas join forces and band together to repel these foreign intruders and form a new state resembling Tetsuo's, the Akira Greater Tokyo Empire (*Daitōkyō Teikoku Akira*). In the (new) final image, Kaneda rides off into the city in an exaggerated perspectival shot that outdoes even the earlier panorama from the top of the building. In this new final image, the road extends infinitely to a clean vanishing point, while the city buildings rise dramatically and geometrically on either side. In a collapse of present and future, the buildings seem to be rebuilding themselves from the rubble. So plot-wise, the idea of friendship and community (*nakama*) is transformed into the rebuilding of a state, or city-state. In terms of its formal elements, the manga's second ending has an architectural solution that is even more clearly expressed and more optimistically inflected: we can locate ourselves geometrically and geographically in the city, we can restore the city's clean lines from the rubble, and we can chart our own future direction.[27]

If the anime seems to be better at expressing the confusion of Japanese postwar politics with this inability to see ahead, it cannot find any way out of this confusion (visually or narratively) except through this rather contrived transcendence of a divine light. The manga seems more optimistic, even constructive, with this third dimension that gives us some perspective on our problems and our position. But just as that aerial or three-dimensional view has been implicated in the colonial or imperial gaze and all the ideological baggage of the modern, the manga's solution is conservative. It is kind of return to Japanese militarism and nationalism.[28]

Broadening our focus to take in the *Akira* manga and anime at once, we might suggest that these two different media combine to become more sophisticated than either one individually. If the manga falls into one set of traps (the traps of the modern), and the anime falls into another (the traps of the postmodern), maybe when they are read together, they can form something more productive—perhaps a dynamic dialectic if not a stable whole. *Akira* could be regarded as a single text spanning multiple media, media that interrogate each other.

Writing about the bewildering but potentially liberating possibilities of postmodern space, Fredric Jameson suggests hopefully that new kinds of art might serve as a kind of cognitive map for navigating the fraught political and geographic spaces of modernity and postmodernity. For Jameson, such a map might help to relate the coordinates of global knowledge with those of representable experience, enabling "a situational representation on the part of the individual subject to that vaster and properly unrepresentable totality which is the ensemble of society's structures as a whole."[29] In other words, it might enable us to place ourselves in society and in history as well as space. If we consider the anime and manga together, perhaps *Akira* suggests one of Jameson's cognitive maps—one that helps us begin to fix our position, but that also supplies a healthy confusion, a skepticism that keeps us from being too sure of where we stand.

Notes

1. My thanks to Yuko Kanno, whose "initiation tale" in an earlier volume of *Mechademia* was one of the inspirations for this opening. Yuko Kanno, "Implicational Spectatorship: Hara Setsuko and the Queer Joke," *Mechademia* 6 (2011): 288.

2. Ōtomo Katsuhiro, dir., *Akira*, special ed., 2 subtitled DVDs (Pioneer, 2001). For ways the film's production broke new ground in Japan, see the documentary "Akira Production Report" on this DVD. To locate *Akira* within the context of anime and manga's earlier history in North America, see Fred Patten, *Watching Anime, Reading Manga: 25 Years of Essays and Reviews* (Berkeley, Calif.: Stone Bridge, 2004), 52–73, 122–26, 128–29.

3. Simon Richmond, *The Rough Guide to Anime: Japan's Finest from Ghibli to* Gankutsuō (London: Rough Guides, 2009), 36.

4. This move forward and backward is even clearer in the chronology of the *Akira* manga: there, World War III breaks out in December 1982, thirty-seven years after the end of World War II, and the main action takes place in 2019, thirty-seven years after World

War III. December 1982 is also the same month and year the manga began serialization; the anime version and the English-language manga altered the dates to associate the initial explosion and the war with the viewer or reader's own present and locate the main action a generation later.

5. Dave Kehr, "Japanese Cartoon *Akira* Isn't One for the Kids," *Chicago Tribune,* March 30, 1990, D.

6. Noi Sawaragi, "On the Battlefield of Superflat: Subculture and Art in Postwar Japan," trans. Linda Hoagland, in *Little Boy: The Arts of Japan's Exploding Subculture,* exhibition catalog, ed. Takashi Murakami (New York: Japan Society; New Haven, Conn.: Yale University Press, 2005), 204–5; Murakami Takashi, "Earth in My Window," trans. Linda Hoagland, in the same volume, 109.

7. The extensive coverage of the "Little Boy" show in the *New York Times* and elsewhere largely repeated Murakami's arguments about Japanese art and history. Even negative reviews of the show treated the underlying ideas credulously. For examples, see Roberta Smith, "From a Mushroom Cloud, a Burst of Art Reflecting Japan's Psyche," *New York Times,* April 8, 2005, E2:33; Matthew Gurewitsch, "Perpetual Adolescence as a Counterweight to History," *Wall Street Journal,* April 7, 2005, D8.

8. Derrida writes of "the moment when language invaded the universal problematic, the moment when, in the absence of a center or origin, everything became discourse . . . that is to say, a system in which the central signified, the original or transcendental signified, is never absolutely present outside a system of differences. The absence of the transcendental signified extends the domain and the play of signification infinitely." Jacques Derrida, "Structure, Sign, and Play in the Discourses of the Human Sciences," in *Writing and Difference,* trans. Alan Bass (Chicago: University of Chicago Press, 1978), 280.

9. Susan J. Napier, "Panic Sites: The Japanese Imagination of Disaster from Godzilla to *Akira,*" *Journal of Japanese Studies* 19, no. 2 (1993): 327–51. To my knowledge this is the earliest article on anime published in a major Japanese studies journal in the United States.

10. Fredric Jameson, *Postmodernism, or, The Cultural Logic of Late Capitalism* (Durham, N.C: Duke University Press, 1991), 27.

11. Jean Baudrillard, *Simulacra and Simulation,* trans. Sheila Faria Glaser (Ann Arbor: Michigan University Press, 1994), 87.

12. Freda Freiberg, "*Akira* and the Postnuclear Sublime," in *Hibakusha Cinema: Hiroshima, Nagasaki, and the Nuclear Image in Japanese Film,* ed. Mick Broderick (London: Kegan Paul, 1996), 95. Isolde Standish also argues that "*Akira* is, above all else, concerned with the esthetics of movement and destruction, subordinating any sense of narrative sequence to images of the spectacular." Isolde Standish, "*Akira,* Postmodernism, and Resistance," in *The Worlds of Japanese Popular Culture: Gender, Shifting Boundaries, and Global Cultures,* ed. D. P. Martinez (Cambridge: Cambridge University Press, 1998), 64.

13. In 2001 when *Akira* was released on DVD, one reviewer mentioned this confusing quality in a comment that simultaneously addressed *Akira*'s origins, *Akira* as origin, and *Akira* as oblivion: "Animation has gone in various directions, of course, but the film, which alludes to the destruction of Hiroshima and Nagasaki during World War II, helped popularize anime in the United States and remains fresh and startling despite its confused and repetitive plot line." Peter M. Nichols, review of *Akira, New York Times,* July 20, 2001, E27.

14. Napier's early characterization of *Akira* as postmodern (in "Panic Sites") emphasizes this destabilization of the bodily subject as well as the film's open-ended narrative and its paranoid anxiety about capitalist society. After Napier, Freiberg (in "*Akira* and the Postnuclear Sublime") and Standish (in "*Akira*, Postmodernism, and Resistance") characterize the film as postmodern particularly for its fast-paced pastiche of disconnected images. Writing in 2001, Napier summarizes all these ideas: "*Akira*'s postmodern aspects include four major elements: the film's rapid narrative pace (reinforced by its soundtrack); its fascination with fluctuating identity, as evidenced in Tetsuo's metamorphoses; its use of pastiche both in relation to Japanese history and cinematic styles; and its ambivalent attitude toward history." Susan Napier, *Anime from* Akira *to* Princess Mononoke: *Experiencing Contemporary Japanese Animation,* 1st. ed. (New York: Palgrave, 2001), 204–5.

15. See Noi, "Battleground," 202–5.

16. In the wake of the March 2011 earthquake and tidal wave in eastern Japan and the subsequent disaster at the Fukushima nuclear power plants, some critics have sought to locate Fukushima as a new origin, one that sheds new light on Japan's fraught postwar relationship with U.S. nuclear weapons and power, and at the same time marks a turning point or endpoint in postwar Japanese history, perhaps one where antinuclear activism will actually return us to a new era of popular political engagement. This gesture has an undeniable narrative power, but it seems to me to have some political risks: in addition to the kind of reductionism discussed above, inherent in any search for historical origins, it threatens to collapse multiple histories into one by conflating the politics of nuclear weapons and the politics of nuclear power. For a compelling discussion of these issues that treats both the political and theoretical dimensions in a nuanced way, see Margherita Long's discussion of Fukushima and Hagio Moto, elsewhere in this volume.

17. One reviewer wrote, "The film's visual anarchy demands a snarling attitude that never manifests itself in the kids—they are the Sex Pistols as played by the Care Bears." The Sex Pistols and the Care Bears seem to reflect the gap discussed above, between 1960s- or 1970s-style activism and 1980s media culture. John Griffin, "The Mild Bunch," review of *Akira*, *The [Montreal] Gazette,* January 26, 1991, F13.

18. Ōtomo Katsuhiro, *Akira,* 6 vols. (Tokyo: Kōdansha, 1984–93); translated by Yoko Umezawa, Linda M. York, and Jo Duffy, 6 vols. (New York: Kodansha Comics, 2009–11).

19. On publication formats, see Archie Goodwin, "Akira & Otomo," in *Akira* #1 (New York: Marvel-Epic, 1988), n. p. For detailed publication history, see the timeline in Ōtomo Katsuhiro, *Akira Club,* trans. Kumar Sivasubramanian (Milwaukie, Ore.: Dark Horse, 2007), n. p.

20. Standish traces the anime's postmodern fragmentation of the anime's narrative partly to the episodic quality of the manga as a serial genre. Steven Brown argues that *Akira* is postmodern even in comparison with other manga, its multiple competing themes recalling Jean-François Lyotard's characterization of postmodernism as a loss of faith in an overriding historical master narrative, or suggesting the laterally ramified rhizomatic structures described by Gilles Deleuze and Félix Guattari. Standish, "*Akira*, Postmodernism, and Resistance," 64; Steven Brown, *Tokyo Cyberpunk: Posthumanism in Japanese Visual Culture* (New York: Palgrave, 2010), 3–10.

21. Ōtomo relates how, while drawing *Akira,* he collected photographic books with scenes of rubble. *Akira Club,* n. p.

22. An exception that proves the rule comes in a scene where the politician Nezu and the guerrilla Ryū traverse an elevated walkway past some skyscrapers, and the animators try to make one of the background buildings "rotate" realistically as the characters walk past it. This effect—achieved by dividing the building face into multiple sliding layers—is far from realistic. In "*Akira* Production Report," a backdrop painter remarks that if you calculated the scale of the background buildings according to strict or realistic laws of three-dimensional perspective, they would have to be thousands of stories tall.

23. Susan Napier (in "Panic Sites") comments on the darkness of the film, which she associates with a moral atmosphere using the term "Tech noir." Marc Steinberg equates light with weaponry, and notes that as spectators we repeatedly have this light shone in our eyes before we somehow reverse our position and become its bearer, usually by climbing onto or into the vehicles that have these lights mounted. Steinberg's outstanding essay relates this to the classical sublime, in a gesture allows us to link his reading with Jameson's postmodern sublime and Freiberg's postnuclear sublime. Marc Steinberg, "The Trajectory of Apocalypse: Pleasure and Destruction in *Akira* and *Evangelion*," *East Asia Forum* 8/9 (1999–2000): 1–31.

24. Even when it tries, the manga is not very good at portraying this enveloping darkness or the lights. The first volume of the manga tries to depict the night with dark backgrounds, but it is not as successful as the anime, and the bright lights cannot be duplicated on the page. A color version of *Akira* produced by Marvel imprint Epic Comics for release in the United States is only a little more successful in this respect. The history of this color version shows the difficulty of locating a single origin for the *Akira* franchise: it was republished in Japan as the "International Version," with sound effects in roman characters and pages mirrored to read left to right as in the U.S. comic, and with Ōtomo's original Japanese text now replaced by a Japanese reverse-translation of the English translation in the U.S. version(!). Ōtomo Katsuhiro, *Akira*, color Steve Oliff, trans. Umezawa Yūko, English adapt. Jo Duffy, 38 issues (New York: Marvel-Epic, 1988–1995); translated back into Japanese by Kuroma Hisashi as *Furu karaa Akira,* 6 vols. (Tokyo: Kōdansha, 2003–2004).

25. Natsume Fusanosuke also suggests generally that the manga responds to a loss of meaning and political agency characteristic of 1980s Japan, a situation he describes in vocabulary associated with the postmodern; but he is not so optimistic about its ability to find a visual solution to this dilemma. Natsume Fusanosuke, *Manga to sensō* (Tokyo: Kōdansha, 1997), 115–32.

26. This image appears in volume 6 on page 399 of both the Japanese and English editions.

27. Murakami Takashi seems to read this final image as ironic, a pastiche of Tezuka Osamu's utopian city images that also implicitly critiques the utopian conclusion of the anime. It seems to me that Murakami's reading looks at all the right elements, but his conclusions about the irony of the conclusion don't seem to be supported by the way perspective has functioned in the manga up until this point. Murakami, "Earth in My Window," 107–12.

28. For a more optimistic interpretation, see Thomas Lamarre's reading of the Akira Empire of Tokyo as a smaller, more local version of empire, in "Born of Trauma: *Akira* and Capitalist Modes of Destruction," *positions: east asia cultures critique* 16, no. 1 (2008): 131–56.

29. Jameson, *Postmodernism,* 51.

CONTRIBUTORS

STEVEN R. ANDERSON is a clinical research coordinator in New York City.

DALE K. ANDREWS is associate professor at Tohoku Gakuin University.

ANDREU BALLÚS is a PhD candidate in contemporary philosophy at the Universitat Autònoma de Barcelona.

JODIE BECK is a PhD candidate at McGill University in Montreal, Canada.

CHRISTOPHER BOLTON is associate professor of comparative and Japanese literature at Williams College. He is the author of *Sublime Voices: The Fictional Science and Scientific Fiction of Abe Kôbô* and coeditor of *Robot Ghosts and Wired Dreams: Japanese Science Fiction from Origins to Anime* (Minnesota, 2007).

KUKHEE CHOO is faculty of communication at Tulane University. She is the coeditor of *Contents Transformation in East Asia: Popular Culture, Media, and Identity.*

RAYNA DENISON is lecturer and researcher of film, television, and media at the University of East Anglia.

LUCY FRASER received her PhD from the University of Queensland, Australia. She has published translations of literary criticism, short stories, and interviews with Japanese writers.

FUJIMOTO YUKARI is associate professor of global Japanese studies at Meiji University, Japan. She is the author of *Watashi no ibasho wa doko ni aruno?* (Where do I belong?), *Shôjo manga damashii* (The spirit of shôjo manga), *Kairaku denryū* (The electric current of pleasure), and *Aijô hyôron* (Critique of love).

FORREST GREENWOOD is a PhD student in the Department of Communication and Culture at Indiana University Bloomington.

IMAMURA TAIHEI (1911–1986), one of Japan's most renowned and accomplished film critics and theorists, published a broad range of books on cinema, animation, art, literature, and theory, among them *Kiroku eigaron* (1940, Documentary film theory), *Manga eigaron* (1941, Cartoon film theory), *Nihon eiga no honshitsu* (1943, Fundamentals of Japanese cinema), *Eiga riron nyūmon* (1952, An introduction to film theory), *Itaria eiga, sono neoriarizumu* (1953, The neorealism of Italian cinema), and *Shiga Naoya ron* (1970, On Shiga Naoya).

SETH JACOBOWITZ is assistant professor of East Asian languages and literatures at Yale University. He is the translator of the *Edogawa Rampo Reader* and the forthcoming *Writing Technology in Meiji Japan: A Media History.*

JOON YANG KIM is the author of *Animation, Alchemy of Images* and *Empire of Images: Animation on the Japanese Islands.* The latter was awarded the Poranabi Prize from the Japan Foundation. His essays have been published in Korean, Japanese, and English. He is associate editor of *Animation: An Interdisciplinary Journal* and editor of the journal of the Japan Society for Animation Studies. He teaches at Tokyo Zokei University.

THOMAS LAMARRE teaches East Asian studies and art history and communication studies at McGill University. His books include *Shadows on the Screen: Tanizaki Jun'ichirô on Cinema and*

Oriental Aesthetics, Uncovering Heian Japan: An Archaeology of Sensation and Inscription, and *The Anime Machine: A Media Theory of Animation* (Minnesota, 2009).

MARGHERITA LONG is associate professor of comparative literature and foreign languages at the University of California, Riverside. She is the author of *This Perversion Called Love: Reading Tanizaki, Feminist Theory, and Freud.*

MATSUMOTO NOBUYUKI is director of the curatorial planning department and head curator of Asian art at the Tokyo National Museum.

LAURA MILLER is Ei'ichi Shibusawa-Siego Arai Endowed Professor of Japanese Studies and professor of anthropology at the University of Missouri–Saint Louis.

ALEXANDRA ROEDDER received her PhD in musicology from the University of California, Los Angeles.

PAUL ROQUET is an Andrew W. Mellon fellow in the humanities at Stanford University.

BRIAN RUH received his PhD in communication and culture from Indiana University. He writes about Japanese film and animation and is the author of *Stray Dog of Anime: The Films of Mamoru Oshii.*

SHUN'YA YOSHIMI is professor of sociology, cultural studies, and media studies at the University of Tokyo. He is the author of several books in Japanese.

ALBA G. TORRENTS is a PhD candidate in contemporary philosophy at the Universitat Autònoma de Barcelona and in communication studies at the Universidad Nacional de Córdoba.